SECURING AND SUSTAINING THE OLYMPIC CITY

To Jai and Mia

Securing and Sustaining the Olympic City
Reconfiguring London for 2012 and Beyond

PETE FUSSEY
University of Essex, UK

JON COAFFEE
University of Birmingham, UK

GARY ARMSTRONG
Brunel University, UK

DICK HOBBS
University of Essex, UK

ASHGATE

Published by
Ashgate Publishing Limited
Wey Court East
Union Road
Farnham
Surrey, GU9 7PT
England

Ashgate Publishing Company
Suite 420
101 Cherry Street
Burlington
VT 05401-4405
USA

www.ashgate.com

British Library Cataloguing in Publication Data
Securing and sustaining the Olympic city : reconfiguring
    London for 2012 and beyond.
    1. Olympic Games (30th : 2012 : London, England)--Security
    measures. 2. Hosting of sporting events--Security
    measures--England--London. 3. Urban renewal--England--
    London--Case studies.
    I. Fussey, Peter.
    796.4'8'0684--dc22

Library of Congress Cataloging-in-Publication Data
Securing and sustaining the Olympic city : reconfiguring London for 2012 and beyond /
by Pete Fussey ... [et al.].
    p. cm.
    Includes bibliographical references and index.
    ISBN 978-0-7546-7945-5 (hardback) -- ISBN 978-0-7546-9884-5 (e-book)
    1. Olympic Games (30th : 2012 : London, England) 2. Olympics--Security
measures--England--London--Planning. I. Fussey, Peter.
    GV7222012 S43 2010
    796.48--dc22

                                                                    2010038965

ISBN 9780754679455 (hbk)
ISBN 9780754698845 (ebk)

Printed and bound in Great Britain by the
MPG Books Group, UK

Contents

List of Figures

List of Tables

List of Abbreviations

ACOG	Atlanta Olympic Organizing Committee
ACPO	Association of Chief Police Officers
ANPR	Automatic Number Plate Recognition
APD	Atlanta Police Department
ASALA	American Secret Army for the Liberation of Armenia
ATHOC	Athens Organizing Committee for the Olympic Games
BAe	British Aerospace
BALCO	Bay Area Laboratory Co-Operative
BASIS	Biological Aerosol Sentry and Information System
BLF	Big Lottery Fund
BLFC	Big Lottery Funded Clubs
BNP	British National Party
BOA	British Olympic Association
BOCOG	Beijing Organizing Committee for the Olympic Games
BSO	Black September Organization
C4I	Command, Control, Co–ordination, Communication and Intelligence
CBRN	Chemical, Biological, Radiological and Nuclear Terrorism
CCPR	Central Council for Physical Recreation
CCTV	Closed Circuit Television
CO11	Central Operations group 11, the Metropolitan Police Public Order Operational Command Unit
COF	Citizen Organization Foundation
COJO	Comité d'organisation des Jeux Olympiques (see also OCOG)
CONOPS	CONcept of OPerationS
CONTEST	The UK Counter-Terrorism Strategy
COUIC	Coordination, Offensive, Use, Interruptions and Cut
CPO	Compulsory Purchase Order
CPSS	Command Perimeter Security System
CPTED	Crime Prevention Through Environmental Design
CRAM	Comparative Risk Assessment Methodology
DCMS	Department for Culture Media and Sport
DETR	Department for the Environment, Transport and the Regions
DLR	Docklands Light Railway
ETA	Euzkadi Ta Askatasuna (Basque nationalist organization)

FAI	Italian Anarchist Federation
FALN	Fuerzas Armadas de Liberación Nacional (Puerto Rican separatists)
FIBA	Fédération Internationale de Basketball Amateur (International Basketball Association)
FIFA	Fédération Internationale de Football Association (International Football Association)
FLNC	Corsican National Liberation Front
FLQ	Front de Libération du Québec
FRCCTV	Face Recognition Closed Circuit Television
GLA	Greater London Authority
GPS	Global Positioning System
GRAPO	Grupo de Resistencia Antifascista Primo Octobre
HERTI	High Endurance Rapid Technology Insertion surveillance plane
IAAF	International Association of Athletics Federations
IED	Improvised Explosive Device
IOC	International Olympic Committee
IPS	Intelligent Passenger Surveillance
ISAF	International Sailing Federation
JBG	Jewish Board of Guardians
JRA	Japanese Red Army
LAPD	Los Angeles Police Department
LBL	Labour Behind the Label
LC	London Citizens
LDA	London Development Agency
LEED	Leadership in Energy and Environmental Design
LLW	London Living Wage
LOCOG	London Organizing Committee for the Olympic and Paralympic Games
London2012	Bid Team
MANPAD	Man-Portable Air Defence systems
MPA	Metropolitan Police Authority
MPS	Metropolitan Police Service
NaCTSO	National Counter Terrorism Security Office
NAO	National Audit Office
NAOC	Nagano Olympic Organizing Committee
NCVO	National Council for Voluntary Organisations
NGOs	Non-Governmental Organizations
NIJ	National Institute of Justice
NLLDC	New Lammas Lands Defence Committee
NOC	National Olympic Committee
NPC	National Paralympic Committee
NPIA	National Police Improvement Agency
NSSE	National Special Security Event

OCOG	Organizing Committee for the Olympic Games
ODA	Olympic Delivery Authority
ODPM	Office of the Deputy Prime Minister
OGI	Olympic Games Impact
OPLC	Olympic Park Legacy Company
ORN	Olympic Route Network
OSD	Olympic Security Directorate
OSSSRA	Olympic Safety and Security Strategic Risk Assessment
OVP	Olympic Volunteer Programme
PAC	Committee of Public Accounts
PBIED	Person Borne Improvised Explosive Device
PCSOs	Police Community Support Officers
PE	Physical Education
PFLP	Popular Front for the Liberation of Palestine
PIRA	Provisional IRA
RAF	Red Army Faction
RFID	Radio Frequency Identification
RICS	Royal Institute of Chartered Surveyors
RWE	Right Wing Extremism
SBD	Secure by Designs
SFT	Students for a Free Tibet
SMEs	Small and medium enterprises
SMs	Social Movements
SOLEC	State Olympic Law Enforcement Command (Atlanta's 1996 security directorate)
TELCO	The East London Communities Organization
TETRA	Terrestrial Trunked Radio
THG	Tetrahydrogestrinone
TL	Terra Lliure (Catalan separatists)
TS	Total Security
UAV	Unmanned Arial Vehicle
UEL	University of East London
UKBA	United Kingdom Borders Agency
UOPSC	Utah Olympic Public Safety Command
VAT	Value Added Tax
VBIED	Vehicle Borne Improvised Explosive Device
VJE	Violent Jihadi Extremism

Acknowledgements

Pete Fussey would like to thank former colleagues at the University of East London for creating an environment that was both intellectually and geographically suited to this study. I am particularly grateful to Andrew Silke and Anthony Richards for their unfailing collegiality in sharing information, vital contacts and ideas. Special thanks also go to the many practitioners across Olympic planning and other security agencies who kindly donated their time to this research. Much of the analysis exists because of this generosity. Inspiration has also been drawn from colleagues involved in security-based fieldwork on ESRC and EPSRC projects EP/HO230LX/1 and EP/I005943/1.

Many debts have been incurred along the way towards this first book. Some have accumulated via the valued guidance and friendship from numerous academics, particularly Paddy Rawlinson and Chris Crowther-Dowey among others. I am also grateful to Beverley Brown for possessing such astute editing skills. Above all, thanks to my family, to mum and dad, Mo, Jai and Mia for their unfailing encouragement, love and support.

Jon Coaffee would like to thank current and former colleges at the Centre for Urban and Regional Studies (University of Birmingham) and Centre for Urban Policy Studies (University of Manchester). Special thanks also go to Paul O'Hare, Marian Hawkesworth, John and Margret Gold and Ces Moore for their input at various stages of this project. I would also like to acknowledge the assistance of many security and built environment practitioners and policymakers who have given up their time and expertise in the course of carrying out research for this book, as well as the UK research councils for funded support (EP/F008635/1 and 2).

Gary Armstrong: Thanks are due to Natalie Campbell, James Edgerley, Iain Lindsay, Jonathon Milne, Jade Moulden and Emily Stonebridge whose ideas and arguments inspired various chapters in what follow. Thanks are also due to the invaluable technical and formatting skills of Karen Kinnaird.

Dick Hobbs would like to acknowledge the support of Sue, Pat and Nik, and the inspiration provided by the long-suffering citizens of E15.

Introduction
Sustaining and Securing the Olympic City

The Olympic Games is a global idiom attracting the largest global peace-time movement of people. The attendant philosophies of Olympism[1] resonate with humanistic doctrines of dignity, equality and the pursuit of world peace. From their late-nineteenth-century beginnings, the Modern Olympics have had aspirations that extend beyond sport. The Games should thus be considered a political conduit as much as a sporting fixture (Kanin 1981).

In the wider discourse, aspects of sporting evangelism are wrapped around a commentary on mankind. The idea that Olympism may be, or indeed has become, a civil religion has its proselytizers. Pierre Frédy, Baron de Coubertin (1863–1937), the founder of the Modern Olympiad, opined in his *Mémoires Olympiques* (1931) that Olympic sport was a quasi-religion, with its due accompaniments of dogma, ritual and a sense of church. Indeed, Avery Brundage, President of the International Olympic Committee (IOC) from 1952 to 1972 (and a dedicated follower of de Coubertin), proclaimed that 'Olympism is a twentieth-century religion, a religion with universal appeal which incorporates all the basic values of other religions, a modern, exciting, virile, dynamic religion' (cited in Guttman 2002: 3). One could indeed argue that the Olympic Movement[2] attempts to create a civil religion by

---

1   'Olympism' refers to a set of abstract values purporting to connect the Games with the positive aspects of endeavour and competition. These are articulated by the International Olympic Committee in the latest iteration of the Olympic Charter as, 'Blending sport with culture and education, Olympism seeks to create a way of life based on the joy of effort, the educational value of good example and respect for universal fundamental ethical principles' (IOC 2010: 11). For detailed exploration of this issue, see Bale and Christensen (2004) and Girginov (2010). (See also note 4.)

2   The Olympic Movement (sometimes called the 'Olympic Family') comprises a number of different bodies that purport to share the values of Olympism and are integrated into the broader governance of the Olympic Games via regulatory, resourcing or supporting functions. Led by the IOC, other members include international sporting federations (such as the International Cycling Union), domestic Olympic Associations (such as the British Olympic Association), host Olympic organizing committees and the participants themselves.

propagating messages through the medium of sport promoting the pre-determined principles of the Olympic Truce[3] and the Olympic ideal.[4]

Much more than sporting excellence is at stake. Indeed, the Olympics have always been associated with attempts to improve trade, accumulate wealth, demonstrate political power, formulate national status and identity, validate regimes and legitimate systems (Brown 2001). Huge monies and corporate cultures are integral to the Olympic event and, particularly during the past 25 years, the Olympics have become the sporting example of what Barber calls 'McWorld', an idiom that connotes a 'sterile cultural monism' arising out of the transglobal markets' insensitivity to the particularities of local environments in which its commodities are promoted and circulated (2001: xiii). Such homogenizing transcends the commodified, 'cultural' and presentational aspects of the Games, reaching less visible organizational features such as accreditation, logistics and security.

A crucial issue in the twenty-first century is: to what extent, and via what policies, is an event like the Olympics worth hosting and protecting? And in what policing/security milieu should the event be performed? Crucial to such issues is the question: who is putting what into the Olympic collection plate and who is – and is not – welcome in or around the event? In this quasi-religious milieu, one may ask who indeed are the gods? By way of an answer, Olympic economist Preuss suggests that the Olympic Ideal is primarily a means of maintaining IOC hegemony: 'the Olympic aura, nourished by the Olympic Ideals, creates a globally valid ideology. This unique ideology is the basis for the power, the financial resources and the lasting existence of the IOC' (2004: 281).

Often constituting the host nation's largest ever logistical undertaking (see *inter alia* Cashman and Hughes 1999, Samatas 2007), accommodating the Olympics and its attendant security infrastructure brings seismic changes to both the physical and social geography of its destination. Since the 1972 Munich Games and the murder of five athletes and six coaches and judges from the Israeli national team, defence of the spectacle has become *the* central feature of Olympic planning; it has assumed even greater prominence following the bombing of the 1996 Atlanta Games and, most importantly, '9/11'. Indeed, the quintupled cost of securing the first post-9/11 Summer Games, Athens 2004, demonstrates the considerable scale and complexity currently implicated in these operations. Such costs are not only financial. The Games stimulate a tidal wave of redevelopment, ushering in new, often gentrified, urban settings alongside an associated investment that may or

---

3   The Olympic Truce attempts to secure commitment from all IOC members to cease hostilities with other nations or separatist movements for the duration of the Games (see The Olympic Truce Centre 2010).

4   The Olympic Games aim to create a feeling of harmony amongst the participating nations and athletes (Min 1987). This set of ideals, often referred to as 'Olympism', is what has distinguished the Olympics from all other sports events (Schaffer and Smith 2000) and is defined by the IOC as 'a philosophy of life and a state of mind based on equality of sports, which are international and democratic' (Lucas 1992: 211).

may not soak through to the incumbent community. For London 2012, taking the unusual step of developing London's Olympic Park[5] in the heart of an existing urban milieu and the Olympic Delivery Authority's (ODA)[6] commitment to 'community development' and 'legacy' makes these particularly acute issues.

London Calling

The execution of the 7 July bombings in central London a mere 20 hours after the IOC's decision to award the XXXth Olympiad to the city has provided a powerful and symbolic connection between hosting the 2012 Games and fear of terrorist violence. That day, as the front pages of successive editions of *The London Evening Standard* shifted their emphasis from the 2012 Games to the carnage on London's mass transit systems, questions emerged over the capacity to deliver a secure Olympics in the UK's capital. Such questions remain and dominate much of the discourse surrounding planning for the 2012 Games.

This book identifies and analyses the form and impact of the 2012 Games and their security operation on East London. Our analyses sit at the confluence of three interconnected processes: the commitment to hosting the Games, the attendant regeneration programmes and, suffusing these, the security programme installed to defend the spectacle. So far, in addition to sealing Stratford's Olympic Park 'Island Site'[7] from perceived threats, 2012 security operations have also harnessed key staples of Administrative Criminology, community safety and crime reduction (see *inter alia* Newman 1972, Clarke 1997, Felson and Clarke 1988), to generate an ordered space in the surrounding areas. What is more, this book argues, since Munich, Olympic security strategies have become progressively globalized and standardized, a process that, for 2012, introduces externally-defined processes to the local and idiosyncratic milieu of East London. In effect, by anchoring its analysis in the form and impact of the London 2012 Olympic and Paralympic security programme, this book sets out and examines the global processes and local impacts of the Olympics.

Of central importance to the social impact of this programme of securitization are issues of citizenship, engagement and access across urban spaces redeveloped

---

5   The 2012 Olympic Park is located at Stratford in the London Borough of Newham. Given its size, the development also extends into the other 'Olympic Boroughs' of Waltham Forest and Hackney, whilst bordering a fourth, Tower Hamlets.

6   The ODA is a large UK public sector agency established in 2006 to develop the infrastructure to host the 2012 Games; it has broad responsibilities including transport and sustainability. On completion, the Olympic Park will pass to the stewardship of the London Organizing Committee for the Olympic Games (LOCOG), who will host the event.

7   'Island Site' is a term used by developers and other practitioners to refer to the Olympic Park in Stratford. Such language semantically emphasizes the dislocation of this space from its urban context (see Chapters 5–7).

under the themes of defence and commerce (the Olympic Park is being developed
in tandem with what will be Europe's largest purpose-built shopping complex –
'Stratford City' – due to open in 2011).[8] Redefining citizenship through exclusion
has been a consistent theme of Olympic security operations, most notably in
Moscow (1980) and Sydney (2000) where, in the latter case, traditional policing
roles were supplemented with controversial (for Australia) municipal bylaws
to regulate behaviour and public assembly. Concerning 2012, a substantial
securitized traffic-free 'buffer zone' covering the urban areas to the south of the
Olympic Park, from nearby West Ham and Plaistow, has already been approved
– a development which may conflict with official declarations that the Games will
foster community aggrandizement.

Other Work and Our Approach

Our distinctive emphasis on the centrality of security within Olympic planning
processes in relation to many other concerns, and their broader social and operational
implications, develops a nascent area of Olympic-related analyses and is particularly
novel in relation to the 2012 Games. Whilst some studies address the community impacts
of hosting Olympic-sized events, very few consider their security infrastructures and
there are none that examine the social impact of these security operations.

There have been a number of key studies that have ably examined the impact
of sporting mega-events on social and economic renewal and the physical and
governmental challenges of combining the spectacle with other requirements of
branding, community involvement and physical legacy (notably Roche 2000;
Gratton, Dobson and Shibli 2000; Lenskyj 2002, Preuss 2004, Cashman 2006,
Cashman and Hughes 1999, Toohey and Veal 2007, Gold and Gold 2007, 2010).
In terms of the specific socio-spatial context, much has been written on East
London's varied experiments with regeneration. Particular emphasis has been on
the development of London's Docklands since the late 1980s (*inter alia* Foster
1999, Hall 2002) and, latterly, the ambitious Thames Gateway project (*inter alia*
Cohen and Rustin 2008) as well as more wide-ranging analyses adopting a pan-
London focus (*inter alia* Imrie, Lees and Raco 2009). Most recently, a number
of publications seeking to analyse 2012-related regeneration has emerged (*inter
alia* Evans 2007, Poynter 2009, Poynter and MacRury 2009). This text builds
on this literature by both emphasizing and analysing the way in which security
has become embedded in such processes and, critically, the exceptionality and
internationalization of the locality in relation to the 2012 Olympics.

This book thereby contributes to the literature examining urban development
in tandem with the heightened importance of securitized spaces. This includes

---

8   Stratford City is being constructed by the Westfield Group, the company that
recently built a similar development in Shepherds' Bush, West London amid some protests
from local traders and commuters (see BBC 2008c, Chapter 8).

the more general analyses of embedded security features within new models of urban regeneration (*inter alia* Davis 1990, 1998, Atkinson and Helms 2007). More recently, London has become the site of novel and intensified urban 'rebordering' security programmes that operate with far more subtlety than erstwhile (largely North American) approaches that merely 'pad the bunker' (Davis 1998: 364). London, however, has particular expertise in creating urban enclaves that, whilst not physically gated, are symbolically and technologically demarcated from their surrounding environments (Coaffee 2003; Fussey 2007a). Particularly prominent examples include the 'Ring of Steel' encircling the City of London's financial district, erected in response to Provisional IRA (PIRA) attacks of 1992 and 1993 (see Coaffee 2009b) and the similar 'Iron Collar' surrounding Canary Wharf's islands of affluence (see Coaffee, Murakami Wood, and Rogers, 2008, Fussey and Coaffee 2011). Via its specific focus on the Olympics and attendant security architecture, this book extends such existing analyses and, in doing so, accounts for how the specific trajectories of London's security planning collide with the internationalized and mobile forces of standardized Olympic security.

So far, Olympic security has, surprisingly, received scant attention in academic studies, which, largely anchored around terrorism-related threats, are often specific to one particular event and are usually retrospective, such as the studies of Munich (Aston 1983; Reeve 2001), Los Angeles (Charters 1983), Atlanta (Buntin 2000a), Sydney (Thompson 1996, Sadlier 1996), Salt Lake City (Decker et al. 2005, Bellavita 2007) and Beijing (Yu, Klauser and Chan 2009). Other studies seek to undertake a more longitudinal analysis of Olympic security. Normally, such 'histories' often involve a cursory skip through Olympic 'threats', accenting Munich and Atlanta, where 'events' occurred solely within the duration of the Games (*inter alia* Gamarra 2009). Better studies (*inter alia* Sanan 1996, 1997, Thompson 1999, Cottrell 2003, Atkinson and Young 2008, Hinds and Vlachou 2007) adopt a more systematic approach, although often stopping short of theoretical and conceptual interpretation. Most recently, more critical work has begun to emerge (*inter alia* Boyle 2005, Boyle and Haggerty 2009b, Giulianotti and Klausner 2009; Coaffee and Fussey 2011; Fussey and Coaffee 2011, Haggerty and Bennett 2011), seeking to apply conceptual and theoretical frameworks to understand the area of Olympic security, although this field is nascent. Other research directions have scrutinized the way terrorist threats to the Olympics have impacted on factors such as media reporting (Atkinson and Young 2002) and tourism (Taylor and Toohey 2007).

Together, whilst numerous valuable studies have emerged in these three cognate areas – those that try to make sense of economic, social, political and cultural impacts of the Olympics; those analysing large-scale redevelopment projects in East London; and those seeking to analyse some of the issues surrounding Olympic security – these have been largely undertaken in isolation. Adopting a cross-disciplinary perspective, covering human and urban geography, sociology, criminology and terrorism studies, this book aims to draw these three cognate areas together to forge an understanding of the form of London's 2012 security strategy and its impact upon the locale onto which it is imposed. Here, security is viewed both as a primary feature of Olympic planning and an embedded feature of the regeneration projects stimulated by the Games, culminating in a more intensely securitized environment. This analysis is then taken further to develop a theoretical position outlining the contested nature of security – defined in this book as 'the social construction of security'. The 2012 Games can be thus seen to impact on East London's urban geography via the imposition of 'Olympic spaces of exception' that promote selective visions of order. Moreover, drawing on Bauman (2000), the book argues that the application of this security can be seen as 'liquid'. Here, mobile and globalized currents of mega-event security converge, immersing the Olympic neighbourhood and seeping across the wider locale. However, this process is poly-directional. At the same time, these globally instituted processes are to some extent simultaneously shaped by, filtered into and dashed against the specific trajectories and traditions of London's already complex security architecture. Whilst these dilemmas perhaps face all Olympic cities, the more advanced nature of London's extant security infrastructure (particularly when compared to, say, Athens, Sydney, Atlanta and Barcelona) elevates their gravity.

The Book

The book is divided into two main parts. The first part takes a contextual approach to understanding the broader impact of Olympics on its host communities. This is examined over four distinct yet interconnected areas of discussion.

Chapter 1 considers the wider social impacts of grandiose Olympic planning. Analysing both the reconfigurations of other Olympic cities and the current redevelopment of Newham for 2012, this chapter identifies how such developments reverberate through the community. Ever since the first post-WW2 Summer Games, a core part of the Olympic experience for the host city has been the ability to stimulate large-scale redevelopment and rebranding of the city. In more recent Games, particularly the Summer Games in Barcelona in 1992, the regeneration of the city has taken on increased importance as host cities see the Games as a once in a lifetime opportunity to undertake large scale master planning of key development sites. The mantra of London 2012 is very much the 'regeneration Games', using enshrined principles of sustainable development and of sustainable communities. Although ideas of sustainability have traditionally focused upon environmental concerns, or issues of post-event legacy, in the UK sustainability has also become increasingly associated with issues of safety and security. These notions are key features that have been indelibly embedded within the plans for London 2012 with an eye to 'civilizing' the local neighbourhood (as it might be argued for gentrification), to aid community safety through different policing strategies and space design and to protect the Games from terrorist acts. Behind the many hagiographic invocations of Olympic legacies, lie incidences of sterilized environments comprising fragmented and unsustainable community configurations after the Games. Here, the cultivation of new, gentrified, urban environments embedded with overt motifs of crime reduction and security raise important questions that challenge the official utopian articulations of the 2012 legacy and also the post-event retention of safety and security infrastructures.

Chapter 2 undertakes a unique analysis of previous Olympic security operations between 1976 and 2008 and considers the implications for East London over two broad areas of analysis covering both Olympic insecurity and Olympic security. Of particular note is the way Olympic security planning can be seen as an exemplar of increasingly standardized approaches to protecting major sporting events and, as such, contains consolidated generalized and transferable paradigms dislocated from the varying social, political and cultural configurations of the host environments to which they are applied. Moreover, whilst these motifs of security have been transferred across time and place, their direction and intensity have also been shaped by key events, most notably, Munich, the 1996 Atlanta bombing and 9/11. This in turn raises questions concerning the efficacy of planning for retrospective events.

The second part of Chapter 2 outlines and analyses the contemporary anatomy of major event security. Drawing on Beck's conceptualization of a 'protectionist reflex' (1999: 153) in response to generalized late-modern fears, this chapter identifies and examines the key role of 'total security' in protecting sporting mega-events. Such post-millennium tensions not only inform and shape these generalized paradigms of security but also mediate the impermanence of 'states of exception' (Agamben 2005). Key here is the analysis of how the IOC's stated aim of accenting the Games as an athletic event and not an exercise in security is readily discarded in favour of creating fortified urban enclaves. Moreover, this chapter considers the reproduction of such expressions of security via symbolic motifs of protection explored in more detail later in the book. A central aim of this chapter is to develop theoretical ground in explaining Olympic security. This endeavour has two distinct components, both the contested nature of security (the aforementioned 'social construction of security') and its 'liquid' configurations. Here, key questions are asked concerning what is being secured, where the site of security resides, for what period is it applied and which form it occupies. Together, these themes inform a broader debate concerning the contested and partial nature of security that is developed throughout the book. Moreover, in pulling together the disparate and sporadic academic and literature on Olympic security into one place, this chapter will form the first major overview of the area. In doing so, it aims to establish and develop a grounding in the overall contours of Olympic security and the theoretical tools that explain them.

Chapter 3 examines the specific East London context with particular emphasis on its unique and shifting social, cultural, economic and demographic features, impacted by generations of economic change, de-industrialization and war. A key intention of the chapter is to illustrate the context into which the prevailing Olympic regeneration and security processes highlighted in Chapters 1 and 2 are being accommodated (with varying degrees of harmony and dissonance). Despite London becoming the first city to host three Modern Olympiads, the 2012 Games have stimulated an unprecedented reconfiguration of the local area. Connecting the social histories of East London with the 2012 project, the chapter provides a detailed examination that goes beyond the locality's often perceived ecologies of criminality. This provides an important grounding to the issues raised in following chapters concerning the extension of Olympic safety and security to areas often associated with criminality. In doing so, a more complex picture of the continually shifting and contested agglomerations and terrain is presented. Here, further questions arise regarding the plurality of voices and the often more ambiguous nature of contemporary resistance in the contested and continually changing late/post-modern city. Together these discussions suggest how cohesive and totemic notions of East London 'communities' and 'identities' are of declining relevance to the complex and contested milieu of the East End. As such, proclamations of an Olympic legacy for East Londoners become an increasingly complex task. Moreover, these discussions are explicitly connected to one of the book's central themes regarding the 'social construction of security' – the protection of whom, from whom.

Chapter 4 outlines the specifics of the 2012 Olympic bid and how its promises – and budget – have shifted since its original presentation, now beset by competing claims to 2012 dividends and now unsustainable fiscal commitments. Whilst the London 2012 Olympic and Paralympic Games will no doubt deliver on some legacy commitments, questions are raised over whether the benefits will outweigh the costs, and whom are these benefits are for. Safety and security concerns have been a principal driver behind the continually escalating costs of the Games. For example, following the original gross underestimation of the budget needed to defend the Olympic spectacle and the aftermath of 7/7, the safety and security costs of the 2012 Games have quadrupled since their articulation in the 2004 bid document (London2012 2004). Regarding the benefits, key questions can be asked regarding how the ACPO-accredited fortification mechanisms protecting the post-event Olympic Park will fit with other community priorities.

Building on this contextual analysis, Part II of the book examines the ramifications of implementing the bid. Particularly important here is the impact of the safety and security features associated with the 2012 Games. Building on the theoretical model addressing the contested nature of security, what it entails and its potential impact introduced in Chapter 2, Chapters 5–7 examine three central features of the 2012 security operation: the built environment (Chapter 5), the wider policing 'family' in the context of East London (Chapter 6) and technological surveillance (Chapter 7). Throughout, a range of critical themes is developed including the standardization of security, proportionality, the application of routine measures in exceptional times, surveillance and control 'creep', the tensions between expanding security infrastructures and ensuring cohesion and issues of accountability and governance.

Situated as the first of the three substantive chapters examining 2012 Olympic security themes *Chapter 5* first lays out the nationally derived contours of the 2012 security strategy and its constituent parts by examining the form, focus and composition of the UK government's consolidated *London 2012 Olympic and Paralympic Safety and Security Strategy* (Home Office 2009b). In doing so, the mechanisms for capturing and cataloguing potential risks and threats to the Games are identified as well as the risk management approaches.

Then the chapter turns to analyse the provision of security via the physical environment. Planning to maximize the security and safety of participants and visitors has become increasingly important to the design of Olympic sites and now forms a key requisite for candidate cities to be awarded the right to host such events. Drawing from ongoing research into the safety features built into the architecture of the sites of large sporting events, this chapter identifies and examines key strategies adopted to augment such infrastructures and their environs. In doing so, a number of key implications concerning how such physical landscapes shape the behaviour of individuals and the social configurations of groups that engage with it are analysed. At the present time, significant effort is going into plans which will attempt to design-in crime prevention and counter-terrorist features to the Olympic venues. This is notable in terms of materials used in construction as well as the application of measures to restrict vehicular access around the key Olympic sites. Likewise, given the currently high crime rates in the local areas, attempts are being made to embed crime prevention measures into the built fabric. This raises a key point of concern for legacy, with the likelihood that such measures will be retained post-Olympics in order to police one of Europe's largest parkland areas. Other concerns relate to the possibility that the heightened safety and security features of key Olympic sites will make other areas of London more attractive targets of crime and terrorism. This displacement argument, well known in the criminology literature, is a key worry as we move towards the Games. This chapter will examine these claims in order to highlight the intended and unintended impact of crime prevention and counter-terrorism measures being designed into Olympic architectures and how these will impact upon the host community.

Chapter 6 is primarily centred on the colossal policing effort surrounding the Games. Dubbed the 'largest security operation in peacetime' (Thompson 1999), the exceptional nature and scale of the summer Olympics has consistently raised considerable difficulties and dilemmas for those charged with policing the event. In addition to potentially coping with 9 million additional visitors comprising *inter alia* visiting dignitaries, sports enthusiasts and opportunist criminals, such pressures are exacerbated by co-ordinating the temporary coalitions of (sometimes unfamiliar) security agencies. Olympic-wide police forces, inaugurated at the 1994 Winter Games in Lillehammer, have been viewed as both a cohesive multi-agency response to exceptional and complex Olympic security challenges and, as such, a touchstone of organizational best practice. In practice, however, their application has amplified institutional boundaries, perhaps most notably at Atlanta in 1996 and during the 2002 Salt Lake City event. Moreover, in this latter case, the dedication of Utah's police to protecting the Games left the local community more exposed to heightened levels routine criminality. This chapter therefore examines the 'Olympic additionality' of policing roles specifically inaugurated by the

Games. In doing so, the chapter charts the wider ensemble of agencies operating at different governmental levels charged with securing the Games before focusing on local policing issues during the run up to the Games. Conducted across a typology denoting distinct 'actual', 'emergent' and 'imminent' phases, this discussion both frames the local policing environment in Newham, the principal 2012 host borough, and throws into sharp relief key differences between local agendas and capacities and the concerns of regional, national and international agencies.

Chapter 7 examines the third key area of security provision: technological surveillance. Although first instituted at an Olympics during the 1976 Montreal Games and a constant feature at British football grounds since the late 1980s, the use of technological surveillance has gained particular primacy in the post 9/11 era and connects with the IOC's demands to prioritize the sporting event over the policing spectacle. Moreover, this intensified strategic direction has driven exponential increases in the costs of Olympic security – as evinced by the elaborate and expensive 'Olympic superpanopticon' (Samatas 2007) deployed during the Athens Games in 2004.

Also significant for the 2012 Games is the diffusion of these surveillance mechanisms beyond the fortified Olympic Park to the encircling public spaces, both as an embedded component of new commercial developments – such as the Stratford City complex – and the securitized 'buffer zones' imposed on existing spaces. Despite London's unprepossessing status as the most intensively observed city on the planet, the 2012 Games are likely to bring further innovations in the form of biometric and wireless technologies. Against a historical backdrop of such technologies repeatedly being pioneered on East Londoners (including Facial Recognition CCTV and 'Intelligent Pedestrian Surveillance'), these mechanisms may invest new meaning to the 'community focused' discourse surrounding the 2012 Games.

This chapter examines the way technological surveillance has been applied to other Olympic cities (specifically between the 1976 Montreal and 2008 Beijing Games), and to East London, before going on to consider the implications of these processes and practices for 2012. The range of surveillance initiative, from first-generation CCTV systems to second-generation 'video analytics', is analysed before critically assessing their social impact, efficacy and legacy. These discussions are then drawn on in support of a central argument of this chapter that challenges the technologically deterministic accounts common among both supporters and critics of electronic surveillance. Instead, the most important influence upon the function of surveillance and other forms of technological control is argued to be the social context within which they operate.

Chapter 8 discusses resistance to the 2012 Games. One further component of the analysis of the impact of the Olympics and its security infrastructure is the way these developments have been received by the local community. Undermining the ODA's repeated claim that the Games are staged in partnership with residents is the organized protest challenging the proclaimed benefits of the event, benefits that are continually articulated under the rubric of 'legacy' and 'urban regeneration'.

The process, currently underway, of building the Olympic infrastructure and controlling the event at times presents a challenge to local democratic traditions. Such a challenge looks likely to become more pertinent as the opening ceremony approaches. Despite having been continuously promised a rewarding 'legacy' some London citizens have felt the need to mobilize and voice their protests in an attempt to ensure they receive more tangible benefits. The recurrent narrative of this chapter revolves around the importance the State places upon being seen to succeed not only at hosting the Olympic Games but at inviting participation in its process.

At the core of this chapter are two case studies of activist organizations that have taken a sceptical stance towards the 2012 Olympic dream. The first of these is the resistance surrounding the compulsory purchase order placed on the Clays Lane Housing Estate by the LDA in order to develop the Olympic site. Here, the resistance suffered from a failure to articulate their message to more powerful audiences, as well as certain dislocations within the group, that limited the scope and reach of their protest and, ultimately, enabled Olympic authorities to renege on commitments to 'sustaining communities'. The majority of the chapter, however, examines the more powerful and sustained actions of The East London Communities Organization (TELCO) in opposing the Games and considers TELCO'S operation in the context of fragmented street-level politics in the East End.

Chapter 9 concludes the book by drawing together the key themes to articulate how the 2012 Games and its safety and security infrastructure will impact upon East London. The issue of 'legacy' – particularly the functionality and role of the 2012 security provisions after the Games –constitutes an important analytical theme of this chapter. In the first instance, this applies to the national context. Tenders for private contracts to provide security for the 2012 Olympic Park are encouraging companies to supply 'security legacy', thus bequeathing substantial mechanisms and technologies of control to the post-event site. Whilst the security priorities of a high-profile international sporting event attended by millions of people are rather different from those involved in policing a large urban parkland (the future incarnation of the Olympic site), this post-event inheritance of security infrastructures is a common Olympic legacy. Examples of this include the legacy of private policing following the Tokyo 1964 and Seoul 1988 Olympiads and the continuation of 'zero-tolerance'-style exclusion laws after the Sydney 2000 Games. Key to this discussion are the critical themes of legitimacy and control 'creep' as they apply to the post-event site in London. Furthermore, issues of citizenship and community (continually cited by the ODA as the main beneficiaries of the Games) are called into question.

Other social aspects of 'legacy' are also important, and also resonate with the themes of citizenship and community in post-Olympic spaces organized around security and commerce. Another component of the legacy is the much lauded employment opportunities on offer. Alongside the large-scale training of individuals to help build the 2012 site – who were to subsequently compete for jobs in an uncertain post-event construction market – are attempts to cast thousands of individuals in private security roles. Currently, 7,000 private sector agents are estimated to be needed to secure the Games effectively, yet leaders of this industry estimate that, at current levels, collectively only 1,000 individuals could be provided. This has stimulated hastily derived partnerships with further education colleges to divert students towards acquiring the skills needed to match the ephemeral security needs of the Games. The post-event market of meaningful labour for those possessing such skills is less clear.

Another component of the discussion on legacy is an account of what the London security operation means for future sporting mega-events. In the UK context, Glasgow will host the 2014 Commonwealth Games and England will host a number of other international sporting events in the coming years. Internationally, the trend towards the standardization of mega-event security, the mechanisms of ensuring knowledge transfer and the award of Olympic-size events to global cities of a similar stature to London represents a global relevance of the practical and theoretical issues developed in this book.

Many of the discussions, conceptual frameworks and theoretical arguments presented in this book are informed by primary data collected via a range of qualitative methodologies in the course of a number of ongoing empirical projects surrounding 2012. All the authors are currently engaged in empirical research covering this geographic and thematic area. These works-in-progress have largely taken four directions: analysis of the Olympic security ensemble, investigation of criminality stimulated by the Olympic marketplace, the impact of the Games on local policing and the reception of the Games amongst East London's communities. Data used in this book is drawn from interviews and ethnographic work conducted with practitioners, planners, policing agencies and criminal actors in the area and has mainly informed Chapters 5–8. Finally, with decades of experience of living and working in the Olympic neighbourhood, local knowledge has played no small part in framing and informing the discussions that follow.

PART I
2012 in Context

Chapter 1

Secure Regeneration and the Olympics

Ever since the 1908 Summer Games in London, a core part of the Olympic experience for the host city has been the ability to stimulate large-scale redevelopment and rebranding of the city. In more contemporary times, this legacy benefit has been portrayed through a rhetoric of transformational regeneration schemes that are now a key rationale for cities to be awarded the Games by the IOC. In this chapter we focus on more recent Summer Games, whilst also drawing lessons from the earlier London Summer Olympics of 1908 and 1948, to highlight how the regeneration of the city has taken on increased importance as host cities see the Games as a once in a lifetime opportunity to undertake large-scale master planning of key development sites. We will also highlight how the Olympics, now in many circles rebadged as 'regeneration Games', aim to enshrine principles of sustainable development and the creation of 'sustainable communities'. However, whereas ideas of sustainability have previously focused upon environmental concerns, or post-event legacy, sustainability (particularly in the UK context) has now come to be viewed in a more holistic way whereby concerns for safety and security are key for the building of so-called 'sustainable communities' (Raco 2003). In more emotive terms, such a process has also been viewed as attempts to 'civilize' or 'cleanse' an area through processes related to gentrification and high-profile policing in order to reassure the 'incoming' residents that they are relocating to a safe neighbourhood. Commonly, this search for enhanced community safety has resulted in the eviction or removal of 'offending' groups or unwanted businesses that do not suit the legacy criteria for the regenerated neighbourhood, or who are simply deemed 'in the way' of planned change.

These dual concerns of leaving a long-term and sustainable regeneration legacy whilst at the same time ensuring that the areas concerned are 'upgraded' and embedded with security equipment (incorporating different policing strategies and particular space design, often under the guise of protecting the Games from terrorist acts) have a vital place in plans to regenerate large parts of East London as part of the preparation for the 2012 Games. This, we argue through the course of this book, will have significant implications for local communities in the preparatory and event stages of the Games and also raises issue about post-event retention of safety and security infrastructure.

The component parts of this chapter are arranged over three broad areas of discussion.[1] The first highlights issues of legacy and what planning theorists Flyvbjerg, Bruzelius and Rothengatter (2003) describe as the 'mega-project paradox' whereby large-scale planning projects often have hidden implications

---

1 Part of this chapter draws on previously published work by the authors, most notably Coaffee (2007) and Coaffee and Johnston (2007).

for the cost of redevelopment, its legitimacy and legacy. The second section illuminates the evolution of approaches utilized by host Olympic cities to garner regeneration benefits. The third section focuses specifically on how safety and security features have, over time, become increasingly embedded in such regeneration legacies.

The Legacy of Mega-projects

Spectacle – regarded here as 'any form of public display put on for the guidance and edification of a large audience of spectators … created by consciously manipulating space, landscape or objects to produce displays that draw a powerful emotional response from spectators whose participation is part of the experience of spectacle' (Gold and Revill 2003: 38) – has become an integral feature of the Olympic festivals going far beyond the customs and practices of normal sporting competitions (Coaffee and Johnston 2007). Increased commercial concerns have led to even more dramatic displays, ceremonies and urban design, with MacAloon (1981) noting that the Modern Olympics are 'an immense playground, marketplace, theatre, battlefield, church, arena, festival and Broadway of cultural images, symbols and meaning' (cited in Cashman 1999: 5). This development is, however, not without its critics. For many, there is a tension between the contemporary Olympics and the ideals of the founders of the modern Games: the Games have become 'an over-hyped commercial extravaganza' and a 'gross mass spectacle' in which corruption and nationalism are more prominent than high-minded idealism' (MacAloon 1981 cited in Cashman 1999: 8). This is most notably the case with modern Summer Olympics.

Increasingly, though, cities encounter a number of problems in accommodating the spectacles attached to mega-events, not least in assuring safety and security for the 'Olympic Family'. This type of critique is not restricted to the Olympic Games. Rather, it has been generalized to any form of mega-planning project, which often suffers from the 'pathology of the planning process' (Hall 1980: 3) whereby, once started, the project is either abandoned or proceeds with massive cost overruns. Other recent planning theorists have also questioned why such large-scale planning projects continue to be commissioned when there is a strong likelihood that they will be economically unprofitable, environmentally damaging, undemocratic and unaccountable (Coaffee and Johnston 2007).

The Mega-project Paradox

In recent years, the concept of the urban or planning mega-project has generated much attention amongst academics and policy makers alike. Such projects are part of a global trend in which city leaders enthusiastically follow a variety of entrepreneurial strategies in their efforts to develop and promote their cities.

Increasingly, though, there have been conflicts over the predicted and actual cost of such mega-projects, with questions asked about the transparency of the planning decision-making processes and, ultimately, about the appropriateness of risk management protocols utilized by those in charge of such spectacular projects.

Great Planning Disasters by Peter Hall (1980) was perhaps the first text to chart explicitly how large planning projects turn out to be disasters. Hall attributed this tendency to two key variables – overestimation of demand and underestimation of cost. He drew attention to the fact that cost escalation for such planning projects is typically around 50 per cent, further arguing that what he refers to as 'the art of imaginative judgement' which will only be addressed once more effective and transparent forecasting of projected trends is undertaken (1980: 250).

More recent work on the costs and benefits of planning mega-projects has used Hall's basic premise and expanded it to take account of differing social, economic and political contexts, as well as emphasizing the different spatial aims and outcomes of such projects. For example, some analyses have focused on projects directed at specific 'urban islands' or and at gaining sub-regional and regional infrastructure benefits (see, *inter alia*, Swyngedouw, Moulaert and Rodrigues 2002), whilst others have highlighted the 'place promotion' benefits of projects in the form of conventions and major cultural and sporting events (*inter alia* Roche 2000). Further examples can also be drawn from recent research in America. Altshular and Luberoff in *The Changing Politics of Urban Mega–Projects* (2003), for instance, identified the shifts in American urban policy that have led to the recent boom in mega-projects, paralleling this to a similar impulse in the 1950s and 1960s linked to ideas of urban 'boosterism' and local 'growth machines' (Molotch 1976; Logan and Molotch 1987). In so doing Altshular and Luberoff stressed the large-scale cost escalation that many projects in both eras endured, having serious implications for local taxpayers and often leading to community-based resistance and protest – which they termed 'negative pluralism'.

In attempts at conceptualizing the planning of megaprojects, Flyvbjerg, Bruzelius and Rothengatter (2003) provided a detailed exposé of a number of large-scale infrastructure projects and how the concept of 'risk' and its acceptance by the public and private sectors has been central to mega-project development. On one hand, they argued that in recent years the mega-project has become a 'new political and physical animal': such projects have 'witnessed a steep increase around the world in … magnitude, frequency and geographical spread' (2003: 136) and have been financed by 'a mixture of national and supranational government, private capital and development banks' (2003: 3). On the other hand, they also threw into stark relief the fact that such projects commonly have a calamitous history of cost overrun largely as a result of what Huber described as 'a combination of intentional ignorance, megalomania, and in the later stages of such projects – blame shifting' (2003: 595).

In this context, Flyvbjerg, Bruzelius and Rothengatter's central pillar of enquiry was the 'mega-project paradox'; 'At the same time as many more and larger infrastructure projects are being proposed and built around the world, it is becoming clear that many such projects have strikingly poor performance records in terms of economy, environment and public support' (2003: 3). They argued that the main cause of the paradox was 'inadequate deliberation about risk and the lack of accountability in the project decision making process' (2003: 6).

Taken together, this work allows four key themes to emerge as being central to the planning of the contemporary mega-project, in relation to the Modern Olympic Games. First, it is commonly argued that the impact of such projects is, within reason, priceless and that 'some may argue that in the long term cost overruns do not really matter and that most monumental projects that excite the world imagination had large overruns' (Flyvbjerg, Bruzelius and Rothengatter 2003: 4). This, of course, does not take into account the significant risk of municipal bankruptcy and large-scale and long-term local government debt – often leading to higher local taxes – that can ensue.

Second, for decades the costing of mega-projects has lacked realism, underestimating financial contingency and, significantly undervaluing safety and environmental costs (Merrow 1988). In short, 'megaprojects often come draped in the politics of mistrust' (Flyvbjerg, Bruzelius and Rothengatter 2003: 5) with tender estimates often systematically and deceptively hiding the real costs of construction until the project is underway.

Third, while initiators and managers often present their projects to the public in terms of supposed benefits to the environment and to society, as well as citywide and regional economic and employment growth, these legacy 'benefits', however, are routinely exaggerated. In similar vein, there are widespread and recurrent accusations that such projects have been partially funded by, or have had their cost overruns met by, massaging 'mainstream' public service budgets. In this sense, mega-projects often can be seen to exacerbate social disadvantage and inequality.

Finally, the governance of massive public expenditure on mega-projects often lacks financial and democratic accountability, with such projects associated with the development of so-called 'pro-growth regimes' and the closure of local politics to local citizens. In the course of scrutinizing urban mega-projects and associated governance structures, many commentators have argued that the focus by city leaders upon growth, competition and development has necessitated a recasting of the way in which we view the dynamics of urban governance. For example, work on 'urban regime theory' (see *inter alia* Stone 1989) has argued for the importance of understanding local political contingency and highlighted the impact of elite economically driven groups in constructing self-serving urban governance practices that serve both the interests of the public and private sectors in attempts to cope with external threats and deliver common aims.

More recently, other writers, utilizing a strategic relational approach, argue that 'urban governance – its policy paradigms, institutional form, and regime of political representation – can be understood as part of the creation and maintenance of hegemonic projects' (McGuick 2004: 1024). This can be viewed as inculcating strategies that selectively favour elite capital interests, mobilize their resources to realize state capacity via partnerships and do so through interventions aligned with their policy preferences at the urban scale (2004: 1028).

In short, these new institutional arrangements or governance regimes often only involve the 'the usual suspects, namely government experts, administrators and politicians' (2004: 1026) who, between them, dominate the mainly autonomous webs of power relations in a particular place. As Swyngedouw, Moulaert and Rodrigues (2002: 34) commented, these new governing forms are characterized by less democratic and more elite priorities. However, such regimes have become increasingly skilled at giving the impression that their activities are democratic and hence legitimate, even where decision-making processes occur well in advance of any tokenistic consultation with wider communities of interest. As such, theoretical approaches to stakeholder involvement and risk assessment involving deliberative, communicative and collaborative approaches will rarely be successful for megaprojects due to the strong influence of powerful planning actors.

The foregoing analysis has highlighted the characteristics that have plagued the development of mega-projects. Their proliferation, therefore, may seem surprising but they have undoubted value as spectacle. This undoubtedly helps to explain why the number of cities seeking to develop such projects or events such as the Olympics has expanded greatly in recent years. This conceptual frame helps to throw light on the complex relationship between the Olympics and spectacle.

Olympic Mega-projects as Spectacle

The Olympics, especially the Summer Games, are now considered as perhaps the quintessential mega-event, or hallmark event, in which the processes of globalization of both economy and culture are played out in specific localities. As Dunn and McGuirk point out:

> Hosting an Olympic games represents the opportunity to attract enormous investment and consumption spending both during and after the Games. It can also generate significant ongoing local development, particularly in tourism and retail sectors ... A locality's capture of the jewel in the crown of hallmark events becomes a mechanism for driving material land symbolic transformations of place and have profound implications for governance at a local and regional scale. (1999: 23–4)

The interlinking between the Olympics and spectacle is now fundamental to the representation and understanding of the event, especially due to the global reach of television.

Yet, however alluring the large-scale spectacle now associated with the Olympics, accommodating that spectacle cannot avoid the geographies of difference that can occur in a host city (Coaffee and Johnston 2007). The planning rhetoric of recent Olympic cities draws particular attention to the positive 'legacy' elements particularly around regeneration, inward investment, place promotion and tourism (see later parts of this chapter) at the expense of more critical voices that have questioned the very logic and justification for such mega-event-led urban renaissance. Various examples since the 1970s of attempts by urban authorities to use Olympics to stimulate urban development and growth illustrate the 'darker side' (Yiftachel 1994) of accommodating spectacle, in the shape of unethical governance, dubious financial management and the securitization of the public realm.

In the 1970s, Montreal, for instance, seemed to offer the IOC a different model from the emphasis on large host cities. As Chalkley and Essex commented, 'the Games of 1976 [were] awarded to Montreal in 1970s, despite competition from much bigger cities such as Los Angeles and Moscow. The IOC wanted to show that a smaller city could successfully stage the Games and thereby counter criticism of Olympic commercialization and extravagance' (1999: 382). In 1970, the organizers estimated it would cost C$310 million to stage the Games but the Games' finances foundered with the ambition to use Games as an opportunity to develop a series of 'grand projects'. The most notable was the stadium. Designed as architectural spectacle to complement the events that it accommodated, it attempted to implement a retractable stadium roof suspended from an enormous tilting tower that also supplied an observation platform. The construction of this and other monumental Olympic projects was beset by political corruption, mismanagement, labour disputes, inflation and security costs. Overall, the Games proved to be a financial disaster for the city of Montreal and the State of Quebec, which financed a huge building boom, spending the enormous figure of around C$1.5 billion, representing a five-fold increase on original estimates. The Olympic stadium remains a lasting monument to the huge deficit, with its retractable roof and tower only completed after the Games had finished (see *inter alia* Latouche 2007).

Although the Montreal Games have become synonymous in Olympic history with debt substantially incurred in the pursuit of creating and accommodating spectacle, it is worth noting that even Barcelona 1992, often eulogized as the most successful regeneration Games in recent decades, has also been accused of having a 'dark side'. For example, in the short term the Barcelona Games only made $3 billion from $10 billion invested. However, as Garcia-Ramon and Albert (2000) observed, there were also 'shadows in the process' surrounding the 1992 Games. These led to the privileging of physical and design-led intervention, at the behest of pro-growth coalitions, and saw benefits aimed at a global political-economic audience at the expense of locally specific social needs of the most disadvantaged areas of Barcelona.

Analyses of Sydney 2000 and Athens 2004 similarly stress the overestimation of projected benefits and concerns about financial mismanagement amidst attempts to create spectacular Olympics. For example, the national government had to step in to rescue the finances for Sydney 2000 so that the full construction programme might take place, with the predicted long-term 'Barcelona style' tourist boom also failing to materialize. Indeed as Gardiner commented, 'Australia spent AS$1.6billion [£900m] on infrastructure for the Games, but generated just a one per cent increase in Sydney's GDP. Indeed, many of the sporting facilities are still under-utilised creating a burden on the taxpayer estimated at $46m (£19.6m) per year' (2005: 19; see also Demos 2005).

Despite the IOC President Juan Antonio Samaranch hailing the Sydney Olympics as 'the best Olympics ever', other observers pointed to the potential negative consequences of hosting the Games, especially for the city's local communities:

> In the real world – in the street, low income neighbourhoods, homeless refuges, and Indigenous communities – there was indisputable evidence that the staging of the Olympics served the interests of global capitalism first and foremost while exacerbating existing social problems. From this perspective, the best ever label was clearly misplaced. (Lenskyj 2002: 227–8)

Overall, Lenskyj (2002) asserted that Sydney 2000 had suffered a series of 'serious shortcomings'. These included community involvement and democratic decision making; by-passing planning legislation; transparency and accountability of cost with indirect cost omitted from the budget and indirect benefits showcased; extra public subsides given by national government; issues of social equity; and a lack of detailed environmental audits. She concluded that there was:

> [e]xtensive secrecy and obfuscation on the part of Olympic and government officials. In the absence of thorough and accurate financial, social and environmental impact assessment – and in the general euphoria surrounding the 'best ever Olympics' – they are unlikely to engage in any serious post game initiatives that will benefits all … residents. (Lenskyj 2002: 231)

Similar pronouncements were also made after Athens 2004, which saw costs spiral in an astronomical fashion (Samatas 2007).

Overall, the negative side of accommodating spectacle has often seen Olympic venues derided as costly 'white elephants', creating 'island[s] of gentrification' (Garrido 2003: 9) and 'rich ghettos' funded by the private sector (Woodman 2004). Commentators have also drawn attention to the short-term nature of employment prospects and the balance between pursuing growth strategies over destruction of urban green spaces (Marrs 2003). Other evaluations have also noted the major risk of a post-Olympic economic downturn once the special circumstances that accompanied the Games have evaporated (PriceWaterhouseCoopers 2004). Moreover, from the perspective of local governance, researchers have also investigated how planning an Olympic Games bid, or hosting the actual event, is initiated and pursued almost exclusively by a selective coalition of public and private sector elites. Some commentators have argued that this leads to the formation of a pro-growth regime, which is vital to an Olympic bid, by helping, first, to co-ordinate and manage resource flows and, second, to respond to the action and policies of external actors, most notably the IOC, multi-national investors and the national state (Burbank, Andranovich and Heying 2001, Andranovich 2001, Emery

2002). Searle and Bounds (1999), for instance, showed how, following Sydney's success in winning the rights to stage the 2000 Olympics, the organizing committee developed a business-led and pro-growth approach with little consultation outside of elite political and business networks. This was despite concerns raised about the sustainability of planned facilities, which would be built 'at the expense of other developments and other areas of planning in Sydney' under special legislative planning powers to speed up the construction process.

Overall, the tendency, when such an elite regime emerges to drive redevelopment forward at a pace, is that the voice of the average citizen becomes marginalized in Olympic decision-making processes (see Chapter 8). As Burbank, Andranovich and Heying et al reported in a study of bids made by American Olympic cities, 'A common element (in these bids) was that citizens were largely left out of the policy making process (and that) ... in general citizen participation in the process of bidding for organizing an Olympics is minimal' (2001: 164).

Burbank, Andranovich and Heying also indicated that, typically, 'piecemeal resistance' focusing on specific developments linked to environment destruction and simple 'Nimbyism' are recurrent themes in Olympic bids. For example, protest arising from Toronto's bid for the 2008 Games was organized primarily through the symbolically named 'Bread not Circuses' coalition, which argued for what they called 'socially responsible Games' (Bread not Circuses). This protest drew, in part, on work by Lenskyj (2002) that focused on the way the organizers of Sydney 2000 suppressed the real costs and impacts of the Olympics and the exacerbated social problems in the area by suppressing citizen voice and reducing funding to non-Olympic projects. These impacts, indeed, may well persist long after the immediate task of accommodating Olympic spectacle has faded from the city's immediate agenda.

The Summer Olympics and Regeneration Impact

Since the 1960s the importance of what has been termed urban regeneration or urban renewal has risen in prominence within public policy circles as a result of the attempts made at post-industrial restructuring of cities and their economies in the face of urban degeneration. While there is no single agreed definition of the term 'urban regeneration', it might be seen as:

> a comprehensive integrated vision and action which leads to the resolution of urban problems and which seeks to bring about lasting change in the economic, social, physical and environmental condition of an area that has been the subject to change. (Roberts and Sykes 2000: 17)

In recent years the relationship between sport and strategic urban regeneration has grown in importance and is largely attributed to the perceived economic and social benefits of hosting major sporting events and developing the attendant sporting infrastructure. In the UK sports-led or event-led regeneration has increasingly permeated policy-making agendas linked to economic revitalization and the development of sustainable communities (Coaffee and Shaw 2005). In particular, much has been written about the potential for cities to improve and develop urban infrastructure and to stimulate widespread urban revitalization by hosting the Winter Olympics (*inter alia* Teigland 1999, Richie 2000, and Essex and Chalkley 2004) or their Summer counterparts (see *inter alia* Essex and Chalkley 1998, Olds 1998, Tufts 2001, Burbank, Andranovich and Heying 2001 and Searle 2002, Coaffee 2007). Similarly, much has appeared with regard to the impact of Olympic hosting on the marketability of place, with the Olympics seen as offering an unparalleled shop window for inward investment and private sector land development. Both of these impacts have developed in significance and magnitude over time. Indeed, given the continuing effect of economic globalization (and, since 2008, globalized recession) and associated socio-cultural flows, cities hosting Olympics gain a unique opportunity simultaneously to regenerate and to appear on the global stage.

Paralleling the rise in importance of the promotional opportunities associated with hosting the Olympic Games has been a reconceptualization of what planners and other built environment professionals view as 'regeneration and renewal' and their assessment of the current value of mega sporting and cultural events to achieve this end. Whereas, at the beginning of the Modern Olympic Movement regenerative benefits, when they accrued, were associated with physical infrastructure projects, more recently regeneration has been viewed as a holistic intervention targeting a variety of interrelated physical, social, environmental and economic problems in a coordinated fashion linked to ideas of sustainability and 'legacy'. As such, Olympic-led regeneration is now associated with local and national intervention programmes and physical projects that target health, education, employment, local economic development, community cohesion, housing needs, crime reduction and environmental clean up as well as large scale physical development schemes.

The Early Modern Olympics and Urban Impact

When considering the early Games, it is instructive to use the categorization suggested by Chalkley and Essex (1999), who divided the period before 1936 into two segments. The first comprised the Games between 1896 and 1904, which had minimal urban impact. In essence, the organizers of the early Games made little attempt to think about the possibilities of using the Olympics to stimulate urban development.

The second period (1908–32) saw the Games better organized, larger in scale and using facilities constructed specifically for the Olympics. At the 1904 IOC meeting, the fourth modern Games, due to be held in the summer of 1908, was awarded to Rome. Around this time, in 1905 Great Britain and France began organizing a joint trade fair – the Franco–British Exhibition – to be held in London in 1908 with the intention of building and strengthening trading partnerships and where Britain, France and their respective colonies were to be exhibitors (Mallon and Buchanan 1998). However, the eruption of Mount Vesuvius near Naples in 1906 led the Italian government to argue that they could not organize the Games. London was then offered and entrusted with the Games, in large part because of the British experience at hosting sporting events such as the Henley Regatta and the Wimbledon Tennis championships. Meanwhile, the infrastructure planning for the upcoming 1908 Franco-British Exhibition was continuing apace on a 140-acre site at Shepherd's Bush in West London. Architecturally, the site was unique for its time, with gardens, lakes and fountains being used to complement a vast array of innovative buildings with white plaster finishing, leading to the nickname of 'White City' being adopted (Carden 1908). When the decision to award London the 1908 Olympics was made, it was planned that the exhibition should be 'more than just a trade fair' (Mallon and Buchanan 1998: 4) – with the addition of the Olympics as a key element (Mallon and Buchanan 1998: 16). This is in contrast to both 1900 (St Louis) and 1904 (Paris) where the summer Olympic Games were mere side-shows to prestigious trade expositions (Matthews 1980).

The 1908 Games, for the first time, led to purpose-built facilities and transport infrastructure being constructed that could be used post-Olympics (IOC 1908, Chalkey and Essex 1999). Those responsible for organizing the Olympics managed to persuade the exhibition organizers to build the required Olympic stadium in return for three-quarters of the gate receipts. This was seen as a remarkably successful contract for the organizers, as the cost of building the stadium rose five-fold between planning and final construction. This is the same fear that now persists when building contemporary Olympic facilities. That said, the stadium itself was considered to be the finest in the world at that point and provided a partial blueprint for future Olympic venues. Transport infrastructure was also enhanced to coincide with the exhibition and Olympics with a new underground 'tube' stop being added to the network at Wood Street. The exhibition was a great success and had legacy effects both for the host city. As Levin noted:

> the fair grounds, and Olympic stadium, remained and served as the site for future exhibitions and events. White City became a pleasure/amusement park, and the stadium's functions ranged from training Olympic athletes to the site for greyhound dog races until the stadium was demolished. (2001)

London 1908 appeared to create a new model for the development of sport facilities, which was adopted four years later at Stockholm (1912) and in subsequent Games at Antwerp 1920, Paris 1924 and Amsterdam 1928. Los Angeles 1932 also adopted the model of developing a purpose-built sports facility for the Games but also, for the first time, a purpose-built 'athletes' village', which was auctioned for housing needs in the post-Olympic era (Chalkey and Essex 1999: 377).

The Berlin Games of 1936 provided a watershed as far as expenditure on the Games was concerned, although the question of the impact on Berlin was secondary to the incumbent Nazi regime's desire to present a façade to the outside world. The

1936 Games developed facilities and infrastructure of a scale and grandeur far in advance of previous Games, intended to display Germany's architectural prowess and cultural history (*inter alia* Meyer-Kunzel 2007).

In stark contrast to Berlin, the first Games after World War II gave organizers less opportunity to carry out major planning or regeneration works. The 1948 London Olympics were held after the planned Games of 1940 (Tokyo) and 1944 (London) were cancelled due to war. London 1948, held with Britain in the grip of economic recession, required considerable improvisation to provide the necessary facilities. The 1948 Games became known as the 'Austerity Games' as a result of the post-war 'blitz conditions' still faced by Londoners and, to a large extent, became a political project linked to 'returning to normality' as quickly as possible (Baker 1994a: 58). Unlike the last pre-war Games in Berlin in 1936, no new venues, athletes' villages or infrastructure were built with only temporary alterations to existing facilities being carried out. For example, a temporary track was fitted at Wembley Stadium (originally built for the Empire Exhibition in 1924) and local schools, government buildings and military barracks were used to house the athletes. A new road was also built from the stadium to the main station to ease spectator congestion.

The IOC also requested that athletes bring their own food as bread rationing in London only finished the day the Games began (*History Today* 1998). Such austerity, coupled with a downturn in the world economy, put a number of restraints on preparations for the Games, which would leave their future in doubt right up until the final weeks, with fears expressed that the Games would become an unnecessary expense and a 'big bewildering jamboree' (Baker1994b: 108). In particular, critical questions were asked about the appropriateness of London hosting the Games, given the destitute conditions many of its citizens were living in. As Baker noted, this 'pointed to a contradiction between Olympic preparations and the stringent economic circumstances facing the British people' which were 'exaggerated and a case for abandoning the Games established' (1994b: 60). These Games were however important from a geographical point of view in terms of providing an international event which would launch in the post-war world (see for example BOA 1948). The 1948 Games were also the first to be televised, with the BBC paying 100 Guineas for the rights, and also the first to hold Paralympics. Similar rights are expected to cost over £1 billion in 2012.

Overall, the 1948 Games were to have very little effect on the urban structure of London, often being referred to as the 'low impact Games' (Essex and Chalkely 1998: 192), given the relatively modest budget compared to subsequent Games. They did not involve the significant construction of venues or infrastructure as the organizers were under significant pressure to justify the short- and long-term costs and benefits of being an Olympic city. Indeed, the balance between advantage and disadvantage was very much linked to Britain reaffirming its place in the global economy and geopolitics.

Similar 'low impact Games' in Helsinki 1952 and Melbourne 1956 concentrated their activities on sporting facilities and associated athletes' villages. It was from

Rome 1960 onwards that substantial investment in city infrastructure, particularly transport, began to be planned hand-in-hand with new sporting facilities. It is at this time that the idea of city 'legacy' became a key component in planning Olympics venues for Games-time and beyond (Gold and Gold 2008). This changed the way in which municipal authorities perceived the task of hosting the Summer Olympics. As Chalkley and Essex noted, 'the changes produced by the Olympics games led to calls for the next Games to be cancelled because of the scale and complexity of the related urban developments' (1997: 379).

The scale of sporting facilities and associated urban regeneration for host cites was taken to new levels at Tokyo 1964, where the Japanese government saw the Games as an opportunity to invest as much in public transport and utility infrastructures as in sporting stadia and to modernize Tokyo. The city authorities developed many new highways, metro lines, monorail, airport and port facilities, along with improvements in the city's water supply and waste management systems. The areas immediately adjacent to the main stadium were also rejuvenated, with landscaping and the addition of new subway stations.

Urban Entrepreneurialism and Olympic Regeneration

The strategy adopted at Rome and Tokyo would presage the future, although the trend towards the regenerative approach was by no means a linear path. Mexico City 1968, for example, saw a far less lavish and expensive Games than Tokyo, with many critics arguing that investment should be prioritized towards serious socio-economic issues in the country, rather than on updating existing infrastructures or building anew. Although both Munich 1972 and Montreal 1976 invested in both sporting facilities and associated urban and infrastructure elements, neither competed with Tokyo in terms of sheer investment in urban development projects. Moscow 1980, by contrast, made little effort to invest in facilities not directly related to sport, other than a new airport terminal, media centres and hotels (Chalkley and Essex 1999: 384).

In Los Angeles 1984, regeneration was minimal as the focus was on limiting costs while still maintaining the sense of spectacle. The prevailing strategy reflected the fact that the organizing committee ran the Games as a commercial enterprise along private sector lines, given the refusal of taxpayers to foot the cost. The overall approach was to update and use existing sporting and utility infrastructure although the international airport was upgraded (Burbank, Andranovich and Heying 2001).

Although not necessarily obvious at the time, the Olympics also stimulated the development of a regional fibreoptic telecommunications system in Southern California, which provided an advanced regional telecommunications infrastructure that reflected and helped to boost the intense communications activities of the Los Angeles area at a crucial time (Moss 1985). Equally significant were the attempts by the organizers to integrate a community regeneration element into their plans although, cynically, this might also be interpreted as a way of 'encouraging' volunteerism. For example, programmes such as the 'Olympic neighbour program' ran in 1983 introduced youths in south-central Los Angeles to Olympic athletes and served as an impromptu orientation session for those working, or thinking of volunteering to work, at the 1984 Games. Over time such volunteer programmes have become an integral part of Olympic preparation and Games-time activity.

Overall, the 1984 Games were seen as 'great for the city' and 'contributed to a sense that LA was the place to get things done. It also put the lustre back on the Olympics as the mega-event of choice for cities wishing to achieve world-class status' (Burbank, Andranovich and Heying 2001: 80).

This notion of the Olympics as a catalyst for urban 'boosterism' was also fully exploited in 1988 in Seoul where the Games were seen as an ideal opportunity to improve urban infrastructure (particularly transport), revalorize and refurbish the city and undertake environmental clean-up of water systems, parks and open space through pollution abatement programmes and air pollution controls. However, many analysts expressed concern that the Korean authorities had focused on spatial form rather than social process. As Gold and Gold noted:

> the methods chosen to improve the city's built environment and infrastructure … attracted international criticism for paying greater attention to urban form than to social cost. Ideas of improvement centred on the removal of slums and the creation of modernistic, often high-rise, development for high income residential or commercial use. (2005: 203)

The Barcelona Model

The key moment for thinking about the regenerative impacts of hosting Summer Olympics was undoubtedly Barcelona 1992. Indeed, it is now the 'Barcelona Model' of regenerating through the Olympics that provides the blueprint for other cities bidding for Summer Games, as well as offering the conviction that the Olympic legacies can be positive in terms of urban planning and regeneration rather than simply making short-term profits for organizers (Monclus 2003; see also Marshall 1996, Urban Task Force 1999).

For many observers, the Olympic Games were more about bringing about an urban rejuvenation (and associated tourist boom) in Barcelona than about the sporting event, with significant investment required due to a growing population, high levels of unemployment and severe deprivation in particular neighbourhoods. Indeed, the infrastructure operation accounted for 83 per cent of the total budget. Clusa (2000) identified the wide array of infrastructure projects that were developed, which included new and upgraded roads and airport enlargement.

The 'Barcelona model' encompassed a number of key features that other countries have subsequently attempted to replicate (Coaffee 2007). These include strong and long-term strategic visioning, excellence in urban design and the importance of well-funded social programs. Perhaps the most significant aspect of the model with regard to urban regeneration was its focus on long-term and strategic planning rather than the piecemeal and area-specific interventions that had been associated with many of the previous Summer Games.

Underpinning this strategic vision was the strong political and local leadership required to drive the process forward and to develop a flexible approach to regeneration programme management, which allowed the infusion of significant private finance to help fund the renewal projects and alleviate some of the financial risk that Olympic cities faced. The municipal authorities in Barcelona also focused upon good quality urban design and public realm work. The pre-Olympic preparations also significantly focused upon social programmes as well as morphological alterations.

Barcelona's planning and urban design legacy has had profound impacts upon urban regeneration practice in the UK. The UK government's commissioned report *Towards an Urban Renaissance* (Urban Task Force 1999) supported this assertion by highlighting the long-term re-imaging attempts undertaken in Barcelona:

> The Catalonian capital re-invented itself throughout the 1980s and 1990s with a series of urban design initiatives that improved the quality of the public space in the city and radically enhanced its infrastructure. Under Major Pasqual and architect Oriol Bohigas, the city created 150 new public squares at the heart of urban communities. The city succeeded in winning its bid for the 1992 Olympics and coupled this with a strategy of urban regeneration that has paid long term dividends to the citizens of Barcelona, rather than making a short term profit for event organizers. (Urban Task Force 1999: 72)

In contrast to the profound transformations in Barcelona, the 1996 Games in Atlanta returned to the model of Los Angeles 1984 and focused investment into sporting facilities. Lack of public funding and primary reliance on private finance resulted in a lack of lasting and strategic regeneration, with Atlanta's dream of hosting 'the best Olympics ever' whilst at the same time stimulating the social regeneration of the city, turning sour. As Burbank, Andranovich and Heying remarked:

> Major Jackson's dream was to scale the twin peaks of Mount Olympus by staging the best games ever and uplifting the people of Atlanta. In the end, however, the politics of image building and downtown revitalization displaced neighbourhood redevelopment, as well as the needs and dreams of central city residents. (2001: 118)

Nevertheless, the longer-term impact of the Olympics was not wholly negligible. Significant investment for infrastructural improvements flowed into Atlanta, with $371 million of federal money being spent on road, transit and sewer construction and housing projects (2001: 118). The airport received a further runway capable of accommodating international flights at a cost of around $450 million.

Towards a Sustainable Games

For more recent Games of the new millennium, the IOC has laid the requirement on organizing committees to adopt more environmentally and socially responsible approaches to planning, which in turn has influenced how commentators view and evaluate the regenerative legacy of the Olympics. Both Sydney 2000 and Athens 2004 provided tangible examples of attempts by city authorities to follow the model of regeneration through Olympic hosting that was successful in Barcelona and to project themselves to the world as a vibrant 'global city'. At the same time, these cities also focused upon aspects of the experience of Los Angeles 1984 and Atlanta 1996, in particular the concept of developing public–private partnerships to organize the Games.

The twenty-first century has indeed seen host cities focusing on delivering the associated spatial planning and regeneration gains now associated with the Olympics, with a new emphasis on creating an environmentally friendly Games. Sydney received the standard plaudit from Olympic President Juan Antonio Samaranch in his closing speech, as 'the best Olympic ever' but was also heralded by the organizers as 'the sustainable games'. The rhetoric employed in the media leading up to Sydney 2000 revealed great optimism that the Games would leave a lasting and sustainable legacy. Large areas of disused industrial and military land at Parramatta in Western Sydney underwent significant transformation to provide the main location for the sporting venues, showgrounds and Olympic Village (*inter alia* Dunn and McGuirk 1999: 25).

After the event, critical reflection on the regeneration impacts of Sydney 2000 differed markedly from the rhetoric of the 'Green Games' that had preceded the Olympics. Many observers drew attention to the legacy of under-used stadia and facilities. Searle (2002), for instance, noted how subsequent post-Games analysis of the Sydney Olympic stadium legacy showed the lack of profitability of the under-used facilities and argued that, during their construction, the true extent of the financial risks associated with their construction was kept from the public eye. Lenskyj (2002) also indicated how the reduction of funding to non-Olympic planning projects was concealed in the run-up to the Games. The Olympic Park, designed to be Sydney's showcase venue after the Games and the heart of significant and lasting urban transformation, closely resembled a 'ghost town', with little of the planned post-Games construction completed (BBC 2004).

In a similar manner to Sydney, Athens 2004 was seen as an opportunity for the city's authorities to display the Greek capital to the world, to modernize its substandard transport infrastructure and to leave a tangible legacy of regeneration for the city. Here too, and in particular, environmentalist virtues suffused the initial plans for the Games. The organizers claimed that: 'Athens 2004 would be the first Olympiad using 100% green energy' and that 'all projects will be realized with the use of environmentally friendly technologies and materials and this will be a prerequisite in all relevant tenders' (cited in Vidal 2004: 18).

However, the apparently 'green' construction technologies that, it was claimed, would be employed were ultimately largely absent. An environmental audit of the Games that *Greenpeace* carried out argued that, in the construction of the Olympic villages nearly all environmental recommendations were ignored and energy conservation, product recycling, the use of solar energy and natural cooling systems were all dropped from final plans. As a spokesperson argued, 'Instead of moving forward, the Athens 2004 games have gone way back as far as environmental issues are concerned. The International Olympic Committee has called the environment the third pillar of the Olympics, behind sport and culture. Right now, it seems all but invisible' (cited in Vidal 2004: 18).

A report on BBC television aired on 18 June 2005 about the impact of the Games on Athens recognized that the city had gained a positive legacy from staging the Olympics. It noted, for example, the benefits associated with the widening of existing highways and the addition of two extra metro lines, which have contributed to lessening the city's atmospheric pollution problem as well as providing greater accessibility to the revamped beaches. However, this report also drew attention to the increases in the price of basic goods such as food and petrol, which local people had had to suffer, as well at the substantial costs of maintaining the 30 Olympic venues (£40 million per annum). Many venues were redundant, locked or out of bounds. Some were guarded by the police to prevent vandalism. As one local resident interviewed on the BBC programme had noted, 'We had a fantastic Games but no plan for the day after.'

Holistic Regeneration and Urban Remodelling

The infrastructure upgrades and regeneration programmes at Beijing 2008, and the planned urban change accompanying the London 2012 Games demonstrate how host cities must now pay attention to combining lasting regeneration with environmental sustainability – at least at the outset. In China central and municipal governments aimed at, and in many ways succeeded in, transforming Beijing into a world-class global city through major regeneration and construction programmes that aimed to solve the city's inherent environmental and infrastructural problems, and leave a lasting legacy (Ness 2002: 1).

Such challenges, however, took their place alongside other perceived needs that the organizing committee sought to balance. Most notably the development of showcase architecture and property development in order to create a 'modern high tech metropolis' (Royal Institute of Chartered Surveyors 2004). In Beijing most investment was channelled into a 1,215-hectare Olympic Park, including the main stadium, associated venues and training facilities and the athletes' village, all surrounded by a 760-hectare forest and green belt (Cook 2007). The argument was that 'the commercial, residential and infrastructure developments that will accompany the Games will effectively act as a catalyst to change the entire physical structure and planning of the city' (Van de Berg cited in Royal Institute of

Chartered Surveyors 2004). The plans envisaged and delivered spectacular stadia in the north of the city and elsewhere with the aim of stimulating further regeneration of the adjoining areas. This was aided by significant upgrades in existing water recycling, parkland and transport infrastructures, including new subways, urban railways and a new international airport terminal. Although still difficult to assess exactly how much was spent on Games-related regeneration, it has been suggested that this might be as high as $40 billion (Boudehoux 2007) but that this led to a diversion of public funds away from services that have social benefit.

In Beijing, construction and the use of facilities where possible was also undertaken with 'green' standards in mind. For example, the athletes' village was a 'zero emissions' zone exclusively utilizing electric or fuel cell buses and cars, with all buildings constructed to high-energy efficiency standards. The village was the first to be awarded certification under the US Green Building Council's Leadership in Energy and Environmental Design (LEED) for Neighbourhood Development rating system (Clantech 2008).

We should, however, remember that the regeneration of Beijing that has occurred as a result of hosting the Olympics, despite some 'green credentials', has been incredibly resource and energy intensive. Moreover, as with previous Games, the opportunities for regeneration led to the demolition of housing deemed to be substandard on sites key for redevelopment efforts (Cook 2007, Gold and Gold 2008). Some have suggested that over 1.5 million residents have been evicted from their homes as a result of Olympic-led redevelopment and broader attempts to modernize China's capital (BBC 2008d).

Embedding Safety and Security into Sustainable Regeneration

Increasingly, issues or safety and security are becoming integral parts of regeneration schemes in both commercial centres and housing neighbourhoods. As Atkinson and Helms note:

> The interlinking of 'crime and the 'city' is not a new concern, yet a renewed emphasis on the connection between these fields ... has developed to a point where commonsense understandings of how to deal with the renewal of deprived areas, the security of iconic spaces, and broader city economics have become almost synonymous with and agenda of law and order, anti-social behaviour and incivility. (2007: 2)

Although largely driven, in the first instance, by concerns with crime, the threat from international terrorism and the reaction of urban authorities to the events of 9/11 has added further impetus such that traditional safety agendas of crime and fear of crime are being embedded within broader concerns for urban security and connected to an array of other urban policies.

This merging of crime prevention, anti-social behaviour measures and security within an array of policy agendas, underpinned by the rhetoric that we are living in a changing, uncertain and dangerous world, is leading to serious questions over civil liberties and the extent to which Western democracies are moving towards security states and surveillance societies (Coaffee and Murakami Wood 2006). For example, Wekerle and Jackson (2005) have argued with regard to North American cities that numerous policies have 'hitchhiked' on the anti-terrorism agenda and been implicitly and explicitly embedded within many planning policy discourses. Furthermore, exaggeration of urban risk in the global media has seen 'trust replaced with mistrust and as such "the terrorist threat" triggers a self-multiplication of risks by the de-bounding of risk perceptions and fantasies' (Beck 2002: 44). This end result is areas becoming physically and technologically disconnected from the rest of the city (Graham and Marvin 2001) through the development of securitized 'rings of confidence' (Coaffee 2003), threatening the very freedom of movement and intermixing that make cities the engines of civilization.

The response of urban authorities to threat has particularly serious consequences when militarized security perspectives are bound up with neoliberal agendas in urban regeneration schemes. One also cannot ignore the way in which urban security – what is now increasingly being called 'resilience' – exists within a climate of regional, national and global competition between cities for footloose capital, company relocation, cultural assets and visitors. Practices of urban social control are key to mainstream urban governance and strongly connected to competitive economic strategies. However, in a permanent state of emergency (Wood, Konvitz and Ball 2003), the period of resilience can now be seen to be hybridizing into a period in which emergency policy becomes mainstreamed and integrated more strongly with urban social control and economic competitiveness. As such, many cities are now overtly linking security to regeneration, both in terms of the micro-management of new 'cultural quarters' and gentrification initiatives (including measures such as CCTV and gated communities) and the macro-management of urban image through 'city marketing' initiatives increasingly plays on the 'safety' of cities as places of business as vital 'selling points' (Murakami Wood and Coaffee 2007).

Security as Sustainability

The UK government is now adopting a discourse of 'sustainable communities' (ODPM 2003) that seems to be placing 'security' as a key component of, even foundation of, sustainability. Rather than security by design, we have security by sustainable development (Coaffee and Murakami Wood 2006). Here sustainable communities are seen by the UK government as:

> places where people want to live and work, now and in the future. They meet the diverse needs of existing and future residents, are sensitive to their environment, and contribute to a high quality of life. They are *safe* and inclusive, well planned, built and run and offer equality of opportunity and good services for all. (ODPM 2003: 2)

UK government priorities have in recent years focused strongly on issues of 'community safety' as a key element of a broader drive towards lasting regeneration.

Community safety is a broad issue, which has become central to recent government attempts in the UK to create 'sustainable communities' and secure public places (Coaffee et al. 2008). For example, the planning policy guidance document, *Safer Places: The Planning System and Crime Prevention* argues that 'safety and security are essential to successful, sustainable communities' (ODPM 2004). Not only are such places well designed, attractive environments to live and work in but they are also places where freedom from crime and from the fear of crime, improves the quality of life. This guide also identifies seven 'attributes of sustainability' that should be considered 'as prompts' to thinking about promoting community safety (ODPM 2004: 13). These are highlighted in Table 1.1. These attributes draw significantly on ideas of 'crime prevention through environmental design' (CPTED) and 'defensible space', which have been utilized by built environment professionals and law enforcement agencies since the 1970s to make cities safer.

Table 1.1   Attributes of sustainability relevant to crime prevention and community safety

Attribute	Descriptor
Access and movement	Places with well defined routes, spaces and entrances that provide for convenient movement without compromising security
Structure	Places that are structured so that different uses do not cause conflict
Surveillance	Places where all publicly accessible spaces are overlooked
Ownership	Places that promote a sense of ownership, respect, territorial responsibility and community
Physical protection	Places that include necessary, well-designed security features
Activity	Places where the level of human activity is appropriate to the location and creates a reduced risk of crime and a sense of safety at all times
Management and maintenance	Places that are designed with management and maintenance in mind, to discourage crime in the present and the future

Source: adapted from ODPM (2004).

Safer Places shows how planners, developers and other designers can/might use crime-prevention principles to make parks, streets and other public spaces safer. This specifically highlighted (ODPM 2004: 47) the *Secured by Design* initiative launched by the Association of Chief Police Officers (ACPO) in the 1990s, based on a theory that particular kinds of public space design can reduce anti-social behaviour, for example by facilitating 'passive surveillance' (ODPM 2004: 13, 48).

This type of initiative has also included the propagation of community self-help and civic participation in order to promote 'safer communities' and security. This is not, however, an uncontested discourse. For example, Raco (2007: 50) suggested that key attributes of this new approach to crime prevention puts the responsibility on planners and developers to use design for controlling human behaviour in public spaces. Likewise, others have argued that the crime and disorder agenda is actively promoting community obligation and co-option – or the 'responsibilization' of crime control (Garland 1996, Rose 2000). Here individuals, families, firms, organizations and communities are urged to assume responsibility for the security of their property, their persons and for their own families (Rose 2000: 327). Ultimately, as Rose noted, it appears that formal, hierarchical government is increasingly replaced by an emphasis on 'active' citizenship and an encouragement for 'individuals and communities to take more responsibility for their own security, whether this be through "target hardening" or by setting up neighbourhood watch' (2000: 322).

Securitizing Urban Renaissance

More recently, a broadening in the plan for overall urban security has been increasingly embedded with a commitment to more holistic and integrated solutions for city centre rejuvenation. This process is driven from two directions, from the arena of crime control strategy and from within formalized planning processes. Regarding the former, the Crime and Disorder Act 1998 obligated the creation of multi-agency crime-control partnerships, thus drawing in a range of hitherto detached agencies into crime-control policy-making (Fussey 2004). In addition, section 17 of the Act outlines the responsibility of *all* statutory agencies to consider and take action under their respective remits to prevent any possible crime and disorder issues. These developments held particular resonance for urban planners, housing agencies and those involved in regenerating the built environment; likewise, from a planning perspective, more regulatory approaches, including the new Planning Policy Statement 1 (PPS1), Delivering Sustainable Development. PPS1 sets out the overarching planning policies on the delivery of sustainable development through the planning system. Here crime prevention is seen as a central plank, with a key objective being to '[p]romote communities which are inclusive, healthy, safe and crime free, whilst respecting the diverse needs of communities and the special needs of particular sectors of the community' (PPS1 2005: 11).

In the UK, the merging of crime prevention and urban planning agendas is most visible in the newly remodelled urban centres. Since the late 1990s, UK city centres have undergone considerable regeneration in order to reinvigorate and repopulate these previously neglected spaces. Such regeneration, learning from previous less than successful revitalization efforts, has sought to combine a number of design and management issues into a holistic strategy of 'urban renaissance' (Urban Task Force 1999). Urban renaissance has been associated with a design-led approach to regeneration, although implicitly this is connected with new ways of managing the public realm. In recent years, ingredients in contemporary urban renaissance, including public squares, shopping promenades, outdoor cafés and restaurants, increasingly emphasized in urban planning and architectural design, are by design open, flexible and rapidly evolving, a hybrid of commercial and public space. As Rogers and Coaffee have highlighted:

> Urban renaissance can be viewed as an attempt to construct new sustainable urban realms, founded upon the principles of social mixing, sustainability, connectivity, higher densities, walkability, and high-quality streetscapes with the express aim of attracting the suburban knowledge and service industrial demographic back to the city. (2005: 323)

They continue by linking such urban renaissance concerns to broader issues of urban safety:

> In the UK recent policies of design-led urban renaissance have been concerned with making the environment of cities as a whole more attractive whilst at the same time improving the safety, management and governance of public spaces. (2005: 323)

Ongoing urban renaissance has also brought to the fore concerns over the increasingly changing nature of 'publicness', which according to many is being diluted – spatially purified (Sibley 1995) – by design and management processes that prioritize particular commerce-friendly activities and demographics. This is often explicitly linked to ideas of reducing crime and enhancing safety and, as such, security mangers in many urban areas are increasingly utilizing crime management principles, combined with advances in technology, to try and improve the safety and security of the city. In short one of the intentions of city centre regeneration policy has been to make public space safer with 'safety' seen as one of the signs associated with high-quality places and the renaissance of English towns and cities (*inter alia* Lees 2003). Indeed, CCTV has increasingly become a key part of a wider narrative of urban renaissance and is systematically embedded within the regeneration schemes. As Coleman argued:

> The entrepreneurial city is fostering a new urban aesthetic emerging around the creation of privatised spaces for consumption within which proponents of CCTV elaborate a form of 'regeneration-speak' that provides 'confidence' to consumers, tourists and investors ... In the UK, regeneration strategies regularly promote the development and funding of street safety initiatives in which street camera surveillance figures prominently. (2004: 200)

In recent years public space management and the requirement for safety and security have often produced a series of tensions that have implications for the 'right to the city' (Mitchell 2003) and also potentially more negative issues of the active displacement of people and risk. The 'right to the city' premised on a sense of freedom to access streets, shopping malls, river frontages and more, may be circumscribed by the very regeneration schemes and safety and security policies aiming to improve public urban spaces. However, as Columb noted, there is ample evidence pointing to the existence of spatial management policies explicitly designed to control access and revitalize public places by displacing the presence of the 'homeless, street entertainers, beggars and sex workers in the central districts of several British cities' (2007: 16; see also MacLeod 2002, Hubbard 2004).

This approach to public space management is indelibly connected to issues of social control – of restricted access or surveilled spaces and the 'regulating out' of dangerous and risky behaviours. Many such social, symbolic and physical controls over the new kinds of public spaces have their antecedents in US initiatives, such as the 'zero tolerance' policy operated by New York Mayor Rudolph Giulianni and Police Chief William Bratton in the 1980s.

Most critically, this evolving dynamic of social control is commonly described by a number of commentators as 'revanchist' in origin, although this symbiosis between urban revitalization and the retrofitting of defence and control feature was not seen as a new phenomenon. As the 1990s progressed, the 'fortress city' (see Davis 1990) vision spread to other cities as different accounts of the physical and institutional reaction to perceived urban danger were generated, often using emotive metaphors to express how the search for urban safety and security was creating an increasingly fragmented metropolis with serious implications for everyday life. This was perhaps most forcefully encapsulated in Neil Smith's (1996) use of the concept of 'revanchist urbanism', where urban transformation was seen to involve an aggressive and punitive domination and dispossession of the city's poor and the spaces of the city they occupied. Viewing attempts to upgrade particular areas in New York as 'revanchist', Smith drew on the analogy with the right-wing French political movement of the nineteenth century. This political movement of the petit bourgeoisie – reactionary, nationalist and anti-working class – was associated with a revengeful and repressive response to the failed revolutionary challenge of the Paris Commune. Smith suggested that a similarly aggressive attack on the urban poor could be seen emerging in the burgeoning gentrification of the central city.

Subsequent to Neil Smith's (1996) work, the revanchism concept has been illuminated by a number of scholars who have also highlighted the unjust nature of many urban safety and security strategies (*inter alia* Holden and Iveson 2003), particularly for less powerful and less economically viable citizens or 'unsightly user demographics' (Rogers and Coaffee 2005: 324). In particular, the impact of new 'revanchist' urbanism on minority groups such as buskers, street entertainers, leafleters, beggars, skateboarders and the homeless has been commented on widely (see *inter alia* Atkinson 2003). In specific relation to the summer Olympics, Ben Saul (2000) has also documented how, in the run-up to the Sydney Games, restriction on permitted activities in public spaces led to a systematic 'street sweeping' in central Sydney and in and around the Olympic site in Homebush, facilitated by recently enacted legislation that gave the police additional, 'exceptional', powers. This allowed the police to 'move on' members of the public who were causing 'annoyance' or 'inconvenience'. This he argued eroded the 'publicness' of public space and 're-established the powers of criminal nuisance abolished by the Askin Government reforms of 1970, dramatically altering the nature of the modern criminal justice system' (2000: 35).

Outside the renewed city centres, a key element of urban regeneration often associated with major sporting events involves the upgrading of local housing stock. Conversely, such practices have been subject to accusations of gentrification. In both cases, making the city safe for new higher-income residents takes on added significance and raises the question of 'who will be invited back to the renewed neighbourhood?'. This can amount to a catalogue of attempts to 'civilize' low-demand neighbourhoods in order to de-stigmatize them and improve their marketability. In broader terms, the linkages between civil renewal and criminal justice system are made explicit, with a strong focus upon the benefits of proactive neighbourhood policing teams who aim to forge links with local communities and reduce the occurrence of, and importantly the fear of, crime. This can also be achieved, as in the city centre, by embedding surveillance devices and design solutions. As Ward (2003) noted in relation to a disadvantaged housing area in Manchester, UK, that was subject to sports-led regeneration as a result of hosting the 2002 Commonwealth Games, attempt to 'civilize' the city became an active strategy to reassure potential new residents that the area was safe:

> Heavy, time-intensive and intrusive in-your-face policing strategies would form the basis of a wider and sustained effort to perform a civilising of the area ... it was made clear that ... so called 'inappropriate behaviour' would not be tolerated. Where possible, individuals would be arrested. In other cases, alternative, less direct but nevertheless robust policing practices would be used, such as the removal of welfare entitlements or the eviction from social housing. (2003: 122)

As later chapters demonstrate, the imposition of such visions of order is a common adornment to the Olympics.

The Legacy Games

The urban 'legacy' of the Olympics has been an increasingly important part of the rationale for cities to bid to host the Games since the 1960s. Here legacy, implying 'a sense of transfer from one generation to another', has both tangible (material) and intangible (non-material such as enhanced sporting participation) elements (Gold and Gold 2009: 181), which combine as the rationale for city and national governments to target the Olympics as the premier hallmark events to host. For example, launching London's 2012 bid in January 2004, the British Prime Minister also highlighted the urban change mantra of the bid: 'as well as being a wonderful sporting and cultural festival, the Games [would] drive the environmentally friendly regeneration and rejuvenation of East London' (Blair 2004: 1). More specifically, the bid organizers noted, 'the key catalyst would be the development of the 500 acre Olympic Park ... containing the main sporting facilities, would be set in 1,500 landscaped acres – one of the biggest new city centre parks in Europe for 200 years'(London2012 2004).[2] In addition, they stressed that the London Games:

> would form part of the most extensive transformation of the city for generations
> ... and its legacy would transform one of the most underdeveloped areas of
> the country ... All development would form part of an enormous and tangible
> legacy, ranging from sport and venues through to infrastructure and environment.
> London 2012 would change the face of the capital forever. (London2012 2004)

However, beneath the gloss of official announcements and regeneration plans lurks the spectre of the 'mega-project paradox', which highlights the common shortcomings of such a vision. As Gold and Gold noted 'the historic record shows numerous instances where inadequate planning, poor stadium design, the withdrawal of sponsors, political boycotts, heavy cost overruns of facilities and subsequent unwanted stadia leave a legacy that tarnishes rather than enhances the reputation of the host city' (2008: 301). In London specific legacy concerns are being raised that 'islands of prosperity' are being developed in and around the Olympic zones with little thought being given to the broader regeneration of the East End. As Lyndall noted in London's *The London Evening Standard*:

> The Olympic Park risks becoming an 'island of prosperity' amid the deprived
> East End unless greater efforts are made to spread its benefits ... Few jobs have
> gone to unemployed locals, the number of apprenticeships is 'dismal' and there
> are fears that Eastenders will lose out to affluent incomers when the homes
> being built for the athletes' village are sold off after 2012. (*The London Evening
> Standard* 2010b)

Moreover, issues of safety and security are becoming key features of any proposed 'legacy' surrounding the Olympics and other major events. As we will argue in subsequent chapters, the threats from international terrorism, and from low- and high-level criminal activity, are now leading to the production of regeneration plans that explicitly and implicitly embed secure design and technology, most often in the form of security cameras, into existing neighbourhoods on a permanent basis. It is this relationship between the imposition of security and regeneration plans, and what this means for those living in and around the Olympic boroughs in London, that lies at the heart of this book.

---

2   Page reference not included in these citations owing to this being an online source.

Chapter 2
Olympic Impacts: A Safe and Secure Games

As the previous chapter has demonstrated, a key feature of regeneration programmes is the embedding of security features that function to physically protect these spaces and to symbolically promote a particular tenor of order and attract particular types of users. This chapter explores the shape and function of such security practices with particular attention to how they relate to the multiple threats faced by Olympic planners. In doing so, it argues that Olympic insecurities and Olympic securities develop along different trajectories.

Despite the diversity and complexity of Olympic-related threats, since Munich 1972 Olympic security planning has been dominated by the threat of terrorism. Terrorist activity around the Olympics has taken multiple forms. Over the last 22 years, for example, these have included perceived threats from left-wing groups (Barcelona 1992, Athens 2004), left-wing state proxies (Seoul 1988), right-wing extremists (Atlanta 1996), ethno-nationalist separatists (Barcelona 1992), single-issue groups (Albertville 1992), hostile states (Seoul 1988) as well as violent jihadi extremists (Sydney 2000). Since 9/11, such violence has been further defined in terms of the catastrophic potential of a 'postmodern' terrorist attack (Laqueur 1999); hence the 'threat' has been constructed in more wholesale terms based on the vulnerability of crowded places and worst case scenarios (Coaffee 2009b). The selection of this threat from the wider canon of (largely human-constructed) contemporary risks (see Beck 1999) that traditionally accompany such events raises a number of key issues addressed by this chapter.[1]

A key theme here is the primacy accorded terrorism, and the scale of response that it stimulates, in overall Olympic security planning activities. Post-millennium tensions informed by ill-defined (and, in many cases, indefinable), partially knowable, externalized yet potentially catastrophic risks can be seen to shape more generalized approaches to control that become manifest in 'total security' paradigms. This sentiment is clearly central to London's 2012 security project, as articulated by the Metropolitan Police: 'the challenge is to develop

---

1   A key issue when trying to account for threats is the extent to which they are 'Olympic-related'; hence the use of the word 'accompanied'. To avoid anachronistic attribution of motivations and targeting choices to terrorist actors that, in many ways, would be impossible to discern from clandestine activities, the issue is considered broadly. This is because the main purpose of the discussion is to draw attention to the many forms of political violence, and often turbulent contexts, within which many successive Olympiads have been hosted since Mexico 1968. Where evidence of direct and unequivocal threats to the Games (such as threats to athletes or attacks on sponsors) has been found, this is stated.

and deliver a robust overt and covert security framework that provides public confidence and deterrence to attack' (Metropolitan Police Service 2007). Here, Beck's conceptualization of a 'protectionist reflex' (1999: 153) serves as a useful conceptual tool to encapsulate the emphasis on cataclysmic threats and the totality of 'lockdown' responses that have become commonplace in Olympic security operations since 1976.

Notwithstanding the prominent and much discussed attacks at Munich 1972 and Atlanta 1996 that comprise the central focus of many studies of terrorism and the Olympics (*inter alia* Gamarra 2009), and despite (and possibly because of) these 'lockdown' Olympic responses (Coaffee and Fussey 2010), much terrorist activity surrounding the Olympics has occurred outside the time and place of the event itself. The Seoul and Barcelona Olympiads probably experienced the most significant intensity of displaced terrorist violence. More recently, the 2004 Games in Athens also experienced significant terrorist threat in the build-up to the Olympiad – the first post-9/11 Summer Games (see below). To unpack this relationship between terrorist threat and security response at the Olympics, this chapter will first review the ways in which terrorist threats have manifested themselves since Munich before considering the scale and form of the responses they have stimulated. Rather than providing an exhaustive and narrative list of events, what follows is an analysis of some of the broader processes at work and their implications for future security planning. Threat and response are also analysed separately within this chapter to illustrate the argument that, whilst threats develop under myriad logics normally connected to their host environment, response strategies evolve in a more abstracted, consistent and institutional way. This culminates in a standardized approach to security that is deployed into uneven topographies of threat within host cities and nations.

Olympic Insecurities

In analysing Olympic-related threats, two central arguments are made here. First, despite the conspicuous internationalism of the Games, terrorist threats have generally been grounded in specific regional socio-political contexts. Second, despite the propensity of different terrorist ideologies to seek to influence a varied selection of targets (see *inter alia* Drake 1998, Fussey 2010, Coaffee 2010), the Olympics provide a ready and consistent symbolic target for a variety of groups regardless of their ideological, operational and tactical diversity. In addition to creating unprecedented and complex security challenges for the hosts, the diverse utility of the Games for assorted terrorist groups helps to generate an external and totalized vision of threat in need of urgent response.

Disparate Victims: Mexico and Munich

> The confrontations in the streets were getting worse and worse [but] there was a deadline. In 10 days the Olympic Games were going to begin ... We didn't know exactly what the state was capable of. And then, on October 2nd, it became clear. (David Vuelta, protester at the Tlatelolco Massacre, 1968: cited on National Public Radio 2008)

> Before Munich we were simply terrorists. After Munich, at least people started asking 'Who are these terrorists? What do they want?' Before Munich, nobody had the slightest idea about Palestine. (Mohammed Oudeh, planner for Black September's Munich operation: cited in Toohey and Veal 2007: 108)

The above quotes demonstrate the potent symbolism of the Olympics for terrorist actors in recent history. Yet the much discussed tragic events at Munich that culminated in the murder of 11 Israeli athletes, judges and coaches were not the only Olympic massacre of that period. On 2 October, 10 days before the 1968 Games, widespread student protests against the Mexican president Gustavo Díaz Ordaz's repressive rule and his government's diversion of welfare budgets towards Olympic pageantry were met with violent military opposition and a graphic demonstration of the state monopoly on violence. Following the deployment of thousands of soldiers, notably the specially assembled 'Olympia Battalions' and their attendant weaponry, the ensuing Tlatelolco massacre[2] culminated in the murder of hundreds of protestors with thousands of others arrested and assaulted by the state's uniformed representatives (Poniatowska 2003). Whilst such events have not been repeated on such a scale at the Games, exceptional security mobilizations and restrictions on protest (see below), alongside the selective construction of 'threat' at subsequent Olympiads, have ensured their meaning continues to reverberate. Moreover, the marshalling of repressive state machinery to mitigate potential reputational damage – as articulated in President Ordaz's ominous statement 'everything has a limit and I can no longer allow the law to be broken, as it has been in the eyes of the world' (National Public Radio 2008) two weeks prior to the massacre[3] – has continued to occupy an important place in later Olympic security strategies (see below).

It is the Palestinian Black September Organization's (BSO) attack at Munich, however, that has perhaps resonated most completely on conceptions of security and insecurity at succeeding Olympiads. Recounting these tragic events in detail

---

2   Tlatelolco is a suburb of Mexico City. The protests and subsequent massacre happened in the Plaza de las Tres Culturas in the centre of the neighbourhood. For a wealth of qualitative accounts from those present at the time, see Poniatowska (2003) and National Public Radio (2008).

3   Numerous protesters' testimonies in Poniatowska's (2003) collection allude to the establishment of an 'Olympic Truce' between the opposing sides during the Games.

here would add little, given the quantity of extant discussion (including a score of novels, at least two major films – Kevin MacDonald's *One Day in September* (1999) and Steven Spielberg's *Munich* (2005) – and volumes of academic discussion) detailing the actions of that night (see Aston 1983, Reeve 2001). However, what is of note is the relationship between what happened at Munich and the construction of both threat and security at subsequent Olympiads.

With regard to the way terrorists appropriate the Games' symbolism, Munich is perhaps unusual in that the threat was *external* to German politics or issues. As this discussion will argue, at many subsequent Games, terrorist threats have largely been grounded in the more *internal* context of the host nation – yet have been conceptualized in relation to what occurred in 1972. Connected to this is the diverse currency offered by the Olympics for those wishing to make political statements. Alongside the activities of dissident Palestinians, in a less publicized action following 'Bloody Sunday' (the shooting of 27 Catholic protesters in Northern Ireland by the British Army in January 1972), Irish Republican protesters penetrated Munich's Olympic security cordon to attack Noel Taggart, a Northern Irish competitor riding for the Irish Olympic team during the men's cycling road race event (Howard 2006). Away from 1972 and Munich, the BSO attacks on Israeli nationals continue to resonate amongst those with a potential interest in targeting the Games. Documents seized in Afghanistan in 2002, written by Al-Qaeda activist Abu Ubeid Al Qurashi, for example, judge the Munich attack to be the most successful operation of the last 40 years after 9/11 (cited in Silke 2010).

Considering the impact of Munich on subsequent security responses, the BSO's operation was complex, high risk and is unlikely to be repeated. Owing to the additional difficulty of conducting hostage-based action,[4] the BSO went to considerable lengths to develop a plan that still relied on prior accreditation and unfettered access to the Olympic village, achieved by gaining employment within the site in advance of the Games (see Venzke and Ibrahim 2003). By contrast, almost all subsequent Olympic-related terrorist violence has utilized conventional bombing tactics (normally employing conventional explosives) and, rarely, small firearms.[5] At the same time, threats to Olympics have constantly shifted in relation to their own contextual environments and logic, thus raising operational questions over the relationship between future planning on the basis of retrospective events.[6]

---

4   Although now a heightened risk for London 2012 Olympic security planners following the Mumbai attacks of 2008 (see below).

5   In the wake of the Lashkar-e-Toiba attack in Mumbai during 2008, 2012 Olympic security planners placed an added emphasis on the threat of small firearms during recent interviews with the authors.

6   The prevalence of post-hoc planning in Olympic security operations was succinctly put by Crhistopher Bellavita, head of the 2002 Winter Olympic operation, as manifesting a tendency towards 'form follows mistake' (Bellavita 2007: 5).

Following Munich: Innsbruck 1976, Montreal 1976 and Lake Placid 1980

The events in Munich placed additional demands on the next Olympic city, Innsbruck, Austria – a task made more difficult by the fact that, owing to Denver's withdrawal of its candidacy, Innsbruck was selected only three years before the opening ceremony. Having previously hosted the Winter Games in 1964, Innsbruck was considered by the IOC to have adequate extant infrastructure that could be brought into service at late notice. As the official final report for the Games states, Munich was at the forefront of planner's minds: 'the general director for public security, Dr. Oswald Peterlunger, emphasized again and again that all security measures were to be taken to avoid as far a possible a repetition of the Munich tragedy' (OOWI 1976: 281).

Compounding this was continued localized activity from dissident Palestinian groups. During December 1975, less than six weeks before the opening ceremony, six Popular Front for the Liberation of Palestine (PFLP) terrorists took 73 hostages at Vienna's OPEC Headquarters. Although three hostages were killed during the dénouement, the Austrian authorities rapidly submitted to their demands, guaranteeing safe passage out of the country and facilitating asylum for the attackers in Algeria, a measure that drew strong criticism from Golda Meir's Israeli government (Sanan 1997). During the same year, the BSO had conducted three Austrian-based terrorist attacks, hijacking a Vienna–Tel Aviv scheduled flight, a small arms attack against an Austrian Jewish Centre and a hostage siege (Global Terrorism Database).[7] Additionally, the geographically proximate Baader Meinhof/Red Army Faction (with strong Palestinian links)[8] was embarking on an escalated and internationalized campaign, culminating in what became known as the 'German Autumn' the following year. These activities also took place amid a broader tactical shift in terrorist operations at the time. Indeed, the global proliferation of metal detectors at airports (introduced in January 1973), whilst helping to limit airplane hijackings significantly, resulted in terrorist activity becoming tactically displaced into other forms of hostage attack and assassination (Cauley and Im 1988).

These terrorist operations during the run-up to the Innsbruck Games raise a number of key issues. First is the way in which these threats did *not* appear to have generated undue alarm amongst the upper echelons of Innsbruck's security infrastructure. Indeed, Innsbruck's 'Olympic Security Squad' contained a 'Political Crisis [sub-]Squad' comprising the federal Ministers of the Interior and of Justice, the Tyrolean (local) police and provincial governor, the Olympic security chief, Innsbruck's mayor and the chief public prosecutor of Innsbruck. This squad had

---

7   The Global Terrorism Database is a publicly accessible portal operated by the US Department of Homeland Security and the University of Maryland that documents terrorist attacks since 1970.

8   The BSO also demanded the release of Andreas Baader and Ulrike Meinhof during the Munich crisis.

been developed to deal with terrorist and other 'unforeseen incidents' yet was never convened (OOWI 1976). Secondly, despite the prominence of terrorist-related threat, Innsbruck's organizing committee severely underestimated the number of visitors to the Games, with 1.5 million spectators arriving to 'inhale the Olympic aura', as the official report puts it (OOWI 1976: 173), which led to serious crowd densities, bottlenecks and injuries to spectators around key venues.

The fallout radiating from Munich, including criticism levelled at the IOC, led protection from terrorism to become *the* key security concern for Montreal's Olympic organizing committee (COJO) as it geared up for the 1976 summer Olympics. As the discussion in the second part of the chapter illustrates, such concerns in turn had a colossal impact on Montreal's security strategy. A number of analytical points arise from the approach to security at Montreal, which are also relevant to London 2012. First is the issue of the continual mutability of threat. Notwithstanding a recently lapsed threat from the ethno-nationalist Front de Libération du Québec (FLQ) (and a BSO bomb at Montreal's Israeli consulate a week after the Munich Games), questions may be raised concerning the efficacy and appropriateness of planning around retrospective events, particularly given that terrorists have far greater tactical preference for conventional bombing over hostage-taking (over the long term and across groups) (see Global Terrorism Database). Furthermore, despite the unprecedented expense and contemporary sophistication of security operations, both the Olympic village and VIP protection were breached at Montreal. With the help of compatriots, an athlete succeeded in smuggling in and sheltering a friend in the Olympic Village for several days despite its comprehensive security cordon. In another incident, a foreign journalist breached the VIP security ring, approached Queen Elizabeth and handed her a piece of paper as she awaited transportation from an Olympic-related ceremony (COJO 1976). Together, these events demonstrate the difficulties in achieving the 'total protection' promised.

The two Olympiads of Innsbruck and Montreal were the origin of what became the blueprints for subsequent Olympic security programmes and where key security motifs were drafted and shaped. Olympic insecurities, the potential terrorist threats facing the next Games – the XIII Winter Olympics at Lake Placid, New York State – further illustrate their continued mutability. Despite a backdrop of Cold War tensions (without the boycotts affecting the Moscow and Los Angeles Games), and the ongoing Tehran hostage siege,[9] threats to the Games were considered limited. Nevertheless, in the two months leading up to the opening ceremony, Chicago and New York City experienced no less than five bombing attacks (without fatalities), three perpetrated by Puerto Rican separatists (FALN)

---

9 The Tehran hostage crisis began with the seizure by Iranian militants of the American embassy and 66 US nationals during December 1979. The ensuing crisis lasted for 444 days, spanning the Lake Placid and Moscow Olympiads and, despite a calamitous US-led rescue attempt, ended with the release of the remaining 52 hostages during President Reagan's inauguration in January 1981.

over 48 hours against US military installations in Chicago, whilst the remaining two were executed by exiled right-wing Cubans (Omega 7) against the Soviet and Cuban UN missions in New York (Global Terrorism Database). Two key points arise from these events. First, whilst potentially unconnected to the Olympics, these events demonstrate the regional social and political grounding of terrorist activities (and thus how they might constitute risks for security planners) around the Olympics. Secondly, given the current profile of terrorism and its visibility via new 24-hour media formats, five similar bombing incidents in the weeks before London 2012, for example, would likely resonate rather differently.

Cold War Games: Moscow 1980 and Los Angeles 1984

Cold War tensions continued to draw politics into the Olympics during the 1980s at the sequential Moscow 1980 and Los Angeles 1984 Summer Games. Although more significance can perhaps be gleaned from the security operations adopted in these cities (discussed below), many of the contemporaneously perceived threats were intrinsically connected to the activities of the host nations.

For Moscow, information regarding threats to pre-Glasnost Soviet harmony is extremely sparse. It is likely that the chief insecurities of the time were connected with heightened Cold War politics and the Soviet invasion of Afghanistan the previous year (albeit years before the Mujahideen became properly mobilized). This culminated in a boycott by over 50 nations led by the US. Despite this, it is clear that security planning for the Moscow Games was much more introspective and concerned with issues of public order and positive branding for both the city and the USSR (see below).

Los Angeles was awarded the 1984 Games without competition following the withdrawal of Tehran's candidacy. Itself a victim of a Cold War boycott (where the absence of Cuba and the Soviet Union arguably allowed the US to win gold in nine of the twelve Olympic boxing weight categories and to dominate a range of track and field events), threats to the 1984 Summer Games were staged in the context of regional and international disputes filtered through US policies. One year before the Games, the US had been effectively ejected from Lebanon by two mass-casualty suicide attacks in Beirut perpetrated by a nascent Hezbollah, events that followed overt US support for Israel's 1982 invasion. Charters (1983) identifies a number of disparate domestic threats facing the Los Angeles Olympics, including the FALN (dormant since 1982), the Abu Nidal Organization (ANO)[10] and Armenian separatist terrorist groups. Of these, the threat presented by the latter was considered the most significant and, with a diaspora of over 100,000 Armenians in the Los Angeles region (Charters 1983)) (albeit no indicator of terrorist support), was a key focus for the Los Angeles Olympic security

---

10 Although this threat was probably heightened the following year due to ANO's established links to Iraq during the contemporaneous Iran–Iraq war and the US commencement of arms sales to Iran in 1985 as part of the 'Iran–Contra' scandal.

planners. Moreover, according to Harmon (2000) the American Secret Army for the Liberation of Armenia (ASALA) had issued explicit threats to attack Turkish athletes competing at the Games.

Breaking Up: Ethno-nationalism and Territorial Claims at Sarajevo and Calgary

> It was borne in mind that the XIV OWG was the greatest sporting event over to have been held in Yugoslavia and that it would be held in an extremely complex international situation. (Sarajevo Organizing Committee 1984: 159)

Contextual political events continued to play an important role in Olympic security at the 1984 Winter Games in Sarajevo. Although, like Moscow, sources on Olympic planning are sparse, Sanan (1997) noted how the recent post-Tito threat of national fragmentation (that would reach its apotheosis during the 1992–95 conflict) had generated a substantial threat to the Games from Croat extremists. This stimulated the IOC to adopt a more central role in negotiating and advising Olympic security (Sanan 1997). Given the later existential threat to Bosnia following joint Serb and Croat attempts to partition the country (during the aforementioned 1992–95 conflict), alongside the potential for the Games to heighten ethnic tensions by reinforcing perceived grievances of neglect (amid the non-Bosnian, non-hosting regions), such background tensions were extremely significant and, with the exception of the Seoul Games, perhaps constituted the most extreme threat facing a Modern Olympiad.[11]

Ethno-nationalist claims for autonomy were also played out in Canada prior to the 1988 Calgary Winter Olympics. Apparently catalysed by the 1984 Indian military siege of Amritsar's Golden Temple site in Punjab, two Air India flights, both originating from Canada, were attacked within an hour on 23 June 23 1985. Whilst the first bomb exploded prematurely during a lay-over at Narita airport, killing two airport workers, the second exploded during AI Flight 182's passage over the Irish Sea, killing 329 people, an event that remains the largest mass murder of Canadian citizens. Despite a controversial aftermath involving acquitted suspects, accusations of fabricated evidence and bungled investigations, evidence overwhelmingly pointed to the activities of extremist Sikh nationalists operating from British Columbia, as indicated by the eventual sole conviction of Inderjit Singh Reyat for involvement in both attacks (CBC 2008). Such events, however, point to additional complexity when considering threats to the Olympics. Although temporally proximate to the Games, it would be difficult to argue that they were 'Olympic-related'; they would, however, have inevitably informed threat assessment processes related to the Games. Nevertheless, the Calgary Games also

---

11   In a continued merger of this conflict and the 1984 Games in popular consciousness, ex-Bosnian soldiers currently sell tourists maps of the Olympic venues around Sarajevo that have been annotated to include Bosnian Serb artillery positions at the height of the siege between 1992 and1996.

took place amid conflict specifically connected to Alberta, as security planning was devised to meet the widespread protests associated with aboriginal Lubicon land claims (Atkinson and Young 2008).

State-sponsored Terrorism: Seoul 1988

Although 'Olympic terrorism' is largely exemplified by the highly publicized attacks at Munich and Atlanta, the Seoul and Barcelona Olympiads have probably experienced the most significant intensity of terrorist violence explicitly related to and directed at the Games. What is different, however, is the temporal and spatial displacement of this activity outside of and prior to the official events.

In the case of Seoul 1988, both the specific geopolitical setting (of the two hostile nations divided by strained border arrangements) and the geographical features of the host nation (South Korea's *de facto* island status meant Olympic spectators overwhelmingly relied on commercial aviation to reach the event) combined to generate specific terrorist threats against the Games. Here, in attempting to derail Seoul's ability to host the Olympics, North Korean agents and Japanese Red Army proxies launched multiple attacks against South Korea's commercial aviation industry between November 1987 and May 1988, to discourage visitors to the Games (UN Security Council 1988). This manifested in the successful bombing of Korean Airlines flight KAL 858 in November 1987, at the cost of 115 lives, and a disrupted global campaign against Seoul-bound airlines. Although rooted in the geographical and political contexts of contemporary South Korea, this campaign drew a global response, both in the shape of an unprecedented international Olympic-related intelligence operation and in the IOC adopting an enhanced diplomatic function: both have since become staples of Olympic security projects. Together, these factors enabled the IOC to aggrandize its security function and attendant 'knowledge brokering' (Ericson 1994) role.

Regional Games: Albertville, Barcelona and Lillehammer

The XVI Winter Games at Albertville and Savoie, France during February 1992 were staged in the midst of numerous political conflicts being played out in France at that time. Amongst these were the activities of dissident organization Iparretarrak, 'Northern Basques', who conducted 21 explosive operations (all without fatalities) in the 12 months prior to the Games, and the Corsican National Liberation Front (FLNC), who adopted similar tactics to carry out six attacks during this time (Global Terrorism Database). Despite the apparent intensity of such actions, it could be argued that their national distribution indicates that there is little to link them to the Games (although, from a temporal perspective, there was a considerable elevation of Iparretarrak activity around 1991–92).

What received greatest attention, however, was the entry of the PFLP's then leader, George Habash into France to receive medical treatment in January 1992. In what was to prove a highly controversial move, Habash was then allowed to fly to Tunisia without facing any charges six days before the opening ceremony (*New York Times* 1992). Regardless of its outcome, this episode impacted on security risks surrounding the Games. The arrest and retention of Habash in France, for example, would have risked repercussions, whilst his release manifested in elevated tensions amongst the extreme right that was particularly strong in France at that time.

Nevertheless, in a little-publicized incident, politically-motivated sabotage did occur during the 1992 Games. According to the Global Terrorism Database, a group operating with the title Coordination, Offensive, Use, Interruptions, and Cut (COUIC) interrupted the broadcast of the Games' opening ceremony by sabotaging fibre optic cables supplying its television feeds (see also Albertville COJO 1992).[12]

Despite a largely successful pre-Games Franco–Spanish campaign against the leadership of the Basque separatist group Euzkadi Ta Askatasuna (ETA), the Spanish authorities faced terrorist threats to the 1992 Barcelona Games on three fronts between 1986 (in the days following the IOC's award of the Games to Barcelona) and 1992. These originated from the left-wing Grupo de Resistencia Antifascista Primo Octobre (GRAPO), Terra Lliure (Catalan separatists) and ETA themselves. The first group, although extremely small, probably numbering fewer than 25 individuals (Jiminez, 1992), escalated their activity considerably around the time of the Games, conducting five bombings and one small-arms attack (on government offices, business premises and critical national infrastructure) during the first half of 1992 (Global Terrorism Database). Although it is difficult to extract the extent to which the activities of a group that existed 17 years before and eight years after the Games were 'Olympic-related', the double bombing of a Catalan oil pipeline the day before Barcelona's opening ceremony suggests some symbolic value was derived from the Olympics.

The most prominent group, ETA, also undertook a sustained bombing campaign in the run-up to the Games (Galvez Cantero 1991) culminating in a (media-suppressed) attack on the electricity supply to the opening ceremony (see Toohey and Veal 2007). ETA's targeting of the Olympics also extended to Madrid's unsuccessful bid to host the 2012 Games. Most directly, this campaign culminated in bombing Madrid's intended Olympic stadium 11 days before the IOC's final decision – described in

---

12   Despite its potential significance as a politically motivated attack during an Olympic Games, little further information concerning the perpetrators or this action is publicly available. Consistent with the traditional of official Olympic reports in downplaying any experienced problems, what is particularly revealing is the range of threats that were realized at Albertville and that the official report attempts to underplay:

> The risks that had been looked at beforehand, with a view to preventing them, occurred during the Games, but, thankfully at a level of seriousness and frequency far below our anticipated level (theft, breaking and entering, bomb alerts, strange phone calls or telexes, traces of explosives or drugs discovered, scuffles, landslides, power cuts, bad weather, invasion of air space). (Albertville COJO 1992: 239)

the Spanish media as an attack on the 'symbol of Madrid's candidature' (*El Mundo* 2005). Demonstrating the diverse symbolic utility the Olympics has for terrorist groups, ETA's 2005 campaign connected the Games with their enduring operational concerns. As one of the group's spokespersons articulated, 'They planned to continue their campaign against tourism and Spanish economic interests, and Madrid 2012 fulfilled both conditions' (cited in *The Independent* 2005).[13] In addition to these strategic objectives, ETA's antipathy to the Games aligned with their tactical approaches. As Sanan (1996) argues with reference to the 1992 attacks, threatening the Olympics became another instrument of (the enduring tactic of) blackmail in order to extort political concession from the Spanish state.

The 1992 Summer Olympics also connected with terrorist concerns that were more localized, as evinced by the actions of the Catalan nationalists Terra Lliure. With a publicly stated opposition to Barcelona's Olympic candidacy, Terra Lliure escalated their terrorist activities considerably during 1987–92. Although established in 1979 (and operational from 1981) Terra Lliure committed nine attacks (on police, military and business targets) before the IOC announced Barcelona's successful bid to host the Games in late 1986. In the five and a half years between this announcement and the opening ceremony, they undertook 53 further attacks (almost exclusively bombings) (Global Terrorism Database), including the targeting of banks sponsoring the Games.

The first city to host the Winter Games as part of the altered Olympic format that saw the Winter Games alternating with the Summer Games every two years, was Lillehammer during 1994. Despite Norway's general insulation from both global and local terrorist activity, the convergence of this specific location with that particular time generated vulnerabilities related to the ongoing Palestine–Israel conflict. In a quirk of fate linking Lillehammer to the Munich massacre, the Norwegian town had hosted one of the most controversial Israeli reprisals when, in a case of mistaken identity, the innocent Moroccan waiter Ahmed Bouchikhi was killed in 1973 by Mossad agents, believing he was part of the BSO. More contemporaneous was the ill-fated 'Oslo Accords' exactly six months before the Games. This agreement between Israel and the PLO, detailing a now-moribund pathway towards a two-state 'solution', fragmented militancy in the Middle East elevating the status both of Hamas (see Hoffman 2006), who commenced their suicide bombing campaign shortly after, in April 1994, and extremist Zionist groups, most evidently manifest in the massacre at the Cave of the Patriarchs, Hebron, in 1994 and the assassination of Yitzhak Rabin in 1995.

---

13   On 11 March 2004 Madrid's Atocha rail terminus was attacked in the most deadly Al Qaeda-inspired terrorist attack in Western Europe to date, resulting in 191 fatalities. Despite occurring two months before the IOC's short-listing of five prospective hosts for the 2012 Games (for which Madrid was successful), these attacks had little, if any, impact on their application and received no mention in the final IOC Evaluation Commission appraisal of 2012 candidate cities' security (IOC, 2005).

Domestic Extremism from East and West: Atlanta and Nagano

Numerous threats presented concerns for Atlanta's security planners. Just over three years previously, Ramzi Yousef – nephew of Khalid Sheikh Mohammed, widely viewed as the principal organizer of 9/11 – had led a multinational team of extremists who bombed the North Tower of the World Trade Centre in New York City, killing six people.[14] More overtly recognizable Al-Qaeda activity had also occurred three weeks before the Games when US troops stationed in Saudi Arabia were bombed at Khobar Towers, with 19 casualties. In an illustration of how security planning responds to manifest attacks, fears of a repeat at Atlanta led to the hasty construction of a 20-foot-high concrete wall between the Olympic Village and the Interstate I-75 that ran alongside (Buntin 2000a). Yet the escalation of domestic violent right-wing extremism, culminating in Timothy McVeigh's murder of 195 people in Oklahoma in his bombing of the Alfred P. Murrah Federal Building (housing federal offices) during 1995, demonstrates that other severe threats originated from within the US. For Olympic security planners, these events in New York and Oklahoma were particularly influential factors influencing the shape of Atlanta's security strategy (Buntin 2000a, Hinds and Vlachou 2007) in addition to the perceived risk of elevated activity from the city's street gangs during the event (Cottrell 2003).

Eric Rudolph's direct attack on the 1996 Atlanta Games, however, connects with a number of the outlined issues relating to the threats to other Olympiads. In preference to the fortified Olympic site, Rudolph chose to attack Centennial Park, a quasi-public (and therefore less regulated) space hosting sponsors and entertainment in preference to the fortified Olympic site. The fear of similarly displaced attacks against unguarded crowded places has become a key concern for London 2012 security planners (discussed in Part II of this volume). The aforementioned twin themes of the manifold symbolism of the Games and the local socio-political grounding of Olympic threats are further apparent in the Atlanta bombing. Adopting a right-wing single-issue stance, Rudolph attacked the Games due to his opposition to what he saw as the US government's pro-abortion stance (Toohey and Veal 2007). In a written statement presented during his trial, Rudolph articulated how he hoped to:

> confound, anger and embarrass the Washington government in the eyes of the world for its abominable sanctioning of abortion on demand. The plan was to force the cancellation of the Games, or at least create a state of insecurity to empty the streets around the venues and thereby eat into the vast amounts of money invested. (cited in Seegmiller 2007: 517)

---

14   Yousef also led the averted 'Bojinka' plot that planned to destroy 11 airliners (five originating from the US) in midflight during 1995.

Moreover, Rudolph's campaign was ongoing and localized: six months after the Centennial Park attack, he bombed a family planning clinic in an Atlanta suburb before continuing his campaign for another year.[15] The Centennial Park bomb catalysed a number of additional security challenges including more than 100 subsequent bomb threats to the Games (Atkinson and Young 2008) and the 691 suspicious package calls (Buntin 2000b) during the succeeding days. Such incidences demonstrate how the temporal aspects of Olympic security extend both before (as evinced at Seoul and Barcelona) but also after the event.

This attack inevitably generated strategic repercussions for subsequent Games. The next Olympiad, the XVIII Winter Olympics at Naganao, Japan, was similarly played out under the threat of domestic extremism.[16] Although terrorist incidents had declined in Japan during the four years prior to the Games, a number of significant threats remained. Most notably, Aum Shinrikyo[17] had perpetrated a number of high-profile attacks in the years preceding the Games, including the only successful chemical (sarin gas) terrorist attack to date in Matsumoto (located in the Nagano prefecture itself) in 1994 and the subsequent co-ordinated attacks on the Tokyo subway, which killed a dozen commuters. At the time of the Games, Shoko Asahara, Aum's founder, was also awaiting execution following his 1996 arrest and conviction for murder and terrorism-related offences. Other threats were also manifest at this time. As competitors, spectators and officials filed through Tokyo's Narita airport five days before the opening ceremony, left-wing extremists fired three homemade rockets into the complex's cargo area. Whilst Japanese authorities were quick to highlight that the perpetrators, the Revolutionary Workers Association, were protesting against Narita's expansion and therefore not committing an Olympic-related attack (and tarnishing the Games accordingly), its temporal proximity to the event guaranteed a level of global exposure that would have been difficult to achieve without the event's symbolism in the context of pre-9/11 media sensibilities. One additional incident that impacted security planning at Nagano occurred a day after the opening ceremony when the local Olympic organizing committee received a letter, posted in Frankfurt, threatening to bomb the Games. Although the Nagano prefectural police later publicly stated the threat to be a hoax, it stimulated the rapid deployment of additional police and a hasty revision and supplementation of security arrangements at the time (*Washington Post* 1998).

---

15   Another major security breach at Atlanta also occurred. This involved a man armed with a .45-calibre gun who marched into the opening ceremony (Cottrell, 2003). He was dressed as a private security guard and may have gained access due to the confusion and lack of integration between policing agencies at the Games and, potentially, operational problems surrounding the use of metal detectors at the perimeter of the site (see Chapter 7; Buntin, 2000b).

16   The Nagano Games were also billed as the 'Peace Games' with an official 'Peace Appeal From Nagano to the World' (NAOC 1998).

17   Aum Shinrikyo were essentially a Japanese religious cult that ultimately embraced terrorist violence.

Sydney 2000

Despite immunity from a major terrorist attack since 1986 (Sadlier 1996),[18] the events at Atlanta catalysed security planners for the Sydney 2000 Olympic and Paralympic Games to place an intensive focus on political violence. In a wide-ranging pre-event review of terrorism and the 2000 Olympics by the Australian Defence Studies Centre, Thomson (1996) argues that the principal threats stemmed from 'two track terrorism': the simultaneous possibility of what he calls 'amateur'[19] and 'classic' terrorism. As Sydney's security strategy reached an advanced stage, this latter category became refined to emphasize terrorism motivated by religion (Thompson 1999). Within this category, others pointed to the growing internationalized terrorist activity from the Asia Pacific region as the principal threat (Sadlier 1996) although religiously motivated groups, including Jemaah Islamiyah, would only become sufficiently potent in the years following the 2000 Olympics. However, in an antecedent to later events, there was strong evidence that the Sydney Games were targeted by violent Jihadi extremists. During a house search in Auckland in August 2000, New Zealand law enforcement agents uncovered what they claimed to be a plot by Afghan militants to attack the Lucas Heights nuclear reactor, 16 miles from Sydney's Olympic stadium. The incident was played down by Australian officials, with the facility being described as a 'research reactor' and thus of limited disaster potential (*The Independent* 2000).

Other threats to the Sydney Games were more locally focused. A lone-acting right-wing extremist was arrested near the athlete's village by Sydney's Olympic security agencies and charged with possessing explosives with intent to destroy or damage property (Australian Broadcasting Corporation 2000). More controversial was the issue of Aboriginal land rights, leading some to claim that tabled protests by their proponents were repressed in deference to the IOC (Lenskyj 2002), whilst others countered that protests were minimized due to widespread support for the Games amongst Aboriginal populations (Cashman 2006). Other security threats were connected to environmental risks,[20] particularly the introduction of new biological organisms by visitors that could threaten Australia's ecosystems (International Office of Epizootics 2003).

---

18   Notwithstanding incidences of violent right-wing extremism and an individual mail-bombing campaign against government institutions during the 1990s that could be described thus.

19   With the benefit of hindsight, it is difficult not to take issue with Thompson's (1996) characterisation of Ramzi Yousef's 1993 attack on the World Trade Center and the 1995 Aum Shinrikyo sarin attacks as 'amateur', even in Hoffman's (2006) broad sense of the term. Such difficulties potentially undermine the applicability of this model.

20   In her critical review of the Sydney Games, Lenskyj (2002) argues that almost half the funds attributed to security by March 2000 were allocated towards this. However, this is based on the figure of $23 million from an overall budget of $53m, which stands at around one-sixth of the actual final cost of Sydney's security costs (Coaffee and Fussey 2010).

Post 9/11 Olympiads: Salt Lake City 2002 and Athens 2004

The hosting of the XIX Winter Olympic and Paralympic Games in Salt Lake City, just months after 9/11, meant that the attacks at New York, Washington and Pennsylvania dominated the list of threats to the Games.[21] So prominent were these events in the minds of the organizers that their aftermath became fused with the broader symbolism of this particular Olympics, as evinced by the presentation of a flag recovered from the wreckage of the World Trade Center during the opening ceremony (see Atkinson and Young 2008). Exceptional latitude was granted to such expressions and symbolisms of proclaimed US values and attendant nationalism on the Olympic stage. Simultaneously, security discourse was fused with post-9/11 sensibilities regarding the need for total protection against all possible threats (see Atkinson and Young 2002 for a discussion of how these compounds were amalgamated in the global media).

What is striking is the way potential threats to the Games were compiled during the six years of security planning prior to the 9/11 attacks, with a listing of previous threats to a host of sporting mega-events and their coalescence into an expanded model. The head of Salt Lake City's security operation highlighted the historical and transnational focus of this exercise:

> The data for this list – intended more to guide approximations than to be precise – was derived from the 1992 Barcelona Olympics, the 1994 Lillehammer Olympics, the 1994 World Cup, the 1996 Atlanta Olympics, and the 2000 Sydney Olympics. Incidents at events prior to 1992 (such as the Los Angeles Olympics, Lake Placid Games, World University Games, Pan American Games, and Goodwill Games) were also included. (Bellavita 2007: 21)

It could therefore be argued that the generation of post-9/11 uncertainties represents an escalated continuation of the pre-existing approach that similarly totalized and externalized Olympic threats.

One component of this conception of 'total' threat was the enhanced emphasis on bio-terrorism during the Games. Indeed, such fears culminated in the first ever deployment of the now-instituted Biological Aerosol Sentry and Information System (BASIS), a measure that continually monitored the atmosphere across the city for over a month (Heller 2003). Additionally, the real anthrax attacks in New York and Florida during 2001[22] were evoked following a false anthrax reading that stimulated emergency response teams at Salt Lake City's international airport

---

21   These Games also took place amid allegations that Salt Lake City's successful candidacy had been achieved by bribery and corruption (*inter alia* Jennings 2000).

22   Although no-one was ever convicted of these attacks, both the FBI ad US Department of Justice claimed Bruce Edwards Ivins, a micro-biologist working for the US military who committed suicide prior to being formally charged for the attacks, was solely responsible.

four days after the opening ceremony (BBC 2002). Perhaps reflecting the elevated nature of contemporary anxieties, security agencies also contended with 600 reports of suspicious packages during the Games (Atkinson and Young 2008).

Despite such drama, actual disturbances around the Games were comparatively prosaic. These included a slight increase in conventional crime (Decker et al. 2007) and a so-called 'beer riot' involving 20 individuals denied access to an official Budweiser outlet that Lenskyj (2004) argues was left to escalate owing to the over-policing of the peaceful March For Our Lives (whose participants comprised local poor and homeless citizens amongst others) drawing attention to social and economic disadvantage in the city.

Because security planning began seven years before the Games began, and due to its prior accreditation as National Special Security Event (NSSE) status,[23] 9/11 mostly impacted the scale, rather than the form, of the Salt Lake City Winter Olympic security operation (see below and Bellavita 2007). However, this culminated in a security cost of $310 million of which the greatest proportion, 57 per cent, was attributed to personnel (Decker et al. 2005). What is notable here is that this not only comprised an unprecedented *quarter* of the overall costs of staging the Games (Atkinson and Young 2008) but such a cost also exceeded the costs of securing any other Winter Games and also the Summer Games in Sydney two years previously, despite accommodating less than one-third of the spectators.

During the 2004 Summer Olympiad, Hinds and Vlachou (2007) argue, in the main the Athenian security project was geared towards external threats as the primary domestic threat, Revolutionary Organization 17 November (N17), was dormant. It is certainly true that international terrorism was a prioritized threat at the time and has been argued by some to have reduced the turnout of spectators (Pelley and Cowan 2004 cited in Taylor and Toohey 2007). Perhaps most germane here was the seizure of a ship carrying 680 tonnes of explosives in the Ionian Sea during 2003. Subsequently forced into the Greek port of Platiyali (less than 150 miles from Athens), it was revealed that the vessel had been sailing around the Mediterranean for the previous six weeks and was deemed unlikely to have been heading to its logged destination of Khartoum (BBC 2003).

Despite these perspectives and events, domestic threats were most visible. Notably, this included the potential response to the conviction and sentencing of 15 N17 activists during December 2003. Indeed, some have attributed minor bombing of the premises of Olympic sponsors during 2002 and 2003 to N17 militants (Atkinson and Young 2007). Security planning for the Athens Games also coincided with the emergence of the domestic radical group 'Revolutionary

---

23   NSSEs is a system of protecting notable events, such as presidential inaugurations, sporting events and diplomatic summits, instigated under the Clinton administration in 1998 (hence no previous US Olympics had been afforded this status). For events deemed to be of sufficient importance, this effectively shifts the security governance to federal agencies including the secret services, the FBI and FEMA. Such involvement enables effective 'lockdowns' of large areas.

Struggle'. Favouring the targeting of government institutions and publicly opposed to the Games, Revolutionary Struggle detonated five bombs in Athens during the 11 months leading up to the start of the Olympics. These comprised two bombs within minutes at Athens' court buildings on 5 September 2003 and three bombs targeting an Athenian police station on 5 May 2004. This was followed by a series of attacks during 2005–06 culminating in an anti-tank rocket attack against the US Embassy in Athens during 2007 (Global Terrorism Database).

Torino 2006: Anarchism and Environmentalism

Although foreshadowed by internationalized terrorist risks, threats to the 2006 Winter Games in Turin again originated from the specific local context. Indeed, numerous international events had focused security planners towards the risk of violent jihadi extremism, including responses to Italy's participation in the invasion of Iraq (which had produced specific threats by the Abu Hafs al-Masri Brigades in Italy). A hasty review of security arrangements followed the 7 July London bombings (Piaspa and Fonio 2009) and Hussein Osman's flight to Italy after the failed 21 July London bombings. Manifest violent jihadi activity in the region, however, originated from local Moroccan militants as evinced by their attempt to bomb the Milan subway system in 2004.[24]

The most explicit anti-Olympic militancy was connected to overlapping anarchist and environmentalist groups. In particular, three anarchist groups were openly hostile to the Games. Principal amongst these was the Italian Anarchist Federation (FAI). Operating in Turin and Milan, the FAI stepped up a letter bomb campaign against Turin's police during 2005 that continued in the months following the Games. At the same time, there was an environmentalist campaign against a high-speed rail link through the Alps, connecting Turin with Lyon. These protests developed into large-scale demonstrations in the Val di Susa region that linked many of the Olympic venues. This came to a head in violent clashes between hundreds of police and demonstrators and a subsequent police 'militarization' of the area (Piaspa and Fonio 2009, della Porta 2008) two months before the opening ceremony. According to the US State Department these protests connected with a wider anti-Olympics movement[25] and culminated in a FIA flare attack on Turin's official Olympic store (see NBC 2006).

---

24 Three locally-based violent jihadi extremists were arrested in February 2004, a month before the Madrid train bombings, for planning to bomb Milan's central Duomo subway station.

25 However, Piaspia and Fonio (2009) have argued that it is simplistic to view these groups as a synonymous social movement.

Beijing 2008: Reputation and Risk Management

> With the special background of the eve of the Beijing Olympic Games, hostile
> forces at home and abroad will surely act like cornered mad dogs and step up their
> terror and sabotage activities. Nuer Baikeli, Governor of Xinjiang
>
> *The Times* 2008b

According to Yu, Klauser and Chan (2009) security planners at the Beijing Games
considered threats to be organized around three key themes: criminality (local and
transnational), terrorism (despite the above quote, these were related to internal
conflicts rather than international al-Qaeda-inspired forms) and reputation risk.
Regarding the latter, the post-Mao 'Dengist' notions of 'socialism with Chinese
characters' (Cook 2007) – or a state-oriented yet liberalized economy receptive
to the currents of globalization – accented the importance of exporting specific
brand issues of the city. In turn this image management was underpinned by a
strong emphasis on security, as president Hu Jintao clearly articulated prior to the
Games: 'Without security guarantees there cannot be a successful Olympic Games
and without security guarantees the national image will be lost' (cited in *The Times*
2008b). Coupled with the Beijing Organizing Committee for the Olympic Games'
(BOCOG's) official Olympic 'One World, One Dream' slogan, the Games became
an instrument of symbolizing Chinese unity; given the continual internal divisions
and struggles for autonomy, the threats to such a vision become obvious.[26]

Terrorist threats were introspective. Tian Yixang, Director of the military
bureau of the Games' Security Command Centre explained, 'the main danger is
a terrorist attack from three possible threats: East Turkistan [Xinjiang] terrorists,
Tibetan separatists and the evil Falun Gong cult' (cited in Yu, Klauser and Chan
2009: 392). It is clear that the Uyghur militants[27] were active in the lead-up to and
during the Games. Most notably, this involved an intensified campaign (confined
to Xinjiang) that included an improvised explosive device (IED) attack on a police
outpost in Kashgar (killing 16) four days before the Games' opening ceremony
and two further attacks in Kuqa during the first four days of events. Chinese
officials had also previously connected the activities of Uyghur militants to the
2008 Olympics. According to the government, a raid on premises belonging to
Uyghur militants uncovered materials detailing a planned attack on the Games

------

26   The primacy of security planning for the Beijing Games is further underlined by
the appointment of Xi Jinping, then widely seen as Hu Jintao's heir apparent, as head of
Olympic security.

27   Multiple militant Uyghur groups exist that are predominantly based in Xinjiang.
Although historically, they have not necessarily shared the same agenda, one commonality
amongst groups active during this period was an ethno-nationalist claim (often accompanied
by religious overtones) to an autonomous Uyghur state. Their activities have been largely met
by a twin policy of repressive policing and economic development by the Chinese state.

(without specifying which venues) (*The Washington Post* 2008).[28] Other potential threats and disruptions to the Games were also considered to extend beyond organized militant groups to include individuals disaffected by Olympic-related developments, including improper land seizures by the state (see *inter alia* Thompson, 2008). Given the widespread reports of the restriction on protests, the 'overpolicing' of certain populations and the displacement of communities (see *inter alia* Cook, 2007), in this instance the state could perhaps be labelled as holding the monopoly on insecurity.

Terrorist threats look likely to preoccupy Olympic security planning for at least the next three Olympiads, as Part II and the concluding chapter of this book illustrate. For London 2012, the threat of terrorism has become *the* prominent feature of 2012 security planning. Such prioritization is unequivocally articulated in the consolidated *London 2012 Olympic and Paralympic Safety and Security Strategy*: 'the greatest threat to the security of the 2012 Olympic and Paralympic Games is international terrorism' (Home Office 2009: 11).[29] This theme is developed in Part II.

Olympic Threats Reconsidered

The juxtaposition of globalized terrorist risks and local manifestation of threat described above articulates a wider theme of Olympic insecurity. Despite the conspicuous internationalism of the Olympic Games, many of the groups that target them are grounded in specific local socio-political contexts. By contrast, threats to the Games are often characterized as both 'total' and external. This is evinced both generally, as the above examples have demonstrated, and particularly, in respect to what have been the most severe post-1972 threats to the Olympics: those affecting Sarajevo, Seoul and Barcelona. In some part, this is due to the operational demands on Olympic security planners, as highlighted by a senior FBI organizer of the 1996 Atlanta security operation, noting that, prior to Eric Rudolph's telephoned warning, there was no intelligence before the Centennial Park bomb:

> The problem you run into with an event like this is that you can't wait until there's an articulated threat to commit [resources] ... So even if there's no threat or no inference of a threat, you've got to go through all the same steps and planning and putting people in place that you would if there were a threat. (cited in Bellavita 2007: 3)

---

28 A number of other plots to attack the Olympics directly were also described by Chinese officials, including attempts to kidnap athletes, although these have also been viewed sceptically (and as a tool to justify exceptional security measures) by some intelligence analysts (see *The Times* 2008b).

29 This emphasis on terrorism has also been confirmed by senior members of LOCOG and the Metropolitan Police during the authors' ongoing fieldwork into 2012 security.

Borrowing from Said (1993), Olympic threats should perhaps be considered contrapuntally. Here, the (potentially imperialistic) imposition of an international event harbouring specific values and visions of order stimulates manifold discourses of resistance. Such discourses are generated via complex politico-cultural processes that do not easily lend themselves to be cleaved into simple external and internationalized categories of 'threat'. As Said noted, 'the world is too small and interdependent' (2003: 19) for confrontation to be polarized thus. One needs to recognize the confluence of global and local elements, as they constitute Olympic threats. It is in this respect that the 1972 attack at Munich, whilst truly exceptional – both in terms of its complexity and the importation of activism to the host nation –impacted so heavily on subsequent security planning and the constitution of 'threat' as something external and dissident and something that can be, in large part, resolved through the imposition of standardized security models.

The plurality of groups potentially targeting the Olympics also points to further issues. Despite the propensity of different terrorist ideologies to influence a varied selection of targets (see *inter alia* Drake 1998, Fussey 2010), the Olympics provide a ready and consistent symbolic target for many groups regardless of their ideological, operational and tactical diversity. This is seen in their attraction to geographically proximate yet ideologically distinct groups operating in Spain during 1992. The chapter now turns towards an analysis of how these complex and manifold threats have been negotiated and operationalized by Olympic security planners.

Olympic Security

In contrast to the localized vernacular threats examined above, the following discussion argues that paradigms of Olympic security have become progressively standardized since Munich. The process of generalizing, totalizing and externalizing risks,[30] aggrandized by recent post-millennium tensions, can be seen to stimulate a 'protectionist reflex' (Beck 1999: 153) that has increasingly driven Olympic security programmes. To illustrate this process, Olympic security strategies are examined over three areas of discussion. First, approaches to conceptualizing and theorizing the complex and vast endeavour of Olympic security are reviewed. The chapter will then outline key components of previous security operations to serve as a baseline to make visible the reproduction and standardization of subsequent Olympic security strategies. Finally, key elements of these strategies are separated and clarified before a critical analysis of the central practical and conceptual is presented.

---

30   Such processes can be observed from the heavy emphasis given to CBRN (Chemical, Biological, Radiological and Nuclear Terrorism) attacks at every Summer and Winter Olympiad between Atlanta and London.

Conceptualizing and Theorizing Olympic Security

In attempting to make sense of processes of Olympic security, Sanan's (1996) overview of 1972 to 1996 helpfully defines Olympic operations in terms of a number of distinct phases:

- *The 'reaction phase'* (1976–80): heightened emphasis on and militarized approaches to security (particularly at Montreal and Lake Placid) immediately following Munich;
- *The 'hiatus phase'* (1980): essentially, the insularity of Moscow's 1980 security planning;
- *The 'consolidation phase'* (1984–88): internationalization and integration of security across events(including the IOC's enhanced co-ordinating role evident at the Sarajevo and Seoul Olympiads);
- *The 'European phase'* (1992–94): which describes the development of the previous phase with unprecedented transnational co-ordination around the neighbouring Albertville and Barcelona Games and the 1994 Lillehammer Winter Games.

Whilst this model is valuable in its conceptualization of vast security operations deployed in nine countries (Austria, Canada, the US, Russia, Bosnia-Herzegovina [then in Yugoslavia], South Korea, France, Spain and Norway) over 20 years, it contains two major limitations. First, it is too old to account for two of the most significant events impacting Olympic security in recent history – Eric Rudolph's bombing of the Atlanta Games in 1996 and the 9/11 attacks. Secondly, this periodization risks overstating the differences between 'phases' and masks the many continuities between Olympiads since Munich. Moreover, continuing the analysis beyond 1996 makes it clear that particular security *motifs* and their underlying principles have been continually reasserted. What has changed since 9/11, however, is the scale, intensity and scope of these practices. This is mirrored in the spiralling costs of securing such events. For example, Athens' 2004 security operation cost US$1.5 billion, five times that of Sydney 2000 (Coaffee and Fussey 2010). Unravelling this figure reveals further points of interest. Whilst the number of athletes at Sydney and Athens was fairly similar (10,651 and 10,500 respectively), the costs of securing them contrasted sharply. According to one report, athletes attending Sydney received US$16,062 worth of security each. For those competing in Athens it had risen to US$142,857 (Hinds and Vlachou 2007). Equally striking is the cost of security for each visitor, shifting from $34 to $283 per respective visitor to Sydney and Athens.[31] As the later chapters examine

---

31 Applying fairly simple mathematics to this estimate suggests that Hinds and Vlachou may have been inconsistent when calculating the costs of both Games. Nevertheless, their general point concerning the disparities between the security costs of both events remains valid.

in greater detail, these spiralling costs can be connected to growing intensity of surveillance-infused 'lockdown' security models that seek to demarcate the Olympic environment from the contextual milieu of the host city.

This is not to imply a static process. Variations of intensity and form, alongside the penetration of localized security vernaculars (particularly given the importance of occupational cultures in delivering security, see *inter alia* Reiner 2000 and Fussey 2007b) shape the deployment of Olympic security. Nevertheless, such Olympic security processes still mark an exception to prevailing criminological understandings of 'security'. Whilst Zedner correctly noted that, in general, 'universalizing claims about the convergence of crime control practices under the conditions of late modernity (Garland, 2001)' do not 'withstand comparative analysis of the varieties of local culture, organization, and distribution of security between ... nation states' (2009: 11), *Olympic* security is, in fact, more evenly reproduced. Here, a recurrence and reinforcement of key security motifs can be observed that, in effect, constitutes a metastasis of Olympic security orthodoxies. Nonetheless, this overarching homogeneity across time and place necessarily impacts unevenly on its diverse host settings.

There were perhaps two interconnected factors initially driving this progressive standardization. The first can be found in a shift in the governance of Olympic security throughout the 1980s that retains its form today. In 1983 the IOC developed a dedicated 'Security Delegate' role to cover four main functions: conveying the IOC's expectations and guidelines to the host country, adopting an advisory role on security issues, assuming a diplomatic role (for example during North Korea's opposition to the 1988 Seoul Games) (Sanan 1996) and operating as a bridge between local security agencies and organizing committees and the IOC. In practice, this role invests the IOC with considerable oversight over domestic security arrangements and partly explains their spatial and temporal consistencies. Security plans are therefore formulated in close consultation with the IOC's Security Delegate (see NAOC 1998 and Thompson 1996 for respective illustrations from Nagano and Sydney). Formal knowledge transfers between security practitioners working at prior Olympiads reinforce this process. As the following discussion illustrates, this occurs at each Olympics and applies across national, temporal and ideological boundaries.

Second, for host cities, policing the Games is seen as an unprecedented exercise in exceptionality. That London shares this view can be seen from a Metropolitan Police report on 2012 security planning that beings with the statement: 'the 2012 Olympic and Paralympic Games will require the largest security operation ever conducted in the United Kingdom ... The challenge is demanding' (Metropolitan Police 2007). The unprecedented scale and form of this and preceding projects elicits recourse to previous precedents for which the IOC, as the locus of 'institutional memory', is uniquely positioned to broker appropriate knowledge. At the same time, as this and later chapters will demonstrate in further detail, the same private sector security providers are often awarded contracts at successive Games. This particularly applies to large US corporations including IBM, General Electric and

Science Applications International Corporation (SAIC). Indeed, when efforts to favour local companies have been made, as attempted at the 2006 Turin Games, the complexities of procurement and tendering processes left insufficient time to develop and implement an effective security infrastructure, leaving planners to revert to the experienced US providers (Ryan 2007).

The exceptionality of Olympic security, coupled with the transfer of its strategies across time and place, culminates in standardized approaches that are mapped onto the uneven terrain of diverse host cities. Drawing from Bauman (2000), such transferable paradigms operate as a form of 'liquid security', where a shared *lingua franca* of defensible motifs coalesce into strategies that generate securitized spaces dissociated from their geographical contexts. At the same time, these operations and the bordered spaces they create are the products of exceptionality, legitimated on the basis of necessity, atypicality and ephemerality. The threats and vulnerabilities accompanying the Games necessitate substantive action; are unprecedented, requiring a totality of response; and may be temporary. However, as Agamben noted (with a nod to Foucault) in his pioneering work on exceptionality, once established, such states undergo a 'transformation [from] a provisional and exceptional measure into a *technique* of government' (2005: 2, emphasis added). In turn, these techniques realize 'the production of new norms' (2005: 28) that also become installed in a more permanent sense. Although Agamben's focus is more on configurations of governance, the same may be said for places, as such techniques become instituted into the management of both specific spaces and the broader geographies of exception.

A central argument of this book is that accommodating the Games inaugurates securitized 'Olympic spaces of exception' into the host city that, once constructed, generate a particular vision of order, a dislocated uniformity, owing to what Bauman would suggest as 'the lack of overlap between the elegance of structure and the messiness of the world' (2000: 103). With respect to London 2012, the book argues that this standardized development of securitized Olympic spaces, and the selectivity of their constituent security policies, conflicts and contrasts with the idiosyncrasy of East London and the strategies needed to maintain its security (see Chapter 3). Moreover, the requirements for providing temporary security over six weeks of Olympic and Paralympic competition and the role of long-term security legacies bequeathed to East London form an additional tension.

This discussion will now outline and examine key components of Olympic security operations that arose from the crisis at Munich and consider how they became instituted throughout the 1980s to become the staples of subsequent Olympic security strategies.

Blueprints for Olympic Security Operations

everyone was most enthusiastic about the excellent catering service and the superbly organized recreation centre. This enabled the athletes to forget that from the outside the Olympic Village resembled an encampment under siege,

due to the necessary security precautions. (Official Report of the 1976 Innsbruck
Winter Games: OOWI 1976: 175)

Sharply contrasting with Munich's 'low-key' approach, which reflected
contemporary German sensitivities over conspicuous public displays of
social control,[32] the following four Olympiads adopted overt, militarized and
contemporaneously advanced models of security. Following Denver's withdrawal
of its candidacy, the hasty commissioning of Innsbruck's existing Olympic
infrastructure for the 1976 Winter Games left little scope to outfit radically altered
security architectures. Instead, what could be introduced was an inundation of
personnel. Whilst Cottrell (2003) noted there were more police and security guards
than athletes at Innsbruck, this approach no longer appears striking due to its now-
familiar application at all subsequent Olympiads.

Little expense was spared on securing the next Summer Games at Montreal in
1976. Costing US$100 million (equivalent to around US$380 million today and
hence more than expended at Sydney 2000), the security measures deployed at
Montreal have also become particularly resonant Olympic security motifs. Despite
official talk of 'discreet efficiency',[33] Montreal's strategy was, for its time, unique
in scale and placed enormous emphasis on specific strands of security. There was
a heavy accent on preventive measures, a strong and visible presence of security
forces, with particular weight placed on enhanced and integrated surveillance,
communication and decision-making measures (a major failing at Munich and,
later, at Atlanta). Specific measures included isolated transport security corridors,
enhanced accreditation requirements for site workers and, crucially, probably the
first widespread and systematic deployment of Olympic-specific CCTV (COJO
1976). Delineation of Olympic and non-Olympic spaces was thus a key feature
of the Games and drew extensive criticism at the time, including a likening of the
Olympic village to 'a prison camp' (McIntosh 1984: 26 cited in Toohey and Veal
2007: 108).

Such preferences for penal architecture continued at Lake Placid in 1980, evinced
in the Olympic Village's legacy use as a correctional facility (LPOOC 1980). At
the same time, the particular geography that enabled many Winter Games to be
physically separated from their surrounding environment was capitalized on with
the reassertion and refinement of strategies designed to strengthen the perimeters of
Montreal's sites. Central to this endeavour was the deployment of the most advanced
technological measures hitherto used at an Olympics, including 12-foot high touch-
sensitive fencing, voice analysers, ground radar, night vision and improved CCTV
(LPOOC 1980). Together, these represented innovations on surveillance and
security practices previously used to secure military sites and airports and were
subsequently to become strategies emulated at all later Olympics.

---

32   According to Cottrell (2003) Munich's security costs were less than US$2million.
33   Such promises, and their inevitable abandonment, constitute another standard
feature of Olympic security strategies since 1976.

This cross-pollination of security transcended ideological barriers. For example, during 1980, a 'Moscow Doppler' was observable. Previous security themes – such as the deployment of US-made security apparatus, including metal detectors and x-ray scanners (used at previous Games, including at Lake Placid that year) – were incorporated at the same time as newer approaches were refined – such as 'zero-tolerance' style policing strategies and exclusion orders – that have also featured at subsequent Games, notably Sydney (Lenskyj 2002), and Beijing (Peng and Yu 2008), and were embedded in Vancouver's pre-Games Project Civil City (Boyle 2008) (albeit with variations of scale). Another central theme of Moscow's security strategy was the extensive militarization of policing – a strategy that has cut across other Games.

From 1984 to Seoul Policing: Embedding Olympic Security

These specific strategies continued to evolve within their established genus throughout the 1980s to become the DNA of Olympic security operations. As later chapters show, similar surveillance and fortification strategies have continued to be applied at least until London 2012 with some post-9/11 thematic variations around scale, intensity and capability (Chapter 7). The same may be said for securitized enclaves of exception (Chapter 5). Another central feature of such strategies is policing (see Chapter 6). In particular, this broad approach strategy of policing can be seen to comprise three thematic subsets: exceptionally large scales, private policing and militarized policing.

Regarding the first, Montreal's deployment of 20,000 police officers was almost matched by the 16,000 at the Los Angeles 1984 Games, supplemented by an army of 13,000 private police officers (LAOOC 1985). The exceptional ability of single-party states to mobilize agents of social control yielded similar deployments of around 100,000 at the Moscow, Seoul[34] and Beijing Games (see Coaffee and Fussey 2010, SOOC 1989, Peng and Yu 2008 respectively). Whilst these models of policing were intensively militarized (Seoul's security co-coordinator, Major General Yook Wan Sik, described his task as 'very much like preparing for war' (Cottrell 2003: 311)), martial features also became prominent in democratic societies. The advanced perimeter security surrounding Los Angeles Olympic sites was provided by the Pentagon (Cottrell 2003), as it was at Atlanta, and the daily policing of the event was heavily supplemented by the US military. In a demonstration of further connectivity between Olympiads, the US navy also provided water-borne security at Seoul. This militarization, now established, continued throughout the 1990s, evident at Barcelona with the construction of bunkers around the perimeter of the main Olympic Village and tanks situated at strategic locations (Coaffee and Fussey 2010) and at Atlanta with the deployment of

---

34   South Korea had been emerging from a military dictatorship since at least the previous summer.

11,000 troops to help police the Games (Buntin 2000a).[35] This approach continued into the new millennium with the deployment of 4,000 military personnel to protect the Sydney Games, almost equivalent to Australia's geographically proximate East Timor UN peacekeeping commitment[36] (Lenskyj 2002).

The flood of commercialization at the Los Angeles Games also immersed its security infrastructure. Although substantial private security deployment occurred at Tokyo 1964, and was extended at Lake Placid during 1980, it was established on a grand scale at the 1984 Games and then the US' two subsequent Olympiads, in Atlanta and Salt Lake City. Although a long-term staple of US policing strategies, elsewhere this use of non-state-sanctioned actors connects with a number of operational issues relating to standards and integration, in addition to ethical debates concerning accountability, legitimacy and transparency. In the case of Seoul, as at Tokyo, another point of debate concerned the way these Olympic cities experienced post-event retention of private policing agencies (Lee 2004) that the public might not have consented to in less exceptional circumstances.

Together, these developments fed into and cemented the 'total security' paradigm of Olympic security that was firmly in place by 1988 – articulated in the Official Report of the Seoul Olympics as: 'to underscore the priority given to security, "Maximum Security" was chosen as one of the five goals of the Games' (SOOC 1989: 796) – and became a staple of future security projects throughout the next 14 years, as illustrated throughout this discussion.

In sum, since Munich, key security themes introduced to protect the Olympics have become standardized orthodoxies reverberating through the 1980s and 1990s. In particular, these components include strategies based on 'total' or 'exorbitant' security paradigms (Coaffee and Fussey 2010) that seek to delineate the Games from their contextual milieu. These comprise sanitized Olympic 'spaces of exception' or, echoing Bauman's depiction of postmodern urbanism, they represent 'hermetically sealed fortresses/hermitages [that] are in the place but not of it' (2000: 96). These are protected by contemporaneously advanced technologies, the separation of transport modes, target hardening and architectures of 'defensible space', metropolitan militarization, extensive private policing and a commitment to zero-tolerance models of policing. Movement across these borders is, of course, highly regulated and dependent on (physical or fiscal) entitlement.

The coalescence of these strategies was particularly pronounced at the last Olympics of the 'pre-9/11 era', as expressed in the outline of security principles in an unpublished New South Wales Police Olympic planning document about

---

35   There were also particularly hostile disputes between the military and civilian enforcement agencies at Atlanta over their commitment to the Games (see Chapter 7 and also, Buntin 2000a).

36   Australia commanded the UN peacekeeping effort mandated under UNSC Resolution 1264 during East Timor's turbulent passage towards independence from Indonesia between 1999 and 2000. Australia committed 5,500 troops to the operation.

the purpose of policies to secure the Olympics written by the head of the Sydney Games. It is worth quoting in full:

1. Protect the integrity of international entry and accreditation processes to ensure they are consistent with security and Australia's existing policies;
2. Ensure all accredited persons are subjected to appropriate background checking procedures by government authorities;
3. Restrict sensitive areas to accredited persons. Amongst other measures, some form of perimeter fencing should be in place around all venues and sites;
4. Sanitize all Olympic venues and sites for the presence of explosive devices after 'lockdown' of the venue by [the Olympic organizing committee] and re-sanitize as required on the basis of specific risk;
5. Impose random, but carefully targeted, screening procedures using metal detectors and searches of hand carried items, under the supervision of New South Wales Police Officers, for all spectators entering Olympic venues and sites;
6. Apply more thorough checking procedures of all people and items entering higher risk areas such as the Olympic Village;
7. Apply strict and consistent zone controls within each venue and site, aimed primarily at the protection of the Olympic Family and VIPs;
8. Impose strict and consistent controls on the entry of vehicles and commercial materials into all Olympic venues and sites. (cited in Bellavita 2007: 21–2)

Spectacles of Sport and Security: Defending the Olympics after 9/11

Despite their undisputed seismic impact on some areas of law enforcement, particularly the intelligence community (see *inter alia* Bamford 2004), the 9/11 attacks did not drastically change the landscape of Olympic security strategies. Indeed, according to the security co-ordinator of the first post-9/11 Games, at Salt Lake City, the security strategy remained remarkably intact:

> By the time security experts from the national government finished their [post-9/11 Olympic security] review, very little in the plan had changed. Aviation support was expanded, access control procedures were tightened, and a few other elements were slightly modified. It was very easy to get money and people – two resources hard to obtain before the attacks. (Bellavita 2007: 1)

Hence, the main impact of 9/11 was on the availability of human and financial resources. Existing security *motifs* were therefore reasserted, yet their intensity was heightened.[37] More specifically, the underlying principles of the Salt Lake City operation closely map those preceding it, as Senator Mitt Romney, then CEO

---

37   As Chapter 7 illustrates, such trends are present in other forms of crime control and counter-terrorism, particularly the continuation and escalation of extant surveillance

of the 2002 Winter Olympics Organizing Committee highlighted: 'Most Games focus on two security aspects – preventing an attack by hardening the venues and transportation system and ensuring that the resources are in place to respond to an attack' (US Senate Committee on Commerce, Science and Transportation 2004).

To achieve these aims, familiar strategies were deployed at Salt Lake City. The first was the principle of the defined 'security footprint'. In Utah, the collection of Olympic sites was viewed as an 'expanded theatre of operation', rather than the more loosely connected 'venue by venue' model applied at Atlanta (Decker et al. 2005). Alongside the situation of heavily fortified perimeters, further measures were employed to isolate Olympic venues. These included the imposition of a 45-mile 'no fly' airspace radius (Cottrell 2003), the closure of the local airport to commercial traffic and the prohibition of vehicles within 300 feet of protected sites (Toohey and Veal 2007).

From a policing perspective, the 2002 Games also brought together an unprecedented (successful) collaboration between many levels of state and federal law enforcement, costing more than the Atlanta Summer Olympics security operation six years previously. In total, 11,848 individuals worked within the security operation, including 6,553 police officers and 3,500 military personnel (Decker et al. 2005).[38] A key point here relates to local policing capacities. In common with Atlanta and Sydney, local law enforcement agencies carried the bulk of the burden of policing the 2002 Games. Here at Salt Lake City, 40 per cent of Utah's officers were allocated to Olympic duties, leaving other areas under-protected (Decker et al. 2007). Operations of such magnitude also connect with one of the key dilemmas for providing safe and secure Olympiads: the tension between scale and integration. Although largely seen as a successful enterprise, the 2002 Games saw significant problems between the integration of disparate agencies – particularly the tendency for actors to retain intelligence and resources within their own agencies (Decker et al. 2005) and breakdowns in social and technological communication (see Chapter 7). Overall, the creation of Salt Lake City's delineated 'Olympic space of exception', policed by large numbers of law enforcement officers, the military, electronic surveillance and reinforced perimeters, demonstrates an intensified continuation of pre-9/11 Olympic security strategies.

This trend is also particularly apparent in Athens two years later. Despite being the smallest country to host Olympics since 1952, the Greek Olympics set out the most expensive, elaborate and extensive security programme ever deployed at the Games. Indeed, this first post-9/11 Summer Olympiad provided an exemplar (and possibly apotheosis) of the 'total security' paradigm. Quintupling Sydney's security costs, $1.5 billion was expended on the Athenian security project (see

---

strategies during this period (see *inter alia* Ball and Webster 2003, Fussey 2007a and Chapter 7).

38   According to Atkinson and Young (2002: 59) more than 80 per cent of examined global media accounts of 'security/violence matters' at the Games characterized the site as a 'military state'.

inter alia Hinds and Vlachou 2007). Whilst partly attributable to the limited extant security infrastructure prior to the Games, much of this cost can be connected to post-9/11 perceptions of vulnerability and the heavy commitment to technological surveillance (Coaffee and Johnston 2007). As well as being the primary driver of security costs, the elaborate electronic surveillance and communications infrastructure that constituted Athens' 'Olympic superpanopticon' (as Samatas (2007) dubbed it) was also the source of the Games' primary security failures. These events, and their implications for London 2012, are explored in greater detail in Chapter 7.

Forbidden Cities?

The continued trend to standardization was also observable in the less likely setting of Beijing. Hinds and Vlachou (2007) have argued, for example, that much of the strategizing for the 2008 Games was informed by the planning for the 2006 Winter Olympics in Turin, the summer Games in Athens, 2004 and Melbourne's hosting of the 2006 Commonwealth Games. Yet, whilst certain security features and motifs may have been transferred, they were juxtaposed with the specific confluence of global and national processes at that distinct time. In one respect, Beijing's strategy was facilitated by the state's immense power to mobilize security personnel. Other elements included a large and visible military presence (including the deployment of surface-to-air missile batteries within the Olympic Green[39]), a 'broken-windows' variant of policing (dubbed 'sand-pile' policing by its dispatchers, Yu, Klauser and Chan 2009), a 'Olympic Security Law and Order Campaign' to enlist volunteers from local citizens and the delineation of key sites, including additional segregation and securitization of the space around the perimeter of the main Bird's Nest Stadium (Yu, Klauser and Chan 2009). At the same time, the aforementioned liberalization of the economy enabled the infrastructure and machinery of security to be imported, mainly from the US. In particular this centred on the accelerated acquisition of hi-tech security apparatus, particularly technological forms of surveillance (discussed in Chapter 7).

Conclusions

This chapter has argued that, despite pluralities of threat and the diverse local topographies that shape them, strong commonalities can be observed across Olympic security operations over both time and place, summarized in Table 2.1 below. In turn, conceptions of terrorist threat have stimulated 'total security' 'Olympic spaces of exception' that are simultaneously standardized, transferable and mobile. These strategies also risk being dissociated from their host environments. Specifically, they comprise 'exceptional' (temporary, plural

---

39   The Olympic Green was the site of Beijing's main Games venues.

and refocused) policing models that draw heavily on zero-tolerance orthodoxies, the militarization of urban space, extensive private policing, architectural and environmental designs to harden targets and deter transgressive behaviour and heavy reliance on intensive technological surveillance measures.

Contained within this process are a number of dynamics. First, such security exercises are simultaneously oriented towards the future and the past. This 'Janus-faced' dynamic (see Lyon 1994) scans the horizon for future threats – largely externalized – that are negotiated by retrospective security precedents. Indeed, amid early post 9/11 uncertainties, the security co-ordinator of the 2002 Winter Olympics noted, 'all Olympic Games – and by extension other special events – have enough security features in common to permit strategic principles derived from prior events to be used as heuristics for future events' (Bellavita 2007: 2).

This dynamic perhaps also explains the seismic impact of Munich, despite its reduced likelihood of duplication, given contemporary shifts towards less sophisticated forms of political violence that raise operational questions over future planning based retrospectively on past events and ultimately the suitability of this template. Although localized processes, infrastructures and contexts inevitably impact this process, the overarching homogeneity of Olympic security arrangements necessarily result in these strategies impacting unevenly on their hosts. Such asymmetries may relate to issues of efficacy, liberality and applicability.

At the same time, as this chapter has demonstrated, with the exception of the early to mid-1970s at the height of BSO activity, Olympic threats have continually emerged from the fabric of the local Olympic host geography. By contrast, the continual totalizing of terrorist threat as something external and 'othered' invites a contrapuntal reading of this dynamic (Said 1993). As with Said's critique of colonialism and its associated (yet submerged) discourses, a more complex interaction between Olympic 'imperialism and [the] resistance to it', a picture that remains incomplete 'without extending our reading … to include what was once forcibly excluded' (1993: 67). As the above discussion has highlighted, for the Olympics, resistance is present, plural and provincial. Concurrently, Olympic security planning, extrinsically conceived, has become infused with internationally consonant discourses over its ideal form and the total threats it should mediate that in turn stimulate civilizing 'juridical orders' (Agamben 2005: 28) and attendant moral visions.

For London 2012 and beyond, however, further processes are also at play. First, future candidates have noted the currency given by the IOC to the London bid's emphasis on the Games' regenerative 'legacy'. This means that subsequent Olympics Parks are unlikely to become the suburban appendages of the past and more likely, instead, be hosted within existing urban settings. The insertion of new liquid security paradigms into these more idiosyncratic locations is likely to exacerbate their disparity and enhance the isolation, ordering and bordering of such spaces. At the same time the flow of affluent migrants to the wider redeveloped areas may exacerbate the demand to retain Olympic security infrastructures after the event.

A clear example of how this may manifest is in the focus of Olympic policing. As discussed earlier, previous Olympiads have almost unfailingly deployed 'zero-tolerance' models of policing. As such, redefining citizenship through exclusion has been a consistent theme, most notably in Moscow and Sydney where, in the latter case, traditional policing roles were supplemented with controversial (for Australia) municipal by-laws to regulate behaviour and assembly that were also retained after the Games (Lenskyj 2002).

These strategies and their uneven applications can be argued to constitute 'Olympic spaces of exception' that seek to delineate the Games from their contextual milieu. In doing so, particular visions of order are imposed. Echoing Levi-Strauss' (1973) characterization of shifting societal mechanisms for dealing with difference – from the anthropophagic (where difference and otherness is absorbed) to the anthropoemic (the 'vomiting' out, the exclusion or obliteration of difference) – in turn developed and applied to urban spaces by Flusty (1999) and Bauman (2000),[40] Olympic spaces of exception can be seen to play on these countervailing modes. In their most striking aspect, these spaces are overwhelmingly anthropoemic. A particular vision of order is established and difference is excluded via exceptional environmental, legislative, technological and human mechanisms of control that police the Games. At the same time, these mechanisms, along with their broader regenerative projects, are ushered in under anthropophagic discourses of inclusion, diversity and, above all, legacy.

Overlaying such security initiatives are choices regarding the constituency of threat, the shape of response and the type of order that should be created. Olympic risks are thus selectively and socially constructed. The selection of terrorism as the particular threat raises a number of final areas of reflection. From a practical perspective, there is the potential that standardized security responses may fail to map onto to the uneven local topographies of terrorist threat, examined in Part II of this book in relation to London. Conceptually, this selectivity of threat and security can be defined as 'the social construction of security'. Here, questions can be asked concerning what is being secured, where the site of security resides and for what period it is applied. Also particularly important here is the way broader (perhaps more routine) social harms risk being down-played by the emphasis on terrorism. Empirical work has demonstrated that hosting mega-events can routinely generate low- and mid-level offences (Decker et al. 2007) as well as organized criminal activity, particularly those of high exploitation (Fussey and Rawlinson 2009). As such, numerous criminogenic dynamics may be observed in relation to hosting the Olympics. Here, long-standing recognition that global processes impact on local criminal practices – such as the creation of new entrepreneurially-oriented territories of criminality (see *inter alia* Hobbs 2001) – is germane. Hosting mega-events such as the Olympics accelerates these global processes

---

40   See Young (1999a) for critiques of this model as a temporal passage from more inclusive societies and (1999b) for arguments supporting the overlap of inclusion and exclusion in contemporary society.

– including reweighting local markets towards the legal and illegal 'symbolic economies' (Zukin 1995) of the consumer, leisure and service-oriented industries, with their myriad environmental, social and cultural impacts – that, in turn, agitate and impel the development of new criminogenic contexts. Moreover, borrowing from Bauman (1998), such partially-visible movements impact hidden, vulnerable and transitory populations most acutely and, for those it relocates, mobilizes their delineation into protected tourists or policed vagabonds.

These notions of 'what' is being secured also connect with questions about 'where' and 'when' it is being secured. One of the important dynamics affecting attacks on the Olympics is their displacement: the innovative aspects of transgressive behaviour that attempt to circumvent defences rather than overcome them. As the above discussion has illustrated, attacks on and during the Games are rare, whilst those related to the Games, yet are temporally and spatially distinct, are more common. Aside from the more publicized attacks at Munich and Atlanta, the Seoul and Barcelona Olympiads experienced the most significant intensity of terrorist violence yet, in both cases, this activity occurred before the Games and outside of the Park. By targeting the less controlled semi-public Centennial Park, Eric Rudolph's attack on the 1996 Atlanta Games was also arguably spatially displaced away from the more secure Olympic stadium. Nor is temporal displacement limited to the pre-Games period. The Atlanta bombing, for example, triggered a set of post hoc 'risks', with the receipt of 'suspicious package' calls and hoaxes an average of every ten minutes between the explosion and the end of the Games, leading to the examination of over 600 suspicious items and the x-ray or destruction of 450 of them (Buntin 2000b).

In sum, the scale and exceptionality of Olympic security strategies raise a number of social, ethical and practical considerations. Amongst these is a long list of key issues that include frictions between the standardization of Olympic security measures and their insertion into disparate local contexts: policing for protection, policing for reassurance and policing for image maintenance (see Huey, Ericson and Haggerty 2005, Boyle 2005); accountability and privatized security; proportionality; 'control creep'; tensions between expanding security infrastructures and maintaining their cohesion; and the legitimacy of these measures in 'legacy mode'. These themes are explored in greater detail in relation to the London 2012 Olympic security project in Part II of this book.

Table 2.1   Olympic threats and security responses 1972–2016

Olympiad	Perceived/actual threat and/or prior activity	Terrorist/Other politically-motivated attack	Security innovations/models
Munich 1972	• Little perceived threat	• Black September Organization attack, kidnap and murder of 11 Israeli team members. • Violence by Irish protestors during Men's cycling road race	• 'Low intensity' security model
Innsbruck 1976	• PFLP hostage siege, Vienna six weeks before the opening ceremony; • Three BSO operations in Austria during 1973 • Potential Red Army Faction threat	• None, but injuries through poor stadia design and crowd control	• Emphasis on large numbers of personnel (outnumbering competitors). • Relying on existing Olympic architecture
Montreal 1976	• Little (lapsed FLQ threat)	• None, but two security breaches	• Lockdown 'total security' model • Segregated spaces • Blanket surveillance & CCTV deployment • Isolated transport corridors • Visible and militarized security
Lake Placid 1980	• Three FALN attacks, Chicago • Two right wing extremist (Omega-7) bombings, New York. All in the month preceding the opening ceremony		• Developments in the 'bordering' of Olympic sites • Technological advancements • Increased private policing role

Olympiad	Perceived/actual threat and/or prior activity	Terrorist/Other politically-motivated attack	Security innovations/models
Moscow 1980	• Risks associated with prior Soviet invasion of Afghanistan		• Zero-tolerance 'banishments' • Unprecedented military deployment (100,000+)
Sarajevo 1984	• Threat of ethno-nationalism and national fragmentation following the death of Tito • Threats by Croat extremists.		• Largest security force ever deployed at a Winter Olympics up to that point • Enhanced IOC role
Los Angeles 1984	• ASALA makes explicit threats to Turkish athletes • Remaining FALN threats • Cold war tensions • US involvement in Lebanon conflict		• Large-scale private policing
Calgary 1988	• Prior Sikh nationalist activity operating from British Columbia		• Use of security volunteers • Development of security with IOC delegate in a 'conflict free' environment.
Seoul 1988	• Public North Korean hostility • Threats to aviation	• State terrorism (from N. Korea) and proxy Japanese Red Army attacks: • Bombing Korean Airlines KAL 858 at the cost of 115 lives, November, 1987 • Disrupted global campaign against Seoul-bound airlines during 1988	• IOC Diplomacy • US Naval support • Surveillance of *mobilities*

Olympiad	Perceived/actual threat and/or prior activity	Terrorist/Other politically-motivated attack	Security innovations/models
Albertville 1992	• Environmentalist threats • PFLP activity associated with threats to arrest leader George Habash in France • 21 Iparretarrak ('Northern Basques') explosive operations in the 12 months leading up to the opening ceremony • FLNC operations in the lead-up to the Games	• Coordination, Offensive, Use, Interruptions and Cut (COUIC) sabotage of opening ceremony broadcast	• Dispersed/regional Games (since abandoned as a favoured strategy)
Barcelona 1992	• ETA bombing campaign (ETA also attacked Madrid's 2012 bid) • Escalation of Catalan nationalist (Terra Lliure) attacks 1987–92 • Five bombings and one small-arms attack by Grupo de Resistencia Antifascista Primo Octobre (GRAPO) during the first half of 1992	• ETA attack on electricity supply to the opening ceremony • GRAPO double bombing of Catalan oil pipeline the day before the opening ceremony	• Increased militarization
Lillehammer 1994	• Site of Munich-related Mossad murder • Risks associated with the signing of Oslo Accords, 1993		• Dedicated Olympic police force

Olympiad	Perceived/actual threat and/or prior activity	Terrorist/Other politically-motivated attack	Security innovations/models
Atlanta 1996	• 1993 World Trade Center Bombing (Violent Jihadi Extremist (VJE)) • 1995 Oklahoma Bomb (Right Wing Extremist (RWE)) • Khobar Towers attack (VJE) • Risks associated with chlorine transportation under the Olympic press centre. • Soldier guarding the Olympic village shot during independence day celebrations • Security agencies' preoccupation with local gang activity	• Eric Rudolph (RWE) bomb in protest of US Abortion Laws. • Armed man entering the opening ceremony. • Escalation of bomb threats after the Centennial Park bomb (suspicious packages reported every ten minutes until end of the Games)	• Tensions between (a) organising committee (ACOG) and security coalition (SOLEC) (b) state and federal law enforcement and (c) federal law enforcement and the military • Decentralized security arrangements subsequently criticized and abandoned
Nagano 1998	• Aum Shinrikyo attacks in Nagano prefecture during 1995	• Left-wing rocket attack on Narita airport as athletes arrived 4 days prior to opening ceremony • Explicit (hoax) bomb threats to the Games	• Combined Olympic Card: new accreditation scheme (involving domestic registration)
Sydney 2000	• Arrest of a right wing extremist, charged with intent to cause explosions around the Olympic site.	• Alleged violent jihadi extremist attack averted.	• Emphasis on 'biosecurity'

Olympiad	Perceived/actual threat and/or prior activity	Terrorist/Other politically-motivated attack	Security innovations/models
Salt Lake City 2002	• 9/11 • New York and Florida Anthrax attacks 2001	• Anthrax hoax at Salt Lake City airport four days prior to the opening ceremony • So-called 'beer riot'. • 600+ 'suspicious package' scares	• First post 9/11 Games • 'User-pay' model of security (added portion of ticket prices ring fenced for financing public safety initiatives)
Athens 2004	• 9/11 • Threat from VJE • Potential response to sentencing of 17 November 17 activists, December 2003 • 5 bomb attacks by leftist anti-Olympic 'Revolutionary Struggle' group in the 11 months leading to the start of the Games	• Security breached during the Marathon • Hoax bomb threat during opening ceremony • 82 bomb threats	• Technological failure
Turin 2006	• Italian Anarchist Federation (FAI) letter bomb campaign against Turin's police, 2005 • Merging of environmental protest with Olympics • Attempted VJE attacks on Milan's mass transit system, 2004 • Impact of the 7 and 21 July London attacks on security planning • Iraq War (coalition member)	• FAI Anarchist attacks on Olympic store	

Olympiad	Perceived/actual threat and/or prior activity	Terrorist/Other politically-motivated attack	Security innovations/models
Beijing 2008	• Chinese government identify Uyghur militants as principal threat to the Games	• Uyghur militant improvized explosive device (IED) attack in Kashgar, killing 16 people, four days before the Games • Two further attacks in Kuqa during the first four days of the Games	• Beijing's 'Olympic Security Law and Order Campaign'
Vancouver 2010	• No specific threat (although high levels of public fear) • Potential opposition to military deployment in Kandahar as part of the NATO led coalition		
London 2012	• Violent jihadi extremism • Resurgent right-wing extremism • Remaining violent dissident Republicanism		
Sochi 2014	• Geographical proximity to Chechen, South Ossetia and Abkhazian disputes		
Rio de Janeiro 2016	• Local crime. • Local criminal use of terrorist tactics including IEDs and 'man-portable air defence systems' (MANPADs)		

Chapter 3
The East End and London 2012

London, along with Tokyo and New York, is considered a global city (Sassen 2001). Global cities are considered aspirational benchmarks for the international community and, via their pronounced transformations, set the trends in terms of the organization and internationalization of economic activity, social structure and spatial organization. It is widely believed that London was selected as an Olympic host predominantly because of its reputation as a global city. Essentially, this reputation magnifies the profile of the extensive Olympic-related urban regeneration that London and the UK government have committed to. The current level of transformation occurring in the East End of London has not been so high in a global city since London's renewal after the bomb damage inflicted by the Luftwaffe during World War II. Its twenty-first-century transformation seeks to eulogize Olympic design, legacy and urban development in a way that other potential Olympic host cities could not – a consideration clearly not lost on the IOC. Interestingly, despite the London Games being already widely referred to as a Legacy Games, the bid itself lacked a cohesive regeneration model, proffering vagueness instead of lucidity. This included hazy promises about increased youth participation in sport and ambiguous pledges regarding infrastructure and social cohesion. Regeneration can be a narrative or a momentum but fundamentally it will ensure a variety of collateral investment (Gratton 2008). Predictably, it has increased property desirability around the Olympic site and a process of gentrification in the area will accompany the Games. The bidding process saw London's Olympic legacy sold to the UK in general and Londoners in particular as a two-fold stimulus: short-term gains during the delivery process and long-term gains as a result of post-Games inheritance. However, post bid, some local residents feel that London 'winning' the 2012 Olympics has exceeded even their deepest reservations and resulted in their losing their friends, community, businesses and, for some, their sense of identity (see chapter 8). Critics have argued that the promised increase in employment opportunities for local people, via jobs building the Olympic infrastructure, has not materialized and the boost to the local economy appears limited to those dealing with the 'recreational' activities of migrant workers. Despite having been continuously promised benefits, many are realizing that short-term Olympic delivery gains will never materialize. Furthermore, those with the foresight to coldly consider the assured 'legacy' understand that this too is no formality. Rather, it is something that they need to earn, by fighting for. Accordingly, some have mobilized in lawful ways to voice their protests in an attempt to ensure they benefit (see Chapter 8). Others are adopting more creative, illegitimate or illegal, methods as a means of attaining an Olympic benefit that they were led to believe would be theirs – guaranteed. The minutiae of the Olympic impact upon regeneration, resistance, conflict and violence and how these issues are reported and measured, is clearly of both practical and academic concern. This rationale provides the basis for this chapter.[1]

East is East

Prior to London winning the 2012 Olympic bid, the last time East London had enjoyed a global spotlight was World War II. The romantic cliché of East Enders' resilience and communality was born out of a brutal truth – 5,000 East Enders, sandwiched between the twin targets of the docks and the City of London, were killed in what became known as the Blitz. The debris and bomb sites that scarred the area until the 1970s stood as an everyday confirmation of the price the area paid for the Blitz. Recent demolition and excavation around the 2012 Olympic sites throws up periodic reminders of this atrocity over 70 years ago in the shape of ordinance that sank – unexploded – in the mud.

The immediate post-war period brought a dividend to the survivors and offered some respite from the poverty and unemployment that had forged the East End (Gavron, Dench and Morgan 2006). During this period, with near full employment for the first time in its history, East Enders savoured an unprecedented stability, making for a confident community, who bought into domestic and personal consumption while returning Labour MPs with large majorities. The ultimate decline of this populace commenced with the decade-long demise of the indigenous timber and furniture industries between 1961 and 1971 with the loss of over 26,000 jobs in East London (Hall 1962: 72). In the same decade 40,000 jobs were to go in London's clothing and footwear industries, which were centred in the East End (Hall 1962: 44–5). Despite the scale of such job losses, industrial decline took place surreptitiously. Most of the losses were in non-unionized businesses and located in relatively small units of production. However, as we shall discuss later, it was the slow death of the London Docks that marked the end of this classic period of an entrenched pragmatic working-class community. It is in this socio-political milieu that the 2012 Olympics will take place. Never before in Olympic history have the Games been located in such a post-industrial context. Never in the history of UK sport has such investment in sporting infrastructure been thrown at an area manifesting so many indices of poverty.

---

1   The likely impact of the Olympics is explored by Olympic Games Impact (OGI), launched in 2003 by the IOC, who realized that data to measure the impact of the Olympic Games was not being gathered in any systematic way. The Olympic host city is now obliged to collaborate with the OGI as part of their IOC agreement.

Eruptions and Legacies: London 1908

The Olympic Games at one time were hosted in London without promises of legacy or regeneration. The choice of London as the site for the 1908 Olympics, however, was dictated by world events rather than by IOC apparatchiks. The eruption of Mount Vesuvius in 1906 meant that Naples, the intended host for the 1908 Olympic Games, could not sustain the event. At the Interim Games of 1906, Italy's Organizing Committee asked the IOC to re-allocate the event and Lord Desborough, as Chair of the newly formed BOA, offered to host it. What became the 1908 London Games coincided with the Franco-British Exhibition, which meant that the Games were financed by these two powerful nations and primary advocates of the Olympic Movement (Hill 1996). Britain had a proven track record of organizing prestigious sporting events, including the Derby, the Henley Regatta and the Wimbledon tennis tournament and London also had established venues that could host Olympic events (Senn 1999, Killanin 1979). The 1908 Games thus saw 21 sports, 107 events and some 2,035 competitors drawn from 22 countries, making it hitherto the best attended and most diverse Games ever.

In order to stage the main events, a temporary wooden arena seating 68,000, known as the White City Stadium, was hastily erected in west London's Shepherd's Bush district, and dismantled soon after the last event. The Games were controversial by virtue of what one Olympic historian calls 'rampant prejudice by British judging officials', which created a rift between the hosts and American athletes and officials that lasted long after the event (Miller 2003: 53). Noticing there was no American flag flying over the stadium at the opening ceremony, the US discus thrower Martin Sheridan refused to dip the Stars and Stripes before the Royal box during what was the first ever country-by-country procession. The men's 440-yard final was re-run unopposed by the Americans after the disputed disqualification of one of the US runners (Senn 1999). The Complaints made about the bias of British officials included the fact that the British tug of war team were allowed to wear work boots instead of regulation plimsolls. As a result of such controversies all subsequent Games would see a set of 'impartial' judges nominated by each sport's international governing body (Warning 1980). The 1908 Games also left a significant legacy in that they witnessed the first awarding of the gold, silver and bronze medals. The 1908 medals table would be the only time Great Britain ever headed such a league: the 145 Great Britain medals were some four times the medal total Britain was to win in any subsequent Olympic competition (Girginov and Parry 2005).In 1908 the distance for the marathon event was standardized at 26.2 miles following Queen Alexandra's request that the run begin at her Windsor Castle home and finish in the stadium in front of the Royal box.

The Bishop of Pennsylvania remarked that 'The important thing about these Olympic Games is less the winning than the taking part' (Rendall 2004: 27). Such sentiment was to form the basis for Modern Olympics founder Baron de Coubertain's Olympic motto, first used as an inspiration to athletes at the 1920 Antwerp Games: the most important thing in the Olympic Games was not to win but to take part, just as the most important thing in life was not the triumph but to have fought well. But fighting in other contexts brought controversy to peace-time Britain.

The Austerity Games: London 1948

The last Olympic Games to be hosted in London, in 1948, were delivered at a cost of less than £600,000 and a subsequent post-Games profit of £10,000, despite a war-torn London, suffering a housing crisis, having to provide accommodation to 6,000 athletes and tens of thousands of foreign spectators (Roche 2001). Tokyo had been awarded the 1940 Summer Games and Sapporo the Winter Games despite the concerns of many IOC members over Japan's aggressive foreign policy and their 1937 invasion of China (Guttman 2002). When Japan withdrew their offer to stage the Games in July 1938, Finland offered its capital, Helsinki, as a Summer substitute. The alternative Winter event was sought by Garmisch-Partenkirchen in Germany and the unanimous vote for the latter suggests that the IOC had few worries over the 1936 'Nazi Olympics' (Guttman 2002: 75). The post-war revival of the Games fell to London by a 1946 postal ballot of the IOC. For the second time, with less than two years of preparation, London had an opportunity to display its organizational skills. The Games were based in Wembley around the existing facilities built as part of the 1924 Empire Exhibition. A temporary running track was erected in Wembley Stadium. The athletes were housed in army barracks, mainly in Uxbridge, West London. Voices were raised questioning whether staging such an event was wasteful when monies were needed to rejuvenate bombed-out areas of London (Espy 1979) and an editorial in the *London Evening Standard* queried London's indulgence in an 'international weight lifting and basketball jamboree' (cited in Espy 1979: 38). Food was still rationed throughout the UK and many believed the socialist government should have priorities elsewhere. In hindsight, the 1948 Olympics were described as a 'make do' event and today are accorded the title of the 'Austerity Games' (Miller 2003, Hampton 2008). Competing nations brought their own food and some donated their surpluses to local hospitals. The Games were viewed by more people than ever before by virtue of being broadcast. Although television was in its infancy in 1948, the BBC was the first organization to broadcast the event internationally.

The 1948 Games featured 17 sports, 136 events, 59 countries and 4,092 male and female athletes and was the biggest Games to date. The London event helped rescue the Olympic Movement from its disastrous engagement with fascism in the 1930s and 1940s, suggesting instead that the Olympic Movement could play a positive role in promoting international peace (Roche 2000: 152). At the same time, the Games could be considered the beginning of the sporting division between the political philosophies of East and West in what was to become the 'Cold War'. London 1948, in fact, was witness to the first political defection during Olympic competition, with Marie Provaznikova refusing to return to Communist Czechoslovakia (Rendall 2004). Between 1936 and 1948, the IOC had lost two of its former presidents, its founder and his successor, the Belgian Henri de Baillet-Latour, and IOC leadership was passed to Sweden's Sigfrid Edstroem. Increasingly, the IOC had to address political issues; for instance, Arab states objecting to the formation of the state of Israel threatened to boycott the Games and war-ravaged Allied countries objected to the continued membership of Axis countries' representatives on the IOC governing body. The German-born Karl Ritter von Halt and Adolf Friedrich zu Mecklenburg were retained as IOC members despite their links with the Nazis; opposition to their presence was quashed by Edstroem, who considered them 'old friends' of the Olympic Movement, possibly implying that their integrity as IOC representatives outweighed any war-time indiscretions (Guttman 2002).[2]

Reasons to be Cheerful: London 2012

The choice of London, and significantly for the first time ever, East London, for the 2012 Games, was received with jubilation in parts of the metropolis, particularly in political circles. As Whitson and MacIntosh explain, 'Hosting international sporting events has become one of the most effective ways for a country to place itself in front and centre on the world stage, however temporarily, and show itself off as a successful society' (1996: 279). The host city becomes a brand that needs to be marketed, allowing politicians to enter the slipstream of any successful Olympic-related endeavour. The host city thus seeks to present itself as an enticing destination (Chalip and Costa 2005, Stevenson 1997): the decisive selling point of the London 2012 bid was the comprehensive plans proposing the regeneration of East London and an associated renewed transport infrastructure. The candidature file stated, 'By staging the Games in this part of the city, the most enduring legacy of the Olympics will be the regeneration of an entire community for the direct benefit of everyone who lives there' (CF2012 2004: 19).

The promised beneficiaries were to be the East End of London and the long considered development known in its planning stage as the Thames Gateway, projected to run some 15 miles along the north side of the Thames estuary from South Essex to East London. According to most commentators, the Olympic plans were scrutinized a few days later when newspaper editors glanced at maps of London and found that the Games were to be played out not amidst the iconic and fashionable 'East-End', located in districts such as Wapping, Aldgate and Hoxton on the edge of the wealth and glitz of the City of London, but somewhere very different, somewhere more confusing, that lurked beyond the most cocaine-addled imaginations of urban *flâneurs*.

---

2   The limited post-war state infrastructures in Japan and Germany extended to an absence of a recognized elected NOC. The Olympic Charter required a participating country to have a NOC before it could join the 'Olympic Family'.

The potential for stimulating urban regeneration through employment, a new civic image and a concomitant sense of social cohesion through subsidized sporting facilities are assumed correlates (Friedman, Andrews and Silk 2004). The ideal model for the London 2012 bid thus was Barcelona, widely seen as a successful model of a regenerative Olympics.

The term 'regeneration' is broad, all-encompassing – and crucial to 2012. In addition to the sports venues, the most tangible regeneration evident at the conclusion of the Games will arise from the remit of the London Development Agency (LDA). The LDA is responsible for providing 620,000 square miles of commercial space, around 40,000 new 'affordable' homes and open parkland in the Lower Lea Valley area London 2012 Select Committee Report, 2007[3]). The report anticipated that the Lower Lea Valley would be rejuvenated post-Olympics, with citizens wishing to live and grow up in the area and work in up to 12,000 anticipated new jobs. The candidature file stated:

> Creation of wider employment opportunities and improvements in the education, skills and knowledge of the local labour force in an area of very high unemployment. The nature and range of those skills will enable residents of the Lower Lea Valley to have a stake in the economic growth of their region and begin to break the cycle of deprivation in the area. (CF2012 2004: 25)

But, in the months following the winning bid, business closures occurred in East London as a result of London securing the Games and Olympic development work actually produced sizable job losses (Raco and Tunney 2010). Then came the late 2008 world recession. As Travers prophetically explained:

> A 15-year period of economic growth in the UK has created a particularly benign environment for redeveloping the major cities. But the laws of economics have not been suspended. It is inevitable that, at some point, there will be recession. When this happens, the underlying sustainability of the new economies of these cities will be tested. A return to decline would fatally undermine efforts to create self-generating growth and prosperity. (2007: 1)

It could be argued that the laws of economics were suspended the day the 2012 bid was written: London 2012 is currently undergoing the aforementioned economic test.

---

3   Culture, Media and Sport Committee (2007) *The London 2012 Olympic Games and Paralympic Games: Funding and Legacy*, hereafter London 2012 Select Committee Report (not to be confused with other Select Committees that have looked into the 2012 Olympics (see Chapter 4)).

Selling the Games

According to the 2012 Select Committee Report, VisitBritain, the national tourism agency, believed that as much as 50–70 per cent of the net economic benefit that Britain will experience as a result of the 2012 Olympics will be through tourism-generated revenue, estimating a £2 billion contribution from foreign visitors and an even bigger increase in domestic tourism over a seven- to ten-year period. The DCMS (which oversees the Games) however, predicted a slightly lower amount, between £1.4 billion and £2 billion, while an independent Olympic Games Impact Study by PriceWaterhouseCoopers considered the appropriate figure to be merely £762 million, £146 million of which would be generated over the course of the Games themselves (2007).

However, those who do visit will not just visit the traditional London tourist venues of majesty and pageantry but will have to venture to the place that US-born author Jack London christened 'the awful east' in the late nineteenth century. The Olympics in fact touch on five London boroughs – Newham, Hackney, Tower Hamlets, Greenwich and Waltham Forest – chosen against a set of criteria designed by the GLA. Areas seeking to benefit financially, economically and socially from the Games were required to put forward proposals as to why they should be selected. The chosen five were considered to be areas that would benefit most from improved infrastructure, leisure facilities, housing and employment opportunities, as well as gaining from an increased level of 'social cohesion'. Of the five, Newham faces the biggest influx of visitors in 2012 and the longest and most visible legacy in the shape of the Olympic Village and Stadium. Few of the literati or chattering class had ever set foot in this neighbourhood, although the same could be said of those who constituted the UK's Olympic cheerleaders and, indeed, the athletic and sporting establishment. Newham Town Hall is 11 miles by car from Westminster and could certainly benefit from inward investment. The locale can, on a good day, appear enticingly old and seductively shabby. That said, it also embraces enough 40-year-old concrete structures to make all but the most brain-addled modernist seek out a tepee and subscribe to *Caravanning Today*. The projected Olympic Park, in which the Olympic Stadium will be housed, lies in the electoral constituency of the recently re-branded 'Stratford New Town'. Here will also be found the newly-built 'Stratford City', consisting of a massive housing and retail project to complement the Olympic structures, the most notable of which will be the Olympic Village itself, which will consist of 3,600 housing units for Olympic athletes to be made available on the property market one year after the event. Newham will, in places, undoubtedly be transformed.

Itineraries and Indices

Historically the five boroughs have never really been part of tourist itineraries. There are good reasons for this. According to the 2007 Index of Multiple Deprivation,[4] Hackney is the most socio-economically deprived local government borough in England. Life expectancy here, at some four years less than the national average, is the lowest in London. The borough also has a long-term unemployment rate twice the national average (12 per cent and 5.8 per cent respectively) and the worst statistics for levels of child obesity (16 per cent at school reception age). Due to improved transport infrastructure arising out of 2012, the borough will be able to boast a connection to the London Underground for the first time ever in addition to a long overdue upgrade to the city's over-ground rail service. Provision for physical education (PE) and physical activity in Hackney has soared since London won the 2012 bid in 2005. Hackney now boasts one of the most successful junior level basketball teams in the country alongside a junior tennis club who won National Sports Club of the Year in 2006. Thanks to a £1 million investment in 2005, Hackney Marshes is the best-known community football venue in the country with the biggest concentration of pitches in Europe.[5] Academies have been established in basketball, cricket and football, to provide anticipated exit routes into professional sport.

The most prominent commonalities across the five boroughs are the low percentages of physically active people, high percentages of obese children and high rates of unemployment.[6] Of the five, Greenwich has the highest percentage of long-term unemployed and, as of December 2007, PE participation rates in

---

4   The Index of Multiple Deprivation 2007 combines a number of indicators, chosen to cover a range of economic, social and housing issues, into a single deprivation score for each small area in England. This allows each area to be ranked relative to one another according to their level of deprivation. The Indices are used widely to analyse patterns of deprivation, identify areas that would benefit from special initiatives or programmes and as a tool to determine eligibility for specific funding streams. The index is compiled by local council using an identical protocol to obtain information (see Communities and Local Government 2007).

5   £1 million was presented to Hackney Local Council by the LDA for their part in allowing the East Marsh to be turned into a car park for 18 months in the run-up to the Olympic Games. The council reported that it would temporarily relocate the football pitches that were to be paved over but as yet have not released any plans. The £1 million has been used to improve the surfaces and facilities of the other pitches at Hackney Marshes but the number of pitches has been reduced. The LDA is currently accepting proposals for building developments on the site if Hackney Council chooses not to turn the car park back into football pitches.

6   London has gained 24 per cent of all National Lottery sports-related Good Cause money since the Lottery began despite its share of just 14 per cent of the national population (GLA, 2008).

Greenwich were recorded at 78 per cent, making it the second worst performing borough in London for PE (after Tower Hamlets).[7]

A sense of unrealized expectations is evident in Tower Hamlets (see BBC 2008e). In 2005, the council launched the Young Persons Olympic Card, which provided the potential for 25,000 young people to take part in a variety of sport free of charge. The initiative gave children aged 18 or younger a voucher equating to one year's free pass to local council-owned leisure centres. However, fewer than 14,000 regularly used the card. Council officials stated that having a predominantly Muslim community was the main reason as to why take-up was low (see Tower Hamlets BSDF).[8] Sports projects began in Tower Hamlets in 2007, coordinated by the council, religious youth groups and local charities sensitive to socio-religious mores to attract more participation. These included Bengali and Muslim football teams, boxing clubs and gender-segregated gymnastics and dance clubs. However, competitive school sport proved to be a sensitive issue. The majority of state schools in Tower Hamlets do not provide female-only sports facilities and cannot ensure female-only officials for their supervision. In 2007 Tower Hamlets reported a PE participation rate of 65 per cent and targeted a 75 per cent participation rate by 2010. The national average for participation in at least two hours of PE and school sport per week stood at 90 per cent (see Department for Children, Schools and Families 2008).[9]

Eton Manor Park in Leyton is where the Waltham Forest Olympic new build will be sited to host Paralympic tennis and archery. The aim currently is to transform the site – post-Games – into a national hockey, tennis and five-a-side football centre. However, there are already fears that elements of the sporting 'legacy' could fail. In 2007 the council suggested that, if maintenance funding could not be secured after the 2012 Games, it was possible that the site would be sold off to a private leisure club or sports team. Whilst provision of sport in schools in Waltham Forest has improved in both curricular and extra-curricular terms since the 2012 bid, there are still large numbers of pupils (approximately 29 per cent of 5 16 year olds) who are not receiving the government's recommended minimum of two hours of high-quality PE and sport each week. Only one school has its own playing field in Waltham Forest. Despite this, in 2006 the Big Lottery Funded Clubs scheme was set up with a much needed £3.4 million cash injection in after-school sports and activities. Over the next three years schools will offer

---

7   All statistics on the five Olympic boroughs were published in the report *The Five Olympic Boroughs – Key Indicators* by the London Skills and Employment Observatory (2007). Figures cited here were correct at the end of December 2007.

8   The Borough Sports Development Framework document stated that not enough qualitative research was carried out within the community to sufficiently identify the activities that Muslim men and, more specifically, women within the community require that met their health needs but did not contradict or impinge upon their religious beliefs.

9   The document relates that whilst 90 per cent is the national average for participation rates, only 71 per cent of children are receiving two hours of 'high quality' PE.

dance, cheerleading, capoeira, multiskills, cycling, gymnastics and boccia. The three-year extra-curricular programme for primary and secondary schools ensures clubs are targeted at disadvantaged or disaffected young people and those who do not currently participate in PE and sport. In 2008 Waltham Forest Council announced the scheme as very successful so far and identified improvements in concentration, attendance and positive behaviour amongst the programme's merits. In addition to the BLFC scheme, Waltham Forest in 2008 was in its second year of the GirlsActive programme, managed by the Youth Sport Trust, whose ambassador was the two times Olympic Gold medal winner Dame Kelly Holmes.

A third of 2012 Olympic events will be hosted by the Borough of Greenwich despite being divided from the Olympic Park by the River Thames. Greenwich was originally scheduled to deliver events such as shooting at the Royal Artillery Barracks. Gymnastics, Paralympic volleyball, basketball and badminton were scheduled to take place at the O2 Arena in the borough but, due to budget reductions, these events were moved in 2008 to Wembley Stadium, Northwest London. However, equestrian events will take place in Greenwich Park. This has proven very controversial attracting a concentrated and vociferous campaign by local residents to stop the event, which will see the closure of the park to the public for many months of 2012.

While the world of press releases and celebrity visits to the Olympic sites currently concentrates on Newham, not all of the news emanating from the borough makes for good reading. Newham has the least physically active population in the capital and the third lowest nationwide. Only 14.5 per cent of adult residents partake in more than 30 continuous minutes of exercise at least three days a week[10] (the London average is 21.3 per cent). The Newham authorities have delivered initiatives to encourage a new physicality and a £2 million improvement to Newham leisure centres saw membership increase by 7,000 between 2007 and 2008 (*The London Evening Standard* 2008). Sporting participation by the over 16s is bottoming out but participation in school PE is seeing its biggest rise for 10 years (Sport England 2008). The success of summer sports projects has seen schools in Newham thrive on a multitude of PE provisions. Here, an athletics centre and gymnastics club has recently been refurbished and made accessible to local schools and a partnership with Newham's Premier League football club, West Ham United FC, sees schools receiving quality football coaching by club staff both during and outside PE lessons. Two sixth form colleges have opened, with one receiving SportsMark[11] status and the other awarded Specialist Sports College (SSC) status in June 2008. Without the Olympics these statistics and facilities would not be so positive and, as one of the most socio-economically

---

10   See Government Office for London (2007). These figures were correct at the end of December 2007.

11   Introduced in 1996 and re-launched in 2006 by Sport England, SportsMark is a kite mark indicating that a particular school is successfully implementing the present national strategy for PE and school sport.

deprived areas in the UK, Newham is the borough with most to gain from 2012 in terms of physical 'regeneration'.

Common as Muck: Introducing Your Hosts

Most academic attention to the East End of London has focused on the 'old' East End — Whitechapel, Stepney and Bethnal Green – all of which today lie in the borough of Tower Hamlets. At the time that nineteenth-century writers were casting their religious, charitable or journalistic gaze on the 'awful east', the neighbourhoods of Bow and Mile End more closely resembled the industrial landscapes shared with Stratford, whose boundary with Bow was marked by the putrid waters and banks of the River Lea and its associated noxious trades. Coupled with the harsh industrial developments further east on the marshlands and docklands of West Ham, Newham – the epicentre of 2012 Olympic development – stands in many ways in stark contrast to the tawdry Dickensian glamour of the old East End. Yet the two areas are very much reliant upon each other both materially and culturally.

Newham Borough is self-contained by virtue of the Thames in the south, the river Roding in the east, the Lea in the west – split into several small locks and canals – and the proliferation of cemeteries (City of London, West Ham, Manor Park) and the Wanstead Flats grassland to the north. Historically, Newham relied on the Thames to provide for employment and wealth. In 1850 the building of the Royal Victoria Dock was completed, followed by the Royal Albert Dock in 1880 and the King George V Dock in 1921. 'The Royals' was the largest enclosed dock system in the world, bringing work for thousands but making the locality a target for aggressors. Such a vast development was an obvious target for the German air force during World War II, with a devastating loss of life and property in the vicinity. The borough has seen massive post-war changes and now is home to a vast and impressive investment in transport infrastructure. Newham hosts no fewer than 11 British Rail, six London Underground and eight Docklands Light Railway stations. Stratford Train and Bus Station is a major terminal, serving East London and indeed Continental Europe, and London City Airport, which opened in 1987 on the site of the Royal Docks and today operates scheduled flights to 20 European destinations, and boasting a passenger capacity of 2.5 million per year.

Today crowds gather in Newham and just across its Thames borders, not to participate in collective labour but to consume. To the borough's south, on the site of the former Royal Docks, stands the ExCeL Exhibition Centre, which caters for up to 60,000 people via events as diverse as the London Boat Show and arms and weapons exhibitions. Newham's two main shopping centres, in East Ham and Stratford, and smaller areas in Green Street and Canning Town, attract up to 50,000 people at peak times. In the borough stands the home stadium of West Ham United FC, which regularly attracts 30,000-plus spectators to witness games in the English Premier League. Some 25 times a season, this is the place where the mainly white, native-born but long-time escapees to Essex return to wonder, to stare or to fume at the racial diversity of a locale that, while no longer familiar, inspires nostalgic impulses. This temporal cultural conflict is match-day specific rather than an-ongoing contestation over space and these nostalgic impulses can vary between rheumy-eyed narratives of memory, accompanied by a pint of beer or plate of pie and mash to verbal abuse directed at the predominately Muslim shoppers and traders. The borough is also home to one of England's fastest-expanding universities (University of East London), with over 12,000 students.

Any talk of world-class sporting facilities, improved transportation infrastructure and increased tourism tells a politically contentious story. For a start, the demographic of Newham is not one readily associated with Olympic glory. Some 60 per cent of the 2004/5/6 Great Britain athletics team was public-school educated and currently 90 per cent of British Olympic athletes are drawn from AB and C social classes. Newham residents are 43 per cent social class D and E and there are no public schools in the borough. Despite being England's youngest borough, with over one third of residents aged under 25, Newham is also England's third most deprived borough, with 30 per cent of households on income benefit, a massive incidence of social housing rent arrears and around 70 per cent of children living in low-income homes (London Borough of Newham n.d.). Newham's major employers are local government, the Metropolitan police and a sugar refinery. Some 150 languages are spoken in Newham (*The Guardian* 2005) and the white extended family a phenomenon of the imagination of TV soap operas or perhaps evident only in southeast Essex, the traditional haven of East London's working-class escapees. Rated as the UK's most ethnically diverse borough, migrant families and people born outside of the UK comprise the majority of Newham's population. The majority are black African and Asian – the latter primarily from Pakistan. There are 48 mosques within the borough's boundaries – only one is Shi'a. One in three of the population of Newham claim Islam as their religion. Some Muslims are the recently arrived minority Sri Lankan Tamils, while most arrived from Pakistan and India in the 1960s and in 1971 from Uganda when forcibly expelled by the regime of Idi Amin. Initially attracted to the area by cheap housing and the opportunity of employment offered by the vast Ford car factory located some four miles outside the borough, many subsequently took over the corner shop enterprises visible throughout the borough. The total population of the borough is officially 248,000 but it is also the destination for a large proportion of London's 600,000 plus uncounted irregular immigrants (GLA 2009). The past ten years have also seen tens of thousands of young Eastern Europeans arrive to work the economic boom that was London 1992–2008, primarily from Eastern Europe and the Baltic States (*The Daily Telegraph* 2008b), with Newham hosting by far the highest proportion of new national insurance registrations for adult overseas nationals in the UK (Department for Work and Pensions 2009).

Newham today is run by 60 elected councillors representing 20 electoral constituencies. Each electorate has approximately 11–12,000 per ward. In 2006 Labour held a clear majority of the seats with nominal opposition coming from one candidate elected on a Christian People's Alliance ticket. In that same year 31 of the elected councillors were white, eight were black. The rest were Asian, mostly of Bangladeshi and Pakistani origin. George Galloway's Respect Party had three elected Bangladeshi councillors representing Green Street West.

The borough is physically divided in many ways, with the A13 dual carriageway acting as one of the main dividing lines. Those living south of it manifest a very different socio-demographic to those living north. The south still hosts remnants of the much stereotyped white East London working class and those who 'stay on' in spite of the decline of the docks and local industry. This locale is covered by four electoral wards – Beckton, Royal Docks, Custom House and Canning Town South. The population here lives in council housing built in the 1950s and 1960s to replace the bomb-damaged residences. In 2007 Canning Town South ward was represented in local government by a white male, a white female and a black male. By 2010 Labour held 56 of the 60 seats on Newham Council, albeit those voting them in were in some constituencies less than 30 per cent of the electorate. Newham, it can be said, is the living, breathing epitome of English post-industrial urban fragmentation. This area, and others in the borough, is high on indices of poverty and challenging to any notion of social cohesion.

Changing Places

The old East End of contemporary Tower Hamlets is a place of vibrant multi-ethnic poverty and youthful edgy urban investment. Its proximity to the City of London has led to pockets of gentrification, notably in the Spitalfields and Shoreditch districts where, in estate agents' parlance, the properties here permit property buyers to invest in 'authenticity' while residing in 'live and work' spaces. For their money, buyers can obtain access to a chic urban 'lifestyle choice' in an area where, for centuries, silk weavers, seamstresses, cabinet makers and their families lived and worked in fetid, cramped, disease-ridden rooms (Hobbs 2006). Today Britain's New Art icons, such as Gilbert and George and Tracey Emin, live and work here. Several museums, a 'heritage centre' and the Brick Lane Mosque (originally built as a Huguenot chapel and later used as a Methodist chapel and then a synagogue before being converted to its current use in 1976) offer the only real clues to the ethnic succession that defines the Spitalfields proletarian inheritance.

The white and Jewish working classes have left little trace of their one time colonization of this evocative space. The borough's fruit and vegetable wholesale market in Spitalfields closed in the late 1980s (relocated to Leyton and rebranded as 'New Spitalfields'), taking with it some highly sought after well-paid manual jobs. The gentrified 'craft market' that replaced the 'fruit and veg' in 2006 now trades adjacent to the revitalized, and painfully expensive, Huguenot housing. Today the locale is excruciatingly fashionable amongst the young and beautiful, clubbers and fashionistas who flock to the multitude of ethnic restaurants. The same consumers can also enjoy wine in a former brewery that is now a destination for corporate socializing and book launches. Local government tourism officials sell Spitalfields as a 'community' and the culinary thoroughfare that is Brick Lane, has been re-branded as 'Banglatown' – in homage to the thousands of Bengali residents and restaurants (Eade 2002). This collection of streets has evolved into a bazaar of bourgeois delight that comes alive at the weekend, in the evenings and on Sundays. Suburbanites on the roots trail search for a kosher salt beef sandwich and tourists tread wide-eyed in pursuit of an 'authentic' London experience just metres from the backdrop of the corporate cathedrals of global finance that is the City of London. For tens of thousands annually, the area is best known for its 'Jack the Ripper Tours', a tragic tourism of despair that attracts dupes, ghouls and that puzzling breed of inquirers some of whom adopt the nomenclature of 'Ripperologists' (see Samuel 1994: 114, Walkowitz 1992).

Although parts of the borough were chosen as the venue for the marathon, speed-walking and road-cycling events, the Olympics will not change much here; Tower Hamlets will have no new buildings or infrastructure associated with the Games. When not being used for the aforementioned pursuits, the borough's primary thoroughfare, Whitechapel Road, will be used as the main route to and from the Olympic stadium. For some in Tower Hamlets, disappointment is already evident. The borough's initial Olympic dreams, particularly around housing, are destined to remain precisely that. *London 2012 Olympic and Paralympic Games Legacy: Strategy Programme* (Tower Hamlets 2006) outlined the proposed benefits to the borough of hosting the 2012 Games. Research presented in the document indicated that, when housing benefits were excluded from gross annual household incomes, nearly 64 per cent of all households in the borough fell below the threshold level of affordability. The need for more affordable housing is growing at such a rate that an annual shortfall of 3,021 affordable dwellings across the borough was recorded in 2008. Despite the documented overcrowding in the area, none of the proposed 9,000 new properties for the Olympic boroughs will be built in Tower Hamlets.

Future Perfect?

A white flight population shift eastwards from East London has been occurring for many years (Hobbs 1988) and the rebranding and gentrification of the East End has accelerated this process (Watt 2006). Some local histories are documented (Eade 1996), others are wiped out (Gilroy 1987) and some are invented (Hobbs 2006), in this case promoting a 'samosas, saris and steel bands' (Younge 2005) theme park scenario. These processes have combined to create the impression of a blank screen onto which the 2012 Olympics can be projected. What follows attempts to colour in the mosaic that is the East End. In doing so it demonstrates how, here, post-millenium projections of deprivation, deviance and dangerousness have deep-rooted antecedents. The eternal return of moral panics, cumulative disadvantage, demographic fluidity and their attendant frictions foments an uneasy milieu for Olympic-defined 'community legacies'.

The Promised Land? Schmutters and Schnorrers

One of the key narratives of the traditional perception of the East End is that it is a cultural melting pot that, over the centuries has enabled the settlement and assimilation of a variety of diasporas seeking refuge and asylum. This narrative is well documented in relation to the Jewish East End influx. Between 1880 and 1914, 160,000 poor, displaced Jews from Eastern Europe flocked to join the 40,000 established Jews already living in the two square miles of what was to become the 'Jewish East End' in Whitechapel (see Fishman 1979, 1988, Lipman 1990, Newman 1981, Samuel 1994). However, as with most large-scale migration, this Jewification of the East End was far from smooth sailing. Over one-third of the assimilated local Jewish population was 'living on or below the margin of subsistence' (Fishman 1988: 12) and resentment against this large-scale new arrival was inevitable. The established Anglo-Jewry of Sephardic origin, who had arrived in Britain during the seventeenth century and had become well integrated 'socially, culturally, and economically' (Knepper 2007: 72; see also Cesarani 1994). They feared persecution via association and were concerned to 'reduce the pariah or scrounger image so often attached ... to the Jewish immigrant' (Hobbs 1988: 98). However, the Yiddish-speaking new arrivals were accustomed to such intolerant circumstances and brought with them the experience of over two generations living in the Pale of Settlement, marking a severe loss of status in their native land as a result of the industrial change as well as political and religious repression (White 1980: 252, Hobbs 1988: 98–101). They quickly became street traders and worked in small family-orientated workshops or in small sweatshops and factories. Self-sufficiency was encouraged by the Jewish Board of Guardians, formed in 1859 to deal with the 'strange poor' (White 1980: 250) via the funding of charities and self help organizations to provide food, cheap housing, orphanages, heating and provision for the disabled and the elderly. These organizations were especially focused upon making it possible for recently arrived Jews to avoid competing with the indigenous urban poor for scarce resources; between 1900 and 1910, over 26,000 interest-free loans – £7 on average– were made by the Jewish Board of Guardians (JBG) to enable East End Jews to attain self-employed status. This was a direct attempt to *embourgeoiser* an essentially pre-industrial society that had not experienced proletarianization. The result was an entrepreneurial ethic that was to become a clear character trait of East Enders and led to the establishment of monopolies over key markets such as cabinet making and small-scale clothing manufacture (Hobbs 2011 forthcoming).

The proximity of the East End to the City of London, the chance to re-establish their status in an economy marked by pre-industrial production and culture and, most important, the opportunity to achieve the goal of self-employment marked the Yiddish-speaking population of Whitechapel's remarkable ghetto (White 1980, Hobbs 1988). This rather cosy narrative has been important in limiting the scope of many cultural products of the East End to Whitechapel alone.

Murder Most Foul

Old stereotypes re-merged. The most damaging related to vice and the sex trade and was rooted in a stigma established in medieval times (Slater 2007: 53) The notion of the Jew as '[p]rocurer for the white slave trade and living upon the earnings of women' (Gartner 1983: 161) became commonly accepted. Nor did it meet resistance from the Anglo-Jewish establishment establishment who were more concerned with countering indigenous concerns regarding the detrimental impact of Jews on wages and conditions of employment, and colluded with the link between the eastern European Jew and white slavery (Knepper 2006). The late 1880s Whitechapel killings of six women attributed to Jack the Ripper inspired the commonly held belief that the murders and mutilations, 'must have been done by a Jew' (*East London Observer* 1888 cited by Fishman 1979: 84; see also Bermant 1975, Hobbs 1988). The unsolved murders were relatively recent when the Royal Commission on Alien Immigration reported in 1903 and, although it could find no evidence of Jewish immigration having a detrimental impact on the health or employment of indigenous Londoners, the Commission cited dubious data from the Prison Commissioners to confirm the essential criminality of the Jewish community (Knepper 2007: 65).

The Royal Commission laid the foundations for the Aliens Act of 1905, which established the principle of immigration control and government-controlled registration for resident 'aliens'. Crucially, the Act established that entry of non-British nationals to the UK was to be discretionary rather than automatic (Gainer 1972), and established mechanisms for the deportation of 'undesirables' (Feldman 2003, Pellew 1989). In particular, the Act equipped magistrates with the power to deport foreigners convicted of offences linked to prostitution (Slater 2007: 56–9). Given that Jews were connected in the popular imagination with prostitution and its organization, the Act and its aftermath served to institutionalize racist narratives (Hobbs 2011). This example typifies the messy reality of East End life and serves to put some meat on the skeleton of sentiment that so often passes for the area's memory (Kops 1969, Allin and Wesker 1974).

Scatterings and Gatherings: The Luck of the Irish?

The population of London doubled between 1821 and 1851 and doubled again by 1900. The capital's poor were in a state of constant displacement as the City of London shifted eastwards (Stedman-Jones 1971: 162, 171). The dire housing situation in the East End was exacerbated by influxes of the poor from Eastern Europe, Ireland and rural Britain as well as from the redeveloped West End of London. Writers spoke of the place as the 'City of Dreadful Night' (Thomson 2003 [1880]).

The Irish, like the Jews, had a long pre-industrial presence in East London and, like the Jews, suffered considerable religious persecution: anti-Catholic riots occurred in East London in 1736, 1768 and 1786. The Irish were drawn to the area by cheap housing and opportunities for manual labour, particularly in Stepney's riverside hamlets where they became familiar with the casual labour market that dominated river-based manual labour (Hobbs 1988) From the demobbing of Wellington's Army in 1815 and throughout the nineteenth century large numbers of Irish arrived in the East End, forming the core of the floating army of labourers who built the docks. The second significant wave came around 1846, following the potato famine, in a movement known in Irish history as 'The Scattering'. Tens of thousands arrived in East London to join their fellow countrymen in dock building, working in the markets and seeking an income as street traders. Most significantly, however, they joined the surplus of casual labour attempting to obtain what was often daily work in the docks (Hobbs 1988: 95).

The Irish in the rest of England were at the very rump of the factory system and subjected to proletarianization via the harsh disciplines of industrial work (Thompson, 1974: 473). What emerged was a *lumpen* Irish subclass, who colonized harsh and unpleasant manual work 'to which the English worker, successfully moulded by industrial work discipline, was no longer suited, either physically or temperamentally' (Hobbs, 1988: 96). However, East London's Irish population did not experience the gradual transformation from rural peasantry to urban industrial proletariat and in dock work they were offered an ideal opportunity to replicate the experiences of subsistence work they had known so well when working the land, albeit with improved remuneration and freedom of contract (Hobbs 1988: 96). Most important, the 'moral economy of the factory system' (Ure 1835: 17) was not present in East London and, as a consequence, the Irish were not contained or controlled by the proletarian hierarchy that in Britain's industrial heartlands had relegated their countrymen to the lowliest occupations (Roberts 1973: 22).

Similarities in culture between the Irish and East Enders were marked. The former were untainted by the Puritan values of thrift and sobriety that had combined so successfully with factory discipline elsewhere in England. On the north bank of the Thames they were paid by the hour and by the day in flexible occupations where the contract between worker and employer was purely financial. Consequently, the Irish were as untainted by industrialism as both the indigenous East Ender and the Jews who had arrived in the East End to engage in a distinctly pre-industrial mode of production. Distant from coal seams (and hence the mining industry) and hence also heavy manufacturing, the resultant culture exhibited a normative form of proletarianism that denied some of the central tenets that elsewhere defined the industrial working class. The independence and entrepreneurial culture that emerged from self employment and casual work reinforced the pre-industrial culture of East London. This combination, unrestrained by the protocols of industrial life, nurtured varieties of entrepreneurial behaviour. Consequently, manifestations of 'deviance' became a central characteristic and a multitude of transgressions became normalized as an aspect of everyday life (Hobbs 1988). The East London working class appreciated the necessity of networks and enjoyed, and endured, individual economies of boom and bust. Individualism was manifested in negotiating a price for a day's dock work or, in later years, bargaining over the price of a used car.

As the docks spread along the Thames, creating the world's longest (26-mile) waterfront, this mutant culture followed and, in the solid working class areas of Poplar, Canning Town, Silvertown, Plaistow and West Ham, this working culture was replicated, reinforced and unionized, creating powerful traditions of ambivalent resistance. Yet with no viable public transport system, workers could not live far from the markets, the small workshops and the docks all of which required an early start to the day (Hobbs 1988: 104). The flight of the monied and respectable began with the middle classes who took advantage of the newly built railway systems and decamped to the suburbs. For those who had no option but to stay, getting a good deal was the best they could aspire to. As one author succinctly put it: 'They lived on the river and the river meant plunder' (Bermant 1975: 122).

Billericay Dickie: Doing Very Well

Then one day the ships no longer came in. The lottery of casual employment had continued in the docks until 1965, even following the regularizing of work under the 1947 National Dock Labour Scheme. During the post-World War II period the London docks boomed, regular wages were paid and the unions were strong. However, the 1960s brought containerization and new dockside handling methods that reduced the demand for manual – dockside – labour (Hill 1976). Furthermore, massive capital investment in the modernization of the deep-water docks at Tilbury, some 15 miles east, where adjacent land was cheap and plentiful, proved ideal for the storage of containers. This signalled the demise of the industrial East End. By 1971 the Port of London's workforce of registered dockers had shrunk from 26,000 to 6,000. Between 1966 and 1976 London's dockland boroughs (Tower Hamlets, Newham, Southwark, Lewisham and Greenwich) lost 150,000 jobs, mainly in transport, distribution and food/drink processing, all sectors closely associated with Port activity. This represented 20 per cent of all jobs in the area, a figure made more striking when compared with an employment decline of 13 per cent in Greater London and just 2 per cent in the rest of Great Britain (Hobbs 1988, 2006).

Others meanwhile made fortunes without breaking sweat. Between 1960 and 1980 the closing down of London's docks left around eight square miles (21 square kilometres) of derelict land in East London. Unemployment and poverty once again characterized the area. Global capital, and its concomitant branding, changed the East End in the late twentieth century. The term 'London Docklands' was used for the first time in a 1971 government report on redevelopment plans, marking the commencement of a potent rebranding exercise. After the deregulation of the City of London's financial market in 1987, the booming financial services industry voraciously ate up neighbouring cheap land for a mixture of residential, commercial and light industrial development. In densely populated Poplar district established communities that had grown up in the shadows of huge ships became dwarfed by the Disneyesque village that is Canary Wharf on the Isle of Dogs (see Foster 1999, Hobbs 1988: 217–23), where some 63,000 people now work on an

86-million-square-feet site. Only 30 years previously the Islanders had blockaded the two access roads onto the 'Island' and announced a Unilateral Declaration of Independence (Hosteller 2001).

For the past 20 years the East End has proven an especially grotesque Klondike for property developers (Pawley 1986, Hobbs 2006). The rebranding of working-class riverside settlements as 'Docklands' has effectively wiped out any sense of cultural history that is not ratified by an estate agent: the repackaging of labour history is apparent all over the old East End. Nautical themes and structures provide the backdrop for the post-1990s cafes and bars. Seafood festivals are celebrated in corporate venues and the Bryant and May match factory in Bow where, in 1888 1,400 women workers famously organized to oppose the deadly conditions in which they worked (Stafford 1961, Charlton 1999, Fishman 1988), is now Bow Quarter, a chic housing development. Similarly, the various sites of epic labour disputes, be it the 1889 dockers' tanner strike (Champion 1890) or the strikes of the 1960s that finally killed off the obscenity of casualization, are now forgotten or unknown by the newcomers.

The population shift in the 1950s away from the old East End, drawn by the new housing and employment opportunities offered in the more easterly dockland residences of Silvertown, Canning Town, Plaistow and West Ham ensured that such folk memories forged a firm bond between the old iconic East End and the new industrial East End. These districts were populated by the same people, with the same hopes, fears and prejudices. Some, however, sought a new life further east, mainly in the proletarian suburbs and new towns of Essex. This provoked the curiosity of academics and, in the mid-1950s, Cambridge-educated authors Michael Young and Peter Willmott established East London, and specifically Bethnal Green, as a stereotypical British working class community (Young and Willmott 1957). Their analysis concentrated primarily upon matriarchy and, in particular, the extended family. Ethnicity, crime and the world of work received scant attention from this inquiry. However, by the mid-1960s East London contained a black population of approximately 10,000, largely ensconced in rooming houses in Stepney's Cable Street (Downes 1966). A scattering of Black, Asian and Cypriot families was also spread across Tower Hamlets. The resident ageing Jewish population of Spitalfields and Brick Lane declined as second and third generations moved north to Stamford Hill and east to Gants Hill. It was large extended white working-class families that dominated the East End throughout the years that preceded the closing of the docks.

Dirty Secrets: Effluence and the Pursuit of Affluence

The cosy multi-ethnic imagery of the contemporary East End has some dark margins. Political and ethnic conflict marked the East End past and demonized visible minority ethnic populations. Alongside this anger came tragedy via the disastrous impacts of accidents, environmental neglect and work-related danger. Such incidents are seldom referred to as part of the area's official history.

Desperate places produce desperate escape attempts. Some – foreigners – were to die seeking political change; others were to meet their end whilst assembling the munitions to bomb the foreigner. In 1909 a botched armed robbery in Tottenham by Latvian anarchists resulted in the killing of a police officer and a ten year old schoolboy and the wounding of 27 others. The following year a bungled burglary – again by Latvians – saw two police officers shot dead. The aftermath became immortalized in folk memory as the Siege of Sidney Street, wherein the police, reinforced by soldiers from the nearby Tower of London, shot it out with the two remaining anarchists, whilst a top hat wearing Home Secretary by the name of Winston Churchill and an estimated crowd of 100,000 looked on (Rumbelow 1973). The siege triggered an association of Eastern Europeans with crime and violence in the public imagination that would last for generations. Indeed the name 'Peter the Painter', the alias of one of the besieged anarchists whose remains were never recovered from the burnt-out shell of 100 Sidney Street, was invoked as a means of control over generations of East End children. The threat 'Peter the Painter will come and get you' quietened many a truculent child.

Years later some of these truculent children were quieted forever in the Great War of attrition that killed millions of young men in the trenches of Northern France. The same War did not spare the East End munitions workers. On 19 January 1916 an explosion devastated the Brunner Mond munitions factory in Silvertown on the banks of the Thames. The British Army was suffering a shortage of artillery shells in the campaign in north-eastern France and the War Office had opened up what had been (and still is) a caustic soda factory in Silvertown to munitions production. The Brunner Mond board had specifically opposed the production of TNT in such a densely populated urban area; their opposition was ignored. When 50 tonnes of TNT exploded – much of it standing in railway goods waggons awaiting transportation – the munitions plant was instantly destroyed, as were many nearby buildings, including the Silvertown fire station. The burning debris caused fires over a wide area. Some 73 people were killed, over 400 injured and over 70,000 properties damaged, 900 of them totally destroyed or irrevocably damaged; the explosion also damaged buildings eight miles away in the West End of London. The fires generated in the area could be seen in Maidstone, Kent and Guildford, Surrey. The blast was heard some 100 miles away, yet this story is not audible in the sales pitch of the contemporary East End (Hill and Bloch 2003).

East End residents who had travelled far and spoke a different language also had stories to tell – some of which caused moral outrage. The small Chinese population of East London in the early decades of the twentieth century was a product of the East India shipping lines. This community, mainly men, embedded themselves in the dockside communities of Britain's largest ports, and in particular East London's Limehouse district (Waller 1995). Numbering less than 300 by the end of World War I, they proved to be a particular source of fascination and revulsion in what was, at the time, London's most cosmopolitan district (Critchley and James 1987). The requirements of Chinese seaman docked in London dominated this micro-economy, principally laundry facilities and premises for gambling and opium smoking (Seed 2007). Although generations of London's bohemians regularly visited the area's opium dens, World War I instigated a jingoist, anti-foreign sentiment and opium smoking became associated with the seduction and degradation of indigenous white women (Kohn 1992: 27–8). Scandals involving the activities of a handful of Chinese men unfolded and a full scale moral panic ensued (Kohn 1992, Hobbs 2011 forthcoming). New anti-drug laws were introduced and drug use was driven underground, to be associated to this day in the UK with non-white populations.

The river provided, took away and received. Poverty and short life expectancy was the *leitmotif* of the people who drew their living from the Thames but some amongst them were to lose their lives in the most innocent water-based pursuits. Joyful excursions could go horribly wrong; design faults and human error were, and remain, ever present. On 3 September 1878 at 6.15 pm, the *Princess Alice* left Gravesend in Kent intending to return to Woolwich, East London laden with 750 passengers. The 200-foot-long pleasure cruiser was the pride of the London Steamboat Company's fleet. Built in 1865, it was tasked with transporting Londoners to the pleasure gardens that thrived on the banks of the Thames between London and Gravesend. Around 7.45 at Galleons Reach, Woolwich the vessel collided with another, the *Bywell Castle*, an 890-tonne collier, and sank close to the point where the sewage was pumped into the Thames, killing 640 passengers (White 2007: 264, Kemp 2008). This remains the single largest loss of life on a British waterway.

The Thames in the East End was the repository of London's human detritus. The Northern Outfall Sewer, renamed in the mid-1990s – apparently without irony – the 'Greenway', is better known to locals as the 'sewer bank'. It is a huge pipe standing 40 feet high, covered over with grass, and carries London's human waste above the roofs of the terrace houses whose small gardens back onto the sewer's steep sides. Designed by Joseph Bazalgette after an outbreak of cholera in 1853 and 'The Big Stink' of 1858, the sewer bank footpath runs 4.5 miles from Wick Lane in Hackney through Stratford and Plaistow to Royal Docks Road in Beckton, running adjacent to the Olympic Stadium site and possible site of a proposed post-Games culinary district. Life's fundamentals are difficult to ignore when you have a gigantic pipe of effluence at the bottom of the garden. Equally, a certain sense of class awareness is inescapable when the shit is from some of the more affluent parts of London, where sensitivities required sewage to be moved around via *subterranean* means. The sewer bank once served as a barrier between East Enders and another of the area's dirty secrets, the numerous chemical works that once occupied the land today adjacent to the site of West Ham underground station. Local residents' back gardens and the playgrounds of several primary schools were often enveloped in choking yellow acrid emissions from this outcrop of noxious trades. The stink wafting up from the iron gratings on the sewer bank, the sweet acidity from the Yardley's perfume factory and the stench of animal carcasses from the adjacent abattoirs, made for a less than fragrant industrial milieu. Control of smell is a project of modernity. Modernity came late to the East End of London.

LuverlyJubberly: Del Trotter as Cultural Chaperone

The East End has always had its fair share of crime, deviance and generally transgressive behaviour. Its riverside location was pockmarked with wharves, warehouses and lorry parks, which housed the goods that generated a myriad of stolen goods networks (Hobbs 1988). As a travesty of the formal rhetoric of capitalist orthodoxy, this working-class entrepreneurship has been presented in comedic mode in generations of music hall and cinematic representations (Faulk 2004: 24, English and Mitchell 1989, Fisher 1975).

However, although this world of benign predation has gone along with the culture that emerged from the opportunities offered by the river Thames and its environs, some of the language and insolent sharp cultural practices that constituted expressive forms of adaptation and resistance still remain in the outputs of the British entertainment industry. The miniaturization of trading episodes, notably those that involve a distinct locale and just a few key actors, have in the UK created a plethora of media products that simultaneously mock and valorize. The most famous of these products is the BBC's *Only Fools and Horses* (OFH) sitcom. Seven series were originally broadcast in the UK between 1981 and 1991, with sporadic Christmas specials until 2003. OFH holds the record for the highest UK audience (21 million) for a sitcom episode and has been critically and popularly acclaimed, receiving numerous accolades from the British Academy, the National Television Awards and the Royal Television Society. Products such as OFH stress the pretensions that lie behind the petty capitalism of working-class entrepreneurship: by the time the final credits roll, the proletarian protagonists discover that the banknotes are fake, the jewellery turns fingers green or the cheap paint has peeled.

The pretensions of the main characters are also exposed when occupations for which they are unqualified prove beyond their competence, chandeliers fall from the ceilings of stately homes, cheap electrical goods of dubious derivation explode or malfunction. In OFH the two main Jack the Lads are ultimately caught out and left at the bar, glum faced, partially concealed behind a glass of lager festooned with a cocktail umbrella and perhaps a cocktail sausage. Behind the undoubted comic artistry of these performances lies the moral that attempts to join the bourgeoisie via cheating or stealing will ultimately be met by failure; such attempts are no more than futile gestures. Consequently, these stories are unthreatening, as the assembled cast try to make their elusive millions and get it amusingly, but reassuringly, wrong.

The programme and the adoration that it inspires might be considered a template for white working-class Londoners from both sides of the Thames – albeit that the programme is set a few miles across the river in Peckham – and those who have moved out of London to reside on the capital's periphery. Like no other cultural product, OFH provides clues about proletarian entrepreneurial etiquette in a manner similar to the way that the US series *The Sopranos* provides a guide to New York gangster protocol (Gambetta 2009). Decades after its transmission, DVD box sets of OFH enable this lost tribe and their one token black member (who has a Liverpool accent) to evince a language and repertoire of stylistic devices now as dead as, and many would contend, more entertaining than, any passage from Jeeves and Wooster.

Everything All Right?

With an unparalleled history of casual labour, poverty and municipal socialism, Newham established itself as a very particular bastion of proletarianism (Hobbs 2006). These cultural continuities were relatively easy to establish in industrial society, where communities were entrenched and stable. Even with ex-dockworkers at work and play in and around Newham through the 1950s, 1960s and 1970s, their physical presence, with limps and scars and the missing tips of one or two of their fingers, was a constant reminder of the brutally contested nature of the world of work. Stories of how relatives and neighbours had been injured, crippled or killed at work were important in the informal education of young people. These unofficial facts about bosses and workers, conflict and negotiation – Them and Us – were constant and unopposed influences on the young. The power of trade unions in Newham provided a common politicized language for its citizens. Men with the title of 'gangers' were revered members of their neighbourhoods, respected both for their toughness in negotiation and their leadership qualities. Many union activists also stood as local councillors and, as a consequence, the Transport and General Workers Union had a huge impact on housing and education policy. Newham Council's Education Committee placed great emphasis on high quality technical schools, which produced well qualified candidates for the vast number of apprenticeships on Newham's huge Direct Labour force that had rebuilt and revitalized the area's social housing stock through the 1950s, 1960s and 1970s.

However, trade union membership in Newham plummeted. Technical schools and a large Direct Labour force are a distant memory. The world of class communality, where middle-class culture was remote and irrelevant and consumerism underdeveloped, has long gone. When the docks closed, the younger generation of dockers moved eastwards to work at Tilbury. Older workers also moved, but to Essex and retirement, after taking their severance pay. However, a significant number of dockers in their forties and fifties took their severance payments and continued to work in Newham for the local council, as drivers, dustmen, road sweepers and labourers, jobs that required membership of the same trade union. As men with huge experience of negotiating with employers, they revitalized the local council's cleansing department in particular. Disputes were skilfully resolved; union meetings became quorate and pay and conditions at work improved. Newham's citizens were therefore politicized from childhood by the presence of a powerful and pragmatic trade union whose members were active in all aspects of social life, and not only as articulate and confident spokesmen but also in voluntary and community work, notably youth and sports clubs.

Things changed in the late 1970s and national government was the reason. Between 1980 and 1988 Conservative Prime Minister Margaret Thatcher's 'right to buy' policy, enshrined in the 1981 Housing Act, gave council housing tenants the right to buy their homes at a discount. In the UK two million publicly-owned homes were placed on the private market. Long established families, with roots deep in the social and political fabric of the area, bought and later re-sold at a profit and moved out to buy bigger and cheaper properties in Essex. Others on the council waiting list waited longer as the housing stock consequently diminished and those who could not buy and get out were transformed into a resentful and deskilled population. This resentment was exacerbated by the local council's decision in the 1990s to place young single parents (i.e. women with children) in vacant Newham properties. The relative availability of housing in the 1990s – no one now wanted to live there – also attracted newer immigrants to an area whose whiteness had been enforced by an unofficial apartheid in work employment practices (Back et al. 2002). Isolated and often with no links to the area, a fragmented set of cultures emerged that contrasted with the tight-knit but decomposing culture of the remnants. The newcomers' behaviour caused consternation; some of their off-spring were mixed-race. Always a racially conservative area, white residents of Newham, most of whom were of Irish extraction, shifted their politics to the Right. Whilst East London has proved an ideal recruiting base for generations of right-wing organizations, the recent ethnic mix in Newham and Tower Hamlets means that fascism, although far from dead, is no longer publicly nurtured. However, in 2006 the British National Party (BNP) took 12 seats in Newsham's adjacent borough, Barking and Dagenham, which thus became the first UK council to have the BNP as the second party. The central issue during the election was housing, followed by employment.

Contested Legacies

One of the continuously promoted sustainable legacies of the 2012 Games is the building of new homes throughout the Olympic boroughs, homes that were to be clean, safe and affordable. Clean and safe these new apartments may well be; how affordable they are to local residents is debatable. The average price for a one-bedroom flat across the new builds in Stratford is currently over £250,000. Despite Newham Council's agreement with the building contractors that 'local residents' are entitled to be the first to purchase such properties, the market price rules out most Newham residents.

The 2012 Olympics bring employment possibilities but not all those working on Olympic-related projects are local. The Olympic venues have provided employment opportunities in the construction and manufacturing divisions. This is beneficial but we need to ask, what are the longer-term ramifications? Citing the case of the US city of Baltimore, Friedman, Andrews and Silk (2004) illustrate how a society with many construction workers – in this case building a baseball stadium – who subsequently lose employment when works are completed, causes a ripple effect through the community. It raises crime rates and other social ills and causes the higher-paid citizens to migrate. The area's tax base thus erodes, forming a spiral of deterioration. According to Friedman, Andrews and Silk (2004), the construction of a state-of-the-art stadium in Baltimore was intended to reverse this decline and, while its magnificence as a structure is undeniable, it is a distraction from what is truly happening in its shadow; after time, the building's impact upon the city's re-imaging diminished. What this teaches, according to the authors, is that commercial extravagance can dissipate as the novelty decreases, after which the area is left with a sense of responsibility to improve further. The Olympics cannot be solely responsible for sustained socio-economic impact. The 2012 organizers might, however, take heart from a UK example. The issue of job formation and public service investment around Manchester's hosting of the 2002 Commonwealth Games were seen as highly successful (North West Regional Development Agency 2004). This is what the 2012 organizers want to hear.

As for the legacy of sporting participation, the 2012 Select Committee Report stated, 'possibly the greatest prize to emerge from the Games would be a demonstrable increase in participation in sport throughout the community, stimulated by the display and, we hope, by a set of inspiring performances by UK competitors' (2007: 37). Much of this might depend on what facilities the Games leave behind. The predominant difficulty that the 2012 Olympic Stadium will encounter is that, without an anchor tenant such as a significant football or even rugby club, and due to the construction of Wembley and the modernization of Twickenham, in the northwest and southwest of London respectively, the possibility of many large-scale team sports seeking to use the Olympic venue is questionable. In Germany, Australia and Italy the main Olympic stadiums have, since the respective Games, been heavily utilized for one or a number of other sporting functions but this is unlikely to be reproduced in London. The Aquatics Centre could encounter difficulties with community use: studies from post-Olympic Seoul and Athens demonstrate reluctance by the public to utilize facilities that were originally intended for high-performance Olympic training (Hardman 2005).

Sustaining and extending initial popularity is thus a complex task. Indeed, as the London 2012 Select Committee Report confirms, 'no host country has yet been able to demonstrate a direct benefit from the Olympic Games in the form of a lasting increase in participation' (2007: 37). That London is seeking to change this is commendable if a little idealistic. There are many issues around participation and legacy to consider and this is a population that is not agreed on many matters.

Who and what is the East London 'community' that is so regularly depicted as the beneficiary of the Games? The much lauded, and marketed, notion of an E End 'community' is in reality hard to find. The cosy imagery of a c pot, particularly apparent in the public relations campaigns of the 2 organizers, ought to be discarded (Bermant 1975). A more realistic identification is to consider the East End as an area 'racially and class demarcated into white spaces and Asian spaces, middle-class and working-class' (Sharma 2005), producing a socio-political milieu that is a cauldron of vibrant unarticulated discontent that is constantly augmented by new arrivals (Hobbs 2006). This is where the 2012 Olympics will take place. This reality is not apparent in the outpourings of the Olympic Development Authority (ODA) and LOCOG, who prostrate themselves at the feet of the corporate millions whilst simultaneously waxing lyrical about the power of sport to unite both desperate and disparate people and promise a legacy that is mythical, cynical and disrespectful to the citizens of East London.

Chapter 4

The Book of Olympic Promises

On 15 November 2004 15-year-old African-Caribbean East End schoolgirl, Amber Charles handed the London 2012 Olympic candidature file in to the IOC headquarters in Lausanne, Switzerland in an event broadcast live on a variety of British TV channels. This file, also known as the 'bid book', detailed, in some 179 pages, what London was committed to deliver should the UK win the right to host the 2012 Olympics. The document was supported by over 200 covenants and contained signed guarantees from then UK Prime Minister Tony Blair, former Mayor of London Ken Livingstone and all five of the London boroughs that would be most directly involved with, or affected by, the Olympics, along with other local authorities earmarked to host elements of the event. The bid book identified the 2012 Olympic and Paralympic Games as an opportunity for London and the UK to achieve sporting, cultural, economic, social and environmental objectives. Four main themes underpinned this vision: delivering the experience of a lifetime for athletes; leaving a legacy for sport in Britain; benefiting the community through regeneration; and supporting the IOC and the Olympic Movement more widely. This chapter explores the story of the bid to host the 2012 Olympic and Paralympic Games, focusing on what has now become a familiar predicament for successful candidate cities: an enforced commitment to meeting the spiralling costs of hosting the Games.

The bid book spoke of the UK population's adulation of sport of every kind, arguing that 'A devotion to sport unites Londoners and the United Kingdom as a whole' (London2012 2004: I 10). Tony Blair went so far as to state that 'sport is in the lifeblood of the United Kingdom' (London2012: I 4). Then Mayor of London Ken Livingstone argued that the 2012 Games would succeed in 'bringing all parts of our city together to celebrate the unifying force of 'Olympism' (London2012 2004: I 7).

The bid had public support. ICM polls conducted by the bidding team suggested that they had the support of almost 70 per cent of Londoners. Countrywide the figure was over 80 per cent. Findings by the IOC put the national figure at around 65 per cent. A Sports Marketing Survey, presented within the 2004 bid book, identified 73 per cent of Londoners and 68 per cent of the UK population wanting the Games to come to London (Dave 2005).

Indeed, Ken Livingstone could claim that 'the prospect of the Games has united government at every level in support of London's bid' (London2012 2004: I 11). This was an overstatement. Individuals such as veteran Labour MP Gerald Kaufman (then Chair of the Culture, Media and Sport Committee) opposed hosting the Games because of the potential costs such an event would entail (*The London*

Evening Standard 2003). However, his was a rare dissenting voice. Amidst such rhetoric the 2012 Olympic Games were awarded to London in Singapore on 6 July 2005.

Bidding Wars: The Pursuit of 2012

Although Britain had staged the 1908 and 1948 Olympics, it had only ever actually submitted a formal bid for the 1940 Games, which was awarded to Tokyo but, due to World War II, was never staged. Not until the 1992 Birmingham bid did a British city attempt to host the Olympics, and this failed largely due to lack of support from the British government. While Labour had been sympathetic to a Birmingham bid, support became less than forthcoming once the Conservatives took power; sport was not on the agenda of Prime Minister Margaret Thatcher. However, the Premier did allow Secretary of State Kenneth Baker to sign the letter to the IOC guaranteeing the Birmingham bid (Hill 1996: 96–7) and the relatively low-ranking Sports Minister Richard Tracey was sent to represent the UK Government in the final round of bidding presentations. Other bidders, however, notably the French and the Spanish, saw their respective Prime Ministers in attendance: the absence of the UK Head of Government was a major factor in the bid's failure. Furthermore, sport in the UK had been underfunded for years compared with other European countries (Seager 2004). There was also a notable absence of financial support from the City of London (Hill 1996: 96). Birmingham came fifth out of six cities in the first round of voting.

Manchester then bid for the 1996 Games. Reaching the final three cities, Manchester lost out to Atlanta. Andrew Jennings, author and fervent critic of IOC politics, suggested Manchester was an ideal Olympic City, with great character, sporting traditions and a vibrant cultural scene 'but the boutiques didn't impress Olympic wives, too far from London to offer their kind of interesting alternative' (Jennings 1996:37). Manchester bid again for the 2000 Games but again unsuccessfully. Some felt that the Manchester Organizing Committee's catchphrase had backfired – 'Giving the Games back to the athletes' may well have been taken as a jibe at the IOC (Hill 1996). Following these past failures to bring the Games to the UK, it was evident that the only chance of succeeding was with a London bid.

The formal campaign for hosting the 2012 Olympics began in London in 2003. The *idea* for a London Olympics, however, started life in 1997 when the BOA appointed David Luckes, a former Great Britain Olympic Hockey goalkeeper and logistics expert, to write a feasibility report Following three and a half years of research his 400-page report was submitted to the BOA, who decided that hosting an Olympics was plausible. Compiling the bid saw the pursuit of private and public support, financial backing, government guarantees and the assistance of the BOA. The final candidature file was submitted to the IOC), the Olympic Movement's governing body, in May 2005. The cost of the bid from private and public finance was in excess of £25 million.

Political Unity

In February 2005 the IOC Evaluation Commission began its round of four-day visits to each of the five candidate cities. Bidding process reforms introduced in 1999 by the IOC meant that each candidate city was allowed only one formal reception. In London this was held at Buckingham Palace, hosted by the Queen with the Prime Minister and the Mayor of London in attendance, indicating the reverence in which that the Olympic Movement was held by monarch and politicians alike.

Political unity was not always so evident. According to IOC regulations, a bid needs the backing of both the government in charge of the bidding city – in London's case the Mayor – and national government. The IOC also requires governments to underwrite the costs of the Games as a safeguard to cover unforeseen eventualities and ensure facilities are completed to schedule. Taking on the Olympics is a major commitment. The biggest problem for the 2012 bid was securing support from the Labour Party. Understandably sceptical due to the cost of the previous bids and England's unsuccessful bid to secure the 2006 World Cup, the then Deputy Prime Minister, John Prescott, favoured the monies available going towards regeneration in the deprived regions of the north of England. The then Chancellor, Gordon Brown, was well aware of the debts incurred by Montreal in 1976 and, closer to home, the city of Sheffield, whose hosting of World Student Games in 1991 had burdened the taxpayer for the next 20 years. The Prime Minister, Tony Blair, needed to know that the bid was credible, the inference being that another failed sporting bid would be seen as a lack of support for British sport, and might – with a general election planned for 2005 – cost the Labour Party votes. Politicians were rightly wary of the Olympics: would the public support a London-based Games when so many felt that this corner of England already receives more than its fair share of government funding?

An overtly disinterested London politician, Mayor Ken Livingston, saw the Games a catalyst for urban renewal on a massive scale. The Games offered a chance for the recently formed Greater London Authority (GLA) – headed by Livingstone – to demonstrate its new-found power in pushing for massive and much needed redevelopment in London's East End.[1] Mayor Livingstone answered criticisms from northern parliamentary members by adding to the potential funding with a council tax levy for all residents in the capital. Another consideration was

---

1 The London bid would not be without its controversy; Livingstone would be embroiled in a row over comments he made on the eve of the IOC Evaluation visit, when he likened a Jewish journalist to a Nazi concentration camp guard. Such comments have the potential to damage careers but an unnamed senior IOC official was quoted as saying 'it was a storm in a teaspoon (not teacup)' (*The Daily Telegraph* 2005).

the land that would be needed. Although 75 per cent of it was already in the ownership of the London Development Agency (LDA), the remainder would need to be compulsorily purchased. The LDA offered landowners buy-out costs of 20 per cent below the price they had paid for the land two years earlier (*The Guardian* 2007a; see also Chapter 8). The bid then gained support from Tessa Jowell MP, Secretary of State at the Department for Culture, Media and Sport (DCMS), and Richard Caborn, the Sports Minister. Both played their part, along with various stars from the world of sport, in securing government support.

What Am I Bid?

The bidding process for the Olympic host city is complex, elongated and riddled with political intrigue. Major reform around the customs of the IOC bidding process, stressing the need for greater transparency and professionalism, arose from the scandal of Salt Lake City.[2] The visit by the IOC Evaluation Commission, mentioned above, is a key part of the end game. Consisting of representatives from the: IOC, International Sports Federations, National Olympic Committees and other relevant experts, the Evaluation Commission visits the candidate cities, evaluates bids and reports its findings to the IOC. After considering this report and listening to all candidate cities presentation to the IOC session, a secret poll is taken. After each round of voting, the city with the fewest votes drops out. The ballot continues until one candidate possesses an absolute majority.

However, the earlier stages are equally tricky, involving constant dialogue with the IOC – as well as continuing 'domestic' politicking. Once the BOA had secured the required level of official support, it could submit its 'intention to bid' to the IOC. The BOA helped to set up the London 2012 Bid team Team that was responsible for putting the bid together. They selected Keith Mills as Chief Executive and Barbara Cassani, a highly successful American businesswoman and founder of GO! Airways, who agreed to chair the campaign. The decision to head the campaign with an American national was widely criticized, by bid supporters and sceptics alike. Indeed, on occasions, Cassani was asked by reporters to respond to questions regarding the rival New York bid, on the assumption from her accent that she was connected to the US Organizing Committee. In May 2004 Cassani stepped down in favour of former Olympian Lord Sebastian Coe, who was instantly recognizable to the IOC as double Olympic 1500-metre champion in 1980 and 1984; they were probably less aware that he was a former Conservative Party MP. London2012 now had an individual of stature and sporting reputation as the UK's representative.

---

2   Wenn and Martin (2006: 65) document how, 'In November 1998, allegations emerged concerning the use of Salt Lake City (2002) bid committee funds to provide college tuition assistance to Sonia Essomba, daughter of the late René Essomba, an IOC member from Cameroon'.

Table 4.1   Key dates in the bidding process

December 2000	'Luckes report' submitted to the BOA
2003	London 2012 Bid Team formed, led by Barbara Cassani, with Keith Mills as Chief Executive. They will put together the initial 'Applicants Questionnaire', outlining how London would stage the Games.
May 2003	London announces it will bid. Government announces its decision to support the bid.
July 2003	BOA submit London as an official applicant city to the IOC ('intention to bid').
January 2004	London 2012 bid submits 'Applicants' Questionnaire' (also know as 'ptich book'), detailing answers to logistical and other questions.
18 May 2004	IOC announce the five short-listed cities: London, New York, Madrid, Moscow, Paris (Havana, Istanbul, Leipzig and Rio de Janeiro are the unsuccessful candidates). Sebastian Coe takes over as Chair of the London2012 Bid Team, now a company).
15 November 2004	Candidature File ('bid book') submitted to IOC in Lausanne. (The Bid Team now have to 'flesh out' London's bidding proposal, addressing financing, transportation and infrastructure, Games security, post-Game utilization of facilities etc.)
February 2005	IOC Evaluation Commission inspection visit London to assess London's suitability as host for the 2012 Olympics.
May 2005	Final version of London 2012 candidature file submitted. IOC publishes its report.
6 July 2005	The final meeting of the IOC in Singapore. The five cities make their final presentations and the voting is held. London wins by 54 votes to 50. The IOC awards the 2012 Olympic Games and Paralympic Games to London.

Sources: London2012 website (London2012.com); BOA (n.d.).

The Winning Ticket

At the final summit, held in Singapore, voting took place over four rounds, with Moscow eliminated in the first and London taking a one-point lead into the second. By round two Madrid had picked up virtually all of the Moscow votes. *The Times* (2005) put this down to the lobbying done by former IOC President

Juan Samaranch, who used his former Soviet connections established when he was Spain's ambassador to Moscow. New York was the next to go; its bid had floundered when the site of the original stadium near Madison Square Gardens had to be rethought due to a local political dispute. Then Madrid lost out in the third round, and some have speculated that Samaranch's son, Juan Antonio Samaranch Jr, also an IOC committee member, and the focus of intense lobbying by Coe (*The Times* 2005). This left the two heavyweights, London and Paris, in the deciding round. At the decisive moment, Jacques Rogge, the IOC President, added to the tension, fumbling as he attempted to open the envelope, only to reveal that London had triumphed with the votes going 54 to 50 in their favour.

London's final victory caused some surprise. When selected to be amongst the five final candidate cities for the 2012 Olympics, London was widely viewed as only third favourite, with Paris favoured to win. As late as January 2005, a month before the final IOC inspection, 'there was little confidence in government that the games were winnable' (*The Guardian* 2005) and, indeed, it was the opinion of (anonymous) IOC members that the government was 'insufficiently committed to sport to merit the games' (*The Guardian* 2005).

This impression was evidently rectified. Many contend that it was at the final summit that London 2012 members produced their best work. Some 30 London children were flown to Singapore to demonstrate London 2012's commitment to youth development. The focus of the bid played up to the well-established values of the Olympics Movement. Lord's Coe's presentation dealt with Olympic memories, youth development and the multiculturalism and the 'diversity' of London. Alongside Lord Coe, Prime Minister Tony Blair was credited with having won over the IOC voters in the final stages. Arriving in Singapore two days prior to the vote, Blair and his wife conducted one-to-one meetings involving some 30 of the IOC's 116 members in 15-minute intervals. A meeting between the PM and Mr Al-Sabah, the Kuwaiti oil minister and head of the Olympic Council for Asia, was considered key to securing 21 Asian votes in what might have been a return favour for British military support for Kuwait following the Iraqi invasion.[3] The UK Government Minister for Sport, Richard Caborn, had in the 1980s been treasurer to the UK branch of Anti-Apartheid, and his South African connections probably secured the support of the country's former President Nelson Mandela (*The Observer* 2005). The fact that there was no conflict of interest from any Commonwealth countries in bidding for the Games after their experiences at the successful Manchester 2002 Commonwealth Games, may have provided support from former colonies.

Perhaps unsurprisingly, the Paris team, led by President Jacques Chirac, were of the persuasion that Britain's intensive lobbying was inequitable, undemocratic

---

3   The French President Jacques Chirac was criticized by his own press for turning up two days after Blair. With not enough time to meet people and with a presentation that was regarded as staid, containing too much video and dominated by men in suits (*The Times* 2005:2), the French did not impress enough.

and masked the actual quality of the bid (*The Observer* 2005); the *Observer Sport Monthly* described London's victory as the 'Greatest Sporting Mugging of all Time' (2005: 6). The IOC is not obliged to divulge the reasoning behind the voting. The key, however, seems to have been the work, the passions and the personalities attached to the bid.

The Regeneration Game?

However, another important, if less glamorous, factor in London securing the 2012 Games was its claim to be the 'legacy Games'. No doubt, the governments of both London and the UK were using the event for the political purpose of urban regeneration of the capital and, in particular, London's East End and the Thames Corridor in Essex. It was this very aim that would create the now often-cited 'legacy' that the Games would bequeath to London, the South East of England and, indeed, the nation. The bid book suggested the Games would significantly accelerate regeneration already committed to: 'Without the Games, change would still happen, but it would be slower, more incremental and less ambitious from a sporting, cultural and environmental perspective' (London2012 2004: I 23). Regeneration, in this disadvantaged area of East Londo   provide improvements in, amongst others things, healthcare, education, skills and training, housing, the environment and job opportunities (London2012 2004: I). The 9,460 rooms that were to constitute the Olympic Village were, post-Games, to be converted into 3,600 mixed-use permanent homes, with up to 50 per cent to be sold at 'affordable' prices and providing for much needed key workers (London2012 2004: II). Further legacy commitments included provision for schools, a lifelong learning centre and playing fields. Regeneration, coupled with opportunities for creative industries leading to cultural activities such as an Olympic Language Programme, was envisaged to encourage secondary school children to teach their heritage languages to other children. Such engagement between London's schoolchildren would lead to a greater 'understanding and amity' (London2012 2004: III 177).

Any major regeneration project in the twenty-first century must evidence a commitment to environmental principles and the London 2012 bid sought to surpass previous bids by 'setting new standards for sustainable production, consumption and recycling of natural resources' (London2012 2004: I 23). The regeneration process would include reviving and adding to green spaces and wetlands, conserving biodiversity and improving air, soil and water quality. Implementation of 'green' policies in construction, procurement and management of energy, water and waste aimed to achieve long-term benefits and behavioural changes.

Beyond the actual regeneration legacy, the Games themselves were presented as being 'low carbon' (London2012 2004: I 75), with a commitment to a low emission zone and the promotion of sustainable travel during the Games, with 80 per cent of visitors to the Olympic venues predicted to be using rail services (and 100 per cent of spectators using public transport). In addition, a commitment was made for 20 per cent of electricity requirements to be met by local renewable energy sources. As for sports venues, there was a commitment to make maximum use of existing permanent venues wherever possible and appropriate temporary venues where no legacy use was identified. All contractors were to demonstrate the ability to adhere to the LOCOG Sustainability Management System.

Indeed, it appeared that such transformative ambitions were apparently given primacy over the accurate projection of public costs. Deflecting the conflicts over 2012 resources that were already becoming increasingly public, Lord Coe and ODA Chair Roy McNulty announced a joint New Year's message for 2007:

> we are working with Government to ensure issues of budgets and funding are resolved early in the New Year and we are confident they will be. We must not lose sight of the wider benefits of this project. *It is not simply about cost. It is also about value and ambition.* (London2012 2006 emphasis added)

The Olympic Games in London, therefore, are thus not merely a sporting event but a catalyst for social, political and economic change. A successful Olympics leaves a legacy that transcends pure sporting rationale and results in substantial benefits for the hosts. However, as Roche (2000: 139–40) recognizes, the Olympic Games present a complex and risky project, with a wide range of potential social and political costs. Some Games have had negative consequences for the host city and its populace. Lack of preparation, planning, funding and inspiration from central government, can result in an Olympic Games leaving the region in varying levels of political and economical turmoil. At the same time, much lauded and spectacular regeneration schemes often create less visible losers. As Raco and Tunney's (2010) survey of 84 of the 201 businesses operating on the pre-Olympic site in Stratford reveals, many local small and medium enterprises (SMEs) were early casualties of the 2012 project. According to the authors, flagship redevelopment programmes such as these normally visualize spaces as blank canvasses and thus assume there are 'few, if any, socioeconomic activities of value that need protecting or supporting' (2010: 3).

Mind the Gap

One of the most significant consequences of the post bidding process is the dramatic escalation of public finance commitments. Olympic history is littered with instances of final costs exceeding budget (Whitson and McIntosh 1996) to such an extent that former IOC Vice-President Dick Pound labelled bidding documents as the 'most beautiful fiction' (Pound 2004 cited in Jennings 2010). Due to the competitive process surrounding the award to host the Games, Olympic bids have been accused of having substantial embedded 'optimism bias' over both costs and rewards (Jennings 2010). Such fictions have significant connotations in reality, most notably in the considerable burden placed on Montreal's public finances following the 1976 Games.

The UK Government's response to critics is to utter the traditional rhetoric that such costs are contributing to significant investment in regional prosperity and future generations. As Whitson and McIntosh characterize it:

> Public sector debt will repay itself, according to the standard official rhetoric, in private sector opportunities and ultimately in economic growth that will benefit the whole community. Investment in the Games is thus framed as a particular form of public assistance to private accumulation, a post-industrial variant of traditional subsidies to industry. (1996: 283)

As this chapter will demonstrate, London has been no exception to the traditional Olympic sport of budget inflation.

2007: The Secretary of State's Annus Horribilis

> At the time of London's bid to host the Games the estimated gross cost of the Games was £4 billion, comprising £2.992 billion core Olympic costs plus £1.044 billion for infrastructure on the Olympic Park. These costs were to be met by a public sector funding package of £2.375 billion for the core Olympic costs, £1.044 billion Exchequer funding for the infrastructure, plus an anticipated £738 million from the private sector. (NAO 2007: 5)

The 2012 bid budget was, its authors had proclaimed, 'robust, based on conservative revenue and cost forecasts' (London2012: 11). As 2006 came and went, concerns over the £4.036 billion 'robust' budget simmered. On 21 November 2006, considerable cost increases were announced to the CMS Committee by the Secretary of State (summarized in CMS 2007: 20), including £900 million of extra costs relating to the Olympic Park, including security. Yet, under increasing pressure from Parliament, other government departments and the media, she still did not come up with a final budget.

The 2007 CMS report, published in January 2007, began ominously:

> just 18 months after winning the bid, it is clear that many of the cost figures it contained are already seriously outdated. ... we are concerned that costs have arisen which should have been identified at the time of the preparation of the bid. (CMS 2007: 3)

A month later, in February 2007, the National Audit Office Report on *Preparations for the London 2012 Olympic and Paralympic Games – Risk Assessment and Management* (2007a) identified 'the requirement for the budget to be clearly determined and effectively managed' as 'Risk area 3'. Boiling point was reached on Thursday 15 March 2007, when Jowell addressed the House of Commons to reveal that the costs for London 2012 (*excluding* the costs of actually staging the Games)[4] would now be £9.325 billion, 5.289 billion higher than estimated at the time of the bid (NAO 2007: 5). Of this total, ODA 'core' Olympic costs had risen by £1.1 billion, including £570 million 'Programme Management' costs and a £150 million public-sector contribution to the Olympic Village (which in the initial bid budget was to be financed entirely by the private sector). In addition, two separate tranches of contingency provision added £500 million and £2,247 million, with tax (£836 million) and wider policing and security costs[5] (£600 million) (see Chapter 5) adding new headings not included in the bid budget. Of central importance to this text is the later emergence of security as a substantive resource (see below). Table 4.2 summarizes the key changes.

To cover the costs, the public sector funding package at the time of the original bid (November 2004) had been calculated at £2.375 billion plus an additional £1.044 Exchequer funding primarily earmarked for regeneration costs (making a total of £3.4 billion). The balance of costs was to be met through a private sector contribution of £738 million towards the cost of venues and infrastructure. In the March 2007 budget, however, the expected private sector contribution was downgraded to £165 million (less than 2 per cent of the total funding) (PAC 2008: 7). This meant that the load on the public sector correspondingly increased.

To meet the raised costs, and cover the shortfall in private sector funding, would now cost the public sector an additional £5.9 billion, with £4.9 billion of this increase to be met by the Exchequer, £675 million by the National Lottery (bringing the total Lottery contribution to £2.175 billion) and, finally, an extra GLA 'contribution' of £300 million (PAC 2008: 7) (See Table 4.2).

The extra pressure on both Lottery and GLA resources was controversial, with the CMS (2007) report in January being particularly severe. This may explain the recourse to additional Exchequer funding in the March budget. (See below for further discussion of the National Lottery and GLA implications.)

---

4   Staging the Games covers, loosely, the event itself and is the responsibility of The London Organizing Committee of the Olympic Games (LOCOG), which is separate from the Olympic Delivery Authority (ODA). The ODA is the body charged with building the key venues, facilities and infrastructure for the 2012 Games. Much of the discussion on Olympic finances presented in this chapter concerns the budget available to the ODA. LOCOG was established as a private sector organization, although they are exempt from corporation tax following a decision that they operated in the public interest (see below). The LOCOG budget for staging the Games (currently estimated around £2 billion (at 'outturn' prices i.e. as per the bid (£1.5 billion) but updated to take account of inflation etc) is not included in the discussions on financing the Games detailed here – nor has it, as yet, occupied much public attention. LOCOG is intended to be self-financing with the exception of a £66 million government contribution towards the costs of the Paralympics (IOC regulations require the state to meet 50 per cent of the cost of Paralympic Games) (PAC 2008: 7).

5   These are security costs over and above the cost of site security during construction, which had been included in the bid budget at £190 million, increased to £268 million in the March 2007 budget (NAO 2007: 16, Figure 6).

Table 4.2   Olympic costs: 2004 and 2007

	November 2004 bid* budget (£ million)	March 2007 budget (£ million)	Difference (£ million)
ODA budget			
Core Olympic costs	1,996	3,081	1,115
Infrastructure & regeneration	1,684	1,673	(11)
Contingency	included in project budgets	500	500
Subtotal	3,650	5,254	1,604
Other Olympic (non-ODA) provision	386	388	2
Other provisions			
Policing and wider security	Not included	600	600
Tax (corporation tax and VAT)	Not included	836	836
Programme contingency (including VAT)	Not included	2,247	2,247
Subtotal		3,683	3,683
Total	4,036	9,325	5,289

Note: *These figures are 'outturn' figures, taking inflation into account.
Source: Based on information in NAO (2007) and PAC (2008).

In the course of the year, the March 2007 budget would be scrutinized by the National Audit Committee in *The Budget for the London 2012 Olympic and Paralympic Games* (NAO 2007b) published in July with a public warning from the NAO to the DCMS and the ODA that they must iron out budget uncertainties (*The Guardian* 2007i). The budget would be further reviewed, in the light of the NAO report, by the Public Accounts Committee; its report (PAC 2008) was published in April 2008. The PAC oral evidence hearings took place 14 November 2007 and provided some vociferous exchanges, of which more later. But September was to bring further events.

Table 4.3   Public sector funding package

	London2012 ('bid budget')	March 2007
Core costs	*£million*	*£million*
National Lottery	1,500	2,175
GLA council tax precept	625	925 [625 + 300]
LDA	250	250
Exchequer	0	5,975 [includes 1,044]
Total	2,375	9,325
Infrastructure (Olympic Park)		
Exchequer	1,044	
Total	3,419	9,325

Source: NAO 2008 and PAC 2008.

In the News

The original bid had offered promises of both London- and UK-wide economic benefits. The bid book postulated that every sector of the economy would benefit from London staging the Games and the whole of the UK would gain from its 'prosperity'. Along with these economic benefits would come an influx of jobs in both the lead up to and after the event. On 10 September 2007 the Channel 4 programme *Dispatches* offered a series of revelations in its episode on 'The Olympics Cash Machine', with investigation by reporter Anthony Barnett (Channel 4 2007) that challenged these assurances. Whereas the public had been led to believe that 'the country' would benefit from a £2 billion surplus from hosting the Games. However a government- and GLA-commissioned report by Dr Adam Blake, Associate Professor of Tourism at Nottingham University, on the economic impact of the Olympics had found a positive impact of £5.9 billion for London – and a negative impact of £4 billion for the rest of the country. Dr Blake appeared on the programme and predicted that lottery funds, government monies and jobs would be 'sucked into' London and so could cause a damaging economic drain on the rest of the UK. The timing of his report was also significant. It had been completed in October 2004, two months before the submission of the bid document (candidature file) yet the government did not make it public until December 2005 (Blake 2005),[6] six months after London had won the bid. With

---

6   The publicly available version of the report does not explicitly mention the above figures for London and the rest of the country.

the government accused of 'burying' the report and then only part publishing it, in response, the DCMS protested their innocence, claiming they were open and transparent and that the findings in the report had not taken into consideration the wider (non-economic) potential positive impacts of the Games (Channel 4 2007). LOCOG, meanwhile had attempted to withhold financial details on the basis that, as a private company, they were not subject to the Freedom of Information Act; however, they backed down after individuals such as Paul Farrelly of the DCMS said that this was unacceptable (Channel 4 2007).

The *Dispatches* programme had a second, even more embarrassing item, this time concerning the March 2007 budget increases. 'In the course of our investigation, we had uncovered an extraordinary Whitehall memo to Olympics Minister Tessa Jowell, which suggested she had been personally warned about the spiralling Olympic costs long before she told Parliament earlier this year' (Barnett 2007). The document contained the minutes of a high-level confidential Whitehall meeting on 29 November 2005, at which 12 senior officials from the Treasury, the DCMS and the Mayor of London's office met to discuss Olympic costs and seemingly revealed that by September 2004 they had reason to believe that the projected bid budget was 'light' by one billion pounds. By the time of the 2005 meeting the predictions were even higher, according to *Dispatches*, primarily in areas such as infrastructure, environmental commitments and security.

Throughout the Autumn of 2007, there was a united stance. John Armitt, Chair of the ODA, condemned media coverage that suggested Olympic costs had nearly doubled (*The Daily Telegraph* 2007f). Lord Coe was more positive, convinced that the organizers had 'finally got the message across about the distinction between the budgets' through continual reassurance that almost half 'that famous nine billion' was for 'regeneration' (*The Independent* 2007). In the opinion of the IOC's Jacques Rogge, the exclusion of VAT and contingency from the original budget had led the general public to believe there had been an explosion in costs (*The Guardian* 2007b).

MPs continued to barrack Tessa Jowell and the DCMS over the lack of 'transparency' in the ODA and Department for Culture, Media and Sport 2012 operations and budget controls. Jowell had to admitted that, as late as October 2007, 'detailed work on the budget was not complete' (*The Daily Telegraph* 2007f) – which Shadow Olympic Minister Hugh Robertson described as a 'staggering' admission' (*The Guardian* 2007p). In the same month Lord Moynihan (Chair of the BOA and former Minister for Sport) attacked the government over Olympic finances: 'These are everybody's Games, so it is very important that not only do we have the right controls in place but they should be transparent' (*The Daily Telegraph* 2007i). The DCMS replied that they were already fulfilling funding conditions to be 'open' with the Olympic Board (The Guardian 2007o).

Public Accountability and Public Accounts

> a Tory MP on the Public Accounts Committee, Richard Bacon, attacked the
> process as 'Del Boy economics' because the report showed the government had
> failed to allow for VAT, corporation tax or programme management costs in its
> original budget. (*The Guardian* 2007i)

November 2007 saw the hearings ('oral evidence') held by the Public Accounts
Committee (PAC)[7] inquiry into the escalating Olympic costs. This was a far more
public airing of issues than the discreet National Audit Office review (NAO 2007b,
published in July) of the Olympics budget.[8] The questioning of the 'witnesses',
Jonathan Stephens, Permanent Secretary of the DCMS and David Higgins, Chief
Executive of the ODA, involved some lively exchanges that, perhaps unsurprisingly,
were seized upon by excited journalists. The media referred to the uncovering of
'initial bungled calculations which failed to include tax and contingency funding
and underestimated security costs' (*The Guardian* 2007h).[9]

The final PAC report (2008) centred on four central themes: the enormous
escalation of Olympic-related costs, the failure to embed adequately contingency
funding into the programme, the failure to secure sufficient private sector backing
(and the additional burden on public finances that this placed), and the failure to
cost for policing and wider security in the original bid.

Taking these in turn, Olympic cost overruns were criticized on a number
of fronts.[10] This included the accusation that the DCMS had initially published
artificially low figures in the candidature file, with Austin Mitchell, Labour MP
for Great Grimsby asking whether there was a 'deliberate attempt to deceive
or was it just an accidental by-product of excessive optimism?' (PAC 2008:
Ev 15). Indeed, there was some suspicion expressed that the original budget was
set deliberately low to attract public approval for the Games (PAC 2008: Ev 15).
In response Jonathan Stephens, Permanent Secretary of the DCMS, claimed that
such estimates were made given the state of knowledge and development at the
time (PAC 2008: Ev 15). Nevertheless, the now inflated cost of £9.325 billion was
further criticised as a selective interpretation of Olympic costs given that the price
of acquiring the land to accommodate the Olympic Park, resources needed by

---

7   The PAC is appointed by the House of Commons to examine the accounts granted
by Parliament to meet the public expenditure.

8   Formally the PAC was reviewing the budget 'in the light of' the NAO report – and
much of the discussion in the oral evidence referred to 'the report', i.e. NAO (2007b).

9   This was a response to the initial PAC public hearings help in 2007, reproduced in
the later 2008 PAC report.

10   Indeed, further gripes over 'creative' costings have since arisen over the cost of the
Olympic Stadium and Aquatics Centre. The budget for the former had risen from the bid
book estimate of £280 million to £496 million (*The Daily Telegraph* 2007f). The cost of the
Aquatics centre has more than tripled.

government departments working on the Games preparations and legacy planning and the cost of upgrading local transport were all excluded from this budget.

The DCMS were also challenged on the issue of the Olympic contingency budget,[11] both in terms of its absence in the original bid (an omission that was 'contrary to good practice' (PAC, 2008: 5)) and over a lack of detail as to the utilization of contingency funds. (Of the contingency provision of £2.747 billion in the March 2007 iteration of the Olympic budget, £500m was used in the first 12 months.) In addition to providing the recommendation that the DCMS should fully exhaust other funding opportunities before accessing further contingency funds, Edward Leigh, chair of the PAC inquiry, levelled the accusation that this large contingency fund had been incorporated so that the government would have a greater chance of claiming that the Games infrastructure was built to budget. The DCMS did not deny the accusation. Sceptics were correct to be suspicious. DCMS Permanent Secretary Stephens admitted to the 2007 PAC hearings, 'it is realistic to expect that a significant amount, if not all of the contingency, to be required' (PAC 2008: Ev 15). In response, Conservative critics then crowed, this 'blows apart the government's defence that the core costs of the Games have not risen' (*The Daily Telegraph* 2007e).

The DCMS also incurred the wrath of the PAC over what one committee member termed a 'wildly over-optimistic' estimate of private sector contributions (PAC 2008: Ev 2), given that the contribution of £738 million anticipated in the bid budget was dropped to £165 million in the 2007 budget. It had been anticipated that the London 2012 Olympics would have ten first-tier sponsors, 20 to 30 second-tier sponsors and up to 50 third tier sponsors, contributing both money and services (*The Guardian* 2006). Yet it was not until 14 March 2007 (the day before the budget announcement) that the first official private sponsor appeared: Lloyds TSB Bank pledged a sum of £80 million towards what had become the later £165 million projected private-sector funding. In return, Lloyds TSB Bank is the only high-street bank to have marketing rights and the right to use the Olympic logo and became an Official Partner for all the teams who competed at Beijing in 2008 and at the Vancouver Winter Olympics in 2010 and will assist in the sale and distribution of tickets for 2012 (*The Daily Telegraph* 2007b). Within the vast majority of sponsorship deals, the sponsor is expected to provide goods or services in kind in addition to their financial obligations; sponsorship constituted approximately 32 per cent of all Olympic marketing revenue between 2001 and 2004 (Beard 2007).

Despite the importance of private sector construction firms to the 2012 project, the ODA experienced particular difficulties in generating competition for contracts build the major venues. When tendering for the iconic Olympic Stadium, for example, only one credible candidate emerged. Of further importance is that this additional burden on public finances was not met with any guarantees of a commensurate share of Games-related financial benefits.

---

11   The original 2004 budget did allow for some contingency, although this was hopelessly under-resourced.

Of particular interest to this book is the question of why estimates for the cost of policing and wider security (apart from the cost of site security during its construction)[12] were absent in the original bid. As noted above, the March 2007 budget provided an estimate of £600 million (which at the time of writing is supplemented by a £238 million contingency fund).[13] The reasons for this omission can only be speculated upon. One senior police officer whose experience was consulted for the candidature file told the authors there was a sense that London's bid would ultimately fail and this may informed the decision not to thoroughly cost the security requirements for the Games. An alternative explanation may relate to faith in London's extant security infrastructures. Indeed, the candidature file makes a strong play on the sophistication of London's physical and organizational security architectures alongside the capital being a 'low-risk environment' (London2012 2004: 27). The most likely explanation, however, is rooted in the separation of security costs and the likelihood that any Olympic costs that could be divorced from the 'core' building programme were not included in the original bid.

Indeed, the response of the DCMS to the PAC enquiry demonstrates how Olympic security costs were both separated and shrouded in uncertainty. As a result, key thematic areas of security were not included in the original bid. In addition, it may reflect the financial burden of importing standardized security models following a successful Olympic bid.

On this point, the exchanges at the December 2007 hearings are worth quoting at length. In questioning Jonathan Stephens (Permanent Secretary for the Department for Culture, Media and Sport) and David Higgins (Chief Executive of the ODA), Alan Williams of the PAC argued that 'there was no provision whatsoever for security during the Olympics. Had anyone ever mentioned Munich to you? ... I will spell it out to you: M-U-N-I-C-H. There was a little incident there some years ago' (PAC 2008: Ev 19). Jonathan Stevens replied that the omission of broader security costs was due to uncertainty over their final amount:

> If I may say so, my predecessor, the Accounting Officer at the time, wrote to the Committee at the time of the bid and she said: 'While an allowance of £190 million for security costs has also been made, which is covered by the Olympic budget, the Home Office considered that there may be wider costs associated

---

12   The 2004 bid estimate included £190 million for this cost of providing security during construction. This figure also increased (to £268 million) in the March 2007 budget (PAC 2008).

13   Olympic security planners have informed the authors that £1 billion was originally requested for this task. At the time of writing (June 2010) the new coalition government had recently announced a comprehensive public spending review, due for publication during October 2010. In May 2010 it was announced that the overall Olympic budget will be cut by at least £27 million (BBC 2010d). It is likely that the Olympic security budget will be revised a further time on this later occasion.

with policing and counter-terrorism. At present it is not possible to quantify these wider costs precisely'. (PAC 2008: Ev 19)

Alan Williams retorted that the use of the work 'precisely' meant some calculation was possible, 'it may have been wrong but there could have been a calculation' (PAC 2008L Ev 19). In an attempt to provide clarity over the separation of costs, David Higgins of the ODA articulated that

> There are three areas of security. To cover [the] issue of Munich, the cost of securing the Olympic Village and the Games venues during Games time is a LOCOG cost ... The cost of security of the Games venues and infrastructure during the construction of the Games and up until handover to LOCOG during the 60 day period of the Games is covered within the ODA allowance and there always was a budget. There was a budget of some £190 million allowed for at the time of the bid. That has been increased since then ... The cost that we are talking about, the £600 million, is a cost to cover the other security costs which are covered by Home Office or Met Police outside the Olympics. That covers the arrival of dignitaries and securing the rest of UK and London during Games time ... These costs are obviously substantial because of the size and scale of the Olympics ... They are difficult to determine even now (PAC 2008: Ev 19).

This issue of the initial exclusion of security costs therefore raises a number of points. First, the PAC question of why uncertain security costs were not at least project remained unanswered. However, this oral evidence articulates the separation of security funding across Olympic agencies. Sceptics may argue that this allowed any additional Olympic-related security costs to be omitted from the initial 2004 budget. This would fit with the PAC accusation that there was wilful attempt to under-project the costs of hosting the 2012 Games.

Good Causes: Bad Losers?

With the March 2007 £9.325 billion revised budget came the diversion of an additional £675 million from the National Lottery, (as noted above) bringing total Lottery contributions to £2.17 billion. This figure will increase further courtesy of the Olympic Lottery scratch card, launched in 2005. Originally it was thought that some 59 per cent of regular lottery scratch card users would swap to the Olympic cards. In fact 75 per cent converted – thereby reducing the income available to the traditional Lottery-funded beneficiaries in sports, arts, heritage and other causes. This has already affected UK sporting provision. The Central Council for Physical Recreation (CCPR) reported that an estimated loss of £55.4 million from scratch cards sales, which might rise to £72.5 million (*The Guardian*, 2007l). The Big Lottery Fund (BLF), responsible for distributing half the Good Causes Lottery monies, confirmed it would have to re-profile £120 million of its planned UK programmes over the coming year because of the impact of Olympic-diverted income on voluntary and community organizations' initiatives (Warrell 2007a). The biggest loser in National Lottery Good Causes cut backs was the BLF itself, which by 2007 alone had lost £900 million. Then came grassroots 'sport' with a £124 million-reduced budget (Channel 4 2007). Sport England,[14] distributor of lottery funds to sport, explained how, once money was diverted from grassroots sports to Olympic coffers, it would have funds totalling just £150 million to distribute in 2008 compared to £300 million in 2000–01 (*The Guardian*, 2007l).

The PAC had questioned the logic of these financial diversions when the Olympic project was supposed to increase participation in sport (PAC 2008). In response Tessa Jowell claimed that the 2012 Games would act as a catalyst for increasing sporting participation (*The Guardian* 2007g). The BLF also expressed concern that there might be further 2012-related raids on such funds (*Community Care* 2007). This met with pledges from Jowell that the lottery monies would be repaid after the Games from land sales income (*The Guardian*, 2007g) and a promise from James Purnell[15] that 'there will be no further diversions from the lottery good causes' (*The Daily Telegraph* 2008a).

Not all were placated. In 2007 a number of arts, sports and heritage organizations campaigned, along with opposition MPs, against the intention to divert Lottery funds (Jump and Warrell 2007). The National Council for Voluntary Organizations (NCVO) led campaigns lobbying for MPs to vote against any decisions Tessa Jowell made to use more Lottery funding for the Olympics (Thomas 2007). After Jowell confirmed in March 2007 that the additional £675 million would be diverted, a ThirdSector[16] on-line vote reported that 56 per cent of respondents thought Ed Miliband (then Minister for the Cabinet Office) had not done enough to protect them (ThirdSector 2007). Stuart Etherington (Chief Executive of the NCVO) argued that diverting Lottery funds to the Olympics could create insecurity and uncertainty amongst some of the most disadvantaged individuals and communities in the UK and leave roughly 85,000 grassroots projects without funding (*Community Care* 2007).

The National Lottery Good Causes diversions also see also UK arts organizations set to lose £112 million, a sizeable part of the Arts Council's budget (*Strad* 2007: 10). Louise Wylie (Arts Council England) spoke of the cuts affecting organizations in every town, thereby tainting the Arts Council's ability to deliver their cultural remit (*Strad* 2007: 10). However, David Lammy[17] spoke against

---

14   The Government agency responsible for advising, investing in and promoting community sport, whose announced ambition is to get two million people more active in sport by 2012 – and to make sure that such participation is sustained.

15   James Purnell was Secretary of State for Culture, Media and Sport until January 2008 when he became Secretary of State for Work and Pensions.

16   Their website publicity states that 'ThirdSector is the UK's leading publication for everyone who needs to know what's going on in the voluntary and not-for-profit sector'.

17   David Lammy was formerly the Minister for Culture under Tessa Jowell at the DCMS until June 2007 when he was moved to the Department for Innovation, Universities

those who considered the cuts would negatively affect the arts, claiming that only 5 per cent of total yearly income would be lost, that no existing projects would be cut and that the 2012 Games would provide cash and cultural payback such as 'Live Sites'[18] and an International Shakespeare Festival (Lammy 2007: 42–3). According to Lammy, 'The greatest show on earth is not just going to take place in the sports stadiums of Britain' but nationwide via such 'cultural' events (Lammy 2007: 42). Jonathan Stephens (Permanent Secretary to the DCMS) suggested that any impact on Lottery Good Causes would be negated by the £5.2 billion available to Lottery Good Causes: the new lottery licence given to Camelot was on the basis that they would maximize returns to Good Causes (UK Parliament 2007b). PAC member Doug Touhig commented that this strategy was like 'Robin Hood', 'robbing Peter to pay Paul' (PAC 2008: Ev 6).

The Building Blocks: Good Foundations?

When John Armitt took over as Chair of the ODA,[19] he did not seem unduly perturbed by the knowledge that the London Olympic 2012 project was twice the size of the newly completed Heathrow Terminal 5, with a remit to be built in half the time (*The Guardian* 2007j). Yet the PAC report expressed concern that the ODA 'has had difficulty in achieving competition between bidders for contracts to deliver the main venues, with only one bidder emerging for the Main Stadium' (2008: 3). Consequently it could find itself in a position to be exploited on build costs. Their stringent contract pre-qualifications (ODA 2010) have been identified as significant factor in the low number of bidders. For example, according to *The Daily Telegraph*, that was why there was only one bid for the Olympic Stadium contract, by the UK's leading construction company, Sir Robert McAlpine (*The Daily Telegraph* 2007h). At the PAC hearings in November 2007, ODA Chief Executive, David Higgins, argued that it was not easy to gain contractor interest in 'high-profile, iconic structures', especially as there was some 'history' of stadium building across the country (PAC 2008: Ev 10) (Wembley Stadium was ten months late and £200 million over budget) but he remained positive about the ODA's progress (against development deadlines) in gaining contractual commitments and declared himself dedicated to making sure the ODA was 'attractive and efficient as a client'(PAC 2008: Ev 13).

The construction union, the Allied Trades and Technicians (UCATT), was concerned that the ODA had not insisted on the use of directly employed labour in their contracts since self employed/casual workers potentially compromised

---

and Skills to become a Parliamentary Under-Secretary of State.

18   Live Sites has plans for a number of public venues, spread nationally, where people can watch the Olympics. These locations will host temporary large TV screens and provide stages for local arts performances and events (Lammy 2007).

19   His predecessor, Jack Lemley, having left in November 2006 after seven months as part-time head of the ODA (*The Guardian* 2007i).

safety, costs and completion dates, not least due to 'bogus' self-employment being rampant in the construction industry. The ODA, in response, said they were in 'positive negotiations' with construction unions and hoped to include an agreement to maximize the use of directly employed labour in recruiting the expected 20,000 employees expected on the Olympic site (*The Financial Times* 2008).

The bid document had predicted the need for 7,000 full-time jobs before and 12,000 after, for the Olympic Park in Stratford (London2012 2004: I). This positive statistic was undermined, however, by contestations over the impact on local job creation. Fifty per cent of those employed were registered as currently 'living in London' but, again, data failed to enlighten as to whether this included non-British nationals who had re-located to London prior to engagement (PAC 2008: Ev 11. A Freedom of Information request by one Waltham Forest resident in 2010, however, revealed that less than a quarter of the workforce lived in the five Olympic boroughs (*The Evening Standard* 2010). What is more, during 2009 a series of reports revealed that, to be classed as 'local', one only needed to have established an address in one of the host boroughs (*inter alia The Independent* 2009b). With Newham having the highest proportion of new National Insurance registrations for adult overseas nationals in the UK, more than double the second-ranking locality (Department for Work and Pensions 2009: 6; see also Chapter 3), questions were raised over what being 'local' meant. On the plus side, the ODA could detail a comprehensive apprentice training scheme (PAC 2008: Ev 11) and The East London Communities Organization (TELCO) (see Chapter 8) obtained written guarantees from then Mayor Ken Livingstone that all employees of Olympic projects would receive the London Living Wage (LLW).[20]

Not all sectors of the London economy will benefit from Olympic spending. In October 2007 community transport organizations in London lobbied for changes in Olympic-related contracts that they had found disqualified more than 90 per cent of them from submitting tenders. The ODA stipulated that any organization involved in a consortium bidding for a bus service contract (to transport staff between Games venues) must have an annual turnover of at least £5 million. This ruled out all but two of the capital's community transport groups (Warrell 2007). It also stymied the hoped-for bonanza of small businesses in the East End.

Legacy on Track?

With London currently having poorer sporting facilities than many modern capital cities, the influx of sporting infrastructure expected to arrive with the Olympic project should be welcomed and appreciated. The creation of an 80,000-seat Olympic stadium that can be transformed post-Games into a 25,000-seat permanent

---

20   The Mayor of London's office hosts a Living Wage Unit that monitors the level needed for a living wage in London (which has considerably higher living costs than the rest of the UK) (TELCO citizens n.d.).

structure was driven by a bid commitment to leave a 'world class athletics legacy' (*The Guardian* 2007q). But the ODA, as late as 2010, is still indecisive over the eventual legacy use of the Olympic Stadium. Already, some three years ago, IOC President Jacques Rogge urged that the legacy plan be decided quickly (*The Daily Telegraph* 2007f). With track and field not profitable enough to maintain the stadium independently, an anchor tenant must be found. Here, there are also questions about the legacy use of the multiple-use international-standard track (*The Daily Telegraph* 2007h). British Athletics has expressed fears over legacy promises being 'watered down' following a report by management consultants PMP which concluded that, post-Games, there would be no room for a warm-up track and the stadium would have to be shared between athletics and a football club (*The Daily Telegraph* 2007j; see also BBC 2010c).

At the time of writing (late 2010) the future tenancy of the stadium is emerging as a fight between two English Premier League clubs: West Ham United and Tottenham Hotspurs. East London's West Ham, with the backing of Newham Council, is promising to retain the athletics track (to the likely detriment of football spectators). More controversially, North-London based Tottenham Hotspurs, with private-sector financial backing from US leisure firm AEG, propose replacing the existing structure with a purpose-built football stadium and simultaneously redeveloping South London's Crystal Palace athletics stadium.

Certainly, the PAC hearings raised the question whether such uncertainty surrounding future venue ownership (and who would cover the conversion costs) of legacy sites, accounted for the decrease in anticipated private sector support from £738 million to £165 million (PAC 2008: Ev10). The ODA, however, feel they are making good progress, especially in light of the government's Legacy Action Plan, belatedly[21] launched in June 2008 (DCMS 2008b), which sets out what it aims to achieve under each of the five legacy promises published in *Our Promise for 2012*[22] (DCMS 2007).

An Athletics Legacy?

The 2012 London Olympics will not be celebrated primarily in the purpose-built, fenced off, restricted access venue that is Stratford's Olympic Park. Rather it will be hosted via TV broadcast inside the world's living rooms, where the armchair spectator is fleetingly elevated from their unremarkable existence to transitory significance by great exemplars of physical omnipotence. Modernity's dependence upon distanced, media-reliant spectatorship both promotes and

---

21 It had been promised for early 2008 (PAC 2008: 14).

22 The five legacy promises are: 1) to make the UK a world class sporting nation; 2) to transform the heart of East London; 3) to inspire a new generation of young people to take part in local volunteering, cultural and physical activity; 4) to make the Olympic park a blueprint for sustainable living; and, finally, 5) to demonstrate that the UK is a creative, inclusive and welcoming place to live in, visit and to conduct business (DCMS 2007).

facilitates a controlled interpretation of the world's premier sporting events. Commercial interests have identified and cultivated this transition from previous forms of spectatorship: it that facilitates greater control of product placement, unparalleled public endorsement and a level of exposure far greater than that of commercial competitors. Consequently, untold capital is invested in attempts to convince a global audience that, to become a true armchair Olympian, they must eat McDonalds, drink Coca-Cola, drive a Hyundai and pay for everything in-between by Visa card.

The penchant for spectating from afar, with its resonance of reflected glory, and the British public's contentedness with being armchair athletes, are issues that LOCOG has considered only in part. The chair of LOCOG, former Olympian and later Tory MP Lord Sebastian Coe, claims that the 2012 Games will inspire a new generation of UK residents to take up sport. In May 2007, Tessa Jowell spoke of the Games acting as a 'catalyst', increasing participation and announced the first of the government's 'Olympics Legacy Promises' to use the Games 'to make the UK a world-leading sporting nation' (*The Daily Telegraph* 2009). The question on many lips is how this increase will be funded given successive cuts to Sport England's budget.

There are concerns especially that the billions spent delivering the Games will leave no monies for the pledge to get youth playing sport. The constant response is that the Games will make young people 'want' to get involved. Yet there seem to be no concrete plans as to how this will happen. To add to such concerns MPs and sports national governing bodies are even questioning the role of Sport England in delivering the 2012 sporting legacy. At a DCMS Select Committee hearing in 2007, while sports bodies agreed that Sport England should drive the legacy commitment, they were unclear as to its plans.

Such claims also contradict research conducted in 2003 by Sport England, which indicated that ordinary people watching 'models of perfection' (2003: 5) performing on the elite stage are actually put off exercise. It also contradicts the UK Government's 2002 strategy document *Game Plan: A Strategy for Delivering Government's Sport and Physical Activity Objectives*, which concluded that hosting an Olympics would not inspire people to take up sport: 'depending on the scale of the subsidy, it would seem that hosting events is not an effective, value for money method of achieving ... a sustained increase in mass participation' (DCMS/Strategy Unit 2002: 75).

Yet it was not long after the government had come to this conclusion that it was announced in 2003 that London was to bid for the 2012 Games and would be committing billions of pounds of public money towards building the necessary facilities and infrastructure. As former UK Prime Minister Harold Wilson once said, 'A week is a long time in politics'.

Greenery

The 2012 Games pledged to be the greenest Games in modern times. The strategy included green transport, energy-efficient buildings, reuse of construction and destruction materials, cleaning up canals and river courses and reductions in $CO2$ emissions (albeit that the IOC and VIPs would be travelling daily by car) (The Guardian 2007c). As outlined in the bid, there were to be three transport priority levels: Athletes and technical officials took first place, second came the 'Olympic Family', sponsors came third. Athletes, team and technical officials, the accredited media and the members of the IOC (together, the 'Olympic Family'). Reliable congestion-free transport was promised via the Olympic Route Network (ORN), consisting of designated Olympic lanes, traffic and signal plans to ensure journey times were minimal and schedules maintained (London2012 2004: I) and, crucially, would operate from West End five star hotels to the Olympic Park, some nine miles east. In pursuit of this ambition, the 24-hour ORN for the 'Olympic Family' proposed VIP lanes operating from 6 am to midnight throughout the duration of the Games (Games Monitor 2007a). 'Family' members needing to travel outside the Olympic Park would be transported by cars, vans and coaches along the ORN (UK Parliament 2007) and policed by surveillance cameras and enforcement officers with the possibility of £5,000 fines for any ineligible motorists entering the ORN. The efficiency of the system as specified in the bid is reliant on a 15 per cent decline in the rate of traffic recorded in 'normal' years. There was very little clarity about 'what areas of the capital any decline in traffic will take place' (UK Parliament 2007).

The restriction on private car access into Olympic venues to the Olympic Family would leave other (non-Family) spectators walking, cycling or using public transport. A pre-commitment of US$30 billion towards the extension, modernization and refurbishment of public transport services paired with the Olympic Javelin shuttle[23] and planned park-and-ride buses would ideally result in spectators experiencing fast, frequent, reliable journeys (London2012 2004: III) Discussion with local business was said to be underway, with the anticipation of managing commuter traffic, construction works and deliveries and increasing the numbers working from home during the duration of the event.

The Olympic Stadium is to set a 'sustainability pattern' for all future stadiums (*The Daily Telegraph* 2007d). The Commission for a Sustainable London 2012[24] is now in place, but scrutiny has already fallen upon sustainability targets (*The Guardian*

---

23 The new, high-speed 'Olympic Javelin' shuttle train service was projected to provide a direct link from the Olympic Park to central London in just seven minutes' (London2102 2004: I 11).

24 The Commission for a Sustainable London 2012 is an independent body, funded by members of the Olympic Family, with reporting duties to the Olympic Board and the public. It is chaired by Shaun McCarthy, a leading advocate of sustainable business practices, and has 10 people on it holding the title of Commissioner.

2007c). Jack Pringle (President of the Royal Institute of British Architects) wrote in a letter to *The Guardian*:

> Of particular concern is the ODA's sustainability targets for the Olympic village, which lag worryingly behind the government's own proposals. The ODA sustainability strategy states that the village will be 25 per cent more energy-efficient than buildings built today using current building regulations. Yet the government is already proposing that all new housing should meet that target by 2010 – two years before the games take place. Furthermore, the government already proposes that all new homes should be 44 per cent more energy efficient by 2013, and carbon neutral by 2016. The government and the ODA have been lapped by their own targets. (quoted in *The Guardian* 2007c)

In other words, ODA targets are below government aims.

However pleasing projected green targets may look overall, they need more detail. For example, there is an urgent need for a new interceptor tunnel to stop overflow at pumping stations that discharge raw sewage into the Thames when it rains heavily. With hundreds of thousands of tourists expected, one outcome of the Games will undoubtedly be massive increases in human waste. Government proposals in 2007 to build the tunnel are positive; however, it will not be functional until 2014, which means sewage on a massive scale may be discharged into the Thames during the period of the Games (*The Guardian* 2007n).

Olympic Benefits

Although still awaiting the 'proof in the pudding' of Blake's predicted £5.9 billion surplus for London (and £4 billion deficit elsewhere), some Olympic benefits have appeared. When the south coast towns of Weymouth and Portland were confirmed as the Olympic sailing venues, estate agents reported a surge of interest from investment buyers (*The Guardian* 2007k). And, certainly, those individuals charged with delivering the Olympics are well remunerated: Lord Coe takes home an annual salary of £285,000 from LOCOG on top of his earnings from The Complete Leisure Group Limited Plc (Channel 4 2007) and his Vice-Presidency of the International Association of Athletics Federations (IAAF) (*The Daily Telegraph* 2007g).

Some London-based companies have won lucrative Olympic-related contracts. Rockpools is tasked – at a total cost of £2.7 million – with 'head-hunting' the ODA's workforce (Channel 4 2007). Sou Duradiamond Healthcare has won the contract to deliver occupational health (including smoking cessation and diet services) to the 9,000 Olympic Park workers. Controversial – if inadvertent – beneficiaries of Olympic largesse are the ten Travellers' families relocated from the Olympic Park, who each received (in addition to new accommodation) £9,450 compensation from the LDA for moving to make way for Olympic venues (*East London Advertiser* 2007).

The Final Chapter

At the time of writing (mid 2010) some five years have passed since the bid book journey began. A number of pledges have either been altered from the original commitments or are questionable as to their outcome. These discrepancies have been discussed and reported within governmental and parliamentary circles and have also been continually splashed over tabloids and broadsheets.

Tasked with preparing for and delivering the 2012 Games respectively, the ODA and LOCOG have – regularly – been on the receiving end of a fair amount of scrutiny. The ODA in particular has been tainted from the start, with their original Chair, Jack Lemley, leaving after just six months, blaming political infighting between himself, Jowell and Livingstone (*The Guardian* 2007i). Others suggest he was pushed by Jowell following disagreements over delays at Olympic construction sites. LOCOG's battles seem to have been fewer and sparser; an attempt to withhold financial details being one of the most prominent to date. LOCOG claimed that, as a private company, they were not subject to the Freedom of Information Act; however, they backed down after individuals such as Paul Farrelly of the DCMS said that this was unacceptable (Channel 4 2007).

Although there are repeated articulations of unity both between ODA and LOCOG, and of the overall management of the Olympic project security funding is separated across Olympic agencies. At best, this allowed an extremely selective expression of the costs of securing the 2012 Games during London's candidacy stages. Such events reflect on both the temporal factors surrounding the importation of mega-event security and how public acceptability of its features is managed. Rather than advertising security measures to enhance their potential for reassurance, as applies for more routine forms of security, for 2012 a more complex negotiation surrounding the acceptability of security is at play. Here, public support is mediated via the initial presentation of partially visible costs in advance of the highly conspicuous 'spectacular security' (Boyle and Haggerty 2009b) that follows. Such incidences mark an additional point of exceptionality for the Olympic security programme.

The £1,044-billion regeneration budget, having been committed before the London 2012 proposals, saw pledges about the 'renewal' of London's East End. This could have been accomplished regardless of the 2012 Games, albeit the candidature file claims the process would have been less ambitious and more incremental. The Games are thus the catalyst to great change, drawing vast amounts of political will into the process, but the future is not known.

The social configuration of post-Olympic spaces connects with the broader legacy of the Games. The argument that many forms of redevelopment/regeneration reinforce existing social divisions (Sassen 2001) has been borne out by a number of large-scale developments in East London, most notably the Isle of Dogs Docklands development of the late 1980s–1990s (see Hall 2002). Whilst there has been a growing recognition of these issues in planning circles (and the former Mayor of London's policy of incorporating 'affordable housing' into new developments), this pattern is likely to reverberate through the post-Olympic community. As Poynter articulates, the tension between complex institutional and governmental relations surrounding the Games and their operation within extremely constrained contexts of time and place renders it impossible to fulfil the expectations of all stakeholders 'nor effectively integrate or embed these institutions in the local community' (2009: 139). For Poynter, this conflict therefore raises the likelihood that imperatives of commercial viability will outsprint weaker local and civic voices. This process can already be observed in the selling of parts of the Olympic site originally intended as parkland to balance inevitable construction cost overruns. This predictable favouring of private commerce within legacy developments is therefore extremely likely to reinforce and advance existing micro-community-level socio-economic segregation (Poynter 2009: 139).[25] In turn, the re-bordered neighbourhood is liable to bring a host of heightened security demands from the inhabitants of its newly gentrified and splintered enclaves, as has happened so often elsewhere (see *inter alia* Davis 1990, Sennet 1996, Ellin 1999, Bauman 2000, Brenner and Theodore 2002).

There are also less direct post-Games 'legacy' implications relating to East London's labour markets, in particular, the much-lauded employment opportunities on offer. Alongside the large-scale training of individuals to help build the 2012 site – who will subsequently compete for jobs in an uncertain (and currently depressed) post-event construction market – are attempts to cast thousands of individuals into private security roles. Currently, 7,000 private security agents are needed to secure the Games effectively, yet leaders of this industry estimate that, at current levels, only 1,000 individuals could be provided. This has stimulated hastily created partnerships with further education colleges to divert students towards acquiring the skills needed to service the ephemeral security needs of the Games. The post-event market of meaningful labour for those possessing such skills is less clear. As a result, already substantial gaps between socio-economic classes may increase and possibly force some residents to relocate. As such, issues surrounding 'citizenship' and 'community' (continually cited by the ODA as the main benefactors of the Games) and their engagement with these reconfigured post-Olympic spaces may be called into question.[26]

---

25   Ceding redevelopment projects to private governance is also a traditional ideological commitment of the Conservative Party who, regaining government (in coalition) during 2010, are inevitably enabling this process to become reinforced.

26   Just before going to print a number of relevant developments have occurred. The government's spending review has drastically reduced budgets of departments with ministerial authority over key Olympic functions (notably DCMS and the Home Office). Whilst the overall ODA budget has fared well, although, significantly, the wider policing costs for the Games are likely to be slashed from £600 million to £475 million. Just before going to print a number of relevant developments have occurred. The government's spending review has drastically reduced budgets of departments with ministerial authority over key Olympic functions (notably DCMS and the Home Office). Whilst the overall ODA budget has fared well, although, significantly, the wider policing costs for the Games are likely to be slashed from £600 million to £475 million.

PART II
Supplying 2012 Security

Chapter 5

Olympic Architectures of Safety and Security

Having outlined both the more enduring trajectories of urban transformations and the security strategies associated with the Olympics alongside the idiosyncrasies of East London's host geographies, Part II of this text offers a more detailed analysis of how these global and local forces collide. In securing the Games, new technologies and capabilities will be deployed alongside the aggrandizement of local security infrastructures. In doing so, points of harmony and dissonance are created between these globalized and localized forms of security. The following three chapters examine this dynamic in detail via an exegesis of three broad pillars of both Olympic and London-specific security strategies: secured built environments, policing and surveillance technologies. This chapter will first define the broader (national and international) contours of the 2012 security strategy and its constituent parts, before turning to the first of these three central themes of Olympic security, securing the physical environment.

London 2012: The Spoils of Victory

On 6 July 2005, London was awarded the 2012 Olympic Games by the IOC, having persuaded the voting panel that the city could organize the event efficiently and, crucially, safely (Coaffee and Johnston 2007). The candidature file submitted to the IOC in 2004 had argued that London was uniquely placed to offer a secure venue for the Olympics given its many decades of experience with coping with Irish Republican terrorism (London2012 2004: III 31). Although there has been much discussion of the '2012 legacy', this emphasis on security was considered by many to have been a key factor in winning the bid to host the Games (see *inter alia* West 2009).

Despite the idiosyncrasies of East London and its centuries-old evolution of law enforcement, the 2012 security strategy is to be located within the globalized Olympic liquid security paradigm outlined in Part I and further discussed in Chapter 9. Here, standardized and mobile security strategies are deployed that risk being disassociated from the geographies to which they are applied. Indeed, the saturation of London's security programme by these prevailing Olympic paradigms was recently highlighted by the Mayor of London, Boris Johnson, to a Culture, Media and Sport Committee (in January 2008) hearing: 'broadly speaking, there will be quite substantial security and protection around the main Olympic venues of the kind that you would expect, and you will be seeing more detail about that nearer the time, but it will be not unlike what they did in China' (Johnson 2008). Given the inevitability that some localized security vernaculars will penetrate these strategies (particularly given the importance of occupational cultures in delivering security: see *inter alia* Reiner 2000, Sutton and Wilson 2004, Fussey 2007a), the homogeneity of Olympic security arrangements will necessarily impact unevenly. In contrast to many other host cities including Athens, Sydney and Barcelona, one of the notable features of the London Games is their location in the heart of an existing urban milieu (see Chapter 3). Although the segregation of Olympic and non-Olympic venues was readily achieved at previous Games (with the possible exception of Albertville's sprawling terrain in 1992), this extant urban context provides additional security challenges. At the same time, frictions between internationalized Olympic security requirements and local-community-focused policing agendas are likely to intensify.

Whilst it would be easy to draw the conclusion that the standardized Olympic security model therefore represents an external imposition upon East London, there is a complicating factor. Olympic security strategies are not introduced into a vacuum. Instead, as this book has argued, arrangements tend to layer over existing national and international infrastructures (or at least those components that fit the standardized security framework). In the course of over a century of experiencing modern urban terrorism, London – and particularly its eastern, Olympic-focused territories – has a particular track record in creating urban enclaves that, whilst not physically 'gated', are symbolically and technologically demarcated from their surrounding environments (Coaffee 2009b, Fussey 2007b, Chapter 6). London, therefore, has a mature security infrastructure onto which the 2012 programme will be grafted. Indeed, as the then Olympics Minister, Tessa Jowell, very recently stated, 2012-related security measures are rooted in the UK having 'years of experience in both tackling terrorism and hosting major sporting and cultural events' (*The Observer* 2009). In contrast to previous Games where the Olympics were seen as a spur and justification for the introduction and permanent retrofitting of surveillance technologies, London, in securing the 2012 Games, is overtly building on its pre-existing expertise in crime prevention and counter-terrorism.

Priorities

> The OSS [Olympic Security Strategy] rightly assesses the most severe threat to the Games to be terrorism, and much of the strategy focuses on the management of this risk. (MPA 2009).

For London's Olympic planning processes, the execution of the 7 July bombings a mere 20 hours after the IOC's decision to award the XXX Olympiad to the capital powerfully and symbolically connected the fear of terrorist violence with the hosting of the Games. Reflected in the unprecedented expenditure accompanying the (re-launched) UK Government's counter-terrorist (CONTEST) strategy, and the dominance of this agenda in local security budgets, the threat of terrorism has become *the* prominent feature of 2012 security planning. Such prioritization has been publicly and unequivocally articulated in a range of forums. The consolidated Home Office *London 2012 Olympic and Paralympic Safety and Security Strategy*, for example, stated, 'the greatest threat to the security of the 2012 Olympic and Paralympic Games is international terrorism' (Home Office 2009b: 11). Key practitioners have also stressed this linkage, characterizing the Olympic security plan variously as a 'seamless alignment into CONTEST' (Lord West, Parliamentary Under-Secretary of State for Security and Counter-terrorism, 2009) and 'docked with CONTEST' (Robert Raine, Home Office Director of Olympic Safety and Security, 2009).

The conceptual privileging of counter-terrorism is also translated into the structural organization of 2012 security. For the Games, the disparate policing agencies, myriad security foci and governance strata are all filtered through an overarching 'Concept of Operations' (or CONOPS in the official nomenclature; see *inter alia* Quinten 2009).

The CONOPS model (illustrated in Figure 5.1) is organized in terms of five priorities that notionally link together a number of disparate security providers and infrastructures. Whilst the more important of these features are examined throughout this and the two succeeding chapters, what is of immediate interest is the way in which the framing of this strategy further reinforces the emphasis on counter-terrorism. Aside from the 'command and control' component (befitting the management of exceptional sporting mega-events), the remaining four strategic areas replicate the orientation of the UK CONTEST strategy around 'protect', 'prepare', 'pursue' and 'prevent' ('engage' in the Olympic strategy) (see Home Office 2009a). Such intentional structuring of the 2012 Olympic security strategy underscores the primacy afforded to mitigating terrorism and other forms of violent extremism. With the Olympic Park sited in an area that currently hosts the overwhelming majority of UK counter-terrorism-related investigations, and with a resurgence of both Irish Republicanism and right-wing extremism during 2009 and 2010, threats of a terrorist nature are likely to remain dominant concerns for 2012 Olympic security planners.[1]

Capturing and Cataloguing Risk and Threat

Signalling the bleed of corporate risk-management strategies into the public sector (see *inter alia* Beck 1992), analyses of threat across governmental levels normally centre on now-instituted 'risk matrices' or 'risk registers'. Using a very simple arithmetical formula, potential risks are charted on indices of likelihood, impact and vulnerability with attention placed on the highest-scoring threats (see Cabinet Office 2008). For the London Olympics, a similar approach is deployed, notably

---

1   This emphasis on terrorism has also been confirmed by senior members of LOCOG and the Metropolitan Police during the authors' ongoing fieldwork into 2012 security.

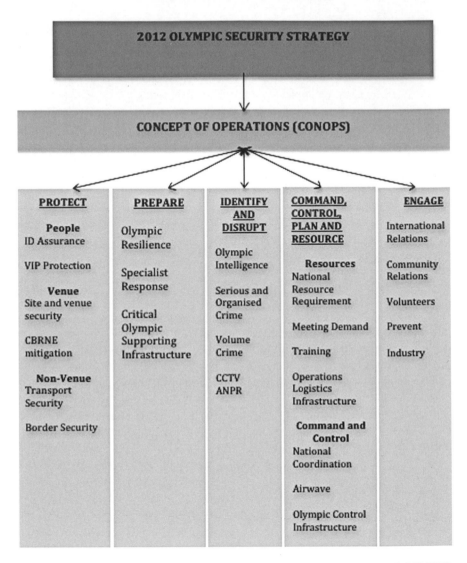

Figure 5.1   London 2012 Olympic Concept of Operations (CONOPS) adapted from Kelly (2009)

the *Olympic Safety and Security Strategic Risk Assessment* (OSSSRA) (see Table 5.1). In this exceptional context, however, there is one crucial difference. Instead of tackling the highest-ranking risks, *any* risk appearing on an OSSSRA matrix (currently around 30) is given attention (Kelly 2009). Risks are then further examined and acted upon via the Comparative Risk Assessment Methodology (CRAM) that applies more focused analyses to each specific venue in addition to identifying and mitigating further residual risks.

Table 5.1   OSSSRA Matrix used for 2012 security planning (simplified version)

⇑ IMPACT ⇑	Catastrophic					
	Significant					
	Moderate					
	Minor					
	Limited					
		Low	Low/med	Medium	Med/high	High
		⇒ LIKELIHOOD ⇒				

Note: Risks to the Games are plotted according to their perceived position on the x and y axes (unattributable source)

This emphasis on all risks is theoretically significant in a number of ways. First, it demonstrates the application of 'total security' paradigms. Accompanying the anthropoemic (exclusionary) physical 'lockdown' infrastructures of 'total security', highlighted in Chapter 2, is an abstracted and conceptual commitment endowed with a rationalized intellectual framework. Secondly, Beck's (1992) argument that innovations to identify risk perpetually generate new threats through their categorization, labelling and subsequent exposure to them is applicable here. These new conceptual and technological techniques of risk identification accompanying 2012 security planning will, in Beck's terms, therefore generate continued risks that will both stretch policing capacity and unremittingly render the resolution of all risks 'just out of reach'. This chapter now focuses attention on the first of the three broad pillars of the 2012 Olympic security strategy: generating security through the built environment.

Olympic Architectures of Safety and Security

Since the 1970s security planning has become an integral and required part of bidding documents and preparation for hosting sporting mega-events, most notably the Summer Olympic Games and Paralympic Games. Moreover, given the perceived threat of international terrorism, physical security planning to minimize the prospect and impact of terrorist attacks has become increasingly important to the design of stadium infrastructure and adjacent crowded places and now forms a key requisite for candidate cities to be awarded the right to host the Olympics. The IOC now makes explicit in guidance to host cities that it is *the city's* responsibility to provide a safe environment for the 'Olympic Family' (competitors, officials and dignitaries), while ensuring that such securitization does not get in the way of the sporting activities or 'spirit' of the Games. As Thompson (1999: 106) observed, 'the IOC has made clear that the Olympics are an international sporting event, not an international security event, and while Olympic security must be comprehensive it must also be unobtrusive.' This, however, often proves a difficult balance to achieve, especially around the main Olympic venues. Here security managers, concerned with the reputational damage that a successful terrorist strike could inflict upon the host city, will often adopt high visibility security operations in order to minimize the vulnerabilities that might be exploited by terrorists. Such operations as they are played out, especially in relation to major events, now have a tendency to construct a siege-like security infrastructure utilizing physical or symbolic notions of the boundary and territorial closure – what one commentator has referred to as 'siege chic' – in a attempt to deter attack (Duffy 2003). Although in recent years much has been written about how security infrastructure may be less visible (see for example Coaffee, O'Hare and Hawkesworth 2009), the tendency amongst security managers is to adopt overt security that can serve the function of assuring the general public (and in the case of the 2012 Games, the 'Olympic Family') that the perceived threat is being taken seriously. The deployment of mass security generates what we might term Olympic 'spaces of exception' (see Chapter 2) that have become standardized across time, place and culture and adopt features that are independent of the security traditions of their host cities (Coaffee and Fussey 2010).

In recent years the heightened need to respond to the threat of terrorism and associated post-9/11 sensibilities has led to the cost of security operations surrounding the Games, increasing dramatically. Since the 2004 Summer Games in Athens a large proportion of this increased cost can be attributed to extra security personal required, as well as the deployment of largely temporary security measures and detailed contingency planning (Coaffee and Johnston 2007). Against this backdrop of 'lockdown' security, militarization and draconian legal procedures often dominate urban spaces. In conceptual terms, this can be viewed as a perfectly rational reaction to perceived risk. Ulrich Beck in his classic work on *Risk* and *World Risk Societies* has outlined how what he terms a 'protectionist reflex' (discussed in Chapter 1) is more often than not adopted by nation states when levels of risk rise and where withdrawal into a safe haven of protected territoriality becomes an intense temptation (Beck, 1999: 153). Such approaches can also be characterized by what Heng (2006) refers to as 'active anticipation and "reflexive" risk management strategies' and are operationalized at a number of scales, leaving a well defined territorial security footprint (Coaffee and Murakami Wood 2006). As this chapter progresses, it will highlight how this 'footprint' is emerging across London and examine key strategies adopted, or planned, to enhance such security infrastructures in and around the 2012 Olympic sites. In doing so, a number of dilemmas facing organizers and security professionals are highlighted, alongside a consideration of the relative merits of such strategies and potential measures to augment their success.

Defending the Soft Target of Mega Sporting Events

In order to defend sporting mega-events from international terrorism, traditional approaches to crime prevention through design modification (most notably Secure by Design (SBD) or Crime Prevention Through Environmental Design (CPTED)) are commonly hybridizing with military security planning to provide protection against explosions at 'at risk' sites. Such attempts to reduce terrorist risk are by no means unprecedented in the UK. During the 1990s, the experience of UK authorities in attempting to 'design out' terrorism was largely confined to efforts to stop car bombing by the Provisional Irish Republican Army (PIRA) against the economic infrastructure in London (Coaffee 2003). Before the events of 9/11, threats of international terrorism in the UK context predominantly came from vehicle-borne improvised explosive devices (VBIEDs) targeting major financial or political centres. In response, attempts to counter terrorism often utilized planning regulations and advanced technology to create 'security zones' or 'rings of steel' where access was restricted and surveillance significantly enhanced (Coaffee 2004, Coaffee et al. 2008). 9/11 and subsequent no-warning attacks, often using person-borne improvised explosive devices (PBIEDs) aimed at causing mass casualties, made such counter-terrorist tactics appear inadequate. National security policy began to shift to proactive and pre-emptive solutions, often involving changes in the way in which design solutions could be permanently and unobtrusively embedded within the cityscape. The theoretical foundations of administrative criminology inform much of the thinking in this area. At its heart is the 'rational choice' approach: a tripartite model that attributes offending behaviour to the convergence of (at least): a motivated offender, an opportunity to commit the crime (or, in this case, terrorism) and the absence of a 'capable guardian' (such as surveillance cameras) (see *inter alia* Clarke and Cornish 1985). Over time, aspects of the theory have been developed to explain (actual and potential) offenders' decision-making processes by reference to notions of the rewards and costs of the offence (see *inter alia* Felson and Clarke 1998). In doing so, the second two components of this rational choice approach (opportunity reduction and capable guardianship) are accented in such planning approaches and subsequently translated into policy, whilst the first element, the 'motivated offender', has received notably less emphasis (beyond the belief that 'hardening' the built environment will reduce an individual's motivation to offend).[2]

Since 9/11, security fears around sporting mega-events have been increasingly magnified, with events such as the Olympics being perceived as 'soft targets' for terrorists, where high crowd densities and large accessible open spaces prevail and where successful terror attacks are guaranteed huge amount of media exposure (Coaffee 2009a).

---

2 Debate does exist, however, over the applicability of crime control strategies to terrorism (see *inter alia* Fussey 2010) and over whether interventions to tackle one particular type of terrorism, such as ethno-nationalism, applies equally to other forms, such as violent jihadi extremism (Coaffee 2003, Fussey 2007b).

Given the changing nature of the terrorist threat, 'securing' the Olympics is increasingly difficult and costly to achieve where increased emphasis is necessarily placed on defending the open and accessible crowded places that make up the sporting venues and their surrounds. Concern has also being expressed about management of the security threat, in particular security procedures for queuing at facilities where rigorous security checks are in force, which may themselves become targets since they are often outside secure areas and could be easily attacked. This latter point, in particular, represents a challenge at major sporting events such as the Olympics where queuing for admission to specific venues will be widespread. Likewise, given the stated aim to make 2012 the 'public transport Games', the security services will be having to cope with a vast array of 'targets' as crowds will inevitably occur at defined locations (venues and transport hubs) and predicable times (pre and post event).

Together, this blend of changing terror methods and targets, especially those directed at crowded places in urban areas and around sporting venues is providing challenges for security professionals and practitioners. Certainly, with London Olympic planning being predicated on an elevated 'severe' level of terrorist threat (West 2009), there is the possibility of seeing core notions of Olympic spectacle to some extent replaced by dystopian images of 'cities under siege', as organizers and security personnel attempt to deliver an Olympics in maximum safety and with minimum disruption to the schedule (Coaffee and Johnston 2007).

For most Olympic organizers, their preparations for the Games necessarily include attempts to equate spectacle with safety and to 'design-out' terrorism, often by relying on highly militarized tactics and expensive, detailed contingency planning (Coaffee 2009). As has been well documented, as a result of increased fears of international terrorism catalysed by the events of 9/11, the cost of security operations surrounding major sporting events, in particular Summer Olympic Games, has increased dramatically.

Hosting the Olympics imposes a burden of security on cities well beyond what they would otherwise face. As has been noted, security planning is now a key requirement of bids submitted to the IOC by prospective hosts and has become a crucial factor in planning the Games. There is now a broadly accepted security management model for the Olympics, which has evolved since the 1980s, developing a set of standardized and mobile security features (Coaffee and Fussey 2010). Such features include governance and organization elements, which seek to forge relationships between the numerous public safety agencies and the local Olympic organizing committee, the planned employment of police and security personnel and the deployment of counter-terrorism techniques of surveillance and design. The impact of such 'exceptional' security operations often serves to reinforce the splintering of the city (Graham and Marvin 2001) where the spaces utilized for sporting festivals have the potential to become dislocated from the wider geographical contexts of the host city.

Such exorbitant levels of security thus temporarily transform the host cityscape into a series of temporary exceptional spaces with displacement of the law by authority as special regulatory regimes are brought to bear so as to control behaviour and maintain order (Agamben 2005). As Browning (2000) observed during the period immediately before the 2000 Games, 'Sydney in September will be under siege.' Likewise, for the duration of the 2004 Games, Athens became a 'panoptic fortress' to give assurances to the rest of the world that the city was safe and secure to host the world greatest sporting spectacle (Samatas 2004: 115).

As highlighted in Chapter 2, Olympic-related threats faced by host cities are increasingly externally defined in terms of international terrorism and, in turn, have inspired strong continuities and commonalities across Olympic security operations over both time and place. As such, we argue that wider shifts towards a 'total security' model comprising continually reproduced security motifs can be observed for the Summer Olympics. As the chapter evolves, we argue that London's hosting of the 2012 Games, as well as following the standardized 'total security' model, brings distinctiveness to the continuing process of Olympic securitization. As discussed in Chapter 5, the pre-existence and maturing of a well defined and tested security infrastructure means that London was uniquely placed to offer assurances to the IOC over their safety and security concerns; this was deemed a particular strength of the city's bid to host the Games (London2012, 2004).

Securing Olympic spectacle and protecting against the dangers of terrorist violence remains the *overriding* concern for Olympic organizers. This has become increasingly stark in the UK as London gears up for hosting the 2012 Games. Particularly important here has been the fallout from the terrorist bomb attacks on London's transport network on July 7 2005 – the day after London was confirmed as host city. As is much emphasized, these attacks have led to a massive increase in perceived security needs and prompted organizers to draw up ever more detailed security plans. At the time of writing, this has led to the security bill escalating from an initial £224 million to over £600 million (plus a further £237 million 'contingency' fund), the planned adoption of advanced biometric security systems to monitor crowds, officials and athletes, special 'measures' to track suspects across the city (see Chapter 7) and, of particular importance to this chapter, a series of efforts to 'design-in' counter-terrorism features to the physical infrastructure of the Olympic venues and environs. This interest in how planners, architects, developers and urban designers, alongside security specialists, can design-out terrorism (or more correctly design-in counter-terrorism features) for Olympic facilities in London is a function not just of the supposed threats against 'crowded places' but also the longer term regeneration vision for the areas in the post-Games period, where issues of safety and security will be paramount within 'legacy' community facilities (Coaffee 2009a).

The Spatial Imprint of the 'Total Security' Model

The spatial imprints of attempts to develop Olympic regimes of 'total security' combine the tactics and techniques of policing, protective counter-terrorism design and technological surveillance and can be articulated as a series of operational characteristics. These are features that also characterize the securitization of many other mega events or conventions and are transferred onto the Olympics (Coaffee et al. 2008; Boyle and Haggerty 2009b). What we can gauge from a study of security planning and design utilized by host Olympic cities (and other major events such as football Word Cups) is a series of normalized event security features that combine temporary physical features and the officious management of spaces with the aim of projecting an air of safety and security not only to visitors but also potential investors (Coaffee et al. 2008).

First, there is intense pre-planning involving the development of control zones around the key venues, procedures to deal with evacuation, contamination and decontamination, and major incident access. Technical information is also scrutinized for all structures and ventures so that any weakness and vulnerabilities can be planned-out in advance. Second, there is the development of 'island security' involving 'locking down' strategic (vulnerable) areas of host cities with large expanses of steel fencing and concrete blocks surrounding the sporting venues (see, for example, Coaffee and Rogers 2008). Island security – now a popular term amongst 2012 security practitioners – combines with a strong police presence, backed up by private security, the Security Services and a vast array of permanent and temporary CCTV cameras and airport-style checkpoints to screen spectators. Often events such as the Olympics are used to field-test 'new' technologies. Third, to back up the intense 'island security', peripheral buffer zones are often set up in advance containing a significant police presence, often with highly visible law enforcement tactics such as police helicopters, a blanket 'no-fly zone', fleets of mobile CCTV vehicles, road checks and stop and search procedures. The result of these measures is that often access to 'public' spaces is restricted to public roads and public footpaths on the grounds of 'security concerns' (Coaffee, O'Hare and Hawkesworth 2008). This creates what security practitioners have long referred to as the 'onion skin effect' (Coaffee 2003) where multiple layers of security combine to reduce the likelihood of successful attack. Fourth, there is increased evidence from major sporting events that one lasting benefit of hosting events is the opportunity for the retrofitting of permanent security infrastructure linked to longer-tem crime reduction strategies and 'legacy' (Coaffee and Murakami Wood 2006). Furthermore, simply bidding to host Olympics is also, in many cases, considered a strong enough stimulus to develop robust and *de facto* permanent security planning procedures.[3]

These features are highlighted below in Table 5.2 and will be reintroduced in later sections of this chapter to articulate how the security preparations for London 2012 converge and diverge from this model in a variety of ways. The argument we are making here is that whilst London is following this standardized security model, it is starting its security preparation from a more mature starting point, having had decades of experience of dealing with the impact of international terrorism through the 'planning-in' of counter-measures (Coaffee 2003).

Table 5.2 Key features of the Standardized Olympic Security Model

Olympic security feature	Operational characteristics
The intense pre-planning for resilience	• To enhance the resilience of the venues and surrounds and the broader host city by technically scrutinizing and planning-out weaknesses and vulnerabilities well in advance of Games time
The development of 'island security'	• The temporary physical 'lockdown' of the key venues or 'at risk' areas through barrier methods of physical security, advanced surveillance and airport-style checkpoints to screen spectators • The real time monitoring of space, often involving the trialling of 'new' technologies
The setting up of peripheral buffer zones surrounding key venues	• Attempts to territorially control spaces using policing or private security • Access restrictions such as restricted public access, vehicle no-go areas and no-fly zones • Methods to monitor and track spectators
Post-event retention of security infrastructures	• Retain security systems for crime reduction legacy purposes

3   For example, as noted in Chapter 9, Cape Town's bid to host the 2004 Games stimulated a large-scale security programme in an effort to project an image that the city could host a safe Olympics. The bid failed but the surveillance and security systems were not removed. Indeed, they found a new justification in terms of the encouragement of foreign tourists, investors and conference delegates (Coaffee and Wood 2006).

London's Pre-existing Security Infrastructure

Commentators have highlighted how, for Olympic-type mega-events, security arrangements tend to layer over extant infrastructures (Jennings and Lodge 2009, Chapter 7), often assisting in their modernization. However, London, in comparison to prior Olympic cities, has a mature security infrastructure which, since the early 1990s, has sought to reduce the real and perceived threat from international terrorism through the adoption of physical, technological and managerial approaches to security at a variety of expanding spatial scales. Security mangers and policy makers in London have also developed a strong strategic capacity to plan counter-terrorism operations and develop a strong resilience to potential terrorist attack through pan-London emergency planning approaches (Coaffee et al., 2008). As outlined below, it is onto this security infrastructure and governance regimes that the 2012 safety and security programme will be grafted.

Perhaps the best-known and most enduring example of counter-terrorist exceptionality in London can be found in the City of London, though its 'ring of steel' which evolved first as a temporary structure following a series of large vehicle-borne explosions in the early-mid 1990s. This formed a delineated security zone that restricted access to the area via vehicle routing, parking and access controls. It was also monitored by CCTV cameras utilizing the latest Automatic Number Plate recording technology (ANPR) (see Chapter 7). The 'ring of steel' was subsequently expanded in geographical scope to cover larger sections of the City of London and made a permanent landscape features in the mid-late 1990s, rendering it the most intensely monitored space in the UK.

This development was underpinned by the need to reassure nervous investors considering the relocation of their businesses to other countries (Coaffee 2009b). Moreover, as the then Metropolitan Police Security coordinator for the 2012 Games highlighted, the City of London's 'ring of steel' was a perfect example of the territorialized security practice he would be trying to enact for the 2012 Games (Ghaffur 2007).

Similar principles were engaged and reproduced in the development an 'iron collar' security cordon for London's second finance zone in the London Docklands following a bomb attack in 1996. As before, this development acted as a staging post for specific concepts and technologies of control prior to their deployment across the wider area (see Chapter 7 for the example of ANPR). This affords the Metropolitan police vast surveillance-gathering capabilities for tracking the movement of traffic and people and, by inference, highlighting potential terrorist threats (Coaffee 2004; Fussey, 2007a).

Another major area of pre-existing counter-terrorist expertise that has been developed in London in recent years is the embedding of principles of resilience into the design and the strategic management of everyday urban spaces. For example, in 2002, in the wake of 9/11, the Metropolitan Police authorities established a London Resilience Forum (LRF) that subsequently developed strategic emergency plans detailing how the authorities in London, the emergency

Figure 5.2   Ring of Steel access

services, utility providers and business and civic communities will cope with, and control, catastrophic incidents (Coaffee and Murakami Wood 2006). In the context of 2012, the LRF has been commissioned to scope the extent of multi-agency and pan-London Olympic resilience preparedness (see also Chapter 1)

This need for managerial resilience corresponds with a further strand of UK, but London-focused, counter-terrorism work around the physical protection of 'crowded

Figure 5.3   Docklands cordon

spaces' from terrorist attack. In the wake of the July 2005 attacks on the London transport network, security experts have sought imaginative solutions to protect crowded locations from terrorist attack. In the UK such crowded places are now defined by the government as 'sites [that] are regarded as locations or environments to which members of the public have access that, on the basis of intelligence, credible threat or terrorist methodology, may be considered potentially liable to terrorist attack by virtue of their crowd density' (Audit Commission, 2010).

Such locations include the following sectors of direct relevance to 2012 security: hotels, sports and entertainment stadia, and major events. These crowded areas have features in common, most notably their easy accessibility, which cannot be altered without radically changing citizen experience. Plans for making the Olympic venues, and London as a whole, more resilient to any potential terror attack, are currently being refined, drawing on Secure by Designs (SBD) techniques that have been utilized for a number of prior London developments (Coaffee 2009b). Moreover, in the wake of the July 2005 attacks, the UK's National Counter Terrorism Security Office (NaCTSO) released a series of specialist guides providing advice on securing crowded places. Of particular note here is the emphasis given to stadium developers, owners and operators: *Counter Terrorism Protective Security Advice for Stadia and Arenas* (NaCTSO 2007), which has become an important resource for 2012 venue designers (see below).

The pre-existing security assemblage set out above to counter the threat of international terrorism provides the context into which the global leitmotifs of Olympic security standards must overlay. At the same time, the (current) £600 million 2012 security budget will generate further opportunities to intensify and embed these practices.

Laminating London's Splintered Spaces

> Despite such experiences, for London's security managers, the scale and form of the Olympic project constitutes an unprecedented peacetime undertaking, requiring the largest security operation ever conducted in the UK. (Metropolitan Police Authority 2007)

In response, these concerns have stimulated an observable series of spatial imprints of different sizes and geographical effects: protecting the Olympic venues and adjoining sites; central London surveillance; and pan-London resilience; all of which are developing what the 2012 security mangers have referred to as a 'onion skin' effect where different layers of security need to be penetrated in order for terrorist attacks to have noticeable impact. This 'onion skin' approach looks at beyond the specific protected site to incorporate the surrounding environment into its security design. Measures include the shaping of the approach to the site (to prevent VBIEDs), installing perimeters, overseeing construction processes, maintaining access controls, designing doors and windows to be both robust and prevent shattering glass and the use of electronic surveillance. Together, this conceptual approach to security stimulates a process whereby the secure design of particular sites brings an additional physical degree of securitization to the surrounding environment. These imprints, summarized in Table 5.3, will be unpacked in the subsequent discussion.

Venue and Site Security

The iconic site for each Summer Olympiad is its main stadium, which becomes an inherently political space – and hence terrorist target – for the duration of the Games. Its architecture is emblematic of the current state of modernity and reflects the political realities and aspirations of State leaders as perhaps best articulated by the Olympic stadiums in Berlin 1936, Montreal in 1976 and Beijing in 2008. Architecture and the built form more generally, have the capacity to transmit a range of dominant ideologies and emotions. The built form is part of how a particular society is materially inscribed in space; equally they possesses the power to condition new forms of subjectivity and everyday public experiences (Coaffee, O'Hare and Hawkesworth 2009). That is why the usual model of Olympic security planning focuses on restricting access and regulating space in and around key facilities and the main stadium.

Table 5.3   The spatial imprint of London 2012 security

Security feature	Spatial imprint for London 2012
Intense pre-planning for resilience	• The development of detailed pre-emptive security plans by an Olympic Security Directorate, in co-ordination with pre-existing resilience plans, to plan out vulnerabilities in advance
The development of 'island security'	• The sealing and securing of the key Olympic sites • Pre Games access restrictions and movement control of public and contractors • Checkpoint security at Games time • Biometric checks, deployment of sensor technologies to scan for explosives, dangerous chemicals and fissile material
The setting up of peripheral buffer zones surrounding key venues	• Large scale access restrictions and control zones • Use of legal measures to restrict public activities • The use of existing ANPR infrastructures • Ticket tracking • Deployment of police and other security personnel drawn from across the UK
Post-event retention of security infrastructure	• The designing-in of permanent security such as CCTV and SBD measures to counter-crime and improve local perceptions of safety

As a result, design has become a key component of security preparedness in and around the main Olympic site in Stratford, East London, where a host of new facilities are being constructed. (Similar principles are also being applied to other 2012 venues outside the Olympic Park.) Security practitioners, planners and urban designers have developed a guidebook for venue security, which utilizes SBD principles to secure the venues territorially, while attempting to ensure that London, and in particular the Olympic Park containing the main venues, is resilient to possible attack without becoming 'siege-like'. In this sense, counter-terrorist security must be comprehensive but also as unobtrusive as possible. As the then Head of 2012 Olympic security, Assistant Police Commissioner Tarique Ghaffur, noted in 2007, 'This is a celebration of what London is about and of the Olympics ... It's not about security or safety. Making the games as accessible as we can without security being obtrusive is the trick we have to pull off' (cited in *The Guardian* 2007e: 15). More recently, UK government ministers have further noted that innovative solutions to counter-terrorism can remove the need for highly visible mass policing by provision of volunteers and technological security (see Chapter 7).

In terms of the design and construction of venues and immediate environs, SBD approaches are being utilized for the Olympics as they have been for a number of recent London developments including Heathrow Terminal Five, the Millennium Dome, Wembley, the Emirates Stadium in North London and Lords Cricket Ground. This involves embedding, at the concept stage, features such as access control and integrated CCTV, the designing-in of 'stand off areas' for hostile vehicle mitigation, as well as the use of more resilient building materials. The aim here is to 'put in place security measures to remove or reduce vulnerabilities to as low as reasonably practicable ...' (NaCTSO 2007: 11).

Venue-specific security is strategically aligned with that of the Olympic Park in which the facilities sit – a large expansive area that is undergoing transformation in preparation for 2012 and which has already been territorially securitized. In July 2007, with little advance warning, the area was 'sealed' and nearby public footpaths and waterways closed to public access. An 11-mile blue perimeter fence

Figure 5.4   Hostile vehicle mitigation at the Emirates Stadium

Figure 5.5   Olympic site access

was put in place for 'health and safety' reasons. (Some, likened this cordon to the Belfast peace walls (*The Guardian* 2007m). In late 2009 this cordon was replaced in large part by electrified security fencing. Access to the site is closely monitored

Figure 5.6   Fencing at the Olympic Stadium

with biometric checks routinely carried out on the construction workforce as they enter the sealed site (*The Guardian* 2009c).

Such a security approach is quickly becoming standard practice in the UK, which has seen potential terror attacks against stadiums (and, moreover, their crowds) elevated to the top of the 'at risk' list. In 2007 the UK's National Counter Terrorism Security Office (NaCTSO), the police unit responsible for providing guidance on business continuity, designing-out vehicle-borne terrorism, the protection of crowded places and reducing opportunities for terrorism through environmental design, released a specialist guide for stadium developers, owners and operators, called *Counter Terrorism Protective Security Advice for Stadia and Arenas* (NaCTSO 2007). Released in the wake of the July 2005 attacks against the London transport network, this guide set out how stadium management and design might be modified, with security designed-in, to restrict the opportunities for terrorism as well as aid evacuation and swift recovery should an attack be successful.

In this context, security planning and design of the stadium is required to take into account the terrorist threat and devise appropriate exterior security and vehicle management for any new building or renovation work. This will allow 'counter-terrorism specifications, for example concerning glazing and physical barriers, to be factored in, taking into account any planning, safety and fire regulations' (NaCTSO 2007: 1). The aim here is to 'put in place security measures to remove or reduce

Figure 5.7   The Olympic security fence 'Sterile Zone'

vulnerabilities to as low as reasonably practicable bearing in mind the need to consider safety as a priority at all times' (NaCTSO 2007: 11). Importantly, in putting security measures in place, care must be taken not to compromise spectator safety. Of particular concern within the NaCTSO guide, and within Olympic preparation, has been the threat posed by VBIEDs or car bombs. As the guide noted:

> They are capable of delivering a large quantity of explosives to a target and can cause a great deal of damage. Once assembled, the bomb can be delivered at a time of the terrorist's choosing and with reasonable precision, depending on defences. It can be detonated from a safe distance using a timer or remote control, or can be detonated on the spot by a suicide bomber. Building a VBIED requires a significant investment of time, resources and expertise. Because of this, terrorists will seek to obtain the maximum impact for their investment. They generally choose high-profile targets where they can cause the most damage, inflict mass casualties or attract widespread publicity. (NaCTSO 2007: 37)

The (amended) guide goes on to state that stadium developers and managers can take a variety of steps to protect against VBIED:

- Ensure basic good housekeeping such as vehicle access controls and parking restrictions. Do not allow unchecked vehicles to park next to or under your stadium
- Consider using physical barriers to keep all but authorized vehicles at a safe distance. Seek the advice of your local police Counter Terrorism Security Adviser (CTSA) on what these should be and on further measures such as electronic surveillance including Automatic Number Plate Recognition (ANPR) and protection from flying glass
- Insist that vehicles permitted to approach your stadium are authorized in advance, searched, and accompanied throughout. The identity of the driver should be cleared in advance
- Do what you can to make your stadium blast resistant, paying particular attention to windows. Have the stadium reviewed by a qualified security engineer when seeking advice on protected spaces, communications, announcement systems and protected areas
- Establish and rehearse bomb threat and evacuation drills. Bear in mind that, depending on where the suspected VBIED is parked and the design of your building, it may be safer in windowless corridors or basements than outside
- Assembly areas must take account of the proximity to the potential threat. You should bear in mind that a vehicle bomb delivered into your building – for instance via underground car parks or through the front of your premises – could have a far greater destructive effect on the structure than an externally detonated device
- Train and exercise your staff in identifying suspect vehicles and in receiving and acting upon bomb warnings. Key information and telephone numbers should be prominently displayed and readily available.(NaCTSO 2007: 37)

What is also clear is that security in the area at Games time will be ratcheted up significantly with an undoubtedly imposing, visibly policed and technologically monitored security cordon encircling the site; while inside the cordon, in the Olympic Park, landscaped security and crime reduction features, infrastructure strengthening (for example bridges and other structures) and electronic devices that scan for explosives, will be embedded in order to 'push' threats away from the main Olympic site. Likewise, concealment points – areas where 'in place' explosives might be hidden – are currently being scrutinized and, where possible, removed (for example bird boxes or litter bins) or sealed (for example, drains).

These security design features are, wherever possible, to be unobtrusive. They are to be kept in place post-Games for legacy purposes in order to deter activities such as joyriding, ram raiding, drug dealing, prostitution and general anti-social behaviour. This means that features that are designed-in specifically for counter-terrorist purposes are, wherever possible, simultaneously invested with crime prevention capabilities for the post-Games period when the park will be fully open to the public. Such initiatives raise important questions over the proportionality and legitimacy of such approaches.

Buffering Venue Security Across London

Stimulated by fears of a terrorist attack that is spatially displaced to an alternative location, security measures are also bleeding through the borders of the 'Island Site' (the Olympic Park) to enable new forms of physical and technological security to permeate across London. Such technological fixes (see Chapter 7) are seen as a soft-touch approach that complements and intensifies the highly visible police presence. An extra 9,000 officers are expected to be on duty in London at peak times, although concern has also been expressed about leaving other parts of the UK vulnerable to attack if police officers are drafted in from other forces.

As Tarique Ghaffur, the then Head of Olympic security, noted in 2007, Olympic security is a pan-London operation:

> The whole rhythm of life in London will change as a result of these events and for 60 days we will have to take charge of that and make it safe in a way that people can enjoy themselves ... 9000 officers at the peak is a heck of an ask. (cited in *The Guardian* 2007e: 15)

In addition to the combination of technological and policing solutions, pre-emptive response planning is also ongoing. In the build-up to the Games, different scenario 'table-top tests' are being increasingly played out for dealing with major incidents, including terrorism, to allow logistics such as the placement of cordons and evacuation routes to be planned in advance. At the same time, securitized traffic-free 'buffer zones' will be located around the main Games infrastructural developments in Stratford.

In sum, the confluence of recent security trends in the capital alongside the particular aims of 2012 Olympic security programme creates a climate that elevates the importance of unobtrusive design and technological strategies. This will apply for the sporting venues as well as other key locations, such as transport hubs and tourist areas. Indeed, as Chapter 7 details, the ODA's (2007) call for 'discrete and proportionate' private security apparatus fits well with the IOC's long-stated aim of presenting the Games as an athletic event and not an exercise in security. What is significant in the context of Olympic security is that 'discretion' and 'proportionality' have often translated into distanciated forms of control and splintered urban spaces.

Legacies of Physical Security

At present the security planning for the 2012 Olympics is ongoing and beginning to focus its efforts upon policing, design and technological challenges, as part of a broader safety and security programme. In particular, this approach will focus upon the need to 'protect the London 2012 Games Venues, events, transport infrastructure, athletes, spectators, officials and other staff and ensure their safe enjoyment of the Games' (HM Government 2009: 13). This is in line with the wider post-Games objective as outlined in the *London 2012 Olympic and Paralympic Safety and Security Strategy*, which highlighted that 'to host an inspirational, safe and inclusive Olympic and Paralympic Games and leave a sustainable legacy for London and the UK' (Home Office, 2009b). Moreover within this strategy:

> safety encompasses the building of the Olympic venues and the placement of the overlay, for example, safety barriers, and the management of crowds within Olympic venues including those relevant aspects of the transport infrastructure … Security encompasses the measures taken to mitigate the identified threats during the build, test, overlay and operational phases and the protection of persons using the venues in Games time, or queuing to enter them, and of the Games themselves. (Home Office, 2009b: 8)

In East London, post-event legacy and the longer-term strategic regeneration of East London has also been a strong consideration when seeking to design-in security to the Olympic venues 'in order to minimize crime and security risks' (Home Office 2009a. As the Chief Inspector of Metropolitan Police noted in 2006:

> we want the security legacy to be us leaving a safe and secure environment for the communities of East London after the Games, on issues such as safer neighbourhoods, lighting and crime prevention. We want a Games legacy that will reduce crime and the fear of crime. (cited in Boyle and Haggerty 2009b: 267)

These measures are both physical and conceptual. In addition to the large-scale deployment of surveillance cameras, physical measures include an overall hardening of the built environment. For 2012, all Olympic structures and the 'white space' between them have been embedded with minimum ACPO standards of SBD. At the same time, these innovations will inform a new code of good practice for similar design projects in the future, thus providing a conceptual security legacy. This, it is hoped, will ensure that a safe and sustainable legacy is delivered to local communities (or incoming communities of the future) who will see benefits such as increased resilience to crime and to anti-social behaviour in the parkland areas as well as increased physical robustness being designed into sporting facilities for use by local people.

Here we should also note that the social configuration of post-Olympic regeneration spaces, and their attendant demands for safety and security, is also important. While there has been a growing recognition of these issues in planning circles, this pattern is likely to reverberate through the post-Olympic community, particularly in relation to issues of potential gentrification – a phenomena which, in the dangerously imagined spaces of East London, will require assurances to be given to 'incomers' that sufficient security is present. This inevitable aggrandizement of private commerce in legacy developments is therefore extremely likely to reinforce and advance existing micro-community level socio-economic segregation (Poynter 2009) with the re-bordered neighbourhood likely to bring a host of new security demands from the new inhabitants of its gentrified and splintered enclaves (see also Chapter 1).

Towards a Permanent Imprint of 2012 Olympic Security

In conclusion, for sporting mega-events the threat from international terrorism is spatially imprinted in 'total security' assemblages that are simultaneously standardized, transferable and mobile, and thus risk being dissociated from their host environments. Such security escalation is perhaps reaching a peak in London as it prepares for the 2012 Summer Games – a process that appears to be altering the standardized Olympic security model in a number of key ways.

First, as we have argued, London is uniquely prepared to counter the threat of terrorism given decades of experience of developing physical, managerial and technological systems to defend particular spaces from attack. As such, measures used to 'protect' Games are being laminated over existing security infrastructures, creating what it is hoped will be unprecedented levels of safety not only within the Olympic venues but across London.

Second, London is pioneering the systematic permanence of many Games-time security features rather than deploying a host of temporary security solutions that have literally swamped prior host cities and in particular the key venues. Permanent design and architectural features intended to counter such threats have emerged during the ongoing redevelopment of sites and venues for the 2012 Games in London as a key priority. This interest in how built environment professionals, alongside security specialists, can design-in counter-terrorism features to Olympic facilities is a function not just of the supposed threats against 'crowded places' but also the longer-term regeneration vision for the area. Such intended permanence of security infrastructure is also being transferred to other Olympic cities, indicating a degree of policy learning and transfer. Most notably, Rio de Janeiro's successful candidacy to host the 2016 Olympic Games drew on a similar plan to that being developed in London:

> A comprehensive security *overlay* will be implemented to ensure the integrity of all Games facilities and prevent unauthorized access. This will include perimeter security, integrated access control and alarm management, coupled with technical surveillance ... The security overlay will be based on Crime Prevention through Environmental Design (CPTED) principles, to be incorporated into the design of all venues. (Rio 2016 2007: 27, emphasis added)

Third, the element of permanent security being initiated in London for the 2012 Games relates directly to another innovative element of securitization, namely the association between security and a community-centred regeneration 'legacy'. This is especially important given the inner city location of the main sites that, the organizers hope, will be transformed physically, socially and economically through the Games. At the same time the flow of affluent migrants to the wider redeveloped area will also exacerbate the demand to retain Olympic security infrastructures in a post-Games capacity. It is also been likely that, post-Games, the whole Olympic Park will be granted SBD status ensuring that a safe and sustainable legacy is delivered to local communities. This legacy extends to the security trained on the inhabitants of the post-Games site. Yet questions over proportionality and control 'creep' mean that the 'benefits' of Olympic legacies are drawn into question.

Come 2012, the Olympic security operation put in place to protect the 'Olympic Family' during the Games will aim for 'customer-sensitive' security to prevail, that is, the highest possible levels of security without having to 'lock down' the entire city, as has happened with other Olympiads (Coaffee 2009b). This approach will be intricately blended with longer-term 'community safety' legacy strategies that are likely to have significant impact upon life in East London across future generations.

Chapter 6

Policing the Olympic Dream

This chapter concentrates on the second major pillar of 2012 Olympic security: the colossal policing effort surrounding the Games. In doing so, the chapter will first examine the broader policing apparatus surrounding the Games before concentrating on how the event impacts on the local context of Newham, the borough where the main Olympic sites are located.

Prefaced by an Olympic Torch run throughout the UK, the 2012 Games will take place over 64 days and cover 11 different police constabulary areas. During this time, 15,000 athletes, 13,000 coaches (together bringing one million pieces of sporting equipment), 20,000 members of the media, 70,000 volunteers and the holders of nine million tickets are due to attend events taking place across 34 venues (see *inter alia* Johnston 2009). At their peak, the Olympic Park venue will house 180,000 people. In addition to providing security for all of the above, the UK state will have to consider protecting the training bases of the 200 plus national Olympic squads and their movements in and out of the Olympic venues. For the disaffected and the politically motivated, as well as the commercially driven, the Games present an ideal opportunity to make a globally-mediated statement. The adoption of the above risk management approaches (Chapter 5) in tandem with their spread across this unwieldy latticework of vulnerabilities stimulates considerable additional demands on the provision of security.

At the same time, conflicting discourses on the existing state of preparedness contest this need for new, intensified forms of security, a tension that can be characterized as the 'business as usual' vs 'Olympic additionality' debate. Regarding the former, numerous Whitehall agencies have been at pains to suggest that the Olympics will not substantially alter current policing and security practices. Bruce Mann, director of the Cabinet Office's Civil Contingencies Secretariat, for example, recently opined that 85 per cent of the UK's resilience infrastructure was already in place for the 2012 Games (Mann 2009). London's mass transit systems continually run at a high capacity: London Underground carries three million passengers every day and 110,000 people flow through Waterloo railway station during average weekday peak hours (Graham 2009). Furthermore, 11 million passengers travel through London's four major airports each month, one of which – Heathrow – serves as one of the world's busiest transport hubs.

London also has considerable experience in hosting (and policing) major events attracting large crowds of people. Every August, close to a million people attend the world's second-largest street carnival in Notting Hill, West London. Over 5000 'major' events have taken place in London since the IOC's award of the Games to London (Broadhurst 2009). These are of both exceptional and routine varieties. Of the former, perhaps the most notable occurred in 2007 when London staged the *Grand Depart* of the Tour de France (on the anniversary of the 7/7 attacks and a week after the failed violent jihadi extremist terrorist attacks at London's Tiger Tiger nightclub and Glasgow airport) drawing an estimated 2 million spectators over three days (Visit London 2007). On a more routine basis, nationally over 13 million people attend England's Premier League football matches each year (see *inter alia* ESPN 2009). Together such events demonstrate substantial capacity and experience in securing major sporting (and other) events.

Nevertheless, whilst a number of the practices and processes are indeed relevant to 2012 planning, significant distinct changes and additions to the scale, form, configuration and governance of London's security infrastructures are observable in the preparation for the Games. Focusing specifically on policing issues, this chapter will first address the form and implications of these changes by first briefly outlining some of the broader organizational shifts before significantly considering the local agencies that will arguably bear the greatest burden of Olympic security.

Policing the Games

Connecting the many components of the 2012 security ensemble is the extended 'policing family'. For London, the Games will necessitate a policing operation of unprecedented form and scale, particularly within the capital's four eastern Olympic boroughs, whose realization will engender considerable difficulties and dilemmas for those charged with its oversight. In addition to coping with an estimated 9 million additional visitors comprising *inter alia* visiting dignitaries, tourists and opportunist criminals, such pressures are exacerbated by co-ordinating the temporary coalitions of (sometimes unacquainted) security agencies. Following the now-instituted example set by the use of a dedicated Olympic police force at the 1994 Winter Games in Lillehammer, Norway,[1] the OSD has been created to address threats related to 2012 and provide overall co-ordination of the Olympic security assemblage.[2] Mirroring the pluralization of crime control governance in the UK (see *inter alia* Fussey 2004, Hughes 2007) the OSD comprises over 30 different agencies, with a high degree of central government control retained by

---

1   Whilst the inauguration of a dedicated Olympic police force at Lillehammer was viewed at the time as an organizational milestone, in practice its applications at subsequent Games have been riven with tensions (see Chapter 7).

2   However, important differences inevitably exist between policing the Lillehammer and London Games. In Norway, 'the police chief and his staff comprised "the central police force for The XVII Olympic Winter Games in Lillehammer"' (LOOC 1994: 52) whereas, since 2008, the governance of the OSD has shifted towards central government.

Home Office leadership.[3] As discussed below, the establishment of this new (for London) and wide-ranging ensemble of actors presents numerous operational issues and challenges that impact upon the local policing of the Games. These include the integration of newly 'responsibilized' agencies (from public, private and voluntary sectors), issues of overload (including the overburdening of existing infrastructures to tackle crime and disorder in Newham) and the application of routinized practices to exceptional events.

Private Policing

For many years the flood of Olympic commercialization has also immersed its security infrastructure as planners have had recourse to private security to meet the exceptional policing demands of the Games. For 2012, practitioners are currently calculating that around 7,000 private security guards will be required for the duration of the Olympic and Paralympic Games to undertake diverse roles such as CCTV monitoring, stewarding, access controls and 'mag and bag' searches (magnetic detector searches of visitors' baggage).[4] However, this figure is likely to multiply when requirements for private security support in the areas of transport, related non-Olympic events and supporting public contingency services are accounted for. When augmented by the integration of the Metropolitan Police's Met Volunteer Programme[5] into the OSD, this will lead to substantial additions to the burgeoning 'policing family' associated with the Olympics.

Such developments generate a range of socio-ethical issues. Amongst these is the theme of *legitimacy*. For example, one of the most valuable areas of agreement across much policy, practice and research is that policing agencies require legitimizing via the consent of the policed (*inter alia* Reiner 2007). A connected issue concerns the way in which these standardized components of mega-event security (such as private and voluntary security) intersect with the particular contexts surrounding policing and legitimacy played out in London over the past 30 years (see below). Another point of debate concerns the tendency for Olympic cities to experience post-event retention of policing agencies and strategies that the public might not have consented to in less exceptional circumstances, such as the legacy of permanent private policing following the Tokyo 1964 and Seoul 1988 Olympiads (Lee 2004).

---

3   There are also other subtle shifts in the governance of 2012 security. For example, in England and Wales, the overall responsibility for policing football matches rests with ACPO. According to one senior practitioner, for 2012, this will shift to the British Transport Police (Graham 2009).

4   Data from interview with one of the directors of 2012 private security operation, 2008.

5   The Met Volunteer Programme is a police-run initiative to augment the Olympic policing operation with security-trained volunteers. The intention is to recruit 12,000 individuals to this programme (interview with Olympic security planner, 2008).

Focus

Beyond debates over the composition of Olympic policing are potential concerns over its focus. Previous Olympiads have almost unfailingly deployed 'zero-tolerance' models of policing (see Chapters 2 and 9). Indeed, redefining citizenship through exclusion has been a consistent theme of these security operations, most notably in Moscow and Sydney where, in the latter case, traditional policing roles were supplemented with controversial (for Australia) municipal bylaws to regulate behaviour and assembly that were retained after the Games (Lenskyj 2002). Moreover, as volumes of literature on policing attest, tensions between maintaining public order and tackling crime are finely balanced (see *inter alia* Crowther 2000). Substantial Olympic-related pressure for the police to clamp down on minor indiscretions around the time of the Games could reverse the shift away from crime control and the move towards 'order maintenance' that followed the rioting at Brixton (1981) and Broadwater Farm, Tottenham (1985). In London, as elsewhere, the legitimacy of policing institutions has long been recognized as an important issue and one that has involved a number of hard lessons (see *inter alia* Scarman 1981, Macpherson 1999). At the same time, more outward-focused Olympic policing has generated additional problems at the local level. As the experience of the Salt Lake City Games relates, the dedication of Utah's police left the local community more exposed to routine criminality (Decker et al. 2007). Locating the 2012 Games in the heart of an existing urban milieu that is densely populated and harbours a thriving market in illegal goods and services will necessarily stretch local policing capabilities (see below). Overall, then, risks of victimization may be faced not only by visitors but also the host communities who are, as so often stated, the intended beneficiaries of the Games.

There are other points of dissonance between local agendas and standardized Olympic security strategies. One notable example is the elevation of perimeter security amongst the list of priorities for securing the Olympics (see Chapter 5). Indeed, 'perimeter is the most important aspect of security', as LOCOG's Director of Security and Resilience recently declared (Johnston 2009). This, one can assume, is a product of the IOC's insistence that additional perimeters are installed around Olympic venues.[6] Not only do these strategies elevate issues of access and entitlement, for practitioners they contrast with the current forms of policing of London's sporting events and necessitate new policing styles entailing the imposition of boundaries, access points, surveillance and control.

---

6   A notable example of this artificial cleaving of space around Olympic venues can be taken from Beijing's iconic 'Bird's Nest' stadium and its imposition of concentric rings of security that cleaved the area into geographies of access and entitlement (see Chapter 2). According to Yu, Klauser and Chan (2009), spectators allowed access into the Olympic Green were kept away from the main stadium via an additional perimeter that could only be traversed by holders of particular tickets, thus creating an insulated and compounded securitized space.

Local Policing

At a local level, in hosting 2012, London will have to adopt a city-wide siege mentality to – we would argue – a degree not yet fully explored or appreciated. Such a mentality has to consider a variety of attack trajectories and political disruptions from a range of socio-political causes whilst simultaneously seeking to accommodate the demands of the IOC that Olympic security be comprehensive yet not overwhelming. The policing traditions of a liberal democracy may well be replaced on occasion by those more akin to dictatorship. The remainder of this chapter now turns to explore how this large-scale project impacts upon the aims, capacity and preparedness of local policing arrangements.

On Your Marks: Initial Planning and Preparedness

The 2012 'bid book' recognized that, with hundreds of thousands of tourists flowing into the capital for the Olympics, there would be a pressing need for stringent security measures. Some words were remarkably pertinent, notably 'though there has been no international terrorist attack in the UK since 1994, the UK remains highly vigilant and devotes extensive resources to intelligence gathering and assessment' (CF2012 2004: III 31).

Key security agencies led by a LOCOG Security Directorate would 'co-ordinate their efforts to ensure a safe and secure Games' (CF2012 2004: III 35), the highest priority of security being members of the 'Olympic Family' and special guests. Some 24 hours after the 2012 Games had been awarded to London the four-pronged suicide bomb attack on the capital's transport system killed 52 innocent commuters and injured a further 700. The feel-good factor generated in the capital because of the winning bid was shattered.

Two weeks later further attempts to bomb London transport failed and the subsequent ever-present threat, enhanced by the UK's involvement in the Iraq and Afghan wars has resulted in an increased awareness around the threats to life and property in the metropolis. This has resulted in an increase in the state's security obligations and the normalization of overt everyday securitization, particularly in London. Given this new environment, security around the 2012 Games has been given an unsurprisingly high profile by the UK government.

The policing strategy, as evidenced in the 2012 Candidature File was rudimentary and based on *realpolitik*. A need for 14,800 police officers was identified along with the ability to call on resources from the UK's other 140,000 police. The athletic contingents were expected to arrive weeks before the opening ceremony, with some remaining up to a week after. Some groups of athletes and officials were expected to prefer to find their own training camp within the M25 that encircles London. Even those who chose to reside in the Olympic Village would still have to make their way to and from airports which would require a 40-mile journey from Stansted, a journey that crosses policing boundaries. One could argue that the policing and security implications for 2012 were not thoroughly scrutinized when the bid was being constructed. As one of the police officer (now retired) who co-authored the police input to the bid informed us, 'No-one thought the London bid had a hope in hell … it [the policing strategy] was written quickly on the equivalent of a cigarette packet'. The awarding of the Games to London over Paris by a margin of four votes surprised more than the police and, in the light of the 7/7 attacks, the original £190 million security budget was amended to a projected £600 million (an ever fluctuating) figure. Denis Oswald, Head of the IOC Co-ordination Commission for London 2012, admitted in 2007 that the budget could be without limits: 'it is impossible for host cities and governments to accurately predict how much they will have to spend on security and policing so far from the start' (*The Daily Telegraph*, 2007c).

Costs and 'Rocks'

What can be predicted is that the scale of 2012 will require deployment of police personnel not seen since the 1984-85 Miners' Strike. Some 5,000 special constables[7] and an unspecified number of foreign firearms officers may need to be recruited specifically for the event (*The Guardian* 2007f). Concerns about a variety of issues have emanated from the MPA,[8] who raised the possibility of foreign firearms officers being needed due to perceived shortfalls in qualified UK-based officers. However, the MPA added that such personnel must 'remain accountable under British law if a shooting incident occurred' (*The Guardian* 2007f). Sovereignty may well be an issue when some Olympic squads decide to bring their own security personnel; diplomatic relations may well be tested around the issue of carrying fire-arms.

In the years, months and then weeks leading up to the opening ceremony, and indeed during the event, the police and politicians have to produce a scenario that accords with the status of 'operational readiness'. The police will have to consider and negotiate:

- What partnerships are to be built, developed and demarcated?
- What policing and security strategies are 'appropriate' and how can they be 'sold' to both legislators and citizens?
- What constitutes a sense of proportionality? What level of contingency plans is required?
- What level of activity constitutes 'operational readiness'? And for how long is this state of affairs to be in place prior to the event?

---

7   A special (police) constable (SC or SPC) is a law enforcement officer who is not a regular member of a police force but a member of a volunteer police auxiliary.

8   The MPA exists to make sure that London's police are accountable for the services they provide to people in the capital. The MPA has 23 members who scrutinize and support the work of the MPS.

While partnership is always stressed in the rhetoric surrounding the staging of the 2012 Games, irritation sometimes shows. Speaking in 2007 at the ACPO Conference, Deputy Assistant Commissioner (DAC) of the Metropolitan Police Service (MPS) Richard Bryan opined that the ODA's decision-making processes and operations were slow, convoluted and not fit for purpose (BBC, 2007).

In *The Guardian* on 17 March 2007, DAC Bryan gave his first interview since taking up the post of the Head of the Olympic Security Directorate the previous week (*The Guardian*, 2007e). He stated that the Olympics would place 'unprecedented demands' on the Met and he sought less of an obsession on the debate around costs and more focus on the benefits the event would bring. But the costs were an issue: the original bid had included £190 million for Olympic security. However, the 7/7 tube bombings meant that a revised budget of £600 million was now the figure talked about (see Chapter 4). At the same time, both the government and senior police officers were agreed that costs for security were impossible to pin down and could rise much higher. For Bryan, the 60 days of the Olympics and Paralympics were not to be seen in isolation. In the same month in London there would be Notting Hill Carnival, the celebrations of the Queen's Jubilee and a plethora of other ceremonial events. In Bryan's estimation, 9,000 (of the Metropolitan Police's 30,000 officers in London) would be required at the peak of the 2012 Olympics, making it the biggest ever policing challenge faced by Britain. The crime threat ranged from public safety and public order demonstrations to petty crime and pickpocketing. Flash mob crowds were expected due to mobile phone technology (*The Guardian* 2007e).

Bryan was to become a much quoted public figure. The launch day of the 'Common Purpose' Volunteer Training Programme hosted in February 2008 at Arsenal FC's Emirates Stadium saw ten individuals from all walks of (London) life permitted two minutes each to present their 'thought pieces' on 2012. The net result was the proliferation of the words 'vision', 'legacy', 'participation' and 'youth/young people'.[9] In his 'thought piece', Bryan voiced his concern that the Olympics risked being 'corporate', 'elitist' and 'monotone in look' and engaged in only by people from the same community. Seeking a 'City that rocks', the challenge for Bryan was making 2012 an event that would make local youngsters want to be part of.

East End Welcomes?

Until the Olympic bid, Newham was the East End's dirty secret (see Chapter 3). It lacked an iconic ghetto identity such as that of Spitalfields and gentrification was largely limited to the installation of central heating and indoor toilets. The café

---

9   Those present included representatives from the MOD, Fire Brigade, police, GLA, Arup Partnership, Marks and Spencer, accounting firms, IT companies, management consultants, Age Concern, armed services veterans, charities, civil servants, public utilities, sports organizations, youth groups, arts and media institutions, hospital trusts and schools.

society of Shoreditch, Spitalfields and Hoxton finds no competition in Newham yet in the three months immediately after the 6 July announcement that London had won their Olympic bid, property prices in Newham rose by 10 per cent (*EasierProperty*, 2007). To put this in context, however, the international courier company DHL, who were one of the first companies to set up in Baghdad after the fall of Saddam and who deliver in Afghanistan, decided that it was unsafe to make deliveries to the Newham districts of Canning Town and Custom House (Hobbs 2006). Buffered from the wealth of the City by Canary Wharf, where property prices have tripled in a decade, Newham was quietly not coping with de-industrialization when the bizarre notion of turning its most toxic sites into a Disneyesque global fantasy was contrived by the Olympic bid (See Chapter 3). But while the main aim is to bring thousands into the area in communion around sport, some celebrations in the vicinity were not wanted.

In 2008, an Islamic sect proposed to build Europe's largest mosque, amid Western Europe's largest Muslim population, very close to West Ham tube station on a brownfield site which once housed a chemical factory and was close to the Olympic Park. The mosque was planned to open in 2012. Tablighi Jamaat was the group supporting the proposal and, as a show of purpose, had previously set up a makeshift mosque on the site. Eschewing a strict interpretation of Islam, the sect with 80 million followers worldwide, unveiled its plan in 2007 and, in response, a 277,000-strong petition opposing the new mosque was presented to the UK government. The petition was largely discredited when links were uncovered between the petition's organizers and the BNP, prompting London's then Mayor Ken Livingstone to condemn the petition for stirring up vitriol:

> It is quite clear that this piece of vicious BNP propaganda, based as usual on entirely fabricated information, is solely designed to damage good community relations. It is wrong that such invented and falsified petitions provide a platform for those who would like to use them to create tensions among Londoners. (*The London Evening Standard* 2007)

The Metropolitan Police opposed the construction of the mosque on grounds of safety, arguing that emergency access in the event of a major incident would be extremely problematic. In January 2010 Newham Council were considering moves to compulsorily purchase the 18-acre site, claiming that planning permission for the land had expired. A spokesman for the Muslim Council of Britain said, 'We would hope that they will be able to work in co-operation with the local council if they wish to set up a mosque in the area. Tablighi Jamaat has no ties to terrorism. They have been subjected to some unfair coverage' (BBC 2010a).

One subtext of opposition to the mosque may be located in a 2006 police raid on a house in Forest Gate, which resulted in the arrest of three men of Pakistani origin on allegations of plotting to bomb London. In the course of the arrest, one suspect was accidentally shot by armed police. The police search did not reveal any explosives, no serious charges were proffered and the suspects were vehement that their treatment was evidence of indiscriminate police raids encouraged by a growing Islamophobia. This event remains contentious; for many in the East End, 'Forest Gate' has become a metaphor for uneven policing.

Policing the Olympic Neighbourhood

The East London district of Newham is the kernel of 2012; the local police are at the epicentre of a policing task whose scale and complexity have never before been witnessed in the UK. The effect the Games would have on the police district of Newham was a subject considered in 2008 by then Divisional Commander, Chief Superintendent Nick Bracken. He contended in interviews with us that policing in Newham needed to consider five stages in relation to the Olympics:

- *Actual:* occurring between 2006/07 until 1 April 2007 when the Olympic Command Unit was established and building work proper began on the Olympic Village
- *Emergent:* April 2007–June 2011 – the four years of infrastructure building, referred to as the 'Klondike' years, which would see up to 20,000, mainly male, construction workers in Newham building Olympic venues
- *Imminent:* June 2011–June 2012 – the 'starting gun' period, which would witness an intensified policing operation
- *Event*: The 'Rostrum Weeks', i.e. the 17 days that encompass the actual Olympic Games, including the opening and closing ceremonies and the 20 days of the succeeding Paralympics
- *Legacy:* the year from July 2012 to July 2013.

The following discussion applies this typology to capture the range of disparate and idiosyncratic issues affecting the policing of Newham in the actual, emergent and imminent phases during the run-up to the Games.

'Actual' Policing Issues

When the 2012 bid was awarded to London, the host borough of Newham had four police stations – Stratford, East Ham, Plaistow and Forest Gate – and total police personnel numbered 760, with 300 'admin' support. Newham was, in the eyes of the senior management team of the Metropolitan Police, a 'failing' policing borough. Crime reduction levels were a worry and the specific crimes of residential burglary, robbery from persons and vehicle crime were in the bottom quartile of Metropolitan Police Key Performance Indicators. Robbery levels made Newham the fifth highest out of the 32 Metropolitan police districts. In the first two weeks of February 2008 the borough suffered 135 robberies (up on the average of 80 in the previous year) thereby awarding Newham the dubious accolade of having the highest levels of recorded robbery of any police district in Europe.[10]

Also of concern was the incidence of wounding, assault and criminal damage. One crime level rather peculiar to the district was theft of vehicle registration plates (5,000 in 2006): Newham was the highest in the country. Stolen vehicle plates were used for the 'drive-off' crime of obtaining petrol without paying and for overcoming the Central London daily pay-as-you-enter congestion charge zone. False registration plates also permitted the perpetrators to avoid paying parking fines. The borough also had a high murder rate in 2006/07; of the eleven murders within its boundaries, three were involved in a single incident of a mother and two children being killed in an Asian 'honour killing'.

The borough's detection rate was low across the board. The 'clear-up' statistic for residential burglary was 40 per cent, a figure considered particularly in need of improvement.[11] As a consequence, Her Majesty's Inspectorate of Constabulary (HIM) had identified the need for a more stringent 'performance management', primarily through proactive policing and a revised Safer Neighbourhoods policy. It also brought in a new divisional commander – Nick Bracken. Integral to his role was balancing the demands of policing and the political reality of Newham and its unique demographics. One meeting in early 2007 indicates the levels of police–public dialogue and the disparity between local and 'Olympic' policing concerns, illustrating the concerns of the local populace some five years before the 2012 Olympics were to make their neighbourhood globally recognized.

In mid-February 2007, West Ham United FC's Boleyn Stadium hosted the Metropolitan Police Authority (MPA) annual meeting for the London Borough of Newham. Titled *Local Policing Issues and Partnership Working*, the two hour meeting was chaired by the MPA's Len Duvall and was attended by 24 people. Of the 24, eight were women. A 15-year-old child attended courtesy of his position as Newham's Youth Parliament representative. Of the 24 present, five were black and two were Asian; the rest were white. Those present represented neighbourhood police, the fire brigade, magistrates, Newham Council's anti-crime unit and the University of East London. Two presentations were made, one by David Burbage from Newham Council, the other by Nick Bracken. The former explained to those present that his talk would inform them of the Council's strategic policies; the latter was to present the realities of the tactical execution of policing policy. Within minutes of opening his talk, Burbage was lavish in his praise for the current council–police partnership, stating that it had 'never been better'. At the same time, he admitted the statistics for crime and disorder in Newham had risen over the previous year. The crime and disorder strategy prioritized behaviours in the following order of seriousness: 1) anti-social behaviour; 2) community reassurance and fear; 3) violent crime (domestic violence, street crime, alcohol-related crime); 4) race-hate crime; 5) a 'basket' of ten key crimes, which included robbery, burglary and motor

---

10   Interview with Chief Superintendent Nick Bracken, 2008.
11   Interview with Chief Superintendent Nick Bracken, 2008.

vehicle crime. Beyond these five were three overarching themes: youth crime, substance misuse and prolific and priority offenders. Burbage spoke of 'targeting resources' and anticipated greater clarity following what was known as the Local Area Agreement due to come into effect on 1 April 2007. Meanwhile, districts in the south of the borough, including Canning Town and Custom House, were to receive £1 million from the London Thames Gateway Development Corporation, whilst the Borough Commander was to receive £50,000 of MPA funding to develop 'partnership working'. Burbage finished his talk stressing crucial the meeting was because accountability in the face of challenges from external agencies was very important to the effective policing of the borough.

The police-council partnership in Newham was then described by Chief Superintendent Bracken as 'both happening and bringing critical results'. To this end, he could state how January 2007 had produced the lowest recorded crime figures for Newham in five years, and went on to list a catalogue of police successes across the range of policing activities. However, Bracken also highlighted a rise in woundings, which he claimed was partly explainable by the presence of 'Lithuanian' males, who came to police attention usually on weekend nights, and who fought between themselves after lengthy drinking sessions. The arrest and detention of such Lithuanians had created a problem for the police, who were tasked with finding interpreters to deal with both victims and alleged perpetrators. The costs of interpreters' services, paid for by the police, were described by Bracken as 'astronomical'; this requirement also delayed both inquiry and detection times. Some months later the possibility that 'Lithuanian' was a flag of convenience for a variety of Eastern European and former Soviet residents was being mooted across Newham, with suggestions that Lithuanian passports were selling for as little as £150 to non-EU immigrants. (Lithuania had acceded to the EU in 2004.) This was not revealed to the public at the meeting, however, although the meeting did hear of a recently discovered Polish website informing aspiring Polish migrants how to 'squat' in Newham Council properties. Because of the large numbers of Polish migrants to the area, a body titled The Newham East European Advisory Group on Housing had been established – the first instance of any such council-led initiative in the UK.

The meeting then engaged with the Borough of Newham's most enduring problem which has hampered the borough for generations. Newham does not have 'Inner London' status and thus does not receive the £70 million of central government funds available to boroughs such as neighbouring Hackney and Tower Hamlets. (This lack of Inner London status also afflicts East London's other Olympic borough, Waltham Forest). This funding issue was crucial to the meeting's final item, which was concerned with the makeup of the borough's population. The meeting learned from the Chair that, according to census data available from the Office of National Statistics (ONS), Newham had lost 5,000 households and its population was 15,000 down on the previous two years. According to ONS intelligence, Newham contained some 92,000 households and a falling population of 248,000. By contrast, figures presented by Newham Council representatives, based on applications for National Insurance numbers for employment purposes and General Practitioners' registration figures, showed population numbers as standing at a minimum of 270,000 and even possibly 295,000. Around 30,000–50,000 people were thus believed to be unaccounted for in government statistics. The counting methodology of the ONS was thus challenged by all in the room. The Chair opined that, whilst everyone in any position of knowledge accepts that the figures were wrong, he was unable to change the figures because the calculating model of the ONS was used nationally. This had huge implications in debates about crime and crime prevention. Newham was not fully resourced across the public sector to cope with this additional population and in policing terms the 'missing' 50,000 did not have the appropriate police resources to police and protect them. Moreover, this gap between law enforcement agencies and the communities they police has long been seen as an intensive criminogenic force. This has been observed both in Newham (Rawlinson and Fussey 2010) and, also, internationally (see *inter alia* Gambetta 1995).

'Emergent' Issues: Images to Record

Our fieldwork in Newham over the past few years indicated that the Olympics constituted but one looming problem among a collection of issues that were rapidly developing in an era of unprecedented change. These issues included the proposed opening of the Eurostar rail link at Stratford, the scheduled Thameslink Bridge and unspecified problems related to demographic reconfigurations in the area. In addition, the building of Stratford City shopping and leisure complex was regarded as likely to bring problems from the construction force and an epidemic of shoplifting when opened. Meanwhile, Newham police had the Olympics about to appear in their backyard: and both the paranoid and pragmatic elements of police occupational culture were evident.

The emergent dimension of policing in Newham began with the turning of the first sod in the district that was to house the Olympic Stadium and Village. The project would be the largest building site in Europe. A workforce projected at its peak at 35,000 was expected to migrate to East London between 2007 and 2012 to build, furnish and maintain the facility, posing the possibility of an assortment of criminality associated with a male workforce operating away from home (*The Independent* 2009a, *The London Evening Standard* 2010a). At the same time, drives to invest the unemployed of East London with new skills through the preferential training and recruitment of local workers were launched. However, behind such community-focused drives are questions over what constitutes 'the local community'. In particular, this discussion is informed by the ease with which one could become a 'local' via temporary residence and National Insurance contributions. Indeed, by early 2009 Newham was host to over 100,000 foreign applicants for new National Insurance numbers (*The London Evening Standard* 2009). Not only was this double that of the next highest municipal area (Waltham Forest), it further agitated the continual motion of London's eastern zones of transition.[12]

Measures implemented in 2008 to assist the construction of the Olympic site saw the ODA initiate electronic fingerprint and iris-scan entries for all working within the Olympic Park. Copies of all foreign workers' passports were also taken and a constant police and UK Borders Agency presence maintained on and around the site.[13] A building project of such magnitude was bound to produce the possibility of theft, fraud, false accounting and breaches of safety at work legislation are perhaps inevitable across Newham. Responsibility for safe practice fell to the major construction companies;[14] the battle between commerce and ethics was about to be played out par excellence within Newham's policing borders.

The police were also lumbered with a ceremonial duty which had public order implications. The Olympic Torch – a legacy of the 1936 Berlin ('Nazi Olympics') Games was wending its way around towards the UK as part of an IOC-inspired symbolic world tour. The Torch inflamed many people and brought logistical problems to the 2012 host borough.

The Olympic Flame

The coming of the Olympic Torch to Newham highlighted the complexities that could emerge from what was, at first glance, the most innocent of symbolic gestures. On Sunday 6 April 2008, the centre of Stratford hosted one of the London legs of the journey of the Olympic Torch relay that was part of the run-up to the Beijing 2008 Olympics. Having been lit in Olympia, Greece, in late March, the Torch was to travel across five continents and be held aloft in 22 cities, one of which was London. Only 72 centimetres high and weighing 985 grams, the Olympic Torch could withstand winds of up to 60 kilometres per hour but was to prove a heavy burden to those tasked with carrying and preserving it.

The Torch relay had created disorder on various legs of its route. In principle, the event was entirely in the spirit of the Olympic rhetoric; an opportunity to celebrate cultural diversity, youth and humanity as all gathered around the symbol of the eternal flame. However, events over the previous month thousands of miles away meant that what might have been an innocuous and agnostic Sunday

---

12   Such transitions not only contribute toward criminogenic contexts (see *inter alia* Shaw and McKay 1942; Sampson, Raudenbush and Earls 1997; Bottoms and Wiles 2002). This fluidity also questions the static nature in which the 'community' (as supposed beneficiaries of the Olympic Legacy) is conceptualised.

13   In 2007 Assistant Metropolitan Police Commissioner, Tariq Ghaffur, spoke of his hope that all 70,000 Olympic volunteers would be added to the fingerprint and iris database.

14   Similar problems have been reported on non-ODA Olympic-related construction projects in other parts of the city (see Rawlinson and Fussey 2010).

afternoon gathering took on the burdens of global *realpolitik*. The activities of the Chinese authorities in Tibet had been brought to the world's attention only two weeks previously, when the Chinese military were believed to have killed over 100 Tibetans protesting against the Chinese occupation of their country. By way of response, the Tibetans had called upon world leaders to boycott the 2008 Beijing Olympic Games and sections of the Western media had taken up the issue, confronting politicians over a possible Olympic boycott. The Torch meanwhile had begun its relay in Greece, the first leg of which was disrupted by Tibetans and pro-Tibet demonstrators. The global media watched as the demonstrators clashed with those carrying the Torch; demonstrators were bundled over by a variety of Chinese and Greek security officials.

In London a total of 80 Torchbearers, including TV and sports celebrities, set off on a route that began at Wembley Stadium and travelled through Notting Hill, Oxford Street, Chinatown, Trafalgar Square, London Bridge and Whitechapel, before ending at the O2 Arena, Greenwich, at 6 pm. The route would see the Torch taken at times by bicycle, boat, bus and, it was suggested – the Docklands Light Railway (DLR). The flame was due to arrive in Stratford in Newham at around 17:00 hours on a Sunday afternoon, where it would pass near the intended 2012 Olympic Village and leave to cross the Thames to enter the O2 Arena for what was described by 2012 promoters as a 'spectacular finale'. A total of seven Torchbearers was scheduled to take turns to carry the flame around Stratford's streets.

To welcome the Torch, Newham Council had arranged for a 'carnival' consisting of performances, music and dance commencing at midday Sunday. The events planned ranged from lantern-making workshops, storytelling from Bangladesh, Africa, Sri Lanka and England, and performances of Eastern European gypsy traditions. Youngsters could also enjoy face painting, a balloon artist and Chinese acrobats, who would also perform a lion dance and martial arts demonstrations. Some 300 schoolchildren were to be part of a mobile carnival consisting of six motorized floats with a 'world music' theme. A primary school samba band would herald the flame's arrival as they stood outside Stratford's railway station. The Newham Young People's Chorus, consisting of 150 primary and secondary school children were to provide a concert, also at Stratford railway terminal. The New Vic Recycled Orchestra would be playing instruments made from recycled items. Not all the entertainment was at ground level. A dance performance by an East London-based dance troupe was scheduled for the roof-top of the Stratford Library. For those seeking a more rarefied atmosphere, a string quartet from the Royal Philharmonic Orchestra and a tea dance were to be hosted in the Old Town Hall.

Sporting demonstrations of the Olympic events of fencing, handball and basketball, and a display of cheerleading, were also to be provided. For those who sought more than spectating, facilities were available to try their hand at cycling, canoeing and rowing. Inside Stratford Shopping Centre, a 40-metre temporary racing track had been set up for short sprint competitions. Adjacent to this, an art display from the Tate Gallery exhibited figures inspired by athletics and dancing. The 'Get Set' London road show was also exhibiting in the shopping centre, jointly managed by the London Development Agency and London 2012. This display promoted London's ambitions for the 2012 Games and sought to provide the curious with an opportunity to see how they would benefit in terms of jobs, skills, culture, business, regeneration and ultimately sporting facilities. Across from this exhibition was one showcasing the 'Changing Face of Stratford', which saw information and exhibits provided by the University of East London, the Stratford Renaissance Partnership and the London Thames Gateway entity. The outdoor market was host to stalls promoting the sporting provision currently available in Newham as well as advising people how to join Newham's Olympic Volunteer Programme. A lot of work and effort had gone into the occasion.

Operational Readiness?

The afternoon's events were planned by the council without detailed discussions with local police. The Chief Superintendent of Newham learned of the full circumstances of the carnival and Torch relay less than two weeks before its arrival. He learned from council officials that the event was anticipated to attract some 50,000 people. Furthermore he learned, none of the roads around the Stratford Shopping Centre would be closed during the day. The Chief Supt was worried about the following four issues: First, the presence of thousands of children, especially as a multitude of events did not sit well with a busy one-way traffic system. Ideally, the road should be closed. Second, the aerial events and those on roofs, though potentially fascinating, did not sit well with a busy one-way system either. Third, late Sunday afternoon had the potential for heavy drinking from midday onwards and with it the potential for a public order situation. Fourth, with so many diverse cultures in Newham, some of whom were not sympathetic to the Chinese authorities or to Western capitalist culture, the opportunity of making a global statement by interrupting the procession was a real possibility. The heightened political atmosphere had obviously been considered at the highest level of British policing but these concerns had not been filtered down to the Chief Supt tasked with the job of keeping public order for this extraordinary Sunday afternoon. The event was the responsibility of the Met Police's specialist public order policy department who carried the title CO11 (Central Operations group 11). The relay, however, would see the Torch crossing five London police districts.[15]

The Chief Supt asked for, and got, the agreement of the council official to meet with him and others both a week later and five days before the event. However, within 24 hours he had, using his own powers of negotiation and persuasion, stopped the proposed rooftop music performances and got permission from

---

15 Fortuitously, an English Premier League fixture between West Ham and Portsmouth, scheduled for the same afternoon at 3 pm, had been moved to 48 hours later, not for public order and safety reasons but because Portsmouth's progress in the FA Cup took precedence over the League fixture. The game would have seen 35,000 people coming into the area to watch the game in the stadium just one mile away from the route of the parade.

Transport for London to close the one-way system for a specified period, this being the route by which the Torch and its associated parade would arrive and leave the area. Stratford police would learn ahead from other policing colleagues as to the time of arrival of the Torch and then stop traffic to allow the Torch a clear passage through the expectant crowds. Furthermore, the Olympic Torch would no longer to be transported from Stratford to Greenwich via the DLR. Not only did the DLR prohibit smoking on both its trains and station platforms, but the Chief Superintendent's years of duty in the British Transport Police afforded him the knowledge that a naked flame of the magnitude of the Olympic Torch was not a good idea or, in fact, permissible in the enclosed environs of a train carriage. The Torch would cross the Thames on a tugboat instead.

The Torch relay did not pass without incident, illustrating the huge scale of the issues that the Olympics could bring. On top of the China–Tibet controversy, the Torch relay attracted protests over Chinese policy in Darfur in Sudan and also from the religious sect Falun Gong which, for ten years, had maintained a permanent vigil outside the Chinese embassy in Central London in support of their followers in China, who had been given custodial sentences for their beliefs. An organization called Students for a Free Tibet (SFT) (an international organization who favour peaceful and law-abiding direct action) were also a worry to the police. SFT announced days ahead that they expected 1,000 exiled Tibetan nationals to protest against the presence of the Torch relay.

On the day, it was the press freedom group Reporters Without Borders who first breached the tight security in the early stages of the Torch procession at Olympia, West London and also interrupted the speech by the Beijing Organizing Committee for the Olympic Games (BOCOG) representative. One Frenchman unfurled a large black flag depicting the five Olympic rings as handcuffs (originally a design used by Amnesty International) before being arrested. High-profile figures invited to the London leg of the Torch relay were then targeted by demonstrators opposed to the Chinese government's policy on Tibet. Together, such events demonstrate the selectivity of the IOC's proclaimed commitment to 'Celebrate Humanity' (IOC 2004).

More than 2,000 police officers were deployed on the route from Wembley Stadium in West London to the O2 Arena in Greenwich. Air, marine and mounted police support was involved in an operation that would cost more than £1 million. Crowd barriers were erected in some areas but much of the 31-mile route would not be sealed off. As a consequence, protestors embarrassed the relay. The former children's TV presenter Konnie Huq announced days before that she was wavering over whether to carry the Torch due to China's human rights record. On the day, she decided that she would but nearly had it snatched from her by a lone, male protestor who had breached the security cordon – and was promptly bundled away by a combination of uniformed police and the Chinese guards who travelled the globe with the Torch. (This specialist security unit provoked much debate in the publicity that ensued following the event.[16])

The Torch arrived in Stratford amidst atrocious weather and no little confusion. The crowds did not flock to the event in the numbers anticipated. Those who were about were primarily shopping, some of these – fewer than 5,000 in the unofficial estimates of the local police – lined the route. The sub-zero temperatures and the flurries of snow did not add to the attractiveness of the event. The Torch was delayed and thus the scheduling was some 40 minutes behind time, which had the knock-on effect of ensuring the lightly-clad children's steel band and the cheerleaders around Stratford rail termini were rather frozen as they performed their arts. When the Torch did finally arrive, it was not on foot but ensconced on a single-decker bus with a multitude of passengers. At various points along the route, the Torch was put on said vehicle and driven to the next gathering of crowds. The vehicle that carried it was part of a cortege but did not have any outstanding feature to differentiate it. Thus those awaiting the arrival of the Torch in Stratford had to guess which vehicle carried the Torch. Many who had waited for over an hour discovered minutes later that the Torch had come and gone.

The first indication that the Torch had arrived in Stratford was the appearance of some 20 police motorcycle outriders. Then came the Olympic entourage, the first element was an open-backed truck containing a bevy of young women wearing tight shorts and T-shirts and advertising a low-brow daily tabloid. The next to arrive was a similar truck, this time with a PA system and young women advertising Coca Cola. Then came a multitude of vehicles; polices cars, ambulances, limousines and a few double-decker buses carrying an assortment of press and 2012 officials. Somewhere amidst this the Torch-bearing bus arrived and then stopped some 100 metres past the Stratford railway esplanade. Out of the vehicle stepped the 20-strong, sky-blue-tracksuit-clad Chinese security team. In their slipstream came uniformed officers of the Metropolitan Police. At one stage, police motorcycle riders got off their bikes and ran in full leather and boots alongside the Torch where the spectators were densest. Carrying the Torch was an individual unrecognized by anyone in the crowd. Celebrity Torchbearers were not present for the Stratford leg of the relay. Yet the relay was cheered and clapped by the waiting crowd as it wended its way around the one-way system before the Torch was placed back on the bus, which then drove away. The Torch had appeared in Stratford for less than ten minutes.

Opponents of the Torch were evident in Stratford. Around two dozen pro-Tibet sympathizers gathered outside Stratford railway station one hour before the scheduled arrival and found themselves corralled by a dozen uniformed police. This did not stop others of similar political sympathy gathering 500 metres away on

---

16   In addition to protests from the public, the Chinese security officers were not appreciated by some senior members of the MPS charged with overseeing the relay, who later raised the issue of who had the right to control procedures and protocol for dealing with demonstrations. Two contrasting traditions of policing the public were very evident.

the one-way system. One of them, on seeing the Torch relay approaching, ran from the pavement into the road, no doubt with a view to disrupting the procession. He was rugby-tackled by a uniformed officer and arrested as the Torch continued past him. The crowds that remained after the Torch had left were considerably thinned out. Those who stayed could enjoy the spectacle of a Chinese dragon dance and a library roof-top display of Eastern martial arts that ended with the artists abseiling down the building. The Mayor of Newham then spoke to his electorate, his words almost incomprehensible by virtue of the poor PA system and the traffic, now resumed on the one-way system. Six carnival floats then drove by, the frozen but still-enthusiastic children on board waving to the departing crowds as the late afternoon darkness shrouded the area. The Olympic Torch had not really lit up the lives of anyone on that winter day in Newham.

The Starting Gun: Towards Imminent Policing

In seeking a secure and incident-free Games, Londoners specifically and much of the wider populace who live within the geographical boundary of the M25 motorway will be subject to buffer zones of containment that may well serve to re-border parts of London, with a concomitant filtering and restriction of the population (see Chapter 5). On top of this will be the desire to police out risks that accrue in these circumstances of exceptionality. The ever-increasing commodification of both public space and sporting stadia will produce zones of supervision and regulation. Integral to these processes will be debates about proportionality and effectiveness of overt security measures and the more subtle forms of deterrence and apprehension. The rhetoric of ensuring public safety will be heard over and above the reality of ensuring a sanitized (and therefore marketable) image of the host city. Overall, these operations aimed at protecting people, property and reputations provides for a logistics labyrinth and a burden that falls heavily on local policing provisions.

Space: The Final Frontier?

The staging of the Games will provoke much debate around whom a city is for and whether a sporting event take over the routine workings of a city and its populace. The issue is in part one of space. Space does not exist as an ontological fact but is endowed with meaning and embodied in regimes of articulation (Lefebvre 1991, Shields 1991). All spaces are resources in which personal and collective expressions of social agency or imperializing impositions of power are realized and exercised. The presence of other spaces or arguments about appropriate use or appropriation may be crucial as such processes exist as counter-points in bestowing meaning (Bailly 1986: 83). The issue can be about notions and processes of arrival and departure as much as about those who routinely use the space. The issue of contestation might best be dichotomized into *locale* and *station*. For Fiske (1993: 11–13) *locales* are spaces that involve 'continuities between interior and exterior, between conscious bodies, places and times and implicitly confront, resist or evade'. In contrast, *stations* are places 'where the social order is imposed upon an individual and self-constitution is denied'. Each of the categories has the potential for time–space specificities and each is loaded with potential power plays as notions of trespass are both constructed and challenged. The defence of physical space-by any one demographic is a symbolic articulation of their social plight which must be considered alongside a more universalist approach that would contend that people are forever contesting issues of social order and tradition (Hall and Jefferson 1976). Places in themselves have little by way of universally accepted representation: it is the way they are 'loaded' with significance that matters. The issue is thus one of constructed meanings and representational systems (Hall 1997:25).

If one accepts these possibilities, then the task of policing becomes one of understanding how cultural contexts are constructed and understood – a task that gains complexity as new agents of Olympic policing are introduced. The socio-cultural histories of a variety of issues are required, as is an explanation as to how they impact upon the protagonists, be it in terms of challenge, avoidance or negotiation. For 2012, not all such contests will be open to debate. The police will have to decide and dictate in many instances. This then provokes debate about citizenship in the new millennium. Citizenship of a place like Newham can no longer be viewed as a status to be granted or achieved once and equally for all (Wacquant 2008: 38) and will be further defined by imposed 2012-inspired visions of control. Citizenship, to follow Wacquant, might best be considered as a contentious and uneven process that 'must continually be struggled for and secured anew' (2008:38). Such struggles are likely to become escalated in Newham's contested spaces of Olympic order.

Challenging Times

The opportunity for a city to host the Olympic Games constitutes an enormous economic, social and cultural commitment with attendant social, political and economic costs. If properly managed and marketed, the event can provide unforgettable moments for both athletes and spectators and bring a number of positive long-term benefits. However, the Games are disruptive, with many of the event's consequences being unintended. The senior police officers tasked with policing Newham do not consider their patch a dangerous one. They prefer the word 'challenging' and two admitted to the authors in late 2009 to having asked to be deployed in Newham because of the variety of populations that make their task so interesting. Meanwhile gossip and rumour concerning the recreational habits of the incomers, in particular the tens of thousands of building construction workers who are occupied on Newham's enormous construction projects, abound. Aerial photographs in 2009 reveal a plethora of somewhat unsophisticated and illegal extensions to the rear of many of Newham's houses. The occupants of such jerry-built structures are believed to be for some of the migrant workers who constitute the 20,000 men now providing the muscle for the Olympic Village as well as the Stratford City complex.[17] Whispers of serious criminal predators, both home grown and international, dipping their toes into the local sex trade remain, for the time being, muted (although see *inter alia* MPA 2009, Fussey and Rawlinson 2009; Chapter 10).

But everything could change. The General Election of May 2010 and the Newham Mayoral election of 2010 were both fought against the background of a catastrophic global economic climate and subsequent cuts to public services. The 2012 Olympic and Paralympic Games take place amidst other large-scale pageantry including the Notting Hill Carnival and Queen Elizabeth's Diamond Jubilee, events marked by expensive and possibly contentious ceremony that will place huge demands on London's police.

The Klondike period is chaotic. Crime data and information on the social conditions of the workforce charged with delivering a pristine Games and a lasting Olympic legacy are confusing and infused with rumour, gossip and the institutional concerns of state agents. At the same time, these national and international interests introduce new concerns that are not necessarily matched by local policing priorities or capabilities. Meanwhile the ongoing state of flux of Newham's population continues the haphazard trajectories that began with the decline of the docks nearly forty years ago. Newham's families, workers and the public sector that serves them hold their breath, cross their fingers and watch in muted astonishment as the shabby but functioning product of a nineteenth-century empire is re-branded and transformed into a temporary global stage. The Olympic legacy is emerging, albeit not totally in accordance with the bid book.

---

17   Our ongoing ethnographic research in Newham indicates that the going rate for a night's stay in one of these illegal structures can be as low as £10.

Chapter 7
Tracking the Field: Technologies of Control

Introduction

Since 1976, one of the key features of Olympic security has been the use of technological surveillance, an approach that has become increasingly central to securing large sporting events in the post-9/11 era and one that also fits neatly with the IOC's demands to prioritize the sporting event over the policing spectacle. For London 2012, the city is likely to reinforce its reputation as a pioneer of such technologies via the deployment of ever more intensified, networked and advanced forms of technological observation. This chapter examines the way electronic surveillance has been applied to secure mega-sporting events since Munich 1972 and the way in which these techniques connect and integrate with the mechanisms deployed to secure the 2012 Games. Following an introductory exploration of what is meant by 'surveillance', this chapter engages in three substantive areas of discussion. First, analysis will focus on the increasing centrality of these surveillance strategies in the overall provision of security for major sporting events, particularly the Olympic Games. The second area of inquiry illustrates how this commitment to technological surveillance is also being retained for London 2012. These two areas of analysis fit together to inform and develop the 'laminating security' perspective outlined in this book. Here, a complex dynamic inviting a collision of local and global security approaches is at play. 'Externally' developed forms of Olympic security strategy are becoming instilled into London's 'internal' pioneering surveillance and security infrastructures. The outcome will be a net increase in the intensity of London's Olympic-approved surveillance embellishments and an intricate mesh of externally levied and locally derived security practices. Finally, the chapter will draw on some of the key analytical issues emerging from these discussions to consider the efficacy, operational context and ethical considerations of surveillance strategies at Olympic-sized events. It will conclude by examining ways in which these converging surveillance mechanisms can be understood, perhaps most successfully via Deleuzian theoretical understandings of the assemblage (Haggerty and Ericson 2000), also considering how the exceptional (and potentially ephemeral) nature of Olympic surveillance strategies impact on such interpretations.

Defining the Terrain: Surveillance Technology and its Application

For practitioners, surveillance strategies are appealing because they can perform myriad functions and connect with existing strategies to tackle crime and terrorism. Although surveillance strategies may take 'informal' and 'low-tech' forms – for example, increasing pedestrian flows, enhancing sight-lines by removing obstacles such as hedges and adopting more open-plan architectural techniques – the most recognizable and debated form of surveillance has been CCTV,[1] cameras that observe defined geographies and feed footage back into a control room for human operators. Yet, as numerous studies have illustrated, this form of observation is far from passive for the observed. For example, ethnographic studies have demonstrated how the subjects of CCTV observations reflexively amend their behaviour in response to their perceived visibility – becoming *active* 'subjects of communication' rather than *passive* 'objects of information' (Smith 2007: 280; see also Norris and Armstrong 1999). Surveillance technologies themselves have also become more active over recent years, adopting second-generation approaches designed to organize, filter or elevate noteworthy signals from the white noise of oversupplied surveillance data. Conversely, 'low-fidelity' traditional surveillance measures are more popular than ever. For the 2012 London Olympics, the unprecedented requirement for private security guards (7,000), in addition to the sizable number of the 70,000 Games volunteers likely to be deployed for security work, means that human surveillance activity will continue to be of considerable importance. Finally, surveillance technologies are not only punitive but, as this chapter demonstrates, aspire to integrate organizations, agencies and actors.

Together, these variegated applications of surveillance technologies raise numerous practical and theoretical questions over their efficacy, their adaptability to new roles (such as Olympic security) and how they interact with their social and operational environments.

Surveillance, Sport and the Olympics before 2001

> it was agreed that the best way to deter suspected trouble-makers was … [one] that would leave no doubt in their minds they were under continual close surveillance.
> (COJO, Official Report of the XXI Olympiad, Montreal, 1976: 559)

---

1   Today CCTV is perhaps more accurately characterized as operating on an *open* circuit rather than a closed circuit. Increasingly, once-bounded networks are not only breaking open to assimilate other extant CCTV schemes (for example, hitherto closed surveillance systems such as those in hospitals, schools and universities are progressively becoming connected to city-centre schemes) but can now be accessed from remote sources such as the internet. As such, 'open circuit television' (OCTV) is probably a more accurate description. However, to ensure parity with existing literature and research on surveillance, the term 'CCTV' is used throughout this chapter to refer to both types of system.

As Chapter 2 details, in the wake of Munich 1972, security for the Montreal 1976 Summer Games was unprecedented. Of further note is the way the three major themes of Montreal's security programme – preventive measures, a visible presence of security forces and enhanced communication systems – were all underpinned by surveillance strategies. Specific initiatives included enhanced accreditation requirements for site workers (COJO 1976: 559), acoustic surveillance devices installed in the Olympic Village (Clarke 1976 cited in Sanan 1997) and, crucially for this discussion, perhaps the first widespread and systematic deployment of CCTV to feature at an Olympics (COJO 1976). Costing US$100 million (equivalent to around US$380 million today), the measures instituted at Montreal have evolved to become staple features of Olympic security planning and marked what was to become the increasing prominence of electronic surveillance at such events.

In common with other motifs of Olympic security, these approaches bridged geographical and ideological barriers to become reproduced and embellished at Lake Placid, Moscow, Sarajevo and Los Angeles. One of the variations on this theme, however, has been the direction of the surveillant gaze. Whereas the observation and hardening of perimeters is have been a perennial features, what emerged in these earlier Olympic security experiments was the monitoring, control and protection of participants (rather than the public). The 1988 Seoul Olympics provides an example of how this focus was preserved. Here, adding to the aforementioned measures, innovations included the surveillance of *mobilities* as well as *geographies*: athletes needed to carry ID cards embedded with coded magnetic strips that could then be checked by sensors across Olympic sites (Cottrell 2003). Indeed, this narrower depth of field (of the few watching the few) was proudly proclaimed by the organizers as comprising:

> a CCTV system to prevent terrorism and to monitor potential saboteurs threatening athletes, officials, related figures, and major facilities at competition sites and venues of functions. The equipment mobilized for the CCTV system included 228 television cameras, 295 monitors, 138 VTRs [video tape recorders], and 41 searchlights, totalling 702 items (SOOC 1989: 746).

The legacy of Munich and fears over the safety of participants has resonated through the continued retention of this focus. Throughout the 1990s, however, and particularly after the Centennial Park bombing at Atlanta 1996, it was supplemented by an emphasis on the protection of crowded spaces. Thus, 1976–2001 can be seen as a period of both reaction and evolution of Olympic security, when practices and processes associated with securing these events became more standardized and internationalized.

Surveillance and Sport in Britain

At the same time, CCTV was becoming a more familiar spectator at many of Britain's football stadia (following a feasibility study of camera surveillance at grounds in the West Midlands during the 1970s (Hancox and Morgan 1975)). Its ubiquity was then assured when the Football Trust financed its installation at all British football clubs throughout the 1980s and 1990s, as well as providing funding for police forces to purchase mobile camera equipment (Armstrong and Giulianotti 1998). Whilst the Football Trust[2] presented the utility of CCTV in maximizing spectator safety (although see below), the main driver was the prevention of fighting and other disorder at the grounds – a fact evinced by the acceleration and escalation of CCTV deployment following the Heysel Stadium disaster of 1985.[3] Such was the extent of football-related CCTV surveillance by 1993 that an official Home Office report on policing football hooliganism stressed that 'football supporters are probably more accustomed to being subjected to camera surveillance than most other groups in society' (Home Office 1993 cited in Marsh et al. 1996). Football supporters effectively had to – silently – consent to being filmed in order to engage with their choice of entertainment. Surveillance and the sporting spectacle had become inseparable.

Other developments in the use of camera surveillance occurred during the mid-1990s around the time that England last hosted a football-related mega-sporting event – the UEFA Euro 96 football championships. A month before the championships were due to commence on 5 May, a number of minor disturbances broke out in Newcastle-upon-Tyne, one of the host cities, as the city's football team had failed to win the Premier League title, having surrendered a once-substantial lead to Manchester United, the eventual winners. In response to the disorder, the police launched 'Operation Harvest', which drew on footage from 16 city-centre CCTV cameras, and proceeded to conduct dawn raids on 30 suspects' homes culminating in the arrest of 19 individuals. At the time this was claimed to have been the biggest policing operation ever to use CCTV technology (*The Independent* 1996). Of interest here is the way entirely separate CCTV systems were becoming co-opted into more integrated meta-networks. Another component of these assemblages was also brought into play during the actual Euro 96 championships: the public. Here, in a technological variation on the long tradition of 'rogues galleries', the media published CCTV stills of those suspected of being involved in public disorder. Another important component of the Euro 96 surveillance strategy was mobility. Mobile surveillance vehicles, so-called 'hoolivans', were extensively deployed throughout the championships (Marsh et al. 1996) and have

---

2   The Football Trust was a part-government funded organization founded in 1979 ostensibly with the aim of providing safety and security at football stadia via grants to particular football clubs. Notably, the Trust was involved in providing resources to clubs obliged to introduce all-seater stadiums following the Hillsborough disaster and, during its lifespan (1979–2000), it was criticized for promoting the excessive criminalization of football supporters (Armstrong 1998).

3   However, in the post-Hillsborough inquiry, Lord Justice Taylor criticised many of these initial systems as being of inadequate quality and staffed by poorly trained operators (Home Office, 1990: 48).

now become a central component of football policing strategies internationally, as evinced at the 2006 FIFA World Cup in Germany (Klauser 2008) and 2008 European Championships in Austria and Switzerland (Hagemann 2008).

Together, these three components – assemblage, mobility and the social environment – demonstrate not only that technological surveillance a multifaceted phenomenon but that by itself it is limited and dependent on its operational context. One event that demonstrates some of the limitations of this technology at football grounds and also underscores the importance of its social environment is the use of CCTV during the Hillsborough tragedy of April 1989. Cameras monitoring the congestion outside the ground led police to open the gates at the Leppings Lane end of the stadium without diverting the flow of fans away from the overcrowded central pens towards less crowded enclosures to the side of the goal; a fatal crush ensued (Home Office 1989). Observers of the ground's CCTV feeds initially misinterpreted this as hooliganism (Armstrong 1998). In the immediate aftermath, Chief Superintendent Duckenfield, in overall command of the policing operation, was reported to have fallen back on CCTV in an vague attempt to attribute culpability to disorderly supporters, as he pointed to one of the control room's CCTV monitors and wrongly claimed, 'That's the gate that's been forced: there's been an inrush' (Home Office 1989: 17). The role of CCTV in these tragic events demonstrates that deploying surveillance systems on their own not only limits their effectiveness but also can generate unforeseen circumstances. Additionally, the misinterpretation of CCTV images of the Hillsborough crowd suggests that these forms of surveillance technologies may be conceptually distinguished from other forms of technological information gathering, such as biometric surveillance or 'smart' ID cards. In these latter modes, through their very existence the technology itself asserts a function by capturing data. With CCTV, such 'capture' is not necessarily assured and, crucially, operators may easily apply an intuitive gloss to its data. Thus, for CCTV, it is not necessarily the technology that does the work but the contingent responses of surrounding actors complete with their human frailties.

Surveillance and Sport Since 2001

Since 2001, Olympic and major sporting event security strategies have continued and built upon many of the themes present at earlier Olympiads. These include the aforementioned strands of target-hardening, ambitions for achieving the 'total security' of designated spaces and the emphasis on technological surveillance. Echoing Ball and Webster's (2004) argument that technological security has been intensified rather than replaced by 9/11, since 2001 Olympic security has seen increases in scale, technological innovation and the centrality of surveillance strategies. Rather than constituting an expression of mere technophilia, this commitment to distanciated electronic surveillance is seen by practitioners as harmonizing with the IOC's longstanding (though often abandoned) aim of projecting the Games as an athletic event and not an exercise in security (see, for example, Thompson 1999). These features are visible across a number of key sporting events during this period, as evinced by the following case studies discussing the 2001 US Super Bowl, the 2004 Olympic Games in Athens and the 2008 Beijing Olympics.

Mega-sporting Events in the US, 2001–2002

One key event in the evolution of surveillance technology occurred during January 2001 during the XXXV Super Bowl at the Raymond James Stadium, Tampa, 2001. Here, Facial Recognition CCTV (FRCCTV) was deployed to monitor the crowd by taking pictures of every ticketholder as they passed through the turnstiles. Algorithms were then applied to the received image to measure facial characteristics such as the distance between the eyes, nose and lips, and the width of nose. This information was then compared against an undisclosed database in an attempt to efficiently identify those matching a similar facial profile belonging to known offenders. Of the 100,000 attendees, the software flagged 19 individuals and was seen as a success by both the authorities (*Los Angeles Times* 2001) and industry representatives (Lyon 2003a). In response, the Florida police rolled the technology out into the public spaces of the city in Ybor City district.[4] However, the numerous difficulties afflicting its operation meant that this deployment was short-lived (see below).

Technological innovation to protect US sporting events continued at the Winter Olympics in Salt Lake City the following year. Although they proved to be a watershed in many areas of security policy, the 9/11 attacks occurred five months before the opening ceremony, at a time when planning was at an advanced stage. As such, the availability of human and financial resources, rather than the overall shape of the strategy, was the most notable impact of 9/11. Nevertheless, common to previous Olympic security strategies, technology was again a central feature. Advanced FBI-supplied communications systems (which failed to work correctly) (Decker et al. 2005), biometric scanners, portable x-ray devices, widespread CCTV and computer monitoring (Atkinson and Young 2008) were all deployed. At the same time, more ambitious technological strategies were brought into service. These included initiatives that sprayed the atmosphere with chemicals that would enable monitoring technology to spot gamma radiation particles more easily (in the event of a radiological or nuclear attack), alongside the BASIS (see Chapter 2) that could capture and examine potentially lethal airborne bacteria and viruses (Heller 2003). Such initiatives reflect an elevated concern over the threat

---

4   Ybor City has both a highly diverse multi-ethnic profile and a reputation for its lively night-time economy. One can assume that the deployment of CCTV in this milieu was not coincidental and reflected the more enduring trend that surveillance cameras are primarily focused on the young and those belonging to particular ethnic minorities (see *inter alia* Norris and Armstrong 1999).

of chemical, biological, radiological and nuclear (CBRN) terrorism or, as one US Health Department official stated, 'Every Olympics event is a potential target of bioterrorism' (Cottrell 2003: 313).

Athens 2004

The Athens 2004 Olympics set out the most expensive, elaborate and extensive security programme ever deployed at the Games. The first post-9/11 summer Olympiad, it provides an exemplar (and possibly the apotheosis) of the 'total security' paradigm. Quintupling Sydney's security costs, $1.5 billion was expended on the Athenian security project (Coaffee and Fussey 2010). In part, some of this unprecedented figure may be accounted for by the limited extant security infrastructure at the time of bidding (when compared to, say, London or Beijing), yet the more direct drivers of this cost can be identified as post-9/11 perceptions of vulnerability and demands for protection from mass-casualty terrorism in addition to the heavy commitment to technological surveillance. Initially, this was borne out by the remarkable levels of international military co-operation and the fact that, as Samatas (2007) noted, one-third of this figure funded electronic surveillance measures. That represented a heavy commitment to preventative measures – a theme at the forefront of Olympic security planning since Montreal.

Dubbed by some the 'Olympic superpanopticon' (Samatas 2007), the Athenian surveillance system was monumental. The flagship development was the C4I ('Command', 'Control', 'Coordination', 'Communications' and 'Integration') programme) (ATHOC 2005, comprising a network of 29 subsystems implemented by the US company, SAIC (see Chapter 2) who had previously worked on the 2002 Winter Olympics. Much of the central focus of this system was on communication between the 135 command centres and the disparate range of security operatives policing the Games. Of the explicitly surveillance-related provisions, the 35 Olympic sites and attendant critical national infrastructure were observed by: an assemblage of thousands of CCTV cameras (estimates range from 1,470 in the official ATHOC (2005) report to almost 13,000 according to Coaffee and Johnston 2008), at least one every 50 metres at Olympic installations; vehicle tracking devices and dedicated CCTV subsystems monitoring roads, motion detectors, underwater sensors guarding Piraeus harbour; deployment of NATO AWACS aircraft; and a leased airship equipped with five cameras that could wirelessly transmit footage to major command centres (Hinds and Vlachou 2007, Samatas 2007). This was complemented by more traditional low-tech information and intelligence gathering strategies. From 2000, a seven-country Olympic Advisory Group facilitated international intelligence sharing (with the UK adopting a co-ordinating role) and the opening of an Olympic Intelligence Centre in the months leading up to the Games (Hinds and Vlachou, 2007).

Beijing 2008

The IOC's decision in July 2001 to award the XXIX Olympiad to Beijing stimulated an unprecedented programme of Olympic-related redevelopment. Although objective statistics on the overall expenditure on the Beijing Games are difficult to verify, estimates suggest that $40 billion was spent upgrading the city's infrastructure with $23 billion of that figure ring-fenced for specific Olympic development (Evans 2007).

Following the awarding of the Games, the Chinese authorities accelerated their acquisition of hi-tech security apparatus. This enabled the deployment of technologically advanced surveillance measures during the Games, including the use of Radio Frequency Identification (RFID) tags in tickets to key events (such as the opening ceremonies) to enable holders' movements to be monitored. Despite these headline-catching technologies, however, the principal emphasis was on developing CCTV networks.[5] This is evidenced by the 2001 launch of the 'Grand Beijing Safeguard Sphere' (running up to the start of the Games in 2008) predominantly focusing on the construct and integration of a city-wide CCTV system covering public and private spaces, which some sources (Security Products 2007) claim has cost over $6 billion. This and related initiatives has led to estimates that Beijing now hosts over 300,000 public CCTV cameras (*inter alia Los Angeles Times* 2008). Also notable is China's recent trend towards hosting international mega-events has driven the deployment surveillance cameras across a number of other cities including Shanghai (relating to 'Expo 2010') and Guangzhou (the 2010 Asian Games). These developments have further catalysed a nationwide 'Safe Cities' programme to establish surveillance cameras in 600 cities (*New York Times* 2007). Overall, such developments, have probably allowed China to claim Britain's dubious accolade of the planet's most intensely observed nation. Moreover, in contrast to the varied hardware quality and often ad hoc (sometimes partially atrophied) networks that constitute many UK systems (see *inter alia* McCahill 2002, Fussey 2007a); the simultaneous deployment of entire networked surveillance infrastructures across China's urban spaces brings a much higher degree of cohesion and hence capacity.

Additionally, it is important to note that Western companies, particularly US technology giants, played a key role in providing much of the technological surveillance apparatus to China. According to *The New York Times* (2007), these include General Electric's Visiowave system, which allowed security personnel simultaneous control of thousands of cameras; a Honeywell system to automatically analyse feeds from cameras deployed at Olympic sites; and a similar IBM system to analyse and catalogue behaviour. What is controversial here is that such transactions can be argued to contravene the spirit (if not the

---

5   Author interviews with CCTV providers for Beijing's 'Bird's Nest' Stadium during April 2008 also confirmed the use of more traditional (albeit high-resolution) CCTV cameras at this location.

letter) of key parts of the Foreign Relations Authorization Act passed by the US Congress in 1990 (colloquially known as the 'Tiananmen Sanctions'). In response to the clampdown and executions connected to the Tiananmen Square protests, this Act prohibited the sale of 'crime control or detection instruments or equipment' to China.

In sum, technological surveillance has been an integral part of Olympic security since Munich 1972, gathering pace in both extent and sophistication since 9/11. Such developments detail the components of the internationalized and standardized security processes to be replayed in London.

Surveilling London for 2012

> London has the most advanced security preparations of any Olympic city...
> Where we can remove the need for people by implementing technology or design, we should. (Lord West, Parliamentary Under-Secretary of State for Security and Counter-terrorism, November, 2009)

The London Olympics will stage the confluence of two broader processes of mega-event securitization that, ultimately, may be coalesced into the Olympic liquid security operation. The first of these are specific trajectories of Olympic security strategies that, as Chapter 2 outlines, transcend temporal, geographical, social, political and cultural boundaries. Together, this constitutes a globalized form of security that may be abstracted and dissociated from the environments that adopt it. For some Olympic cities possessing limited extant security infrastructures when they are awarded the Games (such as Athens in 1997), this stimulates large-scale importation of the materials, mechanisms and motifs of new security orthodoxies. For London, however, the mature, and in many ways pioneering, nature of its security infrastructure, built on decades of experience and experimentation, brings a second process to greater prominence: the lamination and intensification of security mechanisms onto its extant infrastructures.

Laminating London's Surveillance Infrastructure

As Jennings and Lodge (2009) highlight, for Olympic-type events, security arrangements tend to layer-over existing national and international infrastructures or at least those components that fit the standardized security framework (see Coaffee and Fussey 2010). As the head of the 2002 Winter Olympics security operation put it, 'successful security operations are built on what already is in place' (Bellavita 2007: 14). London's oft-accorded status as the most surveilled democratic city in the world (mentioned above) means that an extensive technological surveillance infrastructure currently monitors the capital and, as numerous practitioners attest (*inter alia* Quinten 2009) will by requisitioned to form a key part of the 2012 security ensemble.

Recognizable forms of technological surveillance, such as CCTV, have been permanently deployed in London's public spaces, particularly on Whitehall and around Westminster, since the late 1960s (Williams 2003) and reached saturation point during the 1990s. Here, even a decade ago, economically active Londoners could expect to be filmed by an average of 300 cameras a day (Norris and Armstrong 1999). These developments and their drivers have been extensively discussed elsewhere (*inter alia* Fussey 2007a; Webster 2004) and are thus only given cursory attention here.

'Surveillance 2.0' and the Olympic Boroughs

Such technologies have perhaps been deployed in greatest intensity in London's eastern Olympic territories. Moreover, since the mid-1990s and particularly during the post-Good Friday Agreement[6] and post-9/11 eras potent technologies that had traditionally been 'piloted' in Northern Ireland – such as helicopter monitoring, night vision, sophisticated phone taps and automatic vehicle tracking systems (Matassa and Newburn 2003) have been piloted on East Londoners in the first instance, often in the name of counter-terrorism. Such developments echo Haggerty and Ericson's (2001) concept of 'dual use' technological formats where the capabilities to fulfil military and civil applications are designed into technologies from the outset.[7] Particularly prevalent amongst these later 'martial–metropolitan' technologies have been their asocial and automated forms – 'surveillance 2.0' – such as ANPR, FRCCTV and other 'intelligent' forms of observation.

Because these asocial and automated technologies have been comprehensively discussed elsewhere (*inter alia* Lyon 2003b) as has their deployment across London (*inter alia* Coaffee 2009, Fussey 2007b, 2008), the most notable aspects are only briefly revisited here to enable two distinct points of analysis. The first point is related to the propensity for these technologies to be pioneered into what are generally the poorest areas of London, particularly three of East London's four Olympic boroughs: Tower Hamlets, Hackney and Newham. The potential Olympic intensification of these approaches combined with their likely post-event 'legacy' retention may invest new meaning to the much promoted 'community focused'

---

6   Signed in 1998, the Good Friday Agreement effectively devolved political authority for Northern Ireland to Belfast, leading to a lasting PIRA ceasefire and overall diminution of the attendant conflict.

7   Perhaps the latest example being the deployment of the (potential aneurism-inducing) 'sonic cannon' used to disperse both Iraqi insurgents and the few hundred protesters gathered at Pittsburgh's G20 summit during September 2009 (*The Guardian* 2009a). According to the British Columbia Civil Liberties Association (2009), the Vancouver Police Department acquired a similar appliance with the intention of using it at any protests against the 2010 Winter Games, only to then give assurances that it would not be deployed following pressure from the public and civil liberties groups.

discourse of the 2012 Games. Secondly, these measures constitute surveillance infrastructures that will be co-opted into the wider 2012 security assemblage, particularly in relation to the more populated areas encircling and external to, the Olympic Park.

Following PIRA's bombing of Baltic exchange in St Mary's Axe, City of London, 1992 and the 1993 Bishopsgate bomb, the creation of the City's[8] 'Ring of Steel' fomented a technologically delineated securitized zone that began by monitoring and restricting access to the eastern part of the city (Coaffee 2004). Whilst target-hardening measures such as vehicle routing, parking and access controls altered the urban landscape (see Chapter 5), it was camera surveillance that was viewed by police as being the most important feature of the area's anti-terrorist strategy. All of these were deemed to serve abstract functions (such as 'reassurance') as well as being concrete indicators of security to hesitant investors, tenants and underwriters. Together, these constituted an effort to avoid an exodus that could threaten London's privileged position within global finance markets (Coaffee, Murakami Wood and Rogers 2008). A cornerstone of the surveillance project was the installation of ANPR around the perimeter of the 'Ring of Steel' during 1995.[9] These cameras are able to match vehicle number plates with the identity of drivers, both to verify identity and also raise alarms over any attendant irregularities.

Since the new millennium these cameras have crept across space and function throughout London: ANPR now operates as automated sentries forming a technological boundary surrounding central roads to police London's Congestion Charge.[10] Further afield and demonstrating the perennial 'Janus face' of surveillance (see Lyon 1994), these cameras patrol the wider circumference of Greater London's Low Emission Zone to force owners of high-polluting vehicles to be (substantially) charged for using the capital's roads. Despite this diffusion, ANPR monitoring has noticeably converged eastwards, with the Olympic boroughs of Hackney (Wells 2007) and Tower Hamlets (Coaffee, Murakami Wood and Rogers et al., 2008) hosting distinct concentrations. In the Tower Hamlets, this technology is particularly clustered around Canary Wharf's islands of affluence that, coincidentally, host

---

8   The 'City of London', the 'City', the 'financial district' and the 'square mile' are all labels for the same location and are used interchangeably to describe the small area of to the east of Central London where the majority of its financial industries have traditionally been located. Whilst the 'City of London' is the official name of the local authority administering this space, the 'City' and 'square mile' are commonly used terms.

9   These developments occurred in the midst of a period of rapid and enthusiastic CCTV expansion across Britain, dubbed the 'era of uptake' (Webster 2004). Also of note is the fact that the deployment of the contemporaneously advanced ANPR network occurred during a period of PIRA ceasefire.

10   The congestion charge was instituted in 2003 in an effort to reduce private transport in the centre of the city and raise revenue for public transport initiatives. At present, private cars are charged £8 for entering the city centre during 'peak hours'.

LOCOG and ODA headquarters and are situated geographically, if not socially or culturally, in the Olympic borough of Tower Hamlets.

Other forms of second-generation surveillance strategies – particularly those designed to overcome fallible human attention spans by automatically 'identifying' phenomena deemed suspicious – have also been tested on East Londoners. One notable example first piloted at Mile End Underground station (Tower Hamlets) during 2003 is the Intelligent Passenger Surveillance (IPS) programme that automatically overlays live CCTV feeds onto 'ideal' images (such as an empty platform after a train has departed) and alerts operators of any 'suspicious discrepancies' (such as discarded luggage). Another less-publicized example was the 2006 experimentation with Ipsotek's microphone-equipped cameras in Shoreditch (Hackney) to monitor activity surrounding its thriving night-time economy. Here, manufacturers claimed that they had developed algorithms to distinguish between human screams of pleasure and distress and could automatically alert CCTV operators to the latter – a claim that convinced municipal CCTV managers to allow its deployment into public spaces (Lack 2007) yet arguably presents a rather over-deterministic conception of human action.

Perhaps the most striking use of technology in London's Olympic boroughs has been Newham council's deployment of FRCCTV throughout the 1990s. Widespread networked CCTV coverage was introduced comparatively late into

Figure 7.1   Advertising FRCCTV in Stratford

the area and is more prominently associated with one of the earlier attempts to regenerate Stratford, Newham, during 1995s Stratford City Challenge scheme, which is also at the heart of current 2012-related construction. Conforming to the later Mayor of London Ken Livingstone's approach of developing transport capabilities as the vanguard of subsequent regeneration, the Stratford City Challenge combined upgraded mass transit infrastructures (including work on a new underground line and agreements to link the area to the international cross-channel Eurostar rail network) with investment in local business. In an area that had been unable to escape the label of 'dangerousness' that has historically afflicted much of East London (see Chapter 3), this regeneration stimulated a large deployment of CCTV.[11] FRCCTV followed soon after with the introduction of 300 cameras into the area (*The Guardian* 2002).[12] Officially deployed to counter crime and threats from PIRA, the cameras became operational during 1998, the same year as the Good Friday Agreement that effectively led to the demilitarization of PIRA. It is also important to recognize that Newham's FRCCTV scheme has been controversial. Critics have particularly emphasized the lack of evidence supporting its effectiveness (see *The Guardian* 2002). Following Britain's tradition of committing vast public resources towards technological forms of crime control without sufficient understanding of their capabilities, Newham's flawed FRCCTV system (Visionic's FaceIT scheme) has nevertheless been deployed in other urban centres across the UK, most notably in Birmingham city centre. The difficulties associated with these technologies are explored in more detail below.

'Olympic additionality'

So far, this discussion has demonstrated the considerable scale and sophistication of surveillance infrastructures already operational across East London. However, with the Olympic policing and wider security budget comprising a £600 million 'envelope' with a further £238 million 'contingency'[13] (Raine 2009), bolstered by

---

11 This incorporation of CCTV networks into regeneration projects has been a key feature of urban planning since the 1990s (Coleman 2005; Fussey 2007b).

12 It could be argued that Newham was by no means the first place to experiment with FRCCTV. As Lyon (2003b) noted, the technology has been deployed in numerous controlled spaces, particularly airports (specifically, across Canada, Iceland and into Boston's Logan Airport). In the UK, according to Simon Davies (1996), a prototype version was trialled at Manchester City's former Maine Road Stadium during the mid-1990s, although problems of file compression and subsequent recourse to manually matching photographs to CCTV feeds means this technology was perhaps not as advanced as many commentators and surveillance enthusiasts suggest. Nevertheless, what is interesting about Newham's use of FRCCTV is its deployment in 'uncontrolled' public spaces.

13 One practitioner interviewed by the authors stated that this figure had been revised downwards from an initial proposal of a £1 billion security operation due to limitations on public finances (unattributable source). Of further note is the statement by the Olympic budget is not 'sacrosanct' new Tory Culture minister on his first day in office (*The Guardian*

the incalculable investment entangled amongst the large-scale redevelopment of East London, this indicates a considerable intensification of the area's security framework.

Tender approaches: Procuring Olympic surveillance technologies   Since these foundations have been embedded, private contractors have been invited by the ODA to construct additional and substantial security infrastructures for 2012 via a series of tenders. The first round of these tenders was launched during 2007. This enabled private sector projects to be collated into the consolidated government 2012 security plan developed and finalized during 2008–09 (Home Office 2009b) and thus made it possible to identify the direction of resources within the wider strategy.

These tenders serve as important documents. They articulate the way private sector security contractors are steered towards the key concerns of stakeholders, their desired strategic ambitions and indicate the direction of resources within the 2012 security project. Initially they reveal the intended procurement of private security apparatus in several operational and geographical contexts, each underpinned by a commitment to technology. Concentrating on the 'Island Site' itself (the Olympic Park at Stratford), resources were particularly disseminated towards 'access control systems' (ACS), 'searching and screening', 'command, control and integration' and 'security guarding' (ODA 2007b). To achieve this, the tenders offer steered towards the provision of technological solutions for these problem areas, including the provision of 'ACS comprising RFID token and biometric[s]', a 'combination of technology and physical searching' and 'CCTV, security lighting systems and intruder detection systems to be [established,] integrated with, and form a part of, the perimeter security' (ODA 2007b). The tenders also encouraged suppliers to offer strategies that 'create an integrated security environment that is effective, discrete and proportionate' (ODA 2007b). This focus illustrates the likelihood of a particular climate being generated that favours the deployment of specific technological strategies.

Overall, two further embedded processes were revealed. First, these tenders demonstrate ambitions to provide technologies that bleed across the temporal and spatial boundaries of the Olympic site. Secondly, the continual emphasis on the construction of a secure 'Island Site' (ODA 2007b) is both echoed in other official 2012 discourse (London 2012 2009, Johnston 2009, Quinten 2009) and builds on London's prior experiments with technologically delineated spaces of exception (see Chapter 6). Indeed, perimeter security has now become a key feature of the overall Olympic security plan, particularly given the IOC's request to fence off 2012 sporting venues (see Chapter 5). In doing so, the Island Site's boundaries will be protected by an instituted Command Perimeter Security System (CPSS)

2010d). However, whilst the overall ODA budget has emerged relatively unscathed, the wider policing costs have not (see Chapter 4).

Figure 7.2   CCTV at the perimeter of the Olympic Park

Figure 7.3   Olympic CCTV signage near Hackney Wick

placing CCTV at its heart (ODA 2009). Moreover, the ODA has further indicated that 2012 Olympic CCTV deployment will reflect the configurations of what are perhaps the most intensely monitored and securitized public spaces: airports. More specifically, given the ODA is designing the Olympic Park CCTV network based on recommendations outlined by the government enquiry into airport security following 9/11 (the 'Wheeler Report'[14]), its surveillance capabilities are likely to be powerful and intense (see ODA, 2009 for explicit parallels). Such internal divisions amid a larger securitized space are also reminiscent of Bigo's (2005) characterization of the 'ban-opticon' as mechanism of regulating entitlement and access.

Drone in transition   Perhaps the most controversial deployment of surveillance technology is the use of Unmanned Aerial Vehicles (UAVs), often referred to as 'drones', to patrol the skies above the Games (see Chapter 5). Their proposed use first came to public attention through a 2009 article in The Guardian (2009a) revealing how their initial remit to tackle maritime-related offences had expanded to cover a range of land-based policing activities, including major event security. The results of a subsequent Freedom of Information (FOI) request to Kent Police (2010),[15] however, provides substantive detail on the planning and scope of this initiative.

Comprising a coalition of law enforcement agencies (including Kent Police, Essex Police, the UK Borders Agency and the National Police Improvement Agency) and private sector interests (British Aerospace), the 'South Coast Partnership' became established to pursue a national UAV strategy (Minutes of South Coast

---

14   The 2002 'Wheeler Report' into airport security reviewed extant provisions, considered the impact of the 9/11 attacks in the US and suggested procedural, infrastructure and legislative changes that needed to be made. The report contained a number of recommendations regarding governance and procedure at UK airports (highlighting existing structures as 'inadequate'). In relation to surveillance, it argued for more integrated systems and the wider use of new technologies such as ANPR (see Wheeler 2002).

15   An individual by the name of Marie Koenigsberger made this FOI request in response to the article in The Guardian (2009a). The authors arc grateful to Charles Farrier for making us aware of this source. The following discussion on UAVs draws on seven of the documents made public by this FOI request. All are accessible from whatdotheyknow. com/request/south_coast_partnership_drone_do. The South Coast Partnership, which was formally launched at the Police Aviation Conference in November 2007 at The Hague, is a loose coordination between several police forces in respect to the provision of air support services and also includes other government agencies including the Border and Immigration Agency (Kent Police 2010). Most of the documents discussed here are themselves contained in the Kent Police Freedom of Information Disclosure (2010) but are referred to separately as: South Coast Partnership (2007), Watson (2007), Cambridgeshire, Essex and Suffolk Police Air Support (2008), Thomas (2009) and ACPO (n.d.); BAe (2008) is Appendix 1 to the main disclosure document.

Partnership Meeting, 2007). In the course of this process, a number of options have been considered ranging from military 'High Endurance Rapid Technology Insertion' (HERTI) vehicles, similar to those currently deployed in Afghanistan, to more lightweight 'mini-airship' machines. Of the latter, BAe Systems' (BAe) GA22 is currently viewed as the most likely model for deployment, its advantage being diminutive size. At the time of writing, UAVs under 7 kilograms are not subject to Civil Aviation Authority (CAA) (the body that regulates the use of UK airspace) oversight (CAA 2009), thus enabling the GA22 to avoid being subject to an additional set of regulatory instruments.

Although small, the GA22s surveillance capabilities are potent. Its specific components can be gleaned from prescribed operational requirements outlined by an ACPO Air Support Working Group 'Statement of Requirements for Unmanned Aerial Systems' (ACPO n.d.). Here, in addition to restating the need for sub-7 kilogram machines, ACPO stipulate the need for UAVs to be easily transportable; be equipped with a camera capable of a minimum of 25x optical zoom and, also, thermal imaging; fitted with microphone; and possessing automatic camera targeting capabilities (so a camera can remain trained on a particular subject irrespective of the UAV's movements) (ACPO n.d.). A December 2008 BAe presentation to the South Coast Partnership also accented the GA22's capabilities in networking disparate elements of security ensembles together (BAe 2008).[16] Given such capabilities, it is unsurprising that police-operated UAVs have been considered for myriad applications. Among these, 'event security' is continually mentioned in both the minutes of South Coast Partnership stakeholder meetings (see, for example, South Coast Partnership 2007) and in email communications between its members. One early example can be taken from an email between the police and the CAA during 2008 which stated:

> following discussions with BAE Systems it has been identified that the GA22 may fulfil a useful operational policing function at large public events. In particular Essex Police are responsible for policing the Virgin (V) festival [a major UK music festival] … each August and it is perceived that the GA22 may have a role to play in such an event. (Cambridgeshire, Essex and Suffolk Police Air Support 2008)

Given the auspicious deadline to complete pre-operational testing by 2012, it is clear the London Games are an intended site for deployment. Indeed, this point was clearly expressed by Kent Police Assistant Chief Constable (Special Operations) Allyn Thomas in an email to the CAA Flight Operations Inspectorate:

---

16   A report by *The Daily Mail* (2009) also made unsourced claims that police-operated UAVs are capable of dispersing 'SmartWater' (a unique chemical compound that allows specific suspects to be tracked with appropriate sensors) onto its subjects.

such a system also has considerable potential in the policing of major events, whether they be protests or the Olympics ... I write to seek your support in that there is rather more urgency in the work since [the 2008 terrorist attacks at] Mumbai and we have a clear deadline of the 2012 Olympics. (Thomas 2009)

Such statements unequivocally mark the influence of the Games on the escalation of technological security strategies.[17]

Despite these developments, the current legal landscape surrounding UAVs is contested. However, throughout the South Coast Partnership's planning process there appears to have been an acknowledgement that existing restrictions on the licensing of such aircraft covering urban and populated areas are 'with advances in technology ... expected to be eased over the next 2–3 years' (Watson 2007: 11). Given a recent deployment of similar technology in Liverpool to chase a suspected car thief stimulated a CAA investigation into illegal use of UK airspace by the Merseyside Police (see *The Guardian* 2010b), this relaxation of regulations has yet to occur.

Aside from these privacy-related concerns, this use of UAVs raises additional ethical issues over the governance of law enforcement. Private-sector incursions in the state's delivery of social control have often courted controversy. In this case, the fact that Freedom of Information disclosure over the use of UAVs was mediated by whether it may 'adversely affect Law Enforcement or the legitimate Commercial Interests of third parties such as BAE systems' (Kent Police 2010: 1) indicates the interconnectivity of these sectors. As such, critics have questioned the appropriateness of the potential for these aircraft to undertake additional commercial work to mitigate their overall running costs (*The Guardian* 2009a).

Intensive preparations   To manage the intensified security assemblage, many disparate technological strategies are pulled together in the Metropolitan Police's newly constructed Special Operations Room, a CCTV command centre in Lambeth, South London, inaugurated in 2007. This facility, the largest of its kind in the capital, was ostensibly designed to oversee the security of major events such as the Notting Hill Carnival and large sporting events including the London Marathon and, ultimately, the Olympics. Building on notions of 'nodal governance', this development potentially could be seen in terms of 'nodal security'. Drawing on Castells' (2000) characterization of nodes as the points of confluence for overlapping networks, 'nodal governance' has been developed conceptual tool for understanding how these nodes then exert their influence (see inter alia Burris, Drahos and Shearing 2005). These sites have been characterized as comprising four features: mentalities (mechanisms for thinking about the governed subject/network); technologies (methods for exercising influence);

---

17   According to *The Guardian* (2010a), Olympic-related UAV surveillance has already occurred at the 'Olympic Handover Party' in Central London during 2008.

resources (the means to enable its operation); and institutions (to marshal the mentalities, technologies and resources). The Lambeth control room serves as a conduit, arguably comprising these four elements, in which surveillance footage from the control centres of 32 other London boroughs is filtered. As the network expands, new nodes will arise via the forthcoming development of two similar facilities, one in Hendon, North-West London, and the other in Bow, in the heart of the East End, close to the Olympic Park. Underlining the prominence of terrorism within this definition of 'security' is the integration of the Metropolitan Police's 'Gold Command' (the largely terrorism-focused policing body with overall control of strategy and resources) into the strategic and operational management of this facility, where they are empowered to immediately seize control of the centre during any major incidents.

Partly stimulated by fears of a spatially displaced terrorist attack, security measures will also soak through the 'Island Site's' borders to enable new forms of technological security to permeate both local and regional areas. London authorities will be using advanced surveillance technologies to track suspects across the city. One related proposal here is a ticket trafficking system, which would allow spectators to be tracked from their home (facilitated by the proposed combined entrance and transport ticket) (see for example BBC 2008b).

Similar to the Athenian Olympic security programme, there is substantial investment towards upgrading communications technologies in time for the 2012 Games. This will largely involve a £39 million investment in radio communication for 'blue light' (police, fire and ambulance) agencies that will feed into the existing Airwave network by 2012 (West 2009).[18] The system is also designed to overcome a number of problems afflicting police communications which, historically, have included the lack of secured bandwidth and, perhaps most crucially, limitations on communicating underground (as occurred during the emergency operation following the 7 July bombings, see GLA 2006). Nevertheless, Airwave has been beset by a number of documented operational difficulties, most notably a reported reduced reliability within buildings and from moving vehicles. It is unevenly deployed (GLA 2006). Other difficulties include the extent to which the technology will by rolled-out across the 2012 security ensemble. For example, many non-police, 'civilian' CCTV control rooms are currently not connected to the technology. Other issues include the coalescence of technological infrastructures into a potential single point of failure. More social and operational factors are also relevant, such as common usage strategies and shared forms of expression across different agencies (see below for further discussion on the social environment of technology and related co-ordination issues).

---

18   Airwave is a terrestrial trunked radio (TETRA) system designed with the aim of providing a resilient and common form of communication across different emergency services throughout mainland Britain. Developed by a private company, Airwave Solutions Limited, the technology is leased by the National Police Improvement Agency (NPIA).

From clouds to orbit Accompanying the geographic spread of Olympic surveillance is its potential creep into other 2012 infrastructure. One of the 'legacies' of the Games is a tourist-friendly centrepiece for the Olympic Park. Of the designs reaching the final shortlist was a conspicuous commitment towards augmenting East London's skyline. One particularly attractive candidate was the Digital Cloud (with the tagline 'Broadcasting the Climate of Humanity', see The Cloud 2009). Drawing on postmodern architectural concepts, The Cloud was to comprise a 120-metre tower topped by a series of interlinked transparent spheres (see BBC 2009). These serve a dual function, as an observation deck and a screen to display images and data. The eventual winner, Anish Kapoor and Cecil Balmond's 'Orbit' – a 'vast, snaking steel structure' according to The Guardian (2010c) – is another soaring monument, also 120 metres tall.

London has a long history of capitalizing on 'latent surveillance': investing surveillance measures into potential sites of accommodation. Here, it is not difficult to conceive that such monuments may adopt a dual function of both tourist attraction and surveillance utility. Keenly marketed as an object of 'legacy' for locals by the Mayor of London, the Orbit will be visible from across east London and, by implication, provide a platform whereby the gaze may be returned.

In sum, the confluence of recent security trends in the capital alongside the particular aims of 2012 Olympic security programme creates a climate that elevates the prominence of technological surveillance strategies. Indeed, the ODA's (2007) call for suppliers to offer strategies that 'create an integrated security environment that is effective, discrete and proportionate' echoes the IOC's aforementioned aim giving primacy to the sporting, rather than security, spectacle. What is significant in the context of Olympic security is that 'discretion' and 'proportionality' have often translated into distanciated forms of technological control. As further evidence, this policy direction was confirmed by the then head of the 2012 security strategy, Assistant Commissioner Tarique Ghaffur, as follows: 'One of the main issues will be technology vs people … An event of this scale means technology plays a bigger part in the look and feel of the games and means surveillance will be a major issue that will likely cause debate' (Games Monitor 2007b).

Cumulatively, these approaches both harmonize with and reproduce the standardized *sine qua non*s of Olympic security outlined in Chapter 2 and also, reassert London's tradition of applying technological strategies to 'separated spaces' to tackle crime, terrorism and other risks.

Securing The Olympiad through Technology: Critique and Analysis

Surveillance comprises a key element of the DNA of Olympic security. As the process of centralizing surveillance is reproduced in a series of Olympic cities, a number of inherited errors also recur in successive incarnations and generations. The following discussion presents an analysis of the overarching operational and critical issues germane to 2012. This is conducted over two main areas of discussion. First, it will consider debates around technical capabilities. Second, it will be argued that the efficacy of these initiatives is principally governed by the operational and social contexts within which they are deployed.

Supplying Security: Failures and Technicalities

Since the widespread deployment of CCTV in the UK during the early 1990s, considerable debate has raged over whether its promises of security and crime reduction have ultimately been realized. The debate has taken many forms and been played out in many settings, and is thus too large and multifaceted to be afforded more than cursory attention here (see *inter alia* Welsh and Farrington 2002, Gill and Spriggs 2005, Fussey 2008). For proponents, CCTV provides one or more of many potential and versatile multiple applications, primarily in terms of its deterrent and detection capabilities. However, critics have pointed out that the potential for surveillance to work does not necessarily translate into its actual efficacy (for example, see Tilley 1998). Moreover, even though CCTV may be applicable in many contexts, its performance is unlikely to play out equally over all tasks. In sum, like many crime control strategies, the evidence is ambivalent and, as Tilley (1998: 140) noted, 'mixed findings are the norm'. With regard to terrorism, as Fussey (2007b) noted, it is arguable that CCTV has been more potent in tackling right-wing extremism than violent jihadi extremism (which, in itself is not a static entity).

The contrast between a theoretically effective technological security intervention and its more mixed operational outcome is more pronounced for second-generation technologies. Their limitations largely relate to the same attempted reduction of complex social phenomena (such as behaviour) into amenable, quantifiable categories (governable by algorithms) that has eluded criminologists, and indeed behaviourists of many genres, for centuries. Other difficulties include generating extraneous data, privacy issues, the threshold of 'suspicion' and difficulties in mounting the technology into already functioning networks.

Whilst much of the opposition to these technologies has centred around privacy issues, another pressing debate concerns operational limitations. One of the initial problems with second-generation surveillance strategies is their lack of neutrality. As Introna and Wood (2004) note, in the case of FRCCTV, for example, certain biases are built into the algorithms governing their function. Amongst these is the tendency for the cameras to be more adept at identifying individuals from particular demographic groups, depending on age, race and gender. In particular, older people are more easily detected than younger people, males more than females and those belonging to East Asian and African demographics are more easily identified than white populations.

Broader problems concern the gulf in capability between *confirming* an identity (for example, at an airport check-in) and using this technology to *establish* an identity (for example, picking out a face in the crowd) (Lyon 2004). Such difficulties are evident across public space experiments with FRCCTV. Tampa's post-Super Bowl FRCCTV system (in Ybor City) in 2001, for example, never identified a single individual on its database. This led to its abandonment within three months of operation (ACLU 2002), an issue that received considerably less media coverage than the promises accompanying its initial installation. Other failures in the US (along the US–Mexican border) led to the technology being rejected at the first post 9/11 Olympics, at Salt Lake City. Questions also exist over the proportionality of these strategies. Indeed, in relation to the use of FRCCTV and sport, behind the headline that 19 individuals were 'flagged' by the cameras patrolling Tampa's Raymond James Stadium is the fact that some were false alarms and none had committed anything more serious than ticket touting (ACLU 2002).

One of the central factors governing the effectiveness of FRCCTV is its sensitivity. To generate higher numbers of matches between what the camera observes and its archived images, it needs to be calibrated in a way that lowers the threshold for 'identifications'. The obvious consequence of this, however, is an exponential increase in incorrect identifications – or 'false positives' (FRVT 2006). The incidence of 'false positives' sizeably outstrips the number of 'true positives' (FRVT 2006), a phenomenon that subverts the original resource-saving *raison d'être* of automated filtering and FRCCTV. It also aggravates one of the key tensions of Olympic security: the management of exponential data generation. As a corollary, increased 'false positives' place additional scrutiny upon innocent people.

In the 2012 Olympic neighbourhood, the impact of this can be observed in the reception of low-tech police 'stop and search' strategies amongst East London's suspect communities. Controversy accompanied FRCCTV in the Olympic borough of Newham. Whilst numerous claims were made that crime dropped significantly in the years following its installation in the late 1990s (in fact, mirroring the direction of national crime trends), a more complex set of issues exist. The first is that many of these claims, such as the declaration that burglary in Newham had declined by 72 per cent between 1999 and 2002 (NIJ 2003), are simply false. Moreover, when compared to the neighbouring Olympic borough of Tower Hamlets, many crimes such as robbery had increased at a faster rate in Newham immediately following the introduction of FRCCTV (*The Guardian* 2002).[19] Crime reductions were also expressed misleadingly. For example, in an unpublished internal report into the effectiveness of CCTV (not FRCCTV) in Newham, an impressive-sounding 39 per cent drop in robberies in one particular area masked a reduction of just 14 recorded offences overall (Langstone 2009). Other equally possible explanations could be a prolific offender being arrested or moving to a different area. Such alternative accounts are often absent in evaluations of popular crime control strategies. There are also difficulties in attributing any fluctuations in crime to specific FRCCTV interventions. Particularly striking is the admission of a Newham police officer, with oversight of the local authority's installation of FRCCTV, that the system had never identified a single individual on its database (interviewed in *The Guardian* 2002). An additional problem is the tendency for any surveillance-related successes to be

---

19 Also notable here is that the short 'bedding in' period immediately following CCTV installation is considered by many to be its most effective time (see *inter alia* Tilley 1998).

attributed to FRCCTV. One example, linking the borough's FRCCTV and sport, is an episode in which surveillance cameras assisted the identification and informed denied entry to 12 individuals with Banning Orders[20] into the Boleyn Ground in Newham to watch a Premier League match between West Ham and Leeds United (NIJ 2003). Although FRCCTV was implicated in this operation and lauded as a great 'success' on the basis that 'humans alone could not easily have accomplished such a massive task' according to the borough's CCTV manager (NIJ 2003), it was the more laborious (human) CCTV observation (not FRCCTV) of nearby Upton Park Underground station that was the actual vehicle of identification.

Of these second-generation systems, it is perhaps ANPR that is the most straightforward and effective. Here, scanned images are supplemented with a wealth of additional information. Such cameras penetrate far beyond the visibility of the observed image of a number plate. Whilst proponents point to its utility in tracking suspects and identifying stolen vehicles (Wells 2007), ANPR has also attracted criticism beyond the legions of motorists reluctant to pay for using the capital's roads. In particular, concerns have been raised both over the irrevocable change in what constitutes 'reasonable suspicion' (Nunn 2003) and ANPR's propensity to drain police resources. Regarding the former, the argument is that these cameras have inaugurated a shift away from targeted suspicion and towards an environment where anyone passing through is an object of mistrust, regardless of any preceding action or categorical label. Critics say that this process has transformed the dynamics of how suspicion is projected and received;[21] and analysis here has some resonance with beleaguered Foucauldian characterizations of surveillance. Practical problems also afflict such technologies. In London, large shortfalls caused by the labour required to review the exponential increase in surveillance data generated by these cameras led the Police Authority to request an increase in the Police precept (the quota of council tax revenues apportioned to resource the police) (*The Times* 2008a).

Overall, aspirational claims for second-generation surveillance are not matched by its (at best) mixed results in practice. In turn, such system failures may potentially induce new insecurities and complicate the social and operational contexts in which they are deployed.

---

20   Football Banning Orders involve a suite of potential sanctions applied to those deemed likely to cause violent disruption at football matches in England and Wales. They generally last between two and ten years, normally prohibit entrance to football grounds but may include other provisions such as preventing its subject from visiting particular locations (such as particular bars or transport hubs) on match days.

21   In the US, the Supreme Court has challenged this net-widening strategy. It held in the case of *Kyllo* v US 533 U.S. 27 (2001), which had resulted in a conviction for growing marijuana in a loft, that the police use of undirected thermal imaging scans amounted to an 'unauthorised warrantless search' (Nunn 2003).

The Social Context of Technology

Technology does not operate in a vacuum. Instead, its operation and efficacy are determined in relation to the human contexts with which they function. In the context of security, such uncertain human influences stretch along the entire surveillance continuum from the surveyors to the surveyed. With regard to its subjects, new technologies affect human behaviour in new and often unpredictable ways. One illustrative terrorism-related example is the PIRA's dialectical responses to the British government's attempts to curtail remote bomb detonations. These culminated in the PIRA's use of photographic flash 'slave units' (Hoffman 1994), a measure that, by the end of the conflict, had yet to be countered effectively. The dynamic relationship between technology and human action serves to illustrate how the utopian claims of technological solutions to terrorism need to be treated with caution.

For surveyors, the operational and social context of technological strategies has consistently mediated the provision of Olympic security. What is more, as Decker et al. note, it is this social environment that gains unexpected prominence in difficult circumstances. 'Security networks and organizations have a technical and cultural side. Simply focussing on the technical side may miss the important part, the cultural side and this is likely to become the default response in times of stress and crisis' (2005: 73).

In seeking to understand this issue, it can be argued that a dual dynamic is at play. There are technological failures that stimulate human responses and there are human responses that induce technological failures. These are now explored in the following discussion. Here, four key tensions continually affecting the technological provision of Olympic security are identified and examined: 1) established applications vs. innovation; 2) the technological reinforcement of inter-agency barriers; 3) overload and rising thresholds of action; and 4) socio-ethical issues.

Established applications vs. Innovation　Showcasing new (and potentially untested) security technologies during the short period of Olympic events can prove labour-intensive and costly, and might ultimately undermine the Games' security agenda. In addition to the novelty of some of the technological resources, their concentration into one arena has proved problematic during numerous Olympiads. As the security co-ordinator for Salt Lake City put it, 'Relying too much on a specific technology can also create a single point of failure ... The experiential evidence about the usefulness of innovative technology is fairly one sided. The technology rarely performs as promised or as designed' (Bellavita 2007: 15).

It is the area of communications equipment – the principle technological investment for London 2012 – that has been the most fallible. The emergency response to a collapsed bridge one hour before the opening ceremony of the 1994

FIFA World Cup demonstrates this point. When responders arrived at the scene to extract injured spectators, many realized they lacked the experience and expertise to operate the new state-of-the-art radios they had been provided with for the event (Bellavita 2007: 15). Additionally, parachuting existing technologies into new environments has also proved problematic. At the 2002 Winter Olympics in Salt Lake City sophisticated communications technology supplied by federal agencies failed to work in Utah's mountainous terrain (Decker et al. 2005).

Perhaps the most notable failure of Olympic security technology was at Athens 2004. Despite being the most technologically sophisticated security system ever deployed at an Olympics, and being supplied by a company (SAIC) that had trialled and operated systems at two previous Games (Sydney and Salt Lake City), the technological component of the Athens security operation was severely flawed. These failures were articulated not only by the Greek government when seeking judicial arbitration for SAIC's failure to complete work nearly four years after the 2004 Games ended (Samatas 2007) but also by the provider's own admission of their 'poor performance' (Bartlett and Steele 2007).[22]

Athens' Olympic security system experienced difficulties from the start. The combination of a convoluted open tender process and delays from local construction and telecommunications companies meant that the contract was not awarded until eight months after work was due to commence. Following this, the physical command centres were largely completed on time but, fatally, the software that managed the communications and governed the integration of security failed. Part of the issue related to capacity – despite 800 operators registered to use the C4I (Command, Control, Co-ordination, Communication and Intelligence) system, technical reports indicated that, if more than 80 logged on at the same time, the system crashed, thus rendering it 'operationally useless' (cited in Samatas 2007: 228). What is perhaps more significant is the human and social response to this technological failure. For example, officials supplemented the network by adding more guards and the Greek military, in(correctly) anticipating that the C4I system would not be fully operational in time, deployed its own communication systems (Samatas 2007: 228).

An important operational point related to the relationship of human innovation and technological networks reappears here: technological failures may represent not just the unfortunate denial of an additional service but also incur additional risks. Such risks have escalated in the contemporary technologically saturated post-9/11 era of Olympic security and demonstrate the value of grounding Olympic security strategies within existing and reliable systems.

Technology and the reinforcement of inter-agency barriers The exceptional, temporary and collaborative nature of Olympic security inevitably generates inter-agency tensions. However, the introduction of technology into this milieu

---

22   Bartlett and Steele (2007) argue that this resulted in SAIC losing $123 million on the project.

consistently results in the reflection, amplification and reinforcement of any fractures in these pan-organizational relationships.

In the first instance, institutional tensions have been a consistent part of police and intelligence work for generations. With regard to the Olympics, the best-documented examples can be drawn from the two most recent Games held in the US – at Salt Lake City and Atlanta. In Utah, many agencies were reticent in passing intelligence information across institutional boundaries whilst others displayed a tendency to devalue intelligence received from other, often unfamiliar, security organizations (Decker et al. 2005). Tensions also existed between major security providers, with the Department of Defense appearing unwilling to support the 2002 Winter Olympic security operation until a swift *volte face* following 9/11. The late arrival of such a major player then proceeded to cause considerable organizational and co-ordination difficulties. Problems also existed between disparate private sector organizers and the willingness of the Utah Olympic Public Safety Command to respond to their concerns over national infrastructure protection (The Oquirrh Institute 2002). At the same time, tensions surfaced between federal and government-level agencies, on the one hand, and the (largely rural) incumbent regional police, whom were largely regarded as 'a collection of well meaning, but naive hicks' (Bellavita 2007: 12). In sum, even in Olympic security operations that are deemed highly successful, such as at Salt Lake City, significant tensions between security providers inevitably surface (particularly given unavoidable contestations over resources and status) and remain a substantial obstacle.

Once technological methods of inter-agency 'integration' are introduced to these splintered organizational settings, the fractures increase. This is particularly germane to communication technologies, particularly given their tendency to amplify variations in occupational culture and limitations in technological aptitude. The range of these difficulties was highlighted by the head of the Salt Lake City security operation. He explained:

> even with six years of planning, Department of Defense and Secret Service radios interfered with each other. The Olympic Organizing Committee sold some of its frequency to an international ski team and the frequency interfered with public safety communications. Encrypted radios had a difficult time communicating with non-encrypted radios. Some agencies used coded voice communications; others used plain English. Some disciplines used radios for succinct communications; others used the radio to chat. Those are just a few of the *radio* communication problems. There were analogous technological and human factors difficulties with video, telephone, internet and other modes of communication. (Bellavita 2007: 17)

Such difficulties had been even more pronounced at Atlanta six years earlier. Occurring prior to the Clinton administration's creation of National Special Security Event (NSSE) status to clarify roles and responsibilities during major events, the Atlanta Olympics staged fierce conflicts key security agencies. These conflicts acquired further resonance owing to the decentralized nature of Atlanta's overall Olympic planning. The most serious fault lines occurred between the State Olympic Law Enforcement Command (SOLEC) – roughly equivalent to London's Olympic Security Directorate – and the Atlanta Olympic Organizing Committee (ACOG). Key clashes included ACOG's downward revision of the Games' security funding by around 25 per cent amid accusations that it was balancing its budget by cutting security, an action that lead Atlanta police to threaten a withdrawal of their support for the Games (Buntin 2000a). Other co-ordination problems also surfaced. These included the considerable underestimation of volunteer absenteeism (predicated on 10 per cent, with actual levels nearer 20 per cent, Buntin 2000b), a level that increased further still after the Centennial Park attack. Perhaps most notorious was the failure of the Atlanta Police Department to rapidly convey news of the discovery of Eric Rudolph's (see Chapter 2) suspicious backpack to SOLEC. More specifically, these events surrounded the telephoned bomb threat (to the APD 911 dispatcher), giving an overestimated 30 minutes' notice. Despite being the most significant sporting event ever hosted in that region, a combination of the operator's difficulty in spelling 'Centennial Park' and the Park's absence from the 911 dispatch system resulted in a full 20 minutes elapsing before the 30 minute threat was conveyed to SOLEC.

In common with all other Olympiads since Munich 1972 (see Chapter 2), technologically-assisted perimeter and access security was a central feature of Atlanta's security strategy. Here, the competing priorities of ACOG, who gave primacy to enhancing the flow of visitors through the perimeter, and SOLEC, who emphasized more exacting levels of security, came into conflict via ACOG's refusal to apply SOLEC's heightened 'Secret Service' level settings to the metal detectors at venue entrances. Instead, ineffectually low thresholds were applied at these sites, generating yet more friction as Mike Eason, venue security planner for the Games recalls: 'It was almost like the security was just a show as opposed to real security. [W]e wanted [the machines] to at least detect an AK-47. [W]e wanted security and ACOG didn't' (cited in Buntin 2000b: 5).

It is unclear whether these were the security lapses that allowed an armed man posing as a security guard to attend the opening ceremony (see Chapter 2). Nevertheless, such incidents are germane to the security of the 2012 Games. In the first instance, these competing priorities between access and security remain and, given the record number of private and voluntary security agents due to police 2012, associated tensions may even escalate. Indeed, the division of labour in this specific area of perimeter access security is likely to be repeated, with minimally waged private-sector operators staffing the laborious 'mag and bag' (use of magnetic detectors to search visitors' bags) duties in London (Evans 2010). Also echoing the experiences of Atlanta and Salt Lake City, friction has surfaced between military and policing agencies, which became public during January 2009 when the incoming Commander-in-Chief of Britain's land forces, General Sir David Richards, strongly criticized the Home Office over delays to the 2012 security plan, arguing that it hindered the provision of an already-stretched military capacity. When asked by the Parliamentary Defence Select Committee, 'What keeps you awake at night?', he replied '2012. If we do have to retrain, create new units, IED [improvised explosive device] specialists, all that sort of thing, the sooner we get clarity the better' (*The Times* 2009). Given that the Metropolitan Police Assistant Commissioner for the Olympic and Paralympic Games has stated that London 2012 will be a 'blue games' (Allison 2009) – that is, the primacy of blue light emergency services over the military and other agencies – there is potential for such tensions to continue.

Risk, overload and thresholds of action   The unprecedented scale of Olympic surveillance operations raises two further issues related to operational efficacy: risk identification and overload thresholds for action. Risks are diverse and many. Further questions are generated over the way in which these risks are interpreted and acted upon. Initially, specific risk-averse approaches adopted by both the IOC and domestic Olympic organizing committees harbour inherent tensions between the ambitious aspirations of these mega-events and the overarching commitment to risk mitigation and regulation (Jennings 2010). At the same time, numerous biases and errors are built into the initial mechanisms of risk calculation. Perhaps most notable amongst these are the 'beautiful fictions' of Olympic bid documents (as former IOC Vice-President Dick Pound puts it (cited in Jennings 2010)) that frame present utopian simplifications of Olympic socio-security environments.

At the same time, Beck's (1992) paradox that instituting new methods identifying risks itself generates new risks is applicable here. In the first instance, risks are increasingly anthropogenic (Beck 1999, 2002), radiating from human (rather than natural) origins and thus arguably less quantifiable. The commitment to acting on all and any significant risks to the 2012 Games identified by the OSSSRA mechanism (see Chapter 5) is likely to place further and considerable demands on London's security agencies. As technological surveillance infrastructures expand and these new conceptual mechanisms for identifying and capturing additional risks[23] are implemented, available information increases exponentially. Empirical work examining the decision-making processes surrounding counter-terrorism intelligence work in the UK, for example, demonstrates how this ultimately elevates the threshold for what is deemed significant and hence requiring action

---

23   This unearthing of additional Olympic risks does not diminish the argument that 2012 security is overwhelmingly focused on counter-terrorism (Chapter 2). Additional risks can be continually focused within this selective branch of Olympic (in)security.

(see Herman 2003). This mobility of risk also stands in contrast to the rigidity of standardized security practices.

Together, these events suggest a complex set of issues surrounding technologically induced 'overload'. Exponential increases in technologically produced data place a significant burden on the social and operational environments of security. In turn, this stimulates a number of unanticipated corollary effects, which include the framing of risk and the ability to respond to reports of suspicious activity. At the same time, how humans interface with technology is also important (as seen in the overload of Athens 2004's communication infrastructure). Together, these factors connect with and reinforce the aforementioned 'dual dynamic' in which technological failures stimulate human responses whilst human responses may simultaneously induce technological failures.

Socio-ethical Issues

One of the central features of public, policy and academic discussions around surveillance has been the issue of ethics. In an effort to invest the 2012 Olympic Park's CCTV network with legitimacy and public confidence, or 'to minimize the number of queries from the general public', as the ODA put it (2009: 3), a slim London 2012 *Olympic Park CCTV System Code of Practice* has been formulated by the ODA. Broadly reflecting the raft of similar self-regulatory (and non legally binding) documents in operation across the UK, the code details key points relating to the scheme's rationale, local consultation, data protection issues and how footage is retained. Taking each of these in turn, perimeter integrity is stated to be the focus of the system, as mentioned above. In order to 'protect privacy' – and presumably not penetrate the windows of private dwellings –'electronic masking' will be in place.[24] Local consultation is also promised, although in practice consultations over CCTV installation have historically been abridged in the extreme in both Newham (Langstone 2009) and across the country (Fussey 2004). The code also promises full compliance with the Data Protection Act 1998. To do so, the Olympic CCTV system will need to improve on those installed in a number of other London boroughs that have consistently failed to meet minimum statutory requirements over correct signage (McCahill and Norris 2002) and public access to data. Finally, a related issue is the weight given to data retention. This currently constitutes a key area of tension between CCTV operators and those seeking to regulate them (and will undoubtedly form a key component of the NPIA's CCTV regulation guidance when finalized during 2011). This tension is reproduced here, with the ODA offering to automatically delete stored CCTV footage after 31 days, a limit that more than doubles the Home Office's (2007) recommendation of a 14-day maximum.

---

24 'Electronic masking' blurs the received image and thus prevents CCTV operators from observing particular spaces. This procedure is widely used, notably in the lavatory areas of police custody suites (see Newburn and Hayman 2001).

However, despite their prominence, ethical debates around surveillance are largely limited in scope, often framed by an erroneous trade-off between liberty vs. security and predicated on very generalized and ill-defined notions of civil liberties. With the intensification of London's surveillance infrastructure brought about by the Olympics, these discourses are likely to become more prominent. This book argues that such debates have become somewhat reductionist and fail to capture the complexity of the broader social and cultural impacts of intensified Olympic surveillance. Primarily, such accounts usually harbour an implicit assumption that these measures provide security and/or deny liberty by operating effectively, as if unencumbered by the influences of their operational contexts or other messy social realities. In an effort to refocus the debate as it applies to the Olympics, this book provides five socio-ethical considerations that, it is argued, constitute tangible impacts of the surveillance-infused Olympic security strategies. These are: *legitimacy, locality, listings, legislation* and *legacy* and, given their connectivity with other elements of the 2012 security strategy examined across the second half of the book, are discussed in detail in Chapter 9. Together, manifest issues affecting previous mega-sporting events generate ethical issues extend beyond narrow conceptions of privacy and liberty to include a range of additional social costs. For Olympic-sized events to provide a genuinely beneficial legacy to local communities, these issues need to be defined broadly.

Conclusion

This chapter has illustrated how a diverse range of technological surveillance strategies will be employed to police the 2012 Games. In doing so, points of harmony and dissonance are created between globalized and localized forms of security. Regarding the former, it is evident that the standardized security practices of other Olympiads aimed at creating risk-free 'total security' spaces are being conveyed to and imposed upon East London and its suspect populations. At the same time London's highly developed extant surveillance infrastructure will be buttressed and then coalesced into this strategy with varying degrees of compatibility.

Much has been written on the theoretical implications of new and expanding surveillance networks (see *inter alia* Lyon 2006). In particular, the union of global and local appears to lend some initial support to Deleuzian notions of 'control' and the 'surveillant assemblage' (see *inter alia* Deleuze and Guattari 1987, Deleuze 1995, Haggerty and Ericson 2000). Indeed, the co-option and capitalization of latent surveillance provision, in addition to the supply of new technologies in the capital, represents a shift towards integrated 'flows' of control, factors presenting 'inseparable variations, forming a 'system', as Deleuze puts it (1995: 178). Furthermore, recent developments in video analytics and profiling strategies likely to be deployed for 2012 reduce individuals to abstracted data. Here, the atom of the individual self is split into particular 'dividual' traits and behavioural categories whilst broader population masses are abbreviated to 'samples' and 'data'. Ultimately, for Deleuze, those populating such categories are consigned to move between an interconnected range of modulated 'orbits' within control networks (1995: 180).

For Deleuze, his adherents and other post-Foucauldian theorists (*inter alia* Jones 2000), 'control', seemingly paradoxically, asserts a heightened influence whilst becoming less tangible, an abstract entity or 'a soul, a gas', as Deleuze puts it. In doing so, society's coercive apparatus becomes configured in a less visible way. Where Foucault (1977) famously talked of the tangible 'moulding' of subjects into specific 'normalized' forms, for Deleuze this process is less determinate. Here, technologies of control apply a continual calibration and illimitable 'modulation' to their subjects (Deleuze 1995: 179). However, like many grand narratives of surveillance theory, this explanation is only partial. For London 2012, however, 'control' does not spread in an unrestrained manner. Limitations may be observed across space, purpose and capacity.

Across space, intensified security resources poured into Stratford's surveillance-saturated spaces will inevitably overspill into the surrounding areas (see Chapter 9. However, the specific footprint of the Olympic security programme will mean that control mechanisms largely converge around East London's loosely definable security epicentre.

Regarding the purpose of these control strategies, more subtle and nuanced calibrating (Deleuzian) functions of control are likely to give way to cruder, more formulaic and rigid visions of order (such as those present at other 'theme parks', see Shearing and Stenning 1996 for the example of Disneyland). In turn, these dogmatized blueprints of order are codified in legislation (see the London Olympic Games and Paralympic Games Act 2006, discussed in Chapter 9) and reinforced by zero-tolerance policing strategies.

In terms of capacity, the connectivity of the Olympic surveillance ensemble is also not assured. As the experiences of all prior Olympic security projects have shown, integration has been elusive. In effect, of the four 'C's' of applied to policing mega-event security – command, control, co-ordination and communication – it is the co-ordination and communication components that have proved to be both crucial yet are also the most common points of failure.[25] These blockages may be further aggravated in two ways. First, as the above examples demonstrate, information does not flow evenly between agencies comprising Olympic security coalitions. Secondly, when blockages do inevitably arise, it becomes more difficult to act upon surveillance data that has been captured. In effect, it limits the effective post hoc grouping of data into information 'assemblages' (see Deleuze and Guattari 1987, Haggerty and Ericson 2000). Overall, the converging pull of the Olympic

---

25   It is notable that in the official 2012 strategy these two crucial components of co-ordination and communication are far less explicit than command and control (see Chapter 5).

security ensemble is punctuated by unpredictable and 'messy' human action that resonates throughout the entire operation.

Together, such factors demonstrate support for the central argument of this chapter: the challenge to technological determinism. The most important influence upon the function of surveillance and other forms of technological control is the social context they operate within. Human agents design the algorithmic focus of surveillance technologies, manage their operation and interpret its outputs, even those of second-generation machines. As such, the operations of newly inaugurated technologies are hostage to unpredictable human contingencies. Simultaneously, new technologies also impact and, to some extent, shape their social environment by altering the way in which people work and operate. In sum, an appreciation of these more complex relationships is crucial in developing and understanding both the efficacy of Olympic surveillance strategies and whether the well-documented social costs are worth it.

Chapter 8
Power and Resistance: Contesting London 2012

Contributing to the literature addressing Social Movements (SMs), this chapter[1] addresses the complexities of the processes involved in Londoners' attempts to ensure they receive the maximum benefit from hosting the 2012 Olympic Games. It investigates the SM impact on pre-event politicking via case studies of two of the most prominent resistance organizations. Resistance to the Games has taken a number of forms and, perhaps because of this, has remained fragmented and limited in its ability to articulate precise aims. Such 'movements' are briefly reviewed in the opening sections of the chapter.

By contrast, one organization that existed prior to the Olympic bid, The East London Communities Organization (TELCO), occupies a larger portion of this chapter's analysis. Set up in 1996, TELCO encompasses a diverse alliance of active citizens and community leaders who promote democratically selected causes intended to benefit the local (East London) community. Member institutions include faith groups, schools, student organizations, union branches and charities. Data gathered from attending a variety of community meetings in the Olympic boroughs, and research interviews with stakeholders and activists, is used here to examine the form, direction and efficacy of this particular brand of 2012 resistance. Ultimately, considering both case studies, such analyses reveal much about the power relations inherent in Olympic redevelopment programmes and the strategies used to 'manage' and placate opposition to them.

Spolitics: The Myth of Politically Neutral Sport

Sport is never politically neutral and the Olympics are no exception. American sports sociologist Guttman famously proclaimed that the 'gross social and economic injustices of the imperfect world in which we live do not exist within the Olympic domain', adding that, for the Olympics, there is 'no commercial connivery, nor political chicanery. The rules are the same for everyone, respected by all and enforced impartially' (2002: 28). Not all in the academy – or indeed wider

---

1   The authors are indebted to Iain Lindsay, whose ongoing research into the 2012 Olympics informs some of the ethnographic sections of this chapter. Unless otherwise attributed, quotes in this chapter are from research interviews or research notes from attendance at public meetings.

society – would agree. One key issue is the commercialism that has surrounded the Modern Olympics since its late-nineteenth-century origins, provoking French Marxist Jean-Marie Brohm to state that 'the primary aim of the organizers of Olympic competitions is not sport for its own sake but sport for capitalist profit' (1978: 117). London 2012 promises to be no exception. Equally many examples can be found of chicanery of all sorts. However, these matters are not directly at stake in the current chapter – although awareness of them no doubt inflects the views of at least some of the community resistance described below.

The rhetoric of sports neutrality also has some subtleties. Nigel Crowther, Director of the International Centre for Olympic Studies, argues that, from its outset, the Modern Olympic Games had aspirations beyond sport and that the Games must be considered as much as, if not more than, a political conduit as it is a sporting event (Crowther 2001). Olympic political historian David Kanin suggests that, because the Olympics have 'no *intrinsic* political value, it can be used by any state to demonstrate the physical prowess of the human resources of any ideology or value system' (1981: 2, emphasis added), hence giving the Games huge political malleability. This capacity to promote a vast range of ideals and themes ranges from Nazi German ideals at the 1936 Berlin Games to environmental issues at Sydney 2000.

Most relevant to the concerns in this chapter, Canadian academic and Olympic analyst Helen Lenskyj, has identified a shift in Olympic rhetoric on political neutrality: 'in recent years it appears the rhetoric about keeping politics out of sport has been replaced by the explicit politicizing of the bid process' (1996: 395). For London 2012, key features of this 'explicit politicizing' are community benefits (through the Olympic 'legacy') and community engagement with and support for the Olympics. The London bid team here was simply responding to the Modern Olympiad's blueprint for a successful host, which requires candidate cities to commit to colossal transformations – at a prohibitive and risky, cost – under the heading (or branding) of 'Olympic legacy'.

Three models of regeneration costing were available for London 2012. The Barcelona 1992 model would involve taxing the whole country, with the proceeds invested in the host city. The Athens 2004 model would require £13 billion of EU taxes given by the unaudited Community Support Fund. Finally – and most disturbingly for Londoners –the Montreal 1976 model – in which only the host city populace is taxed and the city administration subsequently goes bankrupt.

Community and Legacy

In 1998 David Stubbs was employed by the UK government to explore and assess the practicalities of a London bid in respect to environment and sustainability. In 2005 Stubbs stated that, to be a credible candidate, London had to 'firstly, get the right experts around us to have a good technical bid and, secondly, engage with the environmental community (sic) so that they felt part of the process. Public support was critical', elaborating that 'The environment chapter embraces a whole range of subjects such as energy, waste, water, biodiversity, cultural heritage, air quality. All of these things had to be looked at' (BBC 2005).

The ever-ambiguous concept of 'public' support – in the case of London strongly tagged to 'community' support – is crucial to any Olympic bid. Equally, the bidding team thus has a responsibility to 'sell' the Olympics to residents of the neighbourhoods where the Games are planned to take place. Stubbs explained that his advisory group – comprising representatives from NGOs, public authorities, academia and business – 'did a lot of work with the voluntary groups to get them involved in the process. By the end, they were really championing the whole thing' (BBC 2005). Significantly, Stubbs divulged no details of the particulars of such 'championing'.

'Olympic championing' by community groups was, according to many Londoners interviewed in this research, falsely portrayed claimed that mass turnouts of local residents in the host boroughs at 'consultation events' indicated clear 'community support' for the Games. One of these events was held at the ExCeL Exhibition Centre in Newham's Royal Docks on 5 February 2006, named the 'Big Sunday', which was attended by over 20,000 people. John Connor, a voluntary sector community development worker based in Newham, stressed that the consultations, which the government claimed as 'Pro-Olympic demonstrations', were nothing of the sort. He explains that the events in Newham were sold to the public as opportunities to raise concerns about the Olympics and to 'consult' with officials who claimed to be directly feeding back to the bid committee. At 'Big Sunday' itself, the reality was that there were too many people in the confined space of the ExCeL Exhibition Centre, with no obvious procedure as to how to express their views. The majority of people left feeling that they had not been able to voice their opinions and, according to Connor, many of them were vehemently opposed to the 2012 Olympic proposal. Yet the impression of widespread 'community support' directly contributed to London's plausibility as an attractive potential host.

Equally, after London won the bid in 2005, followed by increasingly ominous reports of budget 'adjustments' culminating in the March 2007 public announcement of a massive budget re-estimate upwards, this came as no surprise to some of 'the community'. The former head of the Aston Mansfield charity in Newham, Ian Powell, said that it was common knowledge that 'the bid team would've promised to marry your Granny if they thought it might help get your support for the bid, so under-estimating costs was par for the course'.

A significant proportion of the seemingly ever-increasing public-sector investment will cover London's obligation, as an Olympic host, to the massive transformation of East London's infrastructure. These changes, it was promised during the bid (London2012 2004), would underpin urban reform, improve international trade and facilitate a range of innovative social and economic policies, delivering benefits that will far outlast the sporting contest. What 'Londoner' would want to oppose such progress?

Opposing the Games: Resistance is Futile?

As noted above, resistance to the Games has taken a number of forms and, perhaps because of this, has remained fragmented. Moreover, the inability of many of these groups to articulate precise aims, unite with other disaffected groups or connect their grievance to more powerful narratives has rendered them with limited visibility and longevity.

Resistance to the Games have emanated from rural, industrial and residential concerns. Taking these in turn, accompanying the announcement of the London Olympic bid were a series of protests that sought to preserve ancient rights to 'Lammas lands' at Leyton Marshes, East London. Leyton Marshes overlap the Olympic Park and stage a number of access points to the construction site. According to protesters, primarily collected in the 'New Lammas Lands Defence Committee'(NLLDC), Leyton Marshes had been under the protection of a 'Lammas Land' covenant for over 1000 years that allowed the area to be used as a public space with unfettered movement and access.[2] Grievances centered around both the 'inappropriate' use of the land that the construction of the Olympic Park brought, and the erection of fences that partitioned the land in breach of the Lammas Land agreement (NLLDC 2008). Other agrarian-based resistance simultaneously came from plot-holders at the Manor Garden Allotments at the western, Hackney, side of the Olympic development. In brief, the allotments are sited in the heart of the proposed Olympic Park, on a thoroughfare between the proposed Velodrome and Handball arenas and the southern areas of the development containing Olympic Stadium and Aquatics Centre. As of early 2010 plot-holders are awaiting eviction having been promised alternative accommodation for an interim period and then relocation within the Olympic Park after the Games (see Lifeisland 2010 for further details). In addition to forced eviction, further grievances centre around the view that post-Olympic accommodation is inferior to the current allotment facilities. Save for a BBC2 documentary, *Building the Olympic Dream: The last stand at Stratford* aired in May 2009 and a number of small scale protests at Waltham Forest Town Hall neither group has been successful nor achieved widespread recognition.

More prominent was the response of local businesses to the bid. Perhaps most visible was the short-lived 'London 2012 Killing Local Business' campaign which perhaps reached its zenith with its banner display in view of Stratford station's Jubilee Line platforms ahead of the IOC delegate visit there (as part of their visit to all 2012 candidate cities) in February 2005. Despite the limited resonance of the campaign, the impact of the Games was significant for a number of local businesses operating on the future Olympic site. As Raco and Tunney note, the compulsory purchase process meant 'the Olympics ... acted like a tidal wave crashing over local businesses and clearing them away in the first stage of

---

2   Users of Leyton Marshes also had 'grazing rights' for their cattle until 1904, when this was exchanged for recreation or sport (see Games Monitor 2007c).

a longer regeneration process' (2010: 14). The effects were palpable. Throughout this period London experienced acute shortages of business accommodation. Numerous accounts exist of profiteering by future landlords aware of the plight of relocating businesses (Raco and Tunney 2010). Other disadvantages included the loss of local staff and networks of local customers. According to Raco and Tunney, the most potent organization for businesses to act collaboratively was the Marshgate Lane Business Group.[3] Of note here is the way in which businesses felt they had limited traction against the dominant pro-Olympic political discourse and, because of this, they believed significant pressure was being exerted on the media not to spoil the party. Moreover, a belief in the inevitability of the fate awaiting the Marshgate Lane's SME community led many towards a realpolitik of acceptance and negotiation which weakened the movement further (Raco and Tunney, 2010).

Further contestations surrounded the Clays Lane Housing Estate and the compulsory relocation of 425 residents in preparation for the main Olympic construction project. Clays Lane, located to the north of the Stratford's Olympic site in Newham, was the only social housing affected by the LDA compulsory purchase order for the 2012 Olympics. In response to the compulsory purchase order, residents of the estate organized as a group,[4] perhaps belatedly, to launch a sporadic campaign that included on-site rallies, letter writing to MPs and regular on-site meetings with the appropriate authorities. Such actions ultimately failed to prevent the wholesale relocation. Theirs was a fragmented lobby containing some who vehemently opposed the move and some who advocated only moving en bloc as a 'community' but – crucially – there were also residents who readily accepted the proposed relocation and even some who wanted to move as quickly as possible out of fear that they might 'miss the boat' in terms of the superior relocation packages on offer from the council. Ultimately, as people gradually left the estate, the effectiveness of the Clays Lane campaign eroded. Interestingly, Steve Berwick, a member of one of the Gypsy families who formed part of the Clays Lane residents, stated in a research interview (February 2008) that 'the Gypsy ring leaders that could have created a load of trouble during the relocation were given cushy flats over at the Docklands'. People, it seems, can be bought off.

In June 2004, over a year before London became the host city for the 2012 Games, all Clays Lane residents had been assured by the LDA that, if London won the bid, they would be relocated to accommodation 'at least as good as, if not better' than what residents already had (Games Monitor 2008). Referring to this announcement, Mayor Ken Livingstone then opined that he expected them to have improved 'space, quality, standards and amenities', a statement that was later watered down to 'residents would be allocated whatever was available by local authorities' (Games Monitor 2008). Meanwhile, talks of a collective relocation

---

3   When it existed, Marshgate Lane was located towards the west Stratford, near to Newham's border with Hackney and Tower Hamlets.

4   This group might best be categorized as a 'short-term interest group'.

were dropped until after many residents had already left the Clays Lane estate (Games Monitor 2008).

The Clays Lane scenario suggests that, unless a significant proportion of an affected populace mobilizes to object to an issue, any community will be systematically segregated and marginalized, thus limiting the effectiveness of any resisting group. Many Clays Lane residents who relocated while the protest was still ongoing did so in the light of suggestions that any delay would result in their being allocated poorer quality housing than the aforementioned 'as good as, if not better' standard of living assurances expressed by Mayor Livingstone (interview with Julian Cheyenne, former Clays Lane tenant and author of Games Monitor 2008).

As a consequence, the Clays Lane movement became fragmented. This, coupled with the lack of any visible secondary support from outside their immediate vicinity (indicating lower resonance with the wider (i.e. non-resident) community), meant that the action was doomed to fail. Additionally, this represents a nascent organization belatedly established in response to Olympic regeneration plans already in train. The delay in action by Clays Lane residents proved a crucial obstacle to mobilizing wider support and successfully transmitting their objectives. Such processes help pave the way for sanitized Olympic spaces discussed elsewhere in this book.

TELCO and Collective Action

TELCO[5] is an SM[6] that, amongst other causes, seeks to oppose the capitalistic ethos associated with the Olympic-related transformation of East-London in the hope of attaining community benefit. To assess TELCO's significance as a 2012-related SM it is first imperative to investigate their origins.

In 1993 the Reverend Timothy Stevens, representing and funded by, the Church of England diocese of Chelmsford, visited the US to examine The Citizen Organization Foundation,[7] with the intention of transferring the model to major

---

5   Since the fieldwork was completed, TELCO has now become TELCO Citizens, a chapter of the larger coalition of community groups across the capital who go by the name of London Citizens with whom TELCO was already affiliated.

6   TELCO's diverse membership encompasses myriad smaller groups that share a commitment to social change. As such, this shared rationale links the organisation more closely to particular theoretical articulations the Social Movement (SM). For example, as Zirakzadeh notes, 'Participants in social movements not only challenge decisions made by authorities and make demands on authorities but try to make lasting, large-scale and significant changes in the texture of society' (1997: 4).

7   The Citizen Organization Foundation was founded in the 1980s, drawing heavily on the experience of the Industrial Areas Foundation in the US. A registered charity, it aims to generate networks of citizens active in public life, able to influence decisions that impact on their communities and assist in the development of broader citizens' organizations.

Figure 8.1   Anti-2012 Olympics Graffiti, Hackney

UK cities. In 1994, following Stevens' report to the diocese, East London based Reverend Peter Walton took steps to facilitate a similar SM in East London and began recruiting members into what might be considered broad-based community organizing. In November 1996 the organization was launched and the prospective constituent groups, including a variety of religious and community groups, chose the name The East London Communities Organization). Over 1,300 people attended TELCO's launch in November 1996 at York Hall, Bethnal Green including the late Cardinal Hume, Victor Guazelli (Catholic Bishop for East London) and Bishop Roger Sainsbury (Anglican Bishop of Barking). TELCO was the first such organization in London and TELCO's trustees affiliated to the London-wide London Citizens organization in 2002.[8] The organization currently incorporates some 80 London groups that claim to represent London's ethnic diversity.

TELCO is self-funded via membership fees of around £1,800 per annum for each constituent organization and is directed by a board of members elected at an AGM by those in attendance. A percentage of the board (usually one-third) stand down every two years to make way for new blood although the out-going can stand for re-election. The primary motivation of all involved in TELCO is the pursuit of social justice.[9] To this end, they cultivate relationships that enable

---

8   See http://www.londoncitizens.org.uk/pages/about.html.

9   Here, social justice is defined as a collective responsibility to put right what is unjust.

the diverse communities of London to unite and mobilize wherever collective action is perceived to be necessary. TELCO's recruitment revolves around what the former TELCO Chair Paul Regan describes as 'purposive conversation', essentially encouraging members to put the movement in touch with other groups that could then be incorporated into the wider organization. TELCO's membership thus comprises a wide range of smaller groups.

Tangible victories were crucial to TELCO's emerging profile and success would provide prospective members with examples of the possibilities of citizen-initiated social change. For example, in its founding year (1996) one campaign focused on a notoriously 'smelly' factory polluting the environment around Canning Town and Poplar. As a result of TELCO mobilization the factory's owners (Pura Foods) installed a filter at a cost of £1.5 million.

This victory was announced at the first annual TELCO assembly, named the 'People's Assembly', held in York Hall, Bethnal Green. At the start of the assembly, recognition is given to the attending representatives of each member group, who stand up in the audience and are given a round of applause from the other members. The standing members often joined in with their own clapping, singing or cheering dependent upon the voracity and, indeed, ethnicity of its membership. A selected member then ceremonially delivered their membership fee to an official sitting on the stage and the business begins. Former chair Regan believes these 'assemblies' are integral to the continued success of TELCO. Such gatherings are rehearsed beforehand and follow a written order that also specifies how much time each topic and speaker is allocated. TELCO consider this transparency and scheduling crucial to their integrity.[10] Such assemblies and their procedures have proved a catalyst for working relationships to be formed between TELCO and key London figureheads, including Mayor Boris Johnson. Moreover, these assemblies follow carefully choreographed scripts which promotes public declarations of TELCO/ Authority (often governmental, Mayoral or business oriented) agreements[11] – often made behind closed-doors – as an example of accountability.

Conceptualizing TELCO: The Pursuit of Credibility

Community standing, public associations and endorsements are paramount to the credibility of SMs such as TELCO. Questions here include why would groups choose to become part of TELCO? What is the basis of its legitimacy for them? What are the perceived benefits of alignment with organizations such as TELCO? Politically, alignment with groups that are 'champions' of marginalized populaces

---

10   Methods to ensure the time structure is adhered to include a volunteer bell ringer who signals repeatedly when anyone has gone over their allotted time allowance. Each group is generally allowed one minute.

11   An example of this was the presentation of a proposal for an Ethical Olympics agreement between TELCO, the Mayor's office, LOCOG and the LDA –explored in more depth later in this chapter.

may be considered a vote winner, no doubt why new American President Barack Obama flaunted his association with organized labour unions during his successful 2008 election campaign (see Democratic Undergound 2008). Marginalized groups are readily apparent in London, and their susceptibility to exploitation is magnified during the building and planning of mega-event such as the Olympics. If TELCO could cultivate a position as a 'champion' of marginalized groups, they would benefit this subordinate subculture by presenting their causes under the auspices of a united front.

In return, TELCO benefits by attaining greater political appeal and credibility for their movement through vicarious association. This can be seen in TELCO's 'Strangers into Citizens' campaign,[12] which is currently lobbying for changes to immigration policy to enable the naturalization of irregular migrants. A worker with no national insurance number is a worker making no tax contribution to the government. Furthermore, unscrupulous employers imposing imaginary 'taxes' on the earnings of irregular workers increases migrant exploitation further (see *inter alia* Rawlinson and Fussey 2010).

Clearly, a strength of any SM is the ability to mobilize to obtain attention for any cause they deem worthy. The impact of mobilizations, however, can vary dramatically and a group's credibility is often a by-product of the reaction to, and perception of, their action. The mass mobilization of people in public arenas can be an effective tool of social protest but success may also be dependent upon many other – quieter and unobtrusive – factors. To enhance the credibility of their mobilization, demonstrations were often prepared for by TELCO's professional organizers, who would lobby prominent, often religious, members to attend. They would also attempt to ensure a broad demographic cross section s was visibly present in order to emphasize the organization's diversity. Moreover, the more established the groups that form TELCO membership are, the more credible the movement becomes. Consequently, TELCO's ability to mobilize numerous faiths, creeds and cultures is a prerequisite to their standing in London.

TELCO's understanding of the importance to their movement of publicly demonstrable mobilized diversity and inclusivity was evident in their 'Affordable Housing' campaign. During the lead-up to the 2004 London Mayoral elections, the then Mayor Ken Livingstone signed a pledge at a TELCO assembly committing himself to piloting a Community Land Trust (CLT), which theoretically allows for houses to be built and subsequently sold to 'the community' minus the cost of the land, thus making the houses 'affordable' for those assumed to be on low wages. The problem for TELCO was that no location was identified. Nonetheless, this pledge indicated that – within an allotted time – it would be announced which piece of land was to be placed under the ownership of a CLT. However, when Livingstone still did not specify the site by the designated deadline, TELCO decided action was required. TELCO mobilized their members to set up a tented village (50 tents) on the parkland next to the Mayor's headquarters at City Hall,

12   See http://www.telcocitizens.org.uk/strangersintocitizens/index.html.

Westminster. Members present included Catholic Bishops (in their ceremonial clothing) and other prominent multi-faith leaders and community figures. The action attracted a wide variety of print and broadcast media. This mobilization was reasonably successful and led to 'positive' discussions with Livingstone and a further course of meetings. However, the CLT remains an on-going issue and, despite the change of Mayor, no site has yet been specified. TELCO has not given up hope on this issue but has transferred their focus to other issues – one of which is the pursuit of an ethical Olympics.

Pre-bid: The Blueprint for an Ethical Olympics

Following London's success in winning the 2012 bid, a significant amount of TELCO's time has been dedicated to Olympic-related concerns. Indeed, TELCO was already involved during the bidding process. The London 2012 bidding team needed to establish public support to validate their proposals and TELCO was approached by the bidding committee to publicly back the bid. TELCO felt that any public support they offered should be conditional upon clearly specified benefits for the East London populace. Consequently, TELCO developed, through member-driven discourse, a charter for an 'Ethical Olympics'. The end product was a member-produced video and document written by TELCO entitled the 'People's Guarantees' presented to the Olympic bid team in 2004 by a selection of TELCO's school-aged members.

The Ethical Olympics People's Guarantees consisted of six key points:

1. Affordable homes to be built for local people and managed through a Community Land Trust where the value of the land would be removed from the property price making homes more affordable.
2. Olympic development monies to be set aside to improve local schools and health services.
3. University of East London to be the main higher education beneficiary of the sports legacy with a view to becoming a sporting centre of excellence.
4. At least £2 million to be set aside immediately upon winning the bid (to coincide with the first building phase) for a construction academy in Leyton to train local people in employable trades.
5. That at least 30 per cent of construction jobs be set aside for local people, which would require the implementation of a 30 per cent local labour clause with the contractors responsible for construction.
6. The Lower Lea Valley made to be designated 'living wage' zone with all jobs in the defined boundary guaranteed to pay a 'living wage' (set at £6.70 per hour in 2004) (Interview with TELCO activist 2008).

The Ethical Olympics agreement was signed in 2004 on behalf of the Olympic bidding team by Lord Coe, then Chair of the Olympic Bidding Committee, Mayor of London Ken Livingstone and John Biggs, Deputy Chair of the LDA. As a result of this shared commitment, Lord Coe stated, the Games were now 'eminently more winnable' (*The London Evening Standard* 2004). Yet the Ethical Olympics agreement was more a memorandum of agreement than a binding contract, and the signee's carefully worded 'in principle' agreement to the terms ensured room for negotiation should London win the bid.

Post-bid: The Quest for an Ethical Olympics

Once the 2012 bid succeeded, TELCO's priority was to solidify the Ethical Olympics agreement with the relevant parties, notably, the Mayor's Office, the LDA and the then newly formed ODA. Theoretically, the 2012 Olympics necessitated the removal of key elements of local governance by awarding powers to the ODA, which in turn is accountable only to central government. This removed local accountability and ensured freedom from local authority planning controls and regulations.[13]

The LDA, which is the London Mayor's delivery agency responsible for upholding the Olympic pledges of the Mayor, maintained a rapport with TELCO regarding the Ethical Olympics document, holding regular meetings. However, the living wage and the proposed construction academies fell outside the LDA mandate and, consequently, TELCO considered it imperative to interact with the ODA. However, the ODA would not interact with TELCO, and refused even to acknowledge them, on the grounds that the Ethical Olympics had nothing to do with the ODA because it had not been in existence when the agreement was signed; consequently, the ODA referred all interactions to the LDA. TELCO decided that organized collective action was necessary to achieve ODA recognition.

TELCO thus 'ambushed' David Higgins (then Chief Executive of the ODA). Aware of his penchant for high-powered business breakfast meetings at top hotels, it was decided to picket his preferred hotels entrances and exits before and after such meetings. TELCO thus became a nuisance, both to him and to those he met with, and the tactic also attracted media attention to their self-proclaimed 'respectful, civil lobbying' (i.e. non-confrontational lobbying), which established their credibility with the ODA. This led to an ongoing series of meetings with Higgins.

However, the Ethical Olympics campaign plateaued in 2008. TELCO is currently involved in negotiations with the LDA, the ODA and the Mayor's Office in an effort to ensure that the promises agreed during the 2012 bidding process are honoured. Legacy maintenance, however, is beyond the remit of the Olympic

---

13   Facilities intended to be converted for public use after the Olympics, such as the Olympic Village, which has been earmarked for both public and private housing, will need to comply with local authority regulations and this will entail significant modification costs. Also, there is considerable evidence to suggest that contestations among the myriad Olympic stakeholders means that intended public amenities have now been promised to private sector agencies (see Poynter 2009).

deliverers. While momentous consideration is allocated to hosting, comparatively little has been afforded to legacy longevity. However, the newly formed 2012 Olympic Park Legacy Company (OPLC), overseen by American born Andrew Altman is now tasked with dealing with all Olympic legacy-related issues. The OPLC is expected to announce its 'Final Legacy Plan', although details are currently very vague. Ominously for TELCO, neither Altman nor any member of his team turned up to the first meeting between the OPLC and TELCO members scheduled for the 30 September 2009 at Bryant Street Methodist Church. However, Altman did manage to appear in November 2009 at a Legacy Now 'Gains beyond the Games' presentation, principally targeted toward the elite end of academia at the London School of Economics, to stress what a great thing the Olympic legacy is for the local people, or in his words, it will fix 'London's Gash' (his, somewhat unfortunate, definition of the area that stands to be regenerated by the 2012 Olympics).

In 1996 Jane Jacobs published a study that examined regeneration in the Olympic Borough of Tower Hamlets, specifically the area of Spitalfields (Jacobs 1996). The book highlighted the tried and tested formula to make mass regeneration seem more palatable by defining through negative connotations like 'Gash' elicits feelings of gratitude toward the regenerators' community mindedness. However, the Olympic team need little help in this regard; the promised mass transformation of neglected areas has long been legitimized by the Olympic Games. What Londoner could possibly object to the healing of London's Gash?

Power Relations and Information Management

In comparison to other groups opposing the Games, TELCO can be considered a major player in the SM stratosphere. TELCO is actively campaigning for the equal distribution of legacy benefits, which is crucial to determining whether Londoners will benefit from the Games. The ability to make such an assessment, however, is directly dependent upon accurate information – which can often be obtained only directly from the Olympic authorities that can, and do, decide how much information to release and when to release it. There are also complicating processes such as future contestations between private and public interests in the post-Games site that have yet to be resolved (Poynter 2009). Therefore, it is vital to consider how relations of power bear on information management and access to information. Clegg defines such interplay as 'complex organized agents engaged in complex organized games' (1989: 20).

The powerful entities in this analysis are the Olympic authorities given their control of 2012 resources. To attempt to redress the power balance those Londoners seeking to oppose 2012 need to mobilize and harness unity. The amalgamation of smaller entities to construct a more powerful whole – as in the case of TELCO – is a useful method to facilitate strengthening. Crucially, Nash forewarns that redressing the balance of power 'will only succeed with the massive mobilizations of the people' (2005: 2), something that proved beyond the Clays

Lane protestors. Mobilization can occur in a variety of ways, from spectacular street demonstrations to subtle pressures, yet mobilization depends upon the foundations that communities actually have the will, desire and ability to affect, even control, the space and times they live in.

Brown (2007) argues that, in order to motivate communities to become active, it is important for any community organization to deliver a message of collective efficacy, that the organization is 'not in the business to serve you. It is your group. You, the member, are responsible' (2007: 213). This philosophy is vital to enforcing mutual ownership and control and instilling a sense of personal responsibility for the group's advancement. TELCO promote the notion of a member-driven organization by awarding group members the chance to be integrated into all aspects of the movement. This includes rotating the member nominated to chair the People's Assemblies. The assemblies begin at 7 pm, which is the most convenient time for the majority of members. The agendas and minute taking are also tasks undertaken by volunteer members. However, as Kleidman and Rochon (1997) demonstrate, difficulties arise when SMs allow members to be responsible for too many aspects of the movement. This occurs, most notably, in the pursuit of achieving the 'right balance' of appearing to be a professional structure whilst remaining inclusive to all and incorporating well intentioned, but often less able, volunteers. This is a conflict pertinent to TELCO's Olympic meetings and returns us to the immediate question of wresting information from the Olympic authorities.

TELCO's Olympic meetings were intended to gather information in order to assess progress toward objectives. However, the TELCO representatives selected to often had little or no negotiation experience and were unable to comprehend the nuances of debate, something that the people they regularly met with, such as Labour whip and GLA member John Biggs, were masters at. After a meeting in July 2008 that took place on TELCO 'home turf' (their Whitechapel headquarters), Biggs even commented to the group after the meeting that he was shocked at the 'easy ride' they had given him. He had expected that a group of Londoners intent on change would be more fervent or aggressive in their approach.[14] Yet, even after these comments, the post-meeting TELCO discussion (consisting of all members who had been present at the meeting), the 'debate' concentrated upon the 'good' points of the meeting. Members patently ignored the 'elephant in the room', namely the fact that, if they had been better negotiators they might have garnered additional information that Biggs was prepared to divulge.

However, these apparent frailties can be contrasted with examples of acumen in dealing with the capriciousness of public sector representatives and suggests that TELCO will be intermittently influential depending upon which members are available on any given day. Such skills were evident when the issue of longevity of the 2012 legacy was raised at an Olympic legacy meeting held in Newham in 2006.

---

14   As Chapter 3 demonstrates, fervent resistance is a feature of East London's social geography.

The question from a TELCO member directed at Lord Coe was 'who would pay the council tax for the Olympic stadium and the new facilities after the Games finish?' Coe avoided a direct response – he did not appear to know the answer. However, TELCO was prepared. The ubiquitous reluctance of officials from all fields to answer difficult questions had led TELCO to work out a strategy in which members adopt a 'pincer movement' in public meetings. Members spread themselves around the room and barrack the speaker if they avoid answering the question, giving the impression that a wide audience is interested in their response. It is intended to, and in this case did, rattle the speaker. Ultimately, Lord Coe stated that the University of East London (UEL) would pay the council tax on the stadium, at which point, according to TELCO members in the audience, the UEL representative in the room nearly 'fell off of her chair', insisting that would bankrupt the institution. In an interview (July 2008) with John Lock, the Director of Development at UEL, he stated quite categorically that no such discussion of council tax had ever taken place and that the only agreement between the two parties was that UEL would, in principle, like to offer the use of the Velodrome to its students (although this has since expanded towards a more substantial use of the post-2012 Olympic site).

In an attempt to produce the best possible outcomes from their member-driven meetings with a host of assertive, powerful people, TELCO has also cultivated a system to attempt to control the flow of information by requesting, at the outset of every meeting, that the meetings are chaired by a pre-determined TELCO member. This member is briefed by TELCO's paid community organizers as to what points were to be discussed, the amount of time each point would be allotted and who from the group would raise which points about the issues. The procedure required that the chair of the meeting to maintain an organized discussion that would facilitate progression towards a predetermined set of objectives. Theoretically this was sound but in reality it proved futile.

As Srnivasa (2006) states, to use information most effectively, the selective release or withholding of information is crucial. This was clearly evident when, as part of a TELCO action group, a meeting was convened with the then Chief Executive of the ODA, David Higgins, and his assistant Julie King to provide updates on the Ethical Olympics. The meeting was 'chaired' by a 16-year-old schoolboy. The TELCO team comprised a vicar, a schoolteacher, two schoolchildren, local residents, a representative from the Aston Mansfield charity and two community organizers. The balance of power in the hour-long discussion was retained throughout by the ODA delegates, who never deviated from a carefully choreographed script, thereby limiting the information that TELCO received. (For example, TELCO needed hard facts on construction employment figures.) The ODA said that they did not have the relevant information to hand, which could have been true but, equally, could have been avoided. For example, it was abundantly clear from a brief analysis of the pre-meeting bipartisan agreement on the topics to be covered that TELCO should have requested that the information be present at the meeting beforehand. This lack of forethought and, consequently, lack of figures prevented any judgement being made regarding progress. TELCO was assured by the ODA that they would receive more information at a later date via email from the department that 'has those figures to hand'. Short of facts and figures, the ODA did, however, present all the TELCO members a glowing site update leaflet that demonstrated 'excellent' Olympic progress.

TELCO representatives were drawn from a pool of sporadically available members but it was not uncommon for meetings to be attended by a selection of schoolchildren, religious leaders, schoolteachers, the retired, housewives and university students. Such people possessed varying levels of competence and struggled to match the professionalism of London's Olympic agencies. But the real drawback was TELCO's general *modus operandi*, which required representatives to discuss the objectives and the intended direction of a meeting usually only an hour prior to its commencement. Due to this lack of planning, meetings were often disjointed, as member-driven agendas diverged, and thus failed to obtain discernable results other than demonstrating TELCO's 'diversity'. Such diversity is clearly important to the legitimacy of the group. However, it would seem good practice that a precursor to achieving negotiation success is to have all representatives agreed on and aware of clearly delineated objectives prior to each meeting.

This model of pre-prepared negotiation also connects with Flyvbjerg, Bruzelius and Rothengatter's critique of mega-event organization and the risks that accountability and comprehensive public support often become early casualties of the planning process (2003: 3; see also Chapter 1).

TELCO's strengths and weaknesses were evident in June 2008 at Canary Wharf in a meeting with the ODA that was intended to establish an overview of the Ethical Olympics. This included discussing the central Ethical Olympic themes of the living wage and the promise of hiring local residents. On this occasion there was a pre-meeting air of confidence because the group included some strong members who were competent and experienced public speakers, including two religious leaders. However, despite having a 'good team' on paper, the religious leaders did not sing from the same hymn sheet. The ODA maintained that 95 per cent of the workforce was earning over and above the living wage and that guidelines were in place to hire local residents, to the extent of 'requiring proof of residence' from those seeking work on the Olympic site. This point was correctly challenged by one religious leader on the grounds that, because tenure of residency was not stipulated, so-called 'local residents' might have only been living in the area 24 hours before being offered employment (see Chapter 6). The guideline seemed more a way of placating locals rather than actually improving their employment prospects. No answer was forthcoming but, worse, the challenge was actually deflected by the other religious leader, who directed the conversation towards her personal agenda. The issue was thus dropped (until being briefly picked up by the local media in 2009, see *The London Evening Standard* 2009; Chapter 6).

As with most SMs, TELCO comprises a collection of untrained, sometimes ill-informed, individuals prone to following personal concerns rather than clear, long-term united objectives. This evidently raises the likelihood of misshaping intra-group information flows through the occurrence of what Srinivasa calls 'social entropy', a process in which various versions come to be created from the same source item of information (2006: 30). This provides some theoretical explanation as to how TELCO members formulated different interpretations from the same meetings and consequently formed divergent agendas for future progression. (After the Higgins meeting, segments of TELCO considered 'social action', namely public protesting, while others proposed further dialogue). Many of the TELCO members were not able to critically challenge information in the way it was offered. Such issues underline the necessity for adequate planning, reflective group meetings and good leadership often absent in this Olympic opposition movement.

However, Mathew Bolton, one of two full-time paid community organizers' employed by TELCO defends the organization against such accusations. According to him, anyone selected to speak at any meeting is already an 'expert' in their field by virtue of living that reality. TELCO includes many people who know a lot about a little, which, he feels, stands up well to those who know a little about a lot. Further, he argued that all members are as well briefed as possible prior to every meeting and that, at the culmination of every meeting, a period of 'reflective learning' allows those present to use such interaction as learning experiences that ideally are taken back to their individual groups. These provisions, he felt, increased the individual and collective skill sets and, consequently, strengthened TELCO.

An analysis of the exchanges between TELCO and the Olympic authorities indicates that the latter are in the hegemonic pursuit of imposing their vision of 'radical change' and its benefits for Londoners. Following Poulantzas (1973) the Olympic authority, as a hegemon, has the dual function of purporting to represent the general interest of the people/nation whilst maintaining dominance. In or to do so, the authority maintains control and strengthens its position by conceding pre-determined acceptable ground – thereby placating opposition with the illusion of progress whilst maintaining their hegemony. Olympic legacy: who gets what?

TELCO's Olympic struggles revolve around the related issues of 'community benefit' and post-Games 'legacy'. Both issues are considered integral to the wider subject of urban regeneration. The 2012-related proposed regeneration will entail major and continued disruption for Londoners, a disturbance made somewhat palatable by the widely publicized assurances that the community will be recompensed by the after-Games 'legacy'. Such developments are spread across East London's four Olympic boroughs (Newham, Tower Hamlets, Waltham Forest and Hackney),[15] with the epicentre encompassing all facilities within the 500-acre (2-square-kilomtre) Olympic Park and Olympic Village, located in the Lower Lea Valley. A prominent selling point of such a legacy was the intention to convert the

---

15   London's fifth Olympic borough, Greenwich, principally hosting the equestrian events, is located in Southeast London.

Olympic Village into 3,600 apartments, some of which were to be deployed post-Games as 'affordable housing'. However, in an Olympic Park Legacy stakeholders consultation event, held at Stratford Circus on 22July 2008, the Mayor of Newham, Sir Robin Wales, after asking about – and finding that – there were no media reporters present, conceded that many of the legacy promises were 'misleading' and that the mistakes that have been made in terms of delineating legacy were 'very bad indeed'.

When challenged by a member of the audience encouraging him to explain what the legacy actually is, the Mayor stated that £340 million of 'Olympic monies' had been 'ring-fenced' for Newham. He would not, however, divulge the specifics of where this money was coming from, who was ring-fencing it, how the funds were to be allocated or what it would be spent on. Further, in an attempt to justify why things had been left so long to be sorted out, the Mayor stated there was 'little point in discussing legacy before now, whereas now we are in a position to be listened to'. Unsurprisingly, his stance was supported by the LDA spokeswoman, Emma Wheelhouse, who declared that 'no business would commit to investing in legacy until a plan was in place'. This top-down stance suggests the allocation of public money is being invested only into what the LDA and ODA define as appropriate for a successful legacy. Such processes both challenge the wider official declarations that Olympic legacy is something that is being 'done with' the local communities, rather than constituting something 'done to' them (see *inter alia* Department for Communities and Local Government 2009).

It may be inferred that the lack of a clearly defined legacy is in fact a safeguard against being unable to deliver on promises made during the bidding process. If, and when, cutbacks are required, the current belief is that the first things that will be sacrificed are the more public-focused aspects of legacy (see Poynter 2009). Yet here lies a potential banana skin for the Olympic authorities – the very lack of delineation of what is included in the Olympic legacy, coupled with the ubiquitous promise of substantive legacy benefits, has fired the imagination of many susceptible Londoners. At many discussions after the Stratford meeting (above) with the Mayor of Newham, conversation focused only on legacy issues and a high proportion of Londoners spoke out about their fears of losing legacy benefits – despite the fact they could not describe exactly what they might be. Furthermore, many indicated that they were willing to demonstrate against any perceived threat to this concept.

Another controversial legacy issue legacy remains the outlay of vast amounts of money on regeneration that will itself need to be 're-regenerated' via the OPLC immediately after the Games to be fit for public consumption. This possibility was highlighted by Matt Dickinson in *The Times* (2008c), who insisted, 'we are spending £496 million on an 80,000-capacity stadium that … will be downgraded to a 25,000 athletics venue post-Olympics' Evidently, much of the newly built facilities will require millions of pounds of additional public-funded investment before they can be offered to the public. This includes the obvious costs such as the conversion of the Olympic Village into private residences but also other less readily apparent costs, including council tax subsidies levied against the buildings, on top of the expense of converting specialized provisions such as Olympic swimming pools.

Londoners awaiting the promised Olympic legacy treasure are by no means unique. When Sydney bid for the 2000 Games, many residents bought into the Olympic Regeneration concept. However, as Hodgkinson, writing in *The Daily Telegraph* (2007k), argues that, in the aftermath of the Games most Sydney residents who originally regarded the Olympic Park in the Homebush district as a world-class, glitzy collection of stadiums and sports facilities, subsequently changed their opinion.[16] A report by an Australian economic forecaster, *Access Economics* (cited in *The Daily Telegraph* 2007k), explains how the Olympic structures in New South Wales visibly deteriorated in the seven years after Sydney 2000. Many of the stadia built for the Athens Olympics remain closed to the public at the cost of over £1 million per month on upkeep alone.

In the same mould as Sydney and Athens the legacy promises for London include the creation of new sporting facilities intended to benefit 'the community'. To enable such facilities to be built space needed to be created. In May 2006, the Greater London Authority carried out an audit of playing fields in the capital and found that there were around 1500 in total (GLA 2006). The report recognized that in the period between 2001 and 2006 the loss of playing fields, mainly to car parks, had slowed down, but a lack of access, safety and attractiveness of facilities was deterring people from using them. This report formed the basis of the justification to utilize underused public land for the benefit of the Games. However, it remains to be seen whether any new facilities will obtain the required funding for essential maintenance and upkeep to ensure the longevity necessary to enable the promised legacy. Pessimistically, Executive Member for the Regeneration of Newham, Councillor Connor McAuley, when asked by the authors to comment on the community significance of new Olympic facilities, stated that the much-heralded Olympic Aquatics Centre offered nothing more than a 'pretty roof'.

The research drawn on in this chapter has evidenced that the much heralded regeneration has had a less than inspirational impact on the wider London community. This was particularly apparent in an interview with Newham resident, Steve Berwick, 58, who in 2008 argued that, once the Games were over, the only widespread appeal to bring people and more important money, into the regenerated

---

16   Sydney residents' euphoria created by the Olympic Park and the Games swiftly faded, replaced by a feeling of irritation that they are still paying for the Olympics years after the event. Hodgkinson claims that although Sydneysiders recognized that the Olympic Park was a colossal expense, the euphoria of the Games temporarily alleviated these concerns. Similar to what is being heralded for London's host boroughs, Hodgkinson indicates that Sydney's local communities were told that the Olympic Park 'would become a fully-functioning area, but that never happened'. Despite the Aquatic Centre being used regularly, and occasional sporting events and concerts, there is not enough income to pay for the upkeep of the stadiums. Sydneysiders are thus 'lumbered' with the cost.

area would be the newly built John Lewis superstore, located in the Stratford Shopping City. However, whether many of the current local community fit the typical John Lewis customer demographic is doubtful and it may well be designed for the next 'local community' anticipated to repopulate the area post-Games, probably in 'gated communities'. Such developments prompt a number of further points of debate. In the first instance, the globalized retail spaces in Westfield's Stratford City complex raise questions over the fate of the existing functioning and locally focused market hosted by the existing adjacent Stratford Centre mall. When the authors put this question to a representative of Newham Council in 2008 on one of their monthly 'regeneration tours', they received the answer that 'Stratford Centre will be used by local people for everyday things, whilst Stratford City will be used for more extended shopping expeditions.' Although the empirical basis was unclear, this explanation raises further questions. First, many of the proposed retail tenants of Stratford City are likely to be in direct competition with the existing market (in addition to traders in the redeveloped Olympic Fringe commercial areas). Second, arguably, Stratford City will be easier to access from the local transport hub via a newly constructed bridge funnelling prospective consumers from the Underground station, whilst those wishing to enter the existing Stratford Centre must first cross four lanes of Stratford's one-way traffic system and feeder roads, one of east London's busier thoroughfares. Third, in 2008 a similar dynamic accompanied the development of the £1.7 billion Westfield shopping centre in Shepherd's Bush, West London, ultimately generating controversy over the decline of local traders.

The 2012 Games deliverers have created a split within local communities. There are those that blindly accept the assertions that the after Games legacy will counter-balance the upheaval occurred during the construction period and those that feel that the Legacy is a red-herring. This latter group is further split into those that are willing to do something to try to rectify it and those that are not. Predominantly, those that are willing to do something about it feel the Olympics are something that *'is being done to them'*. This group feel that unless the Olympic authority is forced to adjust, the Games, with all its associated peripheries, will continue to be something negative that is being inflicted upon them and over which they have no control. However, whatever stance one takes regarding Legacy, the fact remains that the debate revolves around the issues of its extent, appropriateness, the legitimacy of consultation exercises and, ultimately, its beneficiaries. Revealingly, the Games themselves are ahead of schedule and their progress is attracting praise from visiting IOC dignitaries.

There are also further debates over the fate of the Olympic facilities after the contest. Another issue that may become more pressing for the local community post-Games, common to many of the capital's previous experiments with gentrification and regeneration, is community displacement and the limited role of affordable housing provisions in reversing this trend. Cox, Darcy and Bounds' (1994) investigation into housing inequalities created by major sporting events, for example, provides irrefutable evidence that, in the absence of appropriate policy measures, hallmark events have a negative impact upon low-income private renters. A sceptic might suggest that anyone with a vested interest in the capitalistic revolution of regenerated areas is well aware of this and even relies upon it to facilitate the transition from an impoverished to a more affluent 'gentrified' community. The people in Newham are expected to trust that the legacy will provide benefit to the community, increase local prosperity in the local area and yet, paradoxically, believe that this will strengthen and not jeopardize their place in this revitalized locale.

It will take years following the 2012 Olympics to provide any firm conclusions regarding TELCO's effectiveness in securing a better deal for Londoners. However, what can be clearly ascertained at this juncture is that TELCO has made more progress than many other SMs simply by keeping track of the hierarchical changes and layers of bureaucracies that have been created in response to the Olympic bid. The securing of regular dialogue with all the major players is an achievement in itself and, of course, a necessary precursor to tangible legacy benefits for London's citizens.

Conclusion

As highlighted above, the OPLC, formed in 2009, will lead the transformation of the Olympic Park into its post-Games 'legacy mode'. At the time of writing, the OPLC has indicated a willingness to interact with SMs but, following Haugaard (2002), this generates questions over whether power dynamics will be reset, reconfigured or regressed. Furthermore, will this new order attain greater compliance from SMs simply because it is 'new'? And how much more time will this 'newness' allow the OPLC to reproduce the actions of their predecessors, hinting at legacy progress without ever clearly specifying what exact form it is likely to take? This could be seen as the height of hegemonic bureaucracy, not simply moving the goalposts but changing the teams halfway through the match. At present, the signs are less than encouraging for SM actors. A report by the London Assembly's Economic Development, Culture, Sport and Tourism Committee in early 2010 deemed the OPLC's remit to be extremely restricted and that there was much work to do in ensuring consensus in its decision-making:

> [the] Olympic Park Legacy Company's remit is narrow and it has very little confirmed public funding. Instead, it relies on identifying private funding and partnership working – difficult enough in a boom but almost impossible in the present economic climate. Time is running out. The Mayor and the Olympic Park Legacy Company must act … otherwise an historic opportunity will have been lost. (GLA 2010: 7–8)

Principles observable at past Games should allow future SMs to understand the nuances of negotiation with Olympic organizers. However, the complexities of

Olympic-related concerns are often too advanced for the majority of the players involved in voluntary SMs to engage with. By definition, as this chapter has demonstrated, such arrangements play into the hands of the polished professional structures involved in Olympic delivery. This chapter has also shown how those planning the Games will always begin unilaterally and may then employ placation as a vehicle of marginalization. However, as an hegemonic actors, if Olympic authorities continue to exclude 'the community', they risk escalating malcontent from myriad groups and ultimately foster widespread discontent. Consequently, for such authorities, it is prudent to present the perception to the community of being fluid and changeable and willing to compromise and negotiate, thus keeping malcontents at the negotiating table and away from protesting on the streets.

This reading of the situation is exemplified by the fact that groups that have publicly challenged the authority and legitimacy of the 2012 Olympic movement have been 'rewarded' with placating compensations, such as the Newham campus of the National Construction College, which opened in February 2009, principally funded by the LDA. The deliverers were clearly willing to make such gestures but, rather than delineate community benefits at the outset, they drip them to the community disguised as rewards for malcontents who are thus 'incorporated' into the policy-making process – providing such malcontents can cause 'enough stink', as a member of TELCO often remarked, to suggest being worthy of inclusion.

Naively, SMs often interpret inclusion in the decision-making process as tangible progress. As TELCO community organizer Mathew Bolton summarized when interviewed, 'All we want is a fair piece of the pie and meetings with the relevant agencies is a great start.' However, this impression is carefully cultivated by the Olympic authorities who, by delimiting inclusion, create a value for seats at the discussion table with which they can subsequently 'reward' selected groups, thus creating a sense of gratitude from those 'permitted' inclusion. Consequently, groups 'permitted' access become concerned that, if they remonstrate too strongly, they may jeopardize a relationship they have worked hard to forge. Thus for the Olympic hegemon, opposition from their strongest opponents is minimized.

When such dilemmas were discussed with TELCO luminaries, those in charge openly acknowledge that 'general members' were rarely aware of the complexities of situations. But – significantly – such luminaries were acutely aware of the merry dance they are participating in. They are evidently not a 'mass' movement; neither can they claim to speak for all Newham residents, nor 'East Enders' in general. The critical mass that might have caused the Olympic hegemon to tremble does not exist; a fractured community and one generally apathetic to politics will ensure those charged with delivering the Olympics get their way with little resistance. What is readily apparent, and something that TELCO itself openly acknowledges, is that SMs have to choose their battles carefully and taking on the Olympic industry is proving to be an ambitious decision.

PART III
Conclusions

Chapter 9

Conclusions: Towards 2012 and Beyond

By outlining and analysing the form and impact of the London 2012 Olympic security programme, this book has presented a number of central arguments. In the first instance, specific post-millennium tensions continue to dominate much of the discourse surrounding security planning for the 2012 Games. In turn, as Chapters 2 and 5 outline, these have led to a selective constitution of Olympic risks around catastrophic terrorist attacks. Being both dynamic and diffuse, these risks necessitate complex and uncertain strategies of mitigation. In response, the 2012 security strategy blends cutting-edge technological interpretations of Olympic security traditions with more inert crime control orthodoxies. As the original 2012 security budget more than tripled to address these threats, a range of new formal and informal, human and non-human surveillance-oriented security measures have been hastily shepherded into East London's splintered geographies. Although these spaces have become patrolled by contemporaneously advanced technologies, pre-existing standardized themes of security prevail. These include the deployment of increasingly sophisticated technologies, extensive private policing, a commitment to zero-tolerance models of policing, programmes of metropolitan militarization, target hardening and architectures of 'defensible space' to cleave Olympic neighbourhoods into geographies of access and entitlement. Movement across these borders is, of course, highly regulated and dependent on (physical or fiscal) license. In sum, security innovations, particularly in the areas of technological control, including novel forms of data capture, networking and video analytics, sit atop a bedrock of more permanent underlying orthodoxies.

This convergence of the myriad themes of Olympic (in)security in East London reflects features of a broader genealogy. Regarding perceived risks, as Chapter 2 illustrated, the emphasis on terrorist threats has been a feature of Olympic security planning since Munich. Since 9/11, the Madrid train bombings and London 7/7, a number of recent terrorist attacks on both athletes[1] and spectators[2] have reinforced the powerful symbolic connection between hosting sporting mega-events and

---

1 Including attacks on Sri Lanka's cricket team in Lahore and the ambush of the Togolese national football team in Angola's Cabinda province.

2 Including the murder of 75 spectators at a Pakistani volleyball match during January 2010 and (potentially) Joel Hinrich's apparent suicide attack outside a University of Oklahoma American Football match in 2005. In May 2010, Iraqi security personnel arrested a Saudi national al-Qaeda operative they claimed was, under the co-ordination of Ayman al-Zawahiri, planning to attack the 2010 FIFA World Cup in South Africa (Reuters 2010). However, no further proof or details had emerged at the time of writing.

the fear of terrorist violence. As such, terrorist threats look likely to preoccupy Olympic security planning for years to come. At the recent XXI Winter Olympic Games in Vancouver, for example, numerous reports highlight considerable levels of public fear over terrorist attacks. Indeed, Boyle and Haggerty (2009a) cite one recent survey showing that a quarter of British Columbia's inhabitants believed a terrorist attack was certain to occur before or during the Games. Despite the absence of any specific terrorist threats, Vancouver's provision of security to quell such fears reflects a more enduring trend, which has influenced previous Olympiads and will affect those to come.

With the hosting of the 2014 Winter Games in Sochi, Russia, geographically proximate to Chechnya and the Russo–Georgian disputed territories of South Ossetia and Abkhazia, regional ethno-nationalist concerns are likely to be of principal concern for security providers.[3] For the 2016 Games in Rio de Janeiro, primary attention is likely to be afforded to local crime rather than the explicit threat of terrorism, which organizers currently deem to be a low risk (Rio2016), a model that is also likely for the 2010 and 2014 FIFA World Cups. In the case of Brazil, however, as elsewhere, boundaries between crime and terrorism have become blurred, as evinced by Rio's criminal groups' increasing adoption of terrorist strategies, such as the use of improvised explosive devices, particularly throughout 2006 (sourced from the Global Terrorism Database).

Rio's successful candidacy to host the 2016 Games also draws on the continuities of security outlined in this book. These concerns can be more specifically related to the city's murder rate (that annually stands at triple that of the entire UK) and fear of robberies against tourists. Indeed, a statistical increase in robberies against foreign visitors to the 2009 Carnival also attracted particularly poor publicity (although such statistical variations may also reflect changing policing priorities (see Crowther-Dowey and Fussey 2011) and mask the fact that Cariocas bear the brunt of criminal victimization in their city). Nevertheless, such issues are likely elevate the attention afforded to security, particularly given that in the IOC's pre-ballot review of all 2016 candidate cities, Rio scored poorly in this area, trailing Chicago, Tokyo, Madrid and Doha and ranking only marginally ahead of Baku and Prague (IOC 2008). To mitigate these risks, a familiar plan is being formulated that draws on the principles of CPTED (Rio 2016 2007: 27, Chapter 6) and the insulating of Olympic sites from the wider city. Such imperatives connect international standards of Olympic security with Rio's tradition of delineating 'high-value' spaces from their urban context. Coupled with the location of prestigious sporting sites within an existing urban milieu, it is likely that continued re-bordering of the city risks further splintering Rio's divided spaces and provide a significant challenge to its regenerative aspirations.

The juxtaposition of these local variations with the international standardization of mega-event protection strategies points to a partial, selective and potentially

---

3   Indeed, practitioners engaged in devising Sochi's security strategy have confirmed to the authors that priority is being given to the threat of Chechen violence.

contestable application of security. This 'social construction of security' is characterized not only by its focus but also its temporal and spatial application. Policy discourses on the terrorist threat arguably overshadow other social harms that traditionally accompany such events, including both routine and organized crime (respectively: Decker et al. 2007, Hellenic Republic Ministry of Public Order 2004). Displacement and the diffusion of security measures beyond the fortified Olympic Park (via new commercial developments, and also securitized 'buffer zones', are also points of debate (see below). Temporal factors are wide and varied. Terrorist attacks during the Olympic Games are extremely rare, with a far greater number occurring prior to the actual Games, as highlighted by the events preceding the 1988 and 1992 Games. Security challenges also arise *after* terrorist attacks. Following the Atlanta bomb in 1996, for example, SOLEC were faced with a double crisis. Enhanced public vigilance translated into a dramatic escalation of 'suspicious package' sightings that law enforcement agencies struggled to cope with (see Chapter 2). At the same time, when faced with the prospect of physical danger, Atlanta's low-paid private and volunteer security contingent diminished considerably in the days following the attack (Buntin 2000a).

In making sense of these developments, the book acknowledges Lyon's (2009) provisional exploration of mutable 'liquid surveillance' (albeit with his central emphasis resting on identification) and builds further on Bauman's (2004) characterization of the 'liquefaction' of institutions and frameworks. Bauman's conceptualization of these 'fluids ... so called because they cannot keep their shape for long ... unless they are poured into a tight container' (2004: 51) informs the book's theoretical approach to understanding the institution and operation of security in the context and environment of the Olympics. Here, the 'tight container' is the increasingly standardized and globalized configuration of Olympic security strategies and their sites of application into which the 'liquid' of global and local processes are poured.

Moreover, the unprecedented scale of the 2012 operation has stimulated an inundation of security measures into the Olympic site that overflow its boundaries and soak through into the surrounding neighbourhoods and their well documented suspect communities. A further corollary, of central importance to this book, is the way these processes connect with and abrade against London's more idiosyncratic extant security infrastructures and the communities that host them.

Socio-Ethical Implications

The confluence of Olympic liquid security around East London generates a number of distinct socio-ethical implications. These are now examined over five thematic areas of discussion: *locality, legitimacy, listings, legislation* and *legacy.*

Locality

'Community' has been one of the central motifs of official London 2012 discourse, in terms of both the immediate and long-term 'legacy' beneficiaries of the Games. However, sporting mega-events internationalize the local community and, in doing so, create a security environment aimed at responding to exceptional and external needs. As Lenskyj (2002) notes in the case of Sydney, and Samatas (2007) in respect to Athens, this may stimulate the decline of local control over urban environments. Indeed, during the recent 2008 UEFA European football championships, Klauser (2008) explains how, despite the fact that in one Swiss city selected as host venue for the championships, residents had expressed their opposition to CCTV deployment in two separate referendums, UEFA's requests for the cameras led the municipal authorities to install them. For London, the Games are located in an area with a tradition of scant public consultation over new security measures and, indeed, historically, new control and surveillance measures have been imposed across the city with little more than cursory dialogue with their likely subjects. For broader Olympic-related developments, public engagement, although it does occur, is consistently abridged and often addressed only after key decisions have been taken (see Chapter 8).

Legitimacy

As Chapter 5 argues, political authority and the policing agencies through which it is transmitted, acquires legitimacy via the consent of the policed (see *inter alia* Rose 1979, Reiner 2007). Considering the aspiration to deploy over 7,000 private security guards, police from 11 constabulary areas and representatives from numerous overseas policing agencies in London's Olympic boroughs, these matters gain considerable significance. At the same time, given the likely inequalities in the beneficiaries of East London's Olympic legacies (see Chapters 4, 8 and below) any residual legitimacy of the overall 2012 project may become extremely fragile.

It is probable that London will join the list of Olympic cities that, post-Olympics, retain security architectures that would have struggled to achieve consent in less exceptional circumstances. As Chapter 5 details, previous incidence includes the legacy of private policing following the Tokyo 1964 and Seoul 1988 Olympiads (Lee 2004) and the continuation of zero-tolerance-style exclusion laws after the Sydney 2000 Games (Lenskyj 2002). Together, these themes connect with critical notions of control 'creep' (see *inter alia* Marx 1988). In London, maintaining legitimacy has been a long-standing campaign for the police and one that has been subject to serious challenges. Given that the 'community' is continually cited by the ODA as the main beneficiary of the Games, this perhaps constitutes one of the most important socio-ethical issues.

Listing

Formal social control strategies have a lasting impact on their subjects. Whilst this is often the desired effect, substantial ethical issues arise when these are applied to those innocent of any offence (as seen from the recent European Court of Human Rights ruling on the illegality of UK DNA data retention practices).[4] Connecting with Lyon's (2003b) argument that the most important social cost of surveillance (and, it can be argued, other forms of social control) is the 'sorting' of individuals into categories that could substantially affect their life chances without available mechanisms of redress, the '*listing*' or classification of individuals as a 'risk' has been a component of mega-event security practices in many countries. In addition to debates over the accuracy of the pre-emptive and actuarial processes that define risk (Feeley and Simon 1994), a key concern is the inability of individuals to extricate themselves from the classifications to which they have been assigned. This issue gains importance when considering how such categorizations are often incorrect and/or have a significant effect on one's life chances. For example, Eick and Töpfer's (2008) study of security at the 2006 FIFA World Cup in Germany revealed that police made 8,450 pre-emptive 'contacts' with local people they suspected *might become* involved in hooliganism during the tournament. These contacts often took the form of uniformed officers questioning individuals at their workplace or family environment. Given the trend towards anticipatory control measures, including technological forms of behaviour categorization and 'proactive' zero tolerance policing, that constitute a growing trend in UK law enforcement practices, catalysed by the Olympics, these issues are set to gain greater importance over the coming years.

Legislation and Regulation

This book has highlighted how the hosting of mega sporting events may generate tensions between the requirements of supranational bodies, such as the IOC, and existing provisions enshrined in domestic legislation. This can occur in a number of ways. As demonstrated by the procurement issues surrounding the Beijing

---

4   Flaherty (2010) notes that 21 per cent of profiles on the UK DNA database belong to people who have not been convicted of any crime of offence and that it also holds the profiles of 77 per cent of the UK's young black male population. In the 2008 case of *S and Marper*, the European Court of Human Rights ruled that it was illegal for the UK government to retain DNA samples of individuals innocent of any crime (*S and Marper* v *United Kingdom* 30562/04 [2008] ECHR 1581 (4 December 2008)). Based on much criticized research claiming that innocent constituents of the database were somehow equally likely to commit future offences as those with prior convictions, the government included a provision to retain DNA profiles of the innocent for six years (25 years in the case of those suspected of terrorism) in the 2010 Crime and Security Act. The specific DNA database-related provisions to the Act were never debated in Parliament.

Games, the spirit of domestic laws governing the sales of military and policing apparatus may be bypassed in favour of the huge commercial and reputational benefits to suppliers of Olympic security equipment.

The aesthetics of athletics   Another component of this debate relates to how international branding agendas[5] conflict with local attempts to engage with the Olympic event. Disputes are particularly centred on use of the words 'London 2012', 'Olympics' and 'Olympic', which Olympic authorities have sought to extract and appropriate from vernacular lexicons in order to attach intellectual property rights. Numerous examples abound. During May 2008 the University of East London hosted a conference entitled 'Terrorism and the Olympics' less than 200 metres from the yet-to-be-built Olympic Park. This title remained unchanged despite telephoned warnings from LOCOG (stationed some distance away) that it potentially breached their trademark ownership. Arguably more egregious were the ODA's similar threats to a Stratford Cafe (that caters for many Olympic planners) to remove a homemade banner proudly associating their neighbourhood with the 2012 project. Further afield, Olympic authorities banned enthusiastic students at the University of Brighton from calling a lecture series 'The Olympic Lecture Series'. Despite the official line that they are taking a 'reasonable and proportionate approach to protecting our brand' (The Argus, 2008), such threats represent a very selective and managed interpretation and discourse of what the Olympics means to local residents.[6] Instead, predictably, such local interpretations of – and engagements with – London 2012 Inc.

---

5   The importance of sponsorship and branding to the Olympic organizers was outlined by the Culture, Media and Sport Committee in 2007 as, 'A substantial part of funding for staging the Games – 12% – is expected to be raised through agreements between the International Olympic Committee (IOC) and long-term partners – "*top sponsors*". The IOC therefore requires that steps be taken by host countries and by Organizing Committees to protect the commercial gain through association with the Olympics and Paralympics which *top* sponsors expect in exchange. The Olympic rings – the most powerful symbol for the Games – are already statutorily protected in the UK; 2 71 further measures to protect the Olympic brand were agreed to by Parliament last year and are enshrined in the London Olympic Games and Paralympic Games Act 2006' (2007: 43 emphasis added).

6   The London Olympic Games and Paralympic Games Act Act 2006 also develops previous legislation (notably the Olympic Symbol etc. (Protection) Act 1995) to ensure sponsors' privileged access to Olympic iconography is preserved. In doing so, the Act establishes a 'London Olympics association right' which provides two lists of words. If any of the words from either list are used together it is deemed an infringement of copyright. List one contains the words 'Games', 'Two Thousand and Twelve', '2012', 'Twenty Twelve'; and list two comprises the words 'Gold', 'Silver', 'Bronze', 'London', 'Medals', 'Sponsor', 'Summer'. Also these lists are not exhaustive as an infringement may be made via any association with the London 2012 brand (see LOCOG 2010). A further argument here revolves around the questionable appropriation of words already in common use prior to their 'protection' by the 2006 Act.

acquiesce to the branding needs of sponsors. For 2012 these include the usual suspects of Coca-Cola, McDonalds and Cadburys', the food of corporate athletics, if not of athletes themselves.

Fanning the flame – Olympic legislation and the spread of control   Earlier chapters have described how, for 2012, a substantial securitized traffic-free 'buffer zone', extending over the urban areas to the south of the Olympic Park from West Ham and Plaistow, has already been approved. Despite the security benefits and greater usage of public transportation that this may bring, this development entails additional social repercussions, ones that may challenge official declarations that the Games will foster growth and development for local communities. Whilst such controlled zones may visibly conflict with the area's deep rooted traditions of (extremely laissez-faire) street trading, more attention has been placed on the potential stifling of another East End ritual: rebellion.

Contained within the London Olympic Games and Paralympic Games Act 2006 are a number of sections that restrict the rights of protest, expression and assembly. Particular criticism of this measure has centred on s. 19, focusing on advertising and permitting authorities to cover placards, and s. 22, enabling the police ('or enforcement officer') to 'enter land or premises on which they reasonably believe a contravention of regulations under section 19 is occurring'. This provides legislative powers to constrain both the bearers *and* producers of placards. According to a government spokesperson (cited in *The Guardian* 2009b), these provisions were instigated to curb unauthorized advertising, sales of counterfeit goods and, said without discernable irony, 'over-commercialization' near the Olympic venues. Yet the wording of the Act makes it clear that these measures extend beyond commercial endeavours and can easily encompass political activity, as s. 19(4) demonstrates:

> The regulations may apply in respect of advertising of any kind including, in particular: (a) advertising of a non-commercial nature, and; (b) announcements or notices of any kind.

What is also noteworthy is that such restrictions are not unique to 2012. These practices have been adopted at many other Games across the globe (see Lenskyj 2004 for further examples) and can be argued to be a *condition* of hosting the Games. Restriction on protest in or near Olympic venues, for example, is specified in Rule 51, s. 3 of the IOC's Olympic Charter, which host cities are compelled to adhere to (and may therefore override or contradict enshrined domestic rights) in order for their bids to succeed.

Legacy: The Evolution will be Televised

One of the most frequently articulated concepts in relation to 2012, and a key determinant of London's award of the Games, is the aspect of the 'legacy' that specifically relates to the post-event use of the Olympic site and attendant local regeneration schemes. In the official discourse, this legacy is primarily seen as 'community' focused. One typical articulation of this is the claim by Peter Rogers, Chief Executive of the London Development Agency, that 'we have been working closely with our Olympic partners to ensure a lasting ... legacy. All of this will provide a strong community focus for future generations' (London2012 2009).

This post-Games utility of the Olympic development also extends to the machinery of security. This will also be trained on 'the community'. Questions remain over the comparative security priorities of a high-profile international sporting event attended by millions of people and the degree of infrastructure that will remain behind to police a large urban parkland (the future incarnation of the Olympic site). Indeed, the aforementioned tenders for Olympic Park security providers (see Chapter 7) actively encouraged companies to supply a 'security legacy', thus inevitably bequeathing substantial mechanisms and technologies of control to the post-event site. These measures are both physical and conceptual. In addition to the large-scale deployment of surveillance cameras, physical measures include an overall hardening of the built environment. For 2012, all Olympic structures and the 'white space' between them have been embedded with minimum ACPO standards of 'Secure by Design' (see Chapter 5). At the same time, these innovations will inform a new code of good practice for similar design projects in the future, thus providing a conceptual security legacy.

For other mega-events, such as the 2006 FIFA World Cup, the security legacy consisted of sustained networks of professionals rather than physical control measures (largely due to the deployment of mobile CCTV) (Coaffee and Murakami Wood 2006, Baasch 2008), this post-event inheritance of security infrastructures is a surprisingly common Olympic legacy, as articulated above in relation to private policing and zero-tolerance-style exclusion laws. Indeed, private security providers view the potential to engage in new markets and develop opportunities with the public sector after the Games as a further, and perhaps more compelling, reason for their engagement in the Olympics project.[7] This retention of security mechanisms also adds new resonance to Jacques Rogge's famous maxim 'once an Olympic City, always an Olympic City' (see Rio 2016 2008).

In recent years, just bidding for the Games has been enough to stimulate the installation of mega-event security mechanisms. For example, the attempt by Cape Town, South Africa, to bid (unsuccessfully) for the 2004 Games required the city to be seen as secure enough to host the Olympics. As a result, an extensive security infrastructure was introduced into areas posited as likely venues and visitor

---

7   Data from interview with one of the directors of the British Security Industry Association's 2012 operation.

accommodation centres (Minnaar 2007). After their bid failed, the CCTV systems were not removed; instead they were justified as part of a general programme to combat crime, which in this case was seen as discouraging foreign tourists, investors and conference delegates (Coaffee and Wood 2006).[8]

Overall, key to this discussion are the critical themes of legitimacy and control 'creep' as they apply to the post-event site in London. As such, issues surrounding 'citizenship' and 'community' (continually cited by the ODA as the main beneficiaries of the Games) and their engagement with these reconfigured securitized spaces may also be called into question.

As Chapter 4 articulates, 'legacy' implications are also indirect. With regard to East London's labour markets, the 'Bridging the Gap'[9] scheme, aimed at recruiting the shortfall in the required 7,000 private security guards, will invest swathes of young people with the skills needed to service the ephemeral security needs of the Games. The utility of diverting of thousands of East Londoners towards these specific areas of further education will be ascertained once the post-event employment market for this sector becomes clear.

In addition to containing specific security adornments, Stratford's regenerated spaces may also reinforce existing social divisions that, in turn, generate new demands for security. Combined with the growth of new leisure-oriented symbolic economies (Zukin 1995) and the neoliberal visions of order that normally accompany them (Bauman 2000, Brenner and Theodore 2002) in the area, the re-bordered neighbourhood is likely to stimulate elevated demands for protection from the perceived incumbent 'dangerous populations' by the inhabitants of its newly gentrified compounds (see *inter alia* Davis 1990, Sennet 1996, Ellin 1997, Hall 2002).

Final Thoughts

Throughout the history of urban planning, generally, and specifically since 9/11, issues of security and sustainability have taken different paths. This book has set out a number of arguments relating to both processes as they apply to the 2012 Olympic and Paralympic Games. Given the scale of Olympic-related development and its location amidst human geographies facing acute socio-economic challenges, at the same time as attracting epithets of danger and criminality, these security and regeneration issues interconnect here perhaps more than anywhere in the world at the time of writing. As such, endowing security policies with regeneration considerations before, during and after the event will not only foment

---

8   At the time of writing Cape Town is also compiling a bid to host the 2020 Summer Olympics.

9   'Bridging the Gap' is a scheme largely organized by the British Security Industry Association and further education institutions to train school leavers with the skills to undertake basic security tasks.

a genuinely inclusive legacy, it will also enhance the provision of safe and secure communities.

One of the central arguments of the book has been that the security planning for sporting mega-events (and other) events has become progressively globalized and homogenized. Lessons from 2012 therefore stand to resonate beyond East London and 2012. Security planning is currently underway in Glasgow ahead of the 2014 Commonwealth Games. England will host the 2015 Rugby World Cup and the 2019 ICC Cricket World Cup. Internationally, London's billing as the 'regeneration Games' has been directly influential on Rio's successful bid to host the 2016 Olympics and on the nascent plans of aspiring 2020 hosts (particularly given the strong sentiment within the IOC that the 2020 Games should be hosted in Africa). Together, these trends of standardizing mega-event security, of transferring knowledge between hosts and the award of Olympic-size events to global cities of a similar stature represent the global significance of London's experience.

References

Access Economics Available at: http://www.accesseconomics.com.au/publications reports.

Agamben, G. 2000. *Means Without End: Notes on Politics*. Minneapolis: Minnesota University Press.

Agamben, G. 2005. *State of Exception*. Chicago: University of Chicago Press.

Allin, J. and Wesker, A. 1974. *Say Goodbye: You May Never See Them Again*. London: Cape.

Allison, C. 2009. *The Olympic and Paralympic Safety and Security Programme*, Olympic and Paralympic Safety and Security Conference, Royal United Services Institute, London, 13 November.

Altshular, A. and Luberoff, D. 2003. *Mega-Projects: The Changing Politics of Urban Mega-Projects*. Washington: Lincoln Institute of Land Policy, Brookings Institution Press.

American Civil Liberties Union (ACLU) 2003. Q & A on face recognition. [Online]. Available at: http://www.aclu.org/privacy/spying/14875res20030902. html [accessed: 1 February 2010].

Andranovich, G., Burbank, M.J. and Heying, C.H. 2001. Olympic cities: lessons learned from mega-event politics. *Journal of Urban Affairs*, 23(20): 113–31.

The Argus 2008. Students banned from using the word Olympics by 2012 organisers. [Online, 7 February]. Available at: http://www.theargus.co.uk/news/2025639.0/?act=complaintcid=1109126 [accessed: 10 March 2010].

Armstrong, G. 1998. *Hooligans: Knowing the Score*. Oxford: Berg.

Armstrong, G. and Giulianotti, R. 1998. From another angle: police surveillance and football supporters, in *Surveillance, Closed Circuit Television and Social Control*, edited by C. Norris, J. Moran and G. Armstrong. Farnham: Ashgate, pp. 113–38.

Association of Chief Police Officers (ACPO) n.d. Statement of Requirement (SoR) for small UAS for close air support to standard BCU operations. [Online]. Available at: http://www.whatdotheyknow.com/request/south_coast_partnership_drone_do [accessed: 2 May 2010].

Aston, C. 1983. *A Contemporary Crisis: Political Hostage-taking and the Experience of Western Europe*. Westport, Ct: Greenwood Press.

ATHOC (2005) *Official Report of the XXVIIIth Olympiad: Homecoming of the Games*, Athens: ATHOC.

Atkinson, M. and Young, K. 2002. Terror games: media treatment of security issues at the 2002 Winter Olympic Games. *Olympika: The International Journal of Olympic Studies*, 9: 53–78.

Atkinson, M. and Young, K. 2008. *Deviance and Social Control in Sport.* Champaign, IL: Human Kinetics.

Atkinson, R. 2003. Domestication by cappuccino or a revenge on urban space? Control and empowerment in the management of public space. *Urban Studies*, 40(9): 1829–43.

Atkinson, R. and Helms, G. eds 2007. *Securing an Urban Renaissance.* Bristol: The Policy Press.

Audit Commission 2010. NI 36 Protection against terrorist attack. [Online]. Available at: http://www.audit-commission.gov.uk/localgov/audit/nis/Pages/NI036Protectionagainstterroristattack.aspx [accessed: 12 July 2010].

Australian Broadcasting Corporation (ABC) 2000. Olympics put the country into security [Online, 25 May]. Available at: http://www.abc.net.au/news/olympics/2000/05/item20000524175657_1.htm [accessed: 23 October 2009].

Baash, S. 2008. *FIFA Soccer World Cup 2006: Event-driven Security Policies*, Surveillance and Security at Mega Sport Events: From Beijing 2008 to London 2012 conference, Durham University, 25 April.

Back, L., Keith, M., Khan, A., Shukra, K. and Solomos, J. 2002. New Labour's white heart: politics, multiculturalism and the return of assimilation. *The Political Quarterly*, 73(4): 445–54.

Bailly, A.S. 1986. Subjective differences and spatial representations. *Geoforum*, 17(1): 81–88.

Baker, N. (1994a). Olympics or tests: the disposition of the British sporting public, 1948, *Sporting Traditions*, 11(1): 57–74.

Baker, N. (1994b). The Games that almost weren't: London 1948. *Olympika: International Journal of Olympic Studies*, 3: 107–16.

Bale, J. and Christensen, M. eds 2004. *Post-Olympism? Questioning Sport in the Twenty-first Century.* Oxford: Berg.

Ball, K. 2003. Surveillance after 9/11, in *The Intensification of Surveillance: Crime, Terror and Warfare in the Information Era*, edited by K. Ball and F. Webster. London: Pluto.

Ball, K. and Webster, F. eds 2003. *The Intensification of Surveillance: Crime, Terrorism and Warfare in the Information Era.* London: Pluto.

Bamford, B. 2004. The United Kingdom's 'war against terrorism'. *Terrorism and Political Violence*, 16(4): 737–56.

Bandy, J. and Smith, J. 2005. *Coalitions Across Borders: Transnational Protest and the Neoliberal Order.* Lanham, Md: Rowman Littlefield.

Barber, B. 2001. *Jihad vs. McWorld.* New York: Ballantine.

Barnett, A. 2007. My week. [Online, 24 September]. Available at: http://www.pressgazette.co.uk/story.asp?storycode=38861.

Bartlett, D. and Steele, J. 2007. Washington's $8 billion shadow. [Online]. Available at: http://www.barlettandsteele.com/journalism/vf_washington8_3.php [accessed: 1 February 2010].

Bauman, Z. 2000 *Liquid Modernity.* Cambridge: Polity.

Bauman, Z. 2004. *Identity.* Cambridge: Polity.

Beck, U. 1992. *Risk Society: Towards a New Modernity*. London: Sage.

Beck, U. 1999. *World Risk Society*. Cambridge: Polity.

Beck, U. 2002. The terrorist threat: world risk society revisited. *Theory, Culture and Society*, 19(4): 39–55.

Belina, B. and Helms, G. 2003. Zero tolerance for the industrial past and other threats: policing and urban entrepreneurialism in Britain and Germany. *Urban Studies*, 40(9): 1845–67.

Bellavita, C. 2007. Changing homeland security: a strategic logic of special event security. *Homeland Security Affairs*, 3: 1–23.

Bermant, C. 1975. *Point of Arrival: A Study of London's East End*. London: Eyre Methuen.

Bigo, D. 2002. Security and immigration: toward a critique of the governmentality of unease. *Alternatives*, 5: 63–92.

Bigo, D. 2005. *The Birth of Ban-opticon: Detention of Foreigners in (il)liberal regimes*, Annual meeting of the International Studies Association, Hilton Hawaiian Village, Honolulu, Hawaii, 5 March 2005. [Online]. Available at: http://www.allacademic.com/meta/p70735_index.html.

Blair, A.T. 2004. A Message from the Rt Hon Tony Blair MP in *A Vision for the Olympic Games and Paralympic Games*, London: London 2012.

Blake, A. 2005. The economic impact of the London 2012 Olympics. [Online: Tourism and Travel Research Institute, Nottingham University Business School, Discussion Paper No. 2005/5]. Available at: http://www.nottingham. ac.uk/ttri/discussion/2005_5.pdf.

Bonditti, P. 2004. From territorial space to networks: A Foucauldian approach to the implementation of biometry. *Alternatives*, 4: 465–82.

Bottoms, A. and Wiles, E. 2002. Environmental criminology, in *The Oxford Handbook of Criminology*, edited by M. Maguire, R. Morgan and R. Reiner. Oxford: Oxford University Press.

Boudehoux, A. 2007. Spectacular Beijing: the conspicuous construction of an Olympic metropolis. *Journal of Urban Affairs*, 29(4): 383–99.

Box, S. 1981. *Deviance, Reality and Society*. London: Holt, Rinehart and Winston.

Boyle, P. 2005. Olympian security systems: guarding the Games or guarding consumerism? *Journal for the Arts, Sciences, and Technology*, 3: 12–17.

Boyle, P. and Haggerty, K. 2009b. Spectacular security: mega-events and the security complex. *International Political Sociology*, 3: 257–74.

Boyle, P. and Haggerty, K. 2009a. Privacy Games: The Vancouver Olympics, Privacy and Surveillance, A Report to the Office of the Privacy Commissioner of Canada. [Online]. Available at: http://www.surveillanceproject.org/files/ Privacy%20Games.pdf [accessed: 28 October 2009].

Brenner, N., and Theodore, N. eds 2002. *Spaces of Neoliberalism: Urban Restructuring in North America and Western Europe*. Oxford: Blackwell.

BAe Systems (BAe) 2008. GA22 brief for SCP [South Coast Partnership] meetings. [Online, December 2008]. Available at: http://www.whatdotheyknow.com/request/south_coast_partnership_drone_do [accessed: 2 May 2010.]

British Broadcasting Corporation (BBC) 2002. Anthrax scare at Salt Lake City. [Online, 13 February]. Available at: http://news.bbc.co.uk/1/hi/world/americas/1817831.stm [accessed: 28 October 2009].

British Broadcasting Corporation (BBC) 2003. Sudan hits out at ship's seizure. [Online, 24 June]. Available at http://news.bbc.co.uk/1/hi/world/europe/3015546.stm [accessed: 12 July 2010].

British Broadcasting Corporation (BBC) 2005a. London's green Olympic blueprint. [Online, 12 July]. Available from http://news.bbc.co.uk/1/hi/sci/tech/4299714.stm [accessed: 12 July 2010].

British Broadcasting Corporation (BBC) 2005b. BBC radio interview reported in Rogge Calls 2012 Host City Competition 'Fair' 4 August. [Online]. Available at: http://www.gamesbids.com/cgi-bin/news/viewnews.cgi?category=1&id=1 123175331.

British Broadcasting Corporation (BBC) 2007a. Experts debate Games bid benefits. [Online, 6 March]. Available at: http://news.bbc.co.uk/1/hi/scotland/glasgow_and_west/6422367.stm.

British Broadcasting Corporation (BBC) 2007b. Police warn over Olympic security. [Online, 21 June]. Available at: http://news.bbc.co.uk/1/hi/england/london/6226530.stm.

British Broadcasting Corporation BBC 2008a. Aldershot to host GB Olympic team. [Online, 15 January]. Available at: http://news.bbc.co.uk/1/hi/uk/7188035.stm [accessed: 8 March 2010].

British Broadcasting Corporation (BBC) 2008b. Police announce London 2012 plans. [Online, 5 March]. Available at: http://news.bbc.co.uk/sport1/hi/olympics/london_2012/7277918.stm [accessed: 2 May 2010].

British Broadcasting Corporation (BBC) 2008c. Opposition to Tube closure plan. [Online, 7 January]. Available at: http://news.bbc.co.uk/1/hi/england/london/7175410.stm [accessed: 30 March 2010].

British Broadcasting Corporation (BBC) 2008d. How far will house prices fall? [Online, 12 June 2008]. Available at: http://news.bbc.co.uk/1/hi/business/7445864.stm [accessed: 12 June 2008].

British Broadcasting Corporation (BBC) 2008e. Defiant Beijing family loses home, [Online, 18 July]. Available at: http://news.bbc.co.uk/1/hi/world/asia-pacific/7513289.stm [accessed: 12 July 2010].

British Broadcasting Corporation (BBC) 2008f. Olympic evictions. [Online, 19 July]. Available at: http://www.bbc.co.uk/blogs/thereporters/jamesreynolds/2008/07/olympic_evictions.html.

British Broadcasting Corporation (BBC) 2008g. Are the Olympic boroughs on track? [Online, 26 August]. Available at: http://www.bbc.co.uk/london/content/articles/2008/08/18/five_boroughs_progress_feature.shtml [accessed: 19 September 2008].

British Broadcasting Corporation (BBC) 2009. Digital cloud plan for city skies. [Online, 11 November]. Available at: http://news.bbc.co.uk/1/hi/technology/8350770.stm [accessed: 2 May 2010].

British Broadcasting Corporation (BBC) 2010a. Plans collapse for Britain's biggest mosque in London. [Online, 18 January]. http://news.bbc.co.uk/1/hi/england/london/8465694.stm [accessed: 12 July 2010].

British Broadcasting Corporation (BBC) 2010b. Jowell plays down West Ham's Olympic Stadium hopes. [Online, 17 February]. Available at: http://news.bbc.co.uk/sport1/hi/football/teams/w/west_ham_utd/8519515.stm [accessed: 2 May 2010].

British Broadcasting Corporation (BBC) 2010c. UK develops intelligent CCTV [Online, 11 March]. Available at: http://news.bbc.co.uk/1/hi/uk/8561367.stm [accessed: 11 March 2010].

British Broadcasting Corporation BBC. 2010d AEG Interested in Olympic Stadium. [Online, 4 May]. Available at: http://news.bbc.co.uk/sport1/hi/olympic_games/8658805.stm [accessed: 4 May 2010].

British Broadcasting Corporation BBC. 2010e London Olympic Games budget cut by £27m [Online, 24 May]. Available at: http://news.bbc.co.uk/1/hi/england/london/8701126.stm [accessed: 12 July 2010].

British Olympic Association (BOA) n.d. London 2012 Olympic bid – an eight-year journey. [Online]. Available at: http://www.olympics.org.uk/contentpage.aspx?no=268 [accessed: 12 July 2010].

British Olympic Association (BOA) 1948. *The XIVth Olympiad: London 1948 Official Report*. London: BOA.

Broadhurst, B. 2009. *Policing the Event*, Olympic and Paralympic Safety and Security Conference, Royal United Services Institute, London, 13 November.

Brohm, J.M. 1978. *Sport: A Prison of Measured Time*. London: Ink Links.

Brown, D. 2001. Modern sport, modernism and the cultural manifesto: De Coubertin's Revue Olympique. *The International Journal of the History of Sport*, 18(2): 78–109.

Brown, G. 2007. Statement on Security. Available at: http://www.number10.gov.uk/output/Page12675.asp [accessed: 4 May 2008].

Brown, J.B. 2007. *Building Powerful Community Organisations: A Personal Guide to Creating Groups That Can Solve Problems and Change the World*. New York: Long Hand Press.

Buntin, J. 2000a. *Security Preparations for the 1996 Centennial Olympic Games (B) Seeking a Structural Fix*. Cambridge, MA: John F. Kennedy School of Government, Harvard, Case Program, Case No.C16–00–1589.0.

Buntin, J. 2000b. *Security Preparations for the 1996 Centennial Olympic Games (C) The Games Begin*, John F. Kennedy School of Government Case Program, Harvard, Case No. C16–00–1590.0.

Burbank, M.J., Andranovich, G.D. and Heying, C.H. 2001. *Olympic Dreams: The Impact of Mega-Events on Local Politics*. London: Lynne Rienner.

Burris, S., Drahos, P. and Shearing, C. 2005. Nodal governance. *Australian Journal of Legal Philosophy*, 30(1): 30–58.

Cabinet Office 2008. *National Risk Register*. London: HMSO.

Cambridgeshire,EssexandSuffolkPoliceAirSupport2008.EmailfromCambs,Essex and Suffolk Police Air Support to CAA (1). [Online, 11 November]. Available at: http://www.whatdotheyknow.com/request/south_coast_partnership_drone_ do [UAV DISCLOSURE.pdf] [accessed: 2 May 2010].

Canadian Broadcasting Corporation (CBC) 2008. Convicted Air India bomb-builder Inderjit Singh Reyat gets bail. [Online, 9 July]. Available at: http://www.cbc.ca/canada/british-columbia/story/2008/07/09/bc-air-india-reyat-bail.html [accessed: 20 January 2010].

Carden, R.W. 1908. The Franco-British Exhibition. *Architectural Review*. 24: 32–7.

Cashman, R. 1999. The greatest peacetime event, in *Staging the Olympics: The Event and its Impact*, edited by R. Cashman and A. Hughes. Sydney: University of New South Wales Press, pp. 3–17.

Cashman, R. 2006. *The Bitter-Sweet Awakening: The Legacy of the Sydney 2000 Olympic Games*. Sydney: Walla Walla Press.

Cashman, R. and Hughes, A. eds 1999. *Staging the Olympics: The Event and its Impact*. Sydney: University of New South Wales Press.

Castells, M. 2000. Materials for an exploratory theory of the network society. *British Journal of Sociology*, 51(1): 5–24.

Cauley, J. and Im, E. 1988. Intervention policy: analysis of skyjackings and other terrorist incidents. *American Economic Review*, 78(2): 27–31.

Cesarani, D. 1994. *The Jewish Chronicle and Anglo-Jewry 1841–1991*. Cambridge: Cambridge University Press.

Chalip, L. and Costa, C.A. 2005. Sport event tourism and the destination brand: towards a general theory. *Sport in Society*, 8(2), June: 218–37.

Chalkely, B. and Essex, S. 1999. Urban development through hosting international events: a history of the Olympic Games. *Planning Perspectives*, 14: 369–94.

Champion, H.H. 1890. *The Great Dock Strike*. London: Swan.

Channel 4 2007. Dispatches: The Olympic Cash Machine. 10 September.

Chappelet, J.-L. 2008. The International Olympic Committee and the Olympic system. *International Journal of the History of Sport*, Special issue on Olympic legacies, 14: 1884–1902.

Charlton, J. 1999. *It Just Went Like Tinder: The Mass Movement and New Unionism in Britain 1899*. London: Redwords.

Charters, D. 1983. Terrorism and the 1984 Olympics. *Conflict Quarterly*, 3(4), Summer: 37–47.

Chernushenko, D. 2004. *Sustainable Urban Development in the Beijing Olympic Bid*. Speech given during a private presentation to the Beijing Deputy Mayor and the Beijing Olympic Organizing Committee. [Online]. Available at: http://www.ottawagreens.ca/ottawa-centre2/about/trackrecord/speech-sud_e.php.

Civil Aviation Authority (CAA) 2009. Letter of intent: proposal to amend the Air Navigation Order 2005. [Online]. Available at: http://www.caa.co.uk/docs/33/FOD200923.pdf.

Clark, C. and Hopkins, J. 1970. *A Relevant War Against Poverty: A Study of Community Action Programs and Observable Social Change*. New York: Harper & Row.

Clarke, R. 1980. Situational crime prevention: theory and practice. *British Journal of Criminology*, 20(2): 136–47.

Clarke, R. and Cornish, D. 1985. Modeling offenders' decisions: a framework for research and policy, in *Crime and Justice: An Annual Review of Research*, edited by M. Tonry and N. Morris, 6. Chicago, IL: University of Chicago Press.

Clarke, R. ed. 1997. *Situational Crime Prevention: Successful Case Studies*. Albany, N.Y.: Harrow and Heston.

Cleantech 2008. Beijing debuts green Olympic village. [Online]. Available at: http://cleantech.com/news/3307/beijing-olympic-village-worlds-first-green-neighborhood [accessed: 28 August 2008].

Clegg, S.R. 1989. *Frameworks of Power*. London: Sage.

The Cloud 2009. The Cloud: broadcasting the climate of humanity. [Online.] Available at: http://www.raisethecloud.org/#slides [accessed: 2 May 2010].

Clusa, J. 2000. *The Barcelona Olympic Experience, 1986–1992 and the 2004 Forum Expectations*, The World Direct Investment Forum, Lisbon, 5–6 June.

Coaffee, J. 2003. *Terrorism, Risk and the City*. Farnham: Ashgate.

Coaffee, J. 2004. Recasting the 'ring of steel': designing out terrorism in the City of London, in *Cities, War and Terrorism: Towards an Urban Geopolitics*, edited by S. Graham. Oxford: Blackwell, pp. 276–96.

Coaffee, J. 2007. Urban regeneration and the Olympic experience, in *Olympic Cities: Urban Planning, City Agendas and the World's Games, 1896 to the Present*, edited by J. Gold and M.M. Gold. London: Routledge, pp. 150–64.

Coaffee, J. 2008. Redesigning counter-terrorism for soft targets. *Homeland Security and Resilience Monitor*, Royal United Services Institute, 7(2), March: 16–17.

Coaffee, J. 2009a. Protecting the urban: the dangers of planning for terrorism. *Theory, Culture and Society*, 26(7–8): 343–55.

Coaffee, J. 2009b. *Terrorism, Risk and the Global City: Towards Urban Resilience*. Farnham: Ashgate.

Coaffee, J. and Bosher, L. 2008. Integrating counter-terrorist resilience into sustainability. *Proceeding of the Institute of Civil Engineers: Urban Design and Planning*, 16(2), Issue DP: 75–84.

Coaffee, J. and Fussey, P. 2010. Olympic security and the threat of terrorism, in *Olympic Cities: City Agendas, Planning, and the Worlds Games, 1896 to 2012*, edited by J. Gold and M.M. Gold. London: Routledge.

Coaffee, J. and Johnston, L. 2007. Accommodating the spectacle, in *Olympic Cities: Urban Planning, City Agendas and the World's Games, 1896 to the Present*, edited by J. Gold and M.M. Gold. London: Routledge, pp. 138–49.

Coaffee, J., Moore, C. Fletcher, D. and Bosher, L. 2008. Resilient design for community safety and terror-resistant cities. *Proceeding of the Institute of Civil Engineers: Municipal Engineer*, 161, Issue ME2: 103–10.

Coaffee, J., Murakami Wood, D. and Rogers, P. 2008. *The Everyday Resilience of the City: How Cities Respond to Terrorism and Disaster*. Basingstoke: Palgrave Macmillan.

Coaffee, J. and Murakami Wood, D. 2006. Security is coming home: rethinking scale and constructing resilience in the global urban response to terrorist risk. *International Relations*, 20(4): 503–17.

Coaffee, J. and O'Hare, P. 2008. Urban resilience and national security: the role for planners. *Proceeding of the Institute of Civil Engineers: Urban Design and Planning*, 16(1), Issue DP4: 171–82.

Coaffee, J., O'Hare, P. and Hawkesworth, M. 2009. The visibility of insecurity: the aesthetics of planning urban defences against terrorism. *Security Dialogue*, 40(4–5): 489–511.

Coaffee, J. and Rogers, P. 2008. Rebordering the city for new security challenges: from counter terrorism to community resilience. *Space and Polity*, 12(2): 101–18.

Coaffee, J. and Shaw, T. 2005. The liveability agenda: new regionalism, liveability and the untapped potential of sport and recreation. *Town Planning Review*, 76(2): iv.

Cochrane, A., Peck, J. and Tickell, A. 1996. Manchester plays games: exploring the local politics of globalisation. *Urban Studies*, 33(8): 1319–36.

Cohen, P. and Rustin, M.J. 2008. *London's Turning: The Making of Thames Gateway*. Farnham: Ashgate.

Coleman, R. 2004. Watching the degenerate: street camera surveillance and urban regeneration. *Local Economy*, 19(3): 199–211.

Columb, C. 2007. Unpacking New Labour's 'urban renaissance' agenda: towards a socially sustainable reurbanization of British cities? *Planning, Practice and Research*, 22(1): 1–24.

Comité d'Organisation des Jeux Olympiques (COJO Albertville and Savoie). 1992. *Official Report of the XVI Olympic Winter Games of Albertville and Savoie*. Paris: COJO Albertville and Savoie.

Comité d'Organisation des Jeux Olympiques (COJO Montreal) 1976. *Official Report of the XXIst Olympiad, Montreal 1976*. Ottowa: COJO Montreal.

Committee of Public Accounts (PAC) 2008. *The Budget for the London 2012 Olympic and Paralympic Games*. 14th Report of Session, 2007–08, 31 March. [Online]. Available at: http://www.publications.parliament.uk/pa/cm200708/cmselect/cmpubacc/85/85.pdf.

Community Care 2007. Olympic raid on lottery cash will put thousands of projects at risk. [Online, 1 March]. Available at: http://www.communitycare.

co.uk/Articles/2007/03/01/103592/Olympic-raid-on-lottery-cash-39will-put-thousands-of-projects-at.htm.

Cook, I. 2007. Beijing 2008, in *Olympic Cities: Urban Planning, City Agendas and the World's Games, 1896 to the Present*, edited by J. Gold and M.M. Gold. London: Routledge, pp. 286–97.

Cottrell, R.C. 2003. The legacy of Munich 1972: terrorism, security and the Olympic Games, in *The Legacy of the Olympic Games, 1984–2000*, edited by M. De Moragas, C. Kennett and N. Puig. Lausanne: IOC.

Cox, G., Darcy, M., Bounds, M. 1994. *The Olympics and Housing*. Sidney: Shelter.

Critchley, T.A. and James, P.D. 1987. *The Maul and the Pear Tree: The Ratcliffe Highway Murders, 1811*. London: Sphere Books.

Crowther, C. 2000. *Policing Urban Poverty*. Basingstoke: Macmillan.

Crowther, N.B. 2001. The Salt Lake City games and the ancient Olympics. *The International Journal of the History of Sport*, 19(4): 169–78.

Crowther-Dowey, C. and Fussey, P. 2011. *Researching Crime: Approaches, Method and Application*. Basingstoke: Palgrave.

Culture, Media and Sport (CMS) Committee 2007. *London 2012 Olympic Games and Paralympic Games: Funding and Legacy*. Second Report of Session, 2006–07, I, 24 January. London: HMSO.

Culture, Media and Sport (CMS) Committee. 2008. *London 2012: Lessons from Beijing*. Minutes of evidence. Available at: http://www.publications. parliament.uk/pa/cm200809/cmselect/cmcumeds/25/8100703.htm [accessed: 12 July 2010].

The Daily Mail 2006. London Olympics will cost £15bn says Montreal Olympics guru. [Online, 22 November]. Available at: http://www.dailymail.co.uk/news/article-417889/London-Olympics-cost-15bn-says-Montreal-Olympics-guru.html.

The Daily Mail 2009. Police spy in the sky buzzes BNP summer party, as four protesters are charged following clashes with officers. [Online, 17 August]. Available at: http://www.dailymail.co.uk/news/worldnews/article-1206618/Extremist-banned-entering-UK-BNP-festival.html.

The Daily Telegraph 2005. Livingstone latest to rue careless talk. [Online, 17 February]. Available at: http://www.telegraph.co.uk/sport/othersports/olympics/2355454/Livingstone-latest-to-rue-careless-talk.html. [= bose]

The Daily Telegraph 2007a. Mapp will fight Government over plans to reduce budget. [Online, 11 January]. Available at: http://www.telegraph.co.uk/sport/othersports/olympics/2305929/Mapp-will-fight-Government-over-plans-to-reduce-budget.html.

The Daily Telegraph 2007b. Lloyds TSB becomes Olympic sponsor. [Online, 14 March]. Available at: http://www.telegraph.co.uk/finance/2805703/Lloyds-TSB-becomes-Olympic-sponsor.html.

The Daily Telegraph 2007c. London 2012: Security 'threat to budget'. [Online, 12 December]. Available at: http://www.telegraph.co.uk/sport/othersports/

olympics/2328290/London-2012-Security-threat-to-budget.html [accessed: 12 July 2010].

The Daily Telegraph 2007d. Olympic stadium legacy losing its gloss. [Online, 17 August]. Available at: http://www.telegraph.co.uk/sport/othersports/ olympics/2319172/Olympic-stadium-legacy-losing-its-gloss.html.

The Daily Telegraph 2007e. Sebastian Coe joint first in race for IAAF power. [Online, 23 August]. Available at: http://www.telegraph.co.uk/sport/main. jhtml?xml=/sport/2007/08/23/sobond123.xml.

The Daily Telegraph 2007f. Olympic Stadium costs soar by £216m. [Online, 11 October]. Available at: http://www.telegraph.co.uk/sport/main.jhtml?xml=/ sport/2007/10/11/sofron111.xml.

The Daily Telegraph 2007g Lord Moynihan's broadside at 2012 finances. [Online, 25 October]. Available at: http://www.telegraph.co.uk/sport/othersports/ olympics/2324087/Lord-Moynihans-broadside-at-2012-finances.html.

The Daily Telegraph 2007h. London stadium sustainable but lacks ambition. [Online, 8 November]. Available at: http://www.telegraph.co.uk/sport/main. jhtml?xml=/sport/2007/11/08/soolym208.xml.

The Daily Telegraph 2007i. Olympic organisers unveil £496m stadium. [Online, 8 November]. Available at: http://www.telegraph.co.uk/sport/othersports/ olympics/2325248/Olympic-organisers-unveil-496m-stadium.html.

The Daily Telegraph 2007j. 2007a. Cost of Games under attack. [Online 15 November]. Available at: http://www.telegraph.co.uk/sport/othersports/ olympics/2325815/Cost-of-Olympic-Games-under-attack.html.

The Daily Telegraph 2007k. London 2012 must learn from the £1bn Sydney hangover. [Online, December 12]. Available at: http://www.telegraph. co.uk/sport/othersports/olympics/2307426/London-2012-[accessed: 12 December 2009].

The Daily Telegraph 2008a. From Olympics to obesity, sport gets an airing. [Online, 22 January]. Available at: http://www.telegraph.co.uk/sport/othersports/ olympics/2289684/From-Olympics-to-obesity-sport-gets-an-airing.html [accessed: 12 July 2010].

The Daily Telegraph 2008b. More than 50,000 migrant workers move into Olympics borough. [Online, 13 November]. Available at: http://www.telegraph.co.uk/ sport/othersports/olympics/london2012/3453006/More-than-50000-migrant-workers-move-into-Olympics-borough.html [accessed: 2 May 2010].

The Daily Telegraph 2009. London 2012: serious questions remain about Olympic legacy. [Online, 7 July]. Available at: http://www.telegraph.co.uk/sport/ othersports/olympics/london2012/5758718/London-2012-Serious-questions-remain-about-Olympic-legacy.html [accessed: 12 July 2010].

Dave, C. 2005. *The 2012 Bid: Five Cities Chasing The Summer Games*. Bloomington, Indiana: Author House.

Davies, S. (1996) *Big Brother*. London: Pan.

Davis, M. 1990. *City of Quartz: Excavating the Future in Los Angeles*. London: Verso.

Davis, M. 1998. *Ecology of Fear: Los Angeles and the Imagination of Disaster*. Los Angeles: Vintage.

Decker, S., Greene, J., Webb, V., Rojeck, J., McDevitt, J., Bynum, T., Varano, S. and Manning, P. 2005. Safety and security at special events: the case of the Salt Lake City Olympic games. *Security Journal*, 18(4): 65–75.

Decker, S., Varano, S. and Greene, J. 2007. Routine crime in exceptional times: The impact of the 2002 Winter Olympics on citizen demand for police services. *Journal of Criminal Justice*, 35(1): 89–103.

Deleuze, G. 1995. *Negotiations 1972–1990*, New York: Columbia University Press, pp. 177–83.

Deleuze, G. and Guattari, F. 1987. *A Thousand Plateaus: Capitalism and Schizophrenia*. Minneapolis: University of Minnesota Press.

della Porta, D. 2008. *Eventful Protest, Global Conflicts*, Nordic Sociological Association Conference, Aahrus, August. [Online]. Available at: http://www.bc.edu/schools/cas/sociology/meta-elements/pdf/EventfulProtest.pdf [accessed: 28 October 2009].

Democratic Undergound. 2008. Will Obama deliver for organized labour? [Online, 30 December]. Available at: http://www.democraticunderground.com/discuss/duboard.php?az=view_all&address=367x15866 [accessed: 12 July 2010].

Demos 2005. *After the Gold Rush: A Sustainable Olympics for London*. London: Demos/Institute for Public Policy Research.

Department for Children, Schools and Families 2008. *Record Numbers Now Doing PE and School Sport*. [Online]. Available at http://www.dcsf.gov.uk/pns/DisplayPN.cgi?pn_id=2008_0231 [accessed: 12 July, 2010].

Department for Communities and Local Government. 2009. *London 2012 Olympic Games: Scoping the Analytical and Legacy issues for Communities and Local Government*. London: HMSO.

Department for Culture, Media and Sport (DCMS) 2007. *Our Promise for 2012: How the UK will benefit from the Olympic Games and Paralympic Games*. London: DCMS.

Department for Culture, Media and Sport (DCMS) and Cabinet Strategy Unit 2002. *Game Plan: A Strategy for Delivering Government's Sport and Physical Activity Objectives*. [Online]. Available at: http://www.cabinetoffice.gov.uk/media/cabinetoffice/strategy/assets/game_plan_report.pdf.

Department for Culture, Media and Sport (DCMS) 2007. Olympics Minister Tessa Jowell written ministerial statement – Olympic Delivery Authority budget. [Online, 10 December]. Available at: http://www.culture.gov.uk/Reference_library/Press_notices/archive_2007/dcms_TJ-odabaselinebudget_10dec07.htm.

Department for Culture, Media and Sport (DCMS) 2008. *Legacy Action Plan. Before, During and After: Making the Most of the London 2012 Games*. London: HMSO.

Department for Work and Pensions 2009. *National Insurance Number Allocations to Adult Overseas Nationals Entering the UK, 2008–09*. London: Department for Work and Pensions. Available at: http://research.dwp.gov.uk/asd/asd1/tabtools/nino_allocations_aug09.pdf.

Downes, D. 1966. *The Delinquent Solution: A Study in Subcultural Theory.* London: Routledge and Kegan Paul.

Duffy, D. 2003. Security design and architecture: hidden strengths. *CSO Magazine.* [Online, May]. Available at: www.csoonline.com/read/050103/washington.html [accessed: 1 June 2003].

Dunn, K.M. and McGuirk, P. 1999. Hallmark events, in *Staging the Olympics: The Event and its Impact,* edited by R. Cashman and A. Hughes. Sydney: University of New South Wales Press, pp. 18–34.

Eade, J. 1996. Ethnicity and the politics of cultural difference: an agenda for the 1990s?, in *Culture, Identity and Politics: Ethnic Minorities in Britain,* edited by T. Ranger, Y. Samad and O. Stuart. Farnham: Avebury.

Eade, J. 2002. Adventure tourists and locals in a global city: resisting tourist performances in London's East End, in *Tourism: Between Place and Performance,* edited by S. Coleman and M. Crang. New York: Berghahn, pp. 128–39.

EasierProperty (2007) *House prices in East End rise after Olympic win.* [Online]. Available at: http://www.easier.com/32562-house-prices-in-east-end-rise-after-olympic-win.html. [accessed: 12 July 2010].

East London Advertiser 2007. Bigger payout for travellers over relocation. [Online]. Available at: http://www.eastlondonadvertiser.co.uk.

The East London Communities Organisation (TELCO) citizens. *Ethical Olympics.* [Online]. Available at: http://www.telcocitizens.org.uk/campaigns.html.

Eick, V. and Töpfer, E. 2008. *The Human and Hardware of Policing Neoliberal Sport Events Rent-a-Cops, Volunteers and CCTV at the FIFA Championship in Germany 2006 – and beyond,* Security and Surveillance at Mega Sport Events: from Beijing 2008 to London 2012 conference, Durham University, 25 April.

El Mundo 2005. ETA pone un coche bomba contra el símbolo de la candidatura de Madrid 2012. [Online, 27 June]. Available at: http://www.elmundo.es/elmundo/2005/06/25/espana/1119719063.html [accessed: 28 September 2009].

Ellin, N. ed. 1997. *Architecture of Fear.* New York: Princeton Architectural Press.

Emery, P.R. 2002. Bidding to host a major sports event: the local organising committee perspective. *International Journal of Public Sector Management,* 14: 316–35.

English, A. and Mitchell, L. 1989. *Through The Mill and Beyond.* Basingstoke: Basingstoke Press.

Entertainment Sports Programming Network (ESPN) 2009. English Premier League: Attendance 2008/2009. [Online]. Available at: http://soccernet.espn.go.com/stats/attendance?league=eng.1&year=2008&cc=5739 [accessed: 8 March 2010].

Ericson, R. and Haggerty, K. 1997. *Policing the Risk Society.* Toronto: University of Toronto Press.

Espy, R. 1979 *The Politics of the Olympic Games*. Berkeley, CA: University of California Press.

Essex, S. and Chalkely, B. 2004. Mega-sporting events in urban and regional policy – a history of the winter Olympics. *Planning Perspectives*, 19(2): 201–32.

Essex, S. and Chalkley, B. 1998. Olympic Games: catalyst of urban change. *Leisure Studies*, 17(3): 187–206.

Evans, D. 2010. The role of the private security industry, in *Terrorism and the Olympics: Lessons for 2012 and Beyond*, edited by A. Richards, P. Fussey and A. Silke. London: Routledge. pp 163–179.

Evans, G. 2007. London 2012, in *Olympic Cities: City Agendas, Planning, and the World's Games, 1896 to 2012*, edited by J. Gold and M.M. Gold. London: Routledge.

Faulk, B. 2004. *Music Hall and Modernity: The Late-Victorian Discovery of Popular Culture*. Athens: Ohio University Press.

Feeley, M. and Simon, J. 1994. Actuarial justice: the emerging new criminal law, in *Futures of Criminology*, edited by D. Nelken. London: Sage.

Feldman, David. 2003. Was the nineteenth century a golden age for immigrants?, *Migration Control in the North Atlantic World: The Evolution of State Practices in Europe and the United States from the French Revolution to the Inter-War Period*, edited by A. Fahrmeir, O. Faron and P. Weil. Oxford and New York: Berghahn, pp. 167–77.

Felson, M. 1988. *Crime and Everyday Life*. London: Sage.

Felson, M., and Clarke, R. 1998. *Opportunity Makes The Thief: Practical Theory for Crime Prevention*. Police Research Series, Paper 98. London: Home Office.

The Financial Times 2008. Tax warning over Olympics workers. [Online 8 July] Available at: http://www.ft.com/cms/s/0/a6a1fb3c-2d65-11dc-939b-0000779fd2ac.html [accessed: 12 July 2010].

Fisher, J. 1975 *What a Performance: The Life of Sid Field*. London: Seeley, Service and Co.

Fishman, W.J. 1979. *The Streets of East London*. London: Duckworth.

Fishman, W.J. 1988. *East End 1888: A Year in a London Borough Among the Labouring Poor*. London: Duckworth.

Fiske, J. 1993. *Power Plays/Power Works*. New York and London: Verso.

Flaherty, J. 2010. *The Conviction behind Public Protection: The National DNA Database and Newspaper Debate in the United Kingdom, 1991–2009*, Surveillance Cultures: A Global Surveillance Society? Fourth Biannual Surveillance and Society conference, City University, London, 14 April.

Flusty, S. 1999. Building paranoia, in *Architecture of Fear*, edited by in N. Ellin. New York: Princeton Architectural Press.

Flyvbjerg, B., Bruzelius, N., and Rothengatter, W. 2003. *Megaprojects and Risk: An Anatomy of Ambition*. Cambridge: Cambridge University Press.

Foster, J. 1999. *Docklands: Cultures in Conflict, Worlds in Collision*. London: UCL Press.

Foucault, M. 1977. *Discipline and Punish: The Birth of the Prison*. London: Penguin.

Friedman, M.T., Andrews, D.L. and Silk, M.L. 2004. Sport and the façade of redevelopment in the post-industrial city. *Sociology of Sport Journal*, 21: 119–39.

FRVT 2006 Face Recognition Vendor Test 2006. [Online]. Available at: http://www.frvt.org/FRVT2006/ [accessed: 2 February 2010].

Fussey, P. 2004. New Labour and new surveillance: theoretical and political ramifications of CCTV implementation in the UK, *Surveillance & Society*, 2(2/3): 251–69.

Fussey, P. 2007a. An interrupted transmission?: processes of CCTV implementation and the impact of human agency, *Surveillance & Society*, 4(3): 229–56.

Fussey, P. 2007b. Observing potentiality in the global city: surveillance and counterterrorism in London. *International Criminal Justice Review*, 17(3): 171–92.

Fussey, P. 2008. Beyond liberty, beyond security: the politics of public surveillance. *British Politics*, 3(1): 120–35.

Fussey, P. 2011. 'An economy of choice? Terrorist decision-making and criminological rational choice theories reconsidered', *Security Journal* vol. 24(1): 85–99.

Fussey, P. and Coaffee, J. 2011. Olympic rings of steel: constructing security for 2012 and beyond, in *The Security Games*, edited by K. Haggerty and C. Bennett. London: Routledge.

Fussey, P. and Rawlinson, P. 2009. *Winners and Losers: Post Communist Populations and Organised Crime in East London's Olympic Regeneration Game*, Second Annual European Organised Crime conference, Liverpool, 9 March.

Gainer, B. 1972. *The Alien Invasion: The Origins of the Aliens Act of 1905*. London: Heinemann.

Gamarra, A. 2009. Securing the Gold: Olympic security from a counter-terrorist perspective, in *A New Understanding of Terrorism: Case Studies, Trajectories and Lessons Learned*, edited by M.R. Haberfeld and A. von Hassell. New York: Springer.

Gambetta, G. 2009. *Codes of the Underworld*. Princeton, N.J.: Princeton University Press.

Games Monitor 2007a. Drivers face £5k VIP lane fines. [Online]. Available at: http://www.gamesmonitor.org.uk/node/491.

Games Monitor 2007b. The multinational security games. [Online]. Available at: http://www.gamesmonitor.org.uk/taxonomy/term/65?page=2 [accessed: 23 September 2009].

Games Monitor 2007c. What is Lammas Land? [Online]. Available at: http://www.gamesmonitor.org.uk/node/368 [accessed: 12 July 2010].

Games Monitor 2008. London 2012 Olympic evictions: Jowell's 'Parliamentary' answer and an evictee's response. (by Julian Cheyne, former resident at Clays Lane). [Online]. Available at: http://www.gamesmonitor.org.uk/node/558 [accessed: 12 July 2010].

Garcia-Ramon, M.D. and Albet, A. 2000. Pre-Olympic and post-Olympic Barcelona, a model for urban regeneration today? *Environment and Planning A* 32(8): 1331–34.

Gardiner, J. 2005. The spoils of victory. *Regeneration and Renewal*, 15 July, 18–19.

Garland, D. 1996. The limits of the sovereign state: strategies of crime control in contemporary society. *British Journal of Criminology*, 36(4): 445–71.

Garland, D. 2001. *The Culture of Control: Crime and Social Order in Contemporary Society*. Oxford: Oxford University Press.

Garrido, M. 2003. The Olympic ideal, *Property People*, 19 June, 8–9.

Gartner, L. 1973. *The Jewish Immigrant in England, 1870–1914*. London: Vallentine Mitchell.

Gavron, K., Dench, G. and Young, M. 2006. *The New East End: Kinship, Race and Conflict*. London: Profile.

Ghaffur, T. 2007. Memorandum (8 June) to the House of Lords Constitution Committee, Surveillance: Citizens and the State, Second Report, 2008–09, Written evidence. [Online]. Available at: http://www.publications.parliament.uk/pa/ld200809/ldselect/ldconst/18/18we13.htm.

Gill, M. and Spriggs, A. 2005. *Assessing the impact of CCTV*, Home Office Research Study No. 292. London: Home Office. [Online]. Available at: http://www.homeoffice.gov.uk/rds/pdfs05/hors292.pdf.

Gilroy, P. 1987. *There Ain't No Black in the Union Jack*. London: Hutchinson.

Girginov, V. and Parry, J. 2005. *The Olympic Games Explained: A Student Guide to the Evolution of the Modern Olympic Games*. New York: Routledge.

Girginov, V. ed. 2010. *The Olympics: A Critical Reader*. London: Routledge.

Giulianotti, R. and Klauser, F. 2009. Security governance and sport mega-events: toward an interdisciplinary research agenda. *Journal of Sport and Social Issues*, 34(1): 49–61.

The Global Terrorism Database [Online]. Available at: http://www.start.umd.edu/gtd.

The London Evening Standard 2003. MPs: Olympic bid 'desirable'. [Online, 23 January]. Available at: http://www.thisislondon.co.uk/news/article-3054173-mps-olympic-bid-desirable.do.

Gold, J.R. and Gold, M.M. eds 2004. *Cities of Culture: Staging International Festivals and the Urban Agenda, 1851–2000*. Farnham: Ashgate.

Gold, J.R and Gold, M.M. 2005. *Cities of Culture: Staging International Festivals and the Urban Agenda, 1951–2000*. Farnham: Ashgate.

Gold, J.R. and Gold, M.M. eds 2007. *Olympic Cities: City Agendas, Planning and the Worlds Games, 1896 to 2012*. London: Routledge.

Gold, J.R. and Gold, M.M. 2008. Olympic cities: regeneration, city rebranding and changing urban agendas. *Geography Compass*, 2(1): 300–318.

Gold, J.R. and Gold, M.M. 2009. Future indefinite? London 2012, the spectre of retrenchment and the challenge of Olympic sports legacy, *The London Journal*, 34(2): 180–97.

Gold, J.R. and Gold, M.M. 2010. *Olympic Cities: City Agendas, Planning, and the World's Games, 1896 to 2016*. London: Routledge.

Gold, J.R. and Revill, G. 2003. Exploring landscapes of fear: marginality, spectacle and surveillance. *Capital and Class*, 80: 27–50.

Goverde, H., Cerny, P.G., Haugaard, M. and Lentner, H. 2000. *Power in Contemporary Politics: Theories, Practices, Globalizations*. London: Sage.

Graham, P. 2009. *Securing the Transport Network*, Olympic and Paralympic Safety and Security conference, Royal United Services Institute, London, 13 November.

Graham, S. 2002. Special collection: reflections on cities, September 11th and the war on terrorism – one year on. *International Journal of Urban and Regional Research*, 26:(3): 589–90.

Graham, S. and Marvin, S. 2001. *Splintering Urbanism: Networked Infrastructures, Technological Mobilities and the Urban Condition*. London and New York: Routledge.

Gratton, C., Dobson, N. and Shibli, S. 2000. The economic importance of major sports events: a case study of six events, *Managing Leisure: An International Journal*, 5(1): 17–28.

Gratton, R., Dobson N. and Shibli, S. 2001. The role of major sports events in the economic regeneration of cities, in *Sport in the City: The Role of Sport in Economic and Social Regeneration*, edited by C. Gratton and I. Henry. London: Routledge, pp. 78–89.

Greater London Authority (GLA) 2006. *Playing Fields Investigation*. London: GLA. [Online]. Available at: www.static.london.gov.uk/assembly/reports/environment/playing-fields.rtf [accessed: 12 July 2010].

Greater London Authority (GLA) 2009. *Economic Impact on the London and UK Economy of an Earned Regularisation of Irregular Migrants to the UK*. London: GLA. [Online]. Available at: http://www.london.gov.uk/publication/economic-impact-london-and-uk-economy-earned-regularisation-irregular-migrants-uk.

Greater London Authority (GLA) 2008. *The Impact of the 2012 Games on Lottery Funding in London*. London: GLA. [Online]. Available at: http://www.london.gov.uk/archive/assembly/reports/econsd/lottery-funding.pdf [accessed: 12 July 2010].

Greater London Authority (GLA). 2010. *Legacy Limited? A Review of the Olympic Park Legacy Company's Role*. London: GLA.

The Guardian 2002. Robo cop. [Online, 13 June]. Available at: http://www.guardian.co.uk/uk/2002/jun/13/ukcrime.jamesmeek [accessed: 21 December 2009].

The Guardian 2005. It's all a matter of interpretation. [Online, 26 October]. Available at: http://www.guardian.co.uk/society/2005/oct/26/epublic.technology10 [accessed: 2nd May 2010].

The Guardian 2006. London seeks four sponsors to pledge £50m each for 2012 [Online, 25 January]. Available at http://www.guardian.co.uk/media/2006/jan/25/olympicsandthemedia.marketingandpr [accessed: 12 July 2010].

The Guardian 2007a. Olympic ship plan drifts into troubled water. [Online]. Available at: http://www.guardian.co.uk/environment/2007/jan/04/Olympics 2012.olympics2012.

The Guardian 2007b. London 2012 plans among UK's most complex ever. [Online]. Available at: http://www.guardian.co.uk/uk/2007/feb/06/olympics2012. olympicgames.

The Guardian 2007c. Ringing the changes. [Online, 7 February]. Available at: http://www.guardian.co.uk/environment/2007/feb/07/energy.society.

The Guardian 2007d. Olympic inspectors happy with London despite growing budget. [Online, 2 March]. Available at: http://sport.guardian.co.uk/print/0,329732254-112398,00.html.

The Guardian 2007e. Capital will need 9,000 officers a day to police the Olympics. [Online, 17 March]. Available at: http://www.guardian.co.uk/uk/2007/mar/17/ukcrime.olympics2012 [accessed: 12 July 2010].

The Guardian 2007f. Met may have to use armed police from abroad for Olympics. [Online, 11 June]. Available at: http://www.guardian.co.uk/uk/2007/jun/11/ukcrime.olympics2012 [accessed: 12 July 2010].

The Guardian 2007g. Jowell to tell how Olympics funds will be repaid. [Online, 27 June]. Available at: http://www.guardian.co.uk/society/2007/jun/27/voluntarysector.olympics2012.

The Guardian 2007h. MPs demand tighter rein on Olympic spending. [Online, 10 July]. Available at: http://www.guardian.co.uk/uk/2007/jul/10/olympics2012. olympics2012 [accessed: 11 November 2007].

The Guardian 2007i. Lemley paid off with £388,000 after only seven months at ODA. [Online, 20 July]. Available at: http://sport.guardian.co.uk/london2012/story/0,2130620,00.html.

The Guardian 2007j. John Armitt: railwayman who has to keep Olympics on track. Available at: http://www.guardian.co.uk/business/2007/jul/27/olympics2012. transportintheuk.

The Guardian 2007k. After 180 million years, first 2012 Olympic venue ready for action. Available at: http://www.guardian.co.uk/society/2007/aug/06/communities.olympics2012.

The Guardian 2007l. Lottery sales harming grassroots sport. 8 August. Available at: http://sport.guardian.co.uk/news/story/0,2143616,00.html.

The Guardian 2007m. Cordon blue. [Online, 21 September]. Available at: http://www.guardian.co.uk/society/2007/sep/21/communities [accessed: 21 September 2007].

The Guardian 2007n. Hugh Muir's diary. [Online, Available at: http://www. guardian.co.uk/politics/2007/oct/19/1.

The Guardian 2007o. Government rejects Moynihan's criticism of London 2012 costs. [Online, 26 October]. Available at: http://www.guardian.co.uk/ sport/2007/oct/26/Olympics2012.politics

The Guardian (2007p). We have not lost control of Olympic budget, claims Jowell. [Online, 31 October]. Available at: http://sport.guardian.co.uk/london2012/ story/0,2202122,00.html.

The Guardian 2007q. Plain and practical is aim as London unveils its 2012 stadium. [Online, 8 November]. Available at: http://www.guardian.co.uk/ uk/2007/nov/08/olympics2012.olympics2012.

The   Guardian   2007r.   Woodward's   worth   questioned.   [Online,   21 November].   Available   at: http://football.guardian.co.uk/Columnists/ Column/0,2214484,00.html.

The Guardian 2009a. CCTV in the sky: police plan to use military-style spy drones. [Online, 23 January]. Available at: http://www.guardian.co.uk/uk/2010/jan/23/ cctv-sky-police-plan-drones [accessed: 2 May 2010].

The Guardian 2009b. Police powers for 2012 Olympics alarm critics. [Online, 21 July]. Available at: http://www.guardian.co.uk/uk/2009/jul/21/olympics2012-civil-liberties [accessed: 25 September 2009].

The Guardian 2009c. Biometric tests for Olympic site workers. [Online, 11 October]. Available at: http://www.guardian.co.uk/uk/2009/oct/11/biometric-tests-for-olympic-site [accessed: 11 October 2009].

The Guardian 2010a. Expect the drones to swarm on Britain in time for 2012. [Online, 22 February]. . Available at: http://www.guardian.co.uk/ commentisfree/2010/feb/22/doesnt-work-didnt-ask-why-cameras [accessed: 2 May 2010].

The Guardian 2010b. Eye in the sky arrest could land police in the dock. [Online, 15 February]. Available at: http://www.guardian.co.uk/uk/2010/feb/15/police-drone-arrest-backfires [accessed: 2 May 2010].

The Guardian 2010c. Climb this: Anish Kapoor's massive artwork that will tower over London. [Online, 31 March]. Available at: http://www.guardian.co.uk/ uk/2010/mar/31/anish-kapoor-artwork-tower-london [accessed: 1 April 2010].

The Guardian 2010d. Treasury targets middle-class child benefits in spending cut plans. [Online, 13 May]. Available at: http://www.guardian.co.uk/politics/2010/ may/13/spending-cuts-child-benefits-deficit [accessed: 13 May 2010].

Guttman, A. 2002. *The Olympics. A History of the Modern Games*. Chicago: University of Illinois Press.

Hagemann, A. 2008. *From Stadium to 'Fanzone': The Architecture of Control*, Surveillance and Security at Mega Sport Events: From Beijing 2008 to London 2012 conference, Durham University, 25 April.

Haggerty, K. and Bennett, C. eds 2011. *The Security Games: Surveillance and Control at Mega-Events*. London: Routledge.

Haggerty, K. and Ericson, R. 2000. The surveillant assemblage. *British Journal of Sociology*, 51(4): 605–22.

Haggerty, K. and Ericson, R. 2001. The military technostructures of policing, in *Militarizing the American Criminal Justice System: The Changing Roles of the Armed Forces and the Police*, edited by P. Kraska. Boston, MA: Northeastern University Press.

Haggerty, K. and Gazso, A. 2005. Seeing beyond the ruins: surveillance as a response to terrorist threats. *Canadian Journal of Sociology*, 30(2): 169–87.

Hall, P. 1980 *Great Planning Disasters*. London: Weidenfeld and Nicolson.

Hall, P. 2002. *Cities of Tomorrow: An Intellectual History of Urban Planning and Design in the Twentieth Century*. London: Blackwell.

Hall, P.G. 1962. *The Industries of London since 1861*. London: Hutchinson:

Hall, S. and Jefferson, T. 1976. *Resistance Through Rituals: Youth Sub-Cultures in Post-War Britain*. London: Routledge.

Hall, S. 1997. *Representation: Cultural Representation and Signifying Practices*, London: Sage.

Hammar, T. 1990. *Democracy and the Nation State*. Farnham: Avebury.

Hampton, J. 2008. *The Austerity Olympics: When the Games Came to London in 1948*. Aurum Press.

Hancox, P.D. and Morgan, J.B. 1975. The Use of CCTV for Police Control at Football Matches, *Police Research Bulletin*, 25: 41–44.

Hardy, D. 2003. Inner city blues, Olympic Gold, *Town and Country Planning*, October: 288–90.

Haugaard, M. 2002. *Power: A Reader*. New York: Manchester University Press.

Hellenic Republic Ministry of Public Order 2004. *Annual Report on Organised Crime in Greece for the year 2004*. Athens: Hellenic Republic Ministry of Public Order.

Heller, A. 2003. BASIS counters airborne bioterrorism. *Science and Technology Review*, October: 6–8.

Heng, Y.K. 2006. The transformation of war debate: through the looking glass of Ulrich Beck's *World Risk Society*, *International Relations*, 20(1): 69–91.

Herman, H. 2003. Counter-terrorism, information technology and intelligence change. *Intelligence and National Security*, 18(4): 40–58.

Hill, C.R. 1996. *Olympic Politic: Athens to Atlanta, 1896–1996*. Manchester: Manchester University Press.

Hill, G. and Bloch, H. 2003. *The Silvertown Explosion: London 1917*. Stroud: Tempus.

Hill, S. 1976. *The Dockers*. London: Heinemann.

Hinds, A. and Vlachou, E. 2007. Fortress Olympics: counting the cost of major event security. *Janes Intelligence* Review, 19(5): 20–26.

HM Government (2009) Countering the Terrorist Threat: How Academia and Industry Can Play their Part. London: Office for Security and Counter-Terrorism Directorate, Home Office.

Hobbs, D. 1988. *Doing the Business*. Oxford: Oxford University Press.

Hobbs, D. 2001. The firm: organizational logic and criminal culture on a shifting terrain. *British Journal of Criminology*, 41: 549– 60.

Hobbs, D. 2006. East Ending: dissociation, de-industrialisation and David Downes, in *The Politics of Crime Control: Essays in Honour of David Downes*, edited by T. Newburn and P. Rock. Oxford: Oxford: University Press.

Hobbs, D. 2011. *Populating the Underworld*. Cambridge: Polity.

Hoffman, B. 1994. Responding to terrorism across the technological spectrum. *Terrorism and Political Violence*, 6(3): 366–90.

Hoffman, B. 2006. *Inside Terrorism*. New York: Columbia University Press.

Holden, A. and Iveson, K. 2003. Designs on the urban: New Labour's urban renaissance and the spaces of citizenship. *City*, 7(1): 57–72.

Home Office 1989. *The Hillsborough Stadium Disaster, 15 April 1989: Inquiry by The Rt Hon Lord Justice Taylor. Interim Report*. London: HMSO.

Home Office 1990. *The Hillsborough Stadium Disaster, 15 April 1989: Inquiry by The Rt Hon Lord Justice Taylor. Final Report*. London: HMSO

Home Office 1994. *CCTV: Looking Out for You*. London: HMSO.

Home Office 2007. *National CCTV Strategy*. London: HMSO.

Home Office 2009a. *A Safe and Secure Games for all*. London: HMSO.

Home Office 2009b. *London 2012 Olympic and Paralympic Safety and Security Strategy*. London: HMSO.

Home Office 2009c *The United Kingdom's Strategy for Countering International Terrorism*. London: HMSO.

Home Office 2009d. *Working Together to Protect Crowded Places*. London: HMSO. [Online]. Available at: http://www.london2012.com/documents/oda-industry-days/oda-security-industry-day-presentation.pdf [accessed: 3 December 2008].

Horne, C. 1996. The case for: CCTV should be introduced. *International Journal of Risk, Security and Crime Prevention*, 1(4): 317–26.

Hosteller, E. 2001. *The Isle of Dogs: The Twentieth Century: A Brief History*, II. London: Island History Trust.

Howard, K. 2006. *Territorial Politics and Irish Cycling*, Working Papers in British–Irish Studies, No. 71. Dublin: Institute for British–Irish Studies, University College Dublin.

Hubbard, P. 2004. Cleansing the metropolis: sex work and the politics of zero tolerance. *Urban Studies*, 41(9): 1687–702.

Huber, M. 2003. Review of [B. Flyvbjerg, N. Bruzelius and W. Rothengatter] *Megaprojects and Risk, British Journal of Sociology*, 54(4): 594–96.

Huey, L., Ericson, R. and Haggerty, K. 2005. Policing fantasy city, in *Re-imagining Policing in Canada*, edited by D. Cooley. Toronto: University of Toronto Press, pp. 140–208.

Hughes, G. 2007. *The Politics of Crime and Community*. Basingstoke: Palgrave Macmillan.

Huysmans, J. 2004. A Foucaltian view on spill-over: freedom and security in the EU. *Journal of International Relations and Development*, 7: 294–318.

Imrie, R., Lees, L., and Raco., M. eds 2009. *Regenerating London: Governance, Sustainability and Community in a Global City*. London: Routledge.

The Independent 1996. Euro 96 violence targeted by police. [Online, 25 May]. Available at: http://www.independent.co.uk/news/euro-96-violence-targeted-by-police-1349003.html [accessed: 1 February 2010].

The Independent 2000. Games nuclear plot uncovered. [Online, 26August]. Available at: http://www.independent.co.uk/news/world/australasia/games-nuclear-plot-uncovered-711417.html [accessed: 23 October 2009].

The Independent 2005. Eta targets Spain's Olympic bid with series of bombings [Online, 27 June]. Available at: http://www.independent.co.uk/news/world/europe/eta-targets-spains-olympic-bid-with-series-of-bombings-496723.html [accessed: 12 July 2010].

The Independent 2007. Lord Coe: Osaka could be a write-off but 2012 is all that matters. [Online, 19 August]. Available at: http://www.independent.co.uk/news/people/profiles/lord-coe-osaka-could-be-a-writeoff-but-2012-is-all-that-matters-462155.html [accessed: 23 July 2010].

The Independent 2009a. 90 arrested in illegal Olympic worker crackdown. [Online, 4 December]. Available at: http://www.independent.co.uk/news/uk/crime/90-arrested-in-illegal-olympic-worker-crackdown-1834362.html [accessed: 22 January 2010].

The Independent 2009b. Foreign workers who are classed as 'local'. [Online, 17 February]. Available at: http://www.independent.co.uk/news/uk/home–news/foreign-workers-who-are-classed-as-local-1623788.html [accessed: 2 May 2010].

International Office of Epizootics 2003 *Sydney Olympic Games and Paralympics: Australia's biosecurity measures*. Paris: Office International des Épizooties.

International Olympic Committee (IOC). 1908. *The Fourth Olympiad – London 1908 Official Report*. London: BOA.

International Olympic Committee (IOC). 1989. *Official Report: Organisation and planning XXIVth Olympiad*, Seoul: SSOOC, Vol. 1.

International Olympic Committee IOC (2004) *Celebrate Humanity*. Lausanne: IOC.

International Olympic Committee (IOC) 2005. *Olympic Broadcasting*. [Online.] http://www.olympic.org/uk/organisation/facts/broadcasting/index_uk.asp [accessed: 2 January 2005].

International Olympic Committee (IOC). 2007. *Olympic Charter*. Lausanne: IOC.

International Olympic Committee (IOC). 2008. *Games of the XXXIst Olympiad 2016 Working Group Report*. Lausanne: IOC.

Introna, L.D. and Wood, D. 2004. Picturing algorithmic surveillance: the politics of facial recognition systems. *Surveillance & Society*, 22(3): 177–98.

Jacobs, J. 1996. *Edge of Empire: Postcolonialism and the City*. London: Routledge.

Jennings, A. 1996. *The New Lords of the Rings: Olympic Corruption and How to Buy Gold Medals*. London: Pocket Books.

Jennings, A. 2000. *The Great Olympic Swindle*. London: Simon and Schuster.

Jennings, W. 2010. Governing the Games in an age of uncertainty: the Olympics and organisational responses to risk, in *Terrorism and the Olympics: Lessons for 2012 and Beyond*, edited by A. Richards, P. Fussey and A. Silke. London: Routledge.

Jennings, W. and Lodge, M. 2009. Governing mega-events: tools of security risk management for the London 2012 Olympic Games and FIFA 2006 World Cup in Germany. *Proceedings of the Political Studies Association Conference*.

Jessop, B. 1997. The entrepreneurial city: re-imaging localities, redesigning economic governance, or restructuring capital?, in *Transforming Cities: Contested Governance and New Spatial Divisions*, edited by N. Jewson and S. McGregor. London: Routledge, pp. 28–41.

Johnston, I. 2009. *Staging a Safe and Secure Event*, Olympic and Paralympic Safety and Security Conference, Royal United Services Institute, London, 13 November.

Jones, R. 2000. Digital rule: punishment, control and technology. *Punishment and Society*, 2(1): 5–21.

Jump, P. and Warrell, H. 2007. Charity coalition rallies opposition MPs against Lottery raid to fund the Olympics. [Online]. Available at: http://www. thirdsector.co.uk/channels/Finance/Article/652248/Charity-coalition-rallies-opposition-MPs-against-Lottery-raid-fund-Olympics.

Kanin, D.B. 1981. *A Political History of the Olympic Games*. Boulder, CO: Westview Press.

Kelly, B. 2009. *The London 2012 Olympic and Paralympic Games: Assessing the Risk*, Olympic and Paralympic Safety and Security Conference, Royal United Services Institute, London, 13 November.

Kemp, J. 2008. The COLREGS and the *Princess Alice. The Journal of Navigation*, 61: 271–81.

Kent Police 2010 Freedom of Information disclosure: unmanned aerial vehicles. [Online]. Available at: http://www.whatdotheyknow.com/request/south_coast_partnership_drone_do [accessed: 2 May 2010].

Keohane, R.O. 1984. *After Hegemony: Cooperation and Discord in the World Political Economy*. Princeton, NJ: Princeton University Press.

Killanin (Lord) 1979. *The Olympic Games, 1980: Moscow and Lake Placid*. London: Macmillan.

Klauser, F. 2008. *Exemplifications of Security Politics through Mega Sport Events*, Security and Surveillance at Mega Sport Events: From Beijing 2008 to London 2012 conference, Durham University, 25 April.

Kleidman, R., Rochon, T.R. 1997. *Dilemmas of Organisation in Peace Campaigns*. Boulder, CO: Lynne Rienner.

Knepper, P. 2007. British Jews and the Racialisation of Crime in the Age of Empire. *British Journal of Criminology*, 47(1) 61–79.

Kohn, M. 1992. *Dope Girls. The Birth of the British Drug Underground.*, London: Lawrence and Wishart.

Kops, B. 1969. *By the Waters of Whitechapel*. London: Bodley Head.

Lack, R. 2007. *Ipsotek Video Analytics*, Local Government Agency CCTV Conference: The Development of a National Strategy, Innovative Systems, Effectiveness and Standards, Local Government House, London, 4 July.

Lammy, D. (2007). Culture vultures: will the Olympics really be bad for the arts? David Lammy outlines his plans for the 2012 'Cultural Olympiad'. *New Statesman*, 14 May.

Langstone, D. 2009. Myths, crimes and videotape, in *The Myths of Technology: Innovation and Inequality*, edited by J. Burnett, K. Walker and P. Senker. Oxford: Peter Lang.

Latouche, D. 2007. Montreal 1976, in *Olympic Cities: City Agendas, Planning, and the Worlds Games, 1896 to 2012*, edited by J. Gold and M.M. Gold. London: Routledge, pp. 197–217.

Lebzelter, G. 1981. Anti-Semitism: a focal point for the British radical Right, in *Nationalist and Racialist Movements in Britain and Germany before 1914*, edited by P. Kennedy and A. Nicholls. Oxford: St. Anthony's College.

Lee, C. 2004. Accounting for rapid growth of private policing in South Korea. *Journal of Criminal Justice*, 32: 113–22.

Lee, M. 2006. *The Race For The 2012 Olympics: The Inside Story of How London Won the Bid*. London: Virgin Books.

Lees, L. 2003. Visions of urban renaissance: the Urban Task Force Report and the Urban White Paper, in *Urban Renaissance: New Labour Community and Urban Policy*, edited by R. Imrie and M. Raco. Bristol: Policy Press, pp. 61–82.

Lefebvre, H. 1991. *The Production of Space*. Cambridge, MA: Blackwell.

Lenskyj, H. 2002. *Best Olympics Ever? The Social Impacts of Sydney 2000*. New York: State University of New York Press.

Lenskyj, H. 2004. Making the World Safe for Global Capital: The Sydney 2000 Olympics and Beyond, in *Post-Olympism? Questioning Sport in the 21st Century*, edited by J. Bale and M. Christensen. Oxford: Berg.

Lenskyj, H.J. 1996. When winners are losers: Toronto and Sydney bids for the Summer Olympics. *Journal of Sport and Social Issues*, 20(4): 392–410.

Levin, M. 2001. London 1908. [Online]. Available at: http://www.lib.umd.edu/ ARCH/honr219f/1908lond.html [accessed: 10 February 2004].

Levi-Strauss, C. 1973. *Tristes Tropiques*. London: Penguin.

Lifeisland 2010. Support for Manor Garden Allotments Society. [Online]. Available at: http://www.lifeisland.org [accessed: 12 July 2010].

Lillehammer Olympic Organizing Committee (LOOC) 1994. *Official Report of the XVII Olympic Winter Olympic Games*. Lillehammer: LOOC.

Lipman, V. 1990. *A History of Jews in Britain Since 1868*. Leicester: Leicester University Press.

Logan, J.R. and Molotch, H. 1987. *Urban Fortunes*. Longbeach: University of California Press.

The London Evening Standard 2004. East End to strike gold. [Online, 10 November]. Available at: http://www.thisislondon.co.uk/news/article-14598733-east-end-to-strike-gold.do.

The London Evening Standard 2007. BNP is linked to petition against new 'megamosque'. [Online, 20 July]. Available at: http://www.thisislondon.co.uk/news/article-23405143-bnp-is-linked-to-petition-against-new-megamosque.do.

The London Evening Standard 2008. Fewer people playing sport in Olympics city. [Online, 25 July]. Available at: http://www.thisislondon.co.uk/standard-olympics/article-23521003-fewer-people-playing-sport-in-olympics-city.do.

The London Evening Standard 2009. Influx of 10,000 foreign workers for Olympic jobs. [Online, 4 March]. Available at: http://www.thisislondon.co.uk/standard/article-23657158-influx-of-10000-foreign-workers-for-olympic-jobs.do [accessed: 8 March 2010].

The London Evening Standard 2010a. One in four Olympic site workers is from abroad. [Online, 21 January]. Available at: http://www.thisislondon.co.uk/standard/article-23797966-one-in-four-olympic-site-workers-is-from-abroad.do [accessed: 22 January 2010].

The London Evening Standard 2010b. 'Island of prosperity' fears for 2012 Olympic Park. [Online, 16 February]. Available at: http://www.thisislondon.co.uk/standard/article-23806328-island-of-prosperity-fears-for-2012-olympic-park.do [accessed: 12 July 2010].

London2012 2009. Olympic stadium. [Online]. Available at: http://www.london2012.com/games/venues/olympic-stadium.php [accessed: 2 May 2010].

London2012 2006. Joint New Year Message from Sebastian Coe and Roy McNulty [Online, 28 December]. Available at: http://www.the2012londonolympics.com/forum/printthread.php?t=6657 [accessed: 20 July 2010].

London2012 (Bidding Team) 2004. Candidate File, http://www.london2012.com/documents/candidate-files [accessed: 12 December 2005 and 15 February 2008].

London Assembly 2006. *Report of the 7 July Review Committee*. London: GLA. [Online]. Available at: http://static.london.gov.uk/assembly/reports/7july/report.pdf.

London Borough of Tower Hamlets Council. 2006. London 2012 Olympic and Paralympic Games Legacy: Strategy Programme www.towerhamlets.gov.uk/idoc.ashx?docid=9c4b2307-03d1.pdf.

London Citizens Organisation n.d. About London Citizens. [Online]. Available at: http://www.londoncitizens.org.uk/pages/about.html.

London2012 2009. One year on Olympic Stadium on track as internal work ramps up. [Online, 22 May] Available at: http://www.london2012.com/press/media-releases/2009/05/one-year-on-olympic-stadium-on-track-as-internal-work-ramps-up.php [accessed: 10 March 2010].

London Organizing Committee (LOCOG) 2010. *Brand Protection*, London: LOCOG [Online]. Available at: http://www.london2012.com/documents/brand-guidelines/guidelines-for-business-use.pdf.

London Skills and Employment Observatory 2007. The Five Olympic Boroughs – Key Indicators. London Development Agency (LDA). [Online]. Available at: http://lseo.org.uk/data/local-data.

Los Angeles Olympic Organizing Committee (LAOOC) 1985. *Official Report of the XXIIIrd Olympiad*. Los Angeles: LAOOC.

Los Angeles Times 2001. Super day for Big Brother. 2 February.

Los Angeles Times 2008. Many eyes will watch visitors. [Online, 7 August] Available at: http://articles.latimes.com/2008/aug/07/world/fg-snoop7 [accessed: 2 May 2010].

Lucas, J.A. 1992. *Future of the Olympic Games*. Champaign, IL: Human Kinetics.

Lyon, D. 1994. *The Electronic Eye: The Rise of the Surveillance Society*. Cambridge: Polity.

Lyon, D. 2003a. *Surveillance after September 11th*. Cambridge: Polity.

Lyon, D. 2003b Surveillance as social sorting: computer codes and mobile bodies, in *Surveillance as Social Sorting: Privacy, Risk and Digital Discrimination*, edited by D. Lyon. London and New York: Routledge.

Lyon, D. 2004. Technology vs. 'terrorism', in *Cities, War and Terrorism*, edited by S. Graham. Oxford: Blackwell, pp. 297–311.

Lyon, D. 2009. *Identifying Citizens: ID cards as Surveillance*. Cambridge: Polity.

Lyon, D. ed. 2006. *Theorizing Surveillance: The Panopticon and Beyond*. Cullompton: Willan.

MacAloon, J. 1981. *This Great Symbol: Pierre de Coubertin and the Origin of the Modern Olympic Games*. Chicago, IL: University of Chicago Press.

MacAloon, J. 1984. Olympic Games and the theory of spectacle in modern societies, in *Rite, Drama, Festival, Spectacle: Rehearsals Toward a Theory of Cultural Performance*, edited by J. MacLoon. Philadelphia, PA: The Institute of Human Issues.

MacAloon, J. 1989. Festival, ritual and TV: Los Angeles 1984, in *The Olympic Movement and the Mass Media*, edited by R. Jackson and T. McPhail. Calgary, Al.: Hunford Enterprises.

McCahill, M. 2002. *The Surveillance Web: The Rise of Visual Surveillance in an English City*. Cullompton: Willan.

McCahill, M. and Norris, C. 2002. On the threshold to urban panopticon? Analysing the employment of CCTV in European cities and assessing its aocial and political impacts. (Report to the European Commission Fifth Framework RTD) UrbanEye Literature Review, UrbanEyeWorking Paper No. 2. Centre for Technology and Society, Technical University of Berlin. [Online]. Available at: http://www.urbaneye.net/results/ue_wp2.pdf.

McCarthy, S. 2008. Beijing's green Games? *Building*. [Online, 26 August]. Available at: http://www.building.co.uk/story.asp?storycode=3120949#.

McDonald, M. 2005. Constructing insecurity: Australian security discourse and policy post-2001. *International Relations*, 19(3): 297–320.

McGuirk, P.M. 2003. Producing the capacity to govern a global Sydney: a multi-scaled account. *Journal of Urban Affairs*, 25(2): 201–23.

McGuirk, P.M. 2004. State, strategy, and scale in the competitive city: a neo-Gramscian analysis of the governance of global Sydney. *Environment and Planning A*, 36: 1019–43.

Macko, S. 1996. Security at the summer Olympic games is ready. EmergencyNet News Service, 2–191, 9 July.

MacLeod, G. 2002. From urban entrepreneurialism to a 'revanchist city'? On the spatial injustices of Glasgow's renaissance. *Antipode*, 34(3): 602–24.

MacLeod, G. and Goodwin, M. 1999. Space, scale and state strategy: rethinking urban and regional governance, *Progress in Human Geography*, 23: 503–27.

McPhedran, I. 2007. Armed pilotless planes to protect London Olympics. [Online]. Available at: http://www.Gamesmonitor.org.uk/node/497.

Macpherson, W. 1999. *The Stephen Lawrence Inquiry: Report of an Inquiry by Sir William Macpherson of Cluny*. London: HMSO.

Mallon, B. and Buchanan, I. 1998. *The 1908 Olympic Games*. Jefferson, NC: McFarland & Co.

Mann, B. 2009. *Ensuring Resilience*, Olympic and Paralympic Safety and Security Conference, Royal United Services Institute, London, 13 November.

Maragall, P. 1999. Foreword, in *Towards an Urban Renaissance*, Urban Task Force Department of Environment, Transport and the Regions (DETR). London: E & FN Spon, pp. 5–6.

Marrs, C. 2003. 'The benefits of believing' (London's 2012 Olympic bid and its potential catalyst for regeneration). *Regeneration & Renewal*, 13 June 2003, p. 23.

Marsh, P., Fox, K., Carnibella, G., McCann, J. and Marsh, J. 1996. *Football Violence in Europe*. Oxford: Social Issues Research Centre.

Marshall, T. 1996. City Entrepreneurialism in Barcelona in the 1980s and 1990s, *European Planning Studies*, 4(2): 147–65.

Marx, G.T. 1988. *Undercover: Police surveillance in America*. Berkeley: University of California Press.

Matassa, M. and Newburn, T. 2003. Policing and terrorism, in *The Handbook of Policing*, edited by T. Newburn. Cullompton: Willan.

Matthews, G.R. 1980. The controversial Olympic Games of 1908 as viewed by the New York Times and the Times of London. *Journal of Sports History*, 7(2): 40–53.

Merrow, E.W. 1988. *Understanding the Outcomes of Megaprojects: A Quantitative Analysis of Very Large Civilian Projects*. Santa Monica, Ca: The Rand Corporation.

Metropolitan Police Authority (MPA) 2007. Metropolitan Police Service Olympic programme update. [Online]. Available at: http://www.mpa.gov.uk/committees/x-cop/2007/070201/06/ [accessed: 1 October 2009].

Metropolitan Police Authority (MPA) 2009. Women's safety and the policing of the 2012 Olympics. [Online, 16 July] Available at: http://www.mpa.gov.uk/committees/cep/2009/090716/09/#fn005 [accessed: 9 March 2010].

Meyer-Künzel, M. 2007. Berlin 1936, in *Olympic Cities: City Agendas, Planning, and the World's Games, 1896 to 2012*, edited by J. Gold and M.M. Gold. London: Routledge, pp. 138–49.

Miller, D. 2003. *Athens to Athens: The Official History of the Olympic Games and the IOC, 1894-2004*, Edinburgh: Mainstream Publishing.

Min, G. 1987. Over-commercialisation of the Olympics 1988: the role of U.S. television networks. *International Review for the Sociology of Sport*, 22: 137–41. [Online]. Available at: http://irs.sagepub.com [accessed: 5 December 2007].

Minnaar, A. 2006. *Crime Prevention/Crime Control Surveillance: Public Closed Circuit Television CCTV in South African Central Business Districts CBDs*, Crime, Justice and Surveillance conference, Sheffield, 5–6 April.

Minnaar, A. 2007. The implementation and impact of crime prevention/crime control open street closed-circuit television surveillance in South African Central Business Districts. *Surveillance & Society*, 4(3): 174–207.

Mitchell, D. 2003. *The Right to the City: Social Justice and the Fight for Public Space*. New York: The Guilford Press.

Molotch, H. 1976. The city as growth machine: towards a political economy of place. *American Journal of Sociology*, 82(2): 309–32.

Monclus, F.J. 2003. The Barcelona model: an original formula? From 'reconstruction' to strategic urban projects (1979–2004). *Planning Perspectives*, 18: 399–421.

Moss, M.L. 1985. *Telecommunications and the future of cities*, Landtronics conference, London, June.

Murakami Wood, D. and Coaffee, J. 2007. Lockdown! resilience, resurgence and the stage-set city, in *Securing the Urban Renaissance*, edited by R. Atkinson and G. Helms. Bristol: Policy Press, pp. 91–106.

Nagano Olympic Organizing Committee (NAOC) 1998 *The XVIII Olympic Winter Games Official Report*, Nagano City, Japan: NAOC.

Nash, J. 2005. *Social Movements: An Anthropological Reader*. Oxford: Blackwell.

National Audit Office (NAO). 2007a. *Preparations for the London 2012 Olympic and Paralympic Games: Risk assessment and management*. Report by the Comptroller and Auditor General. HC 490, Session 2006–2007, 2 February. [Online]. Available at: www.nao.org.uk/publications/nao_reports/07-08/0708 490.pdf.

National Audit Office (NAO). 2007b. *The Budget for the London 2012 Olympic and Paralympic Games*. Report by the Comptroller and Auditor General. HC612, Session 2006–2007, 20 July. [Online]. Available at: http://www.nao.org.uk/publications/nao_reports/06-07/0607612.pdf.

National Broadcasting Company (NBC) 2006. Olympic terror concern focuses on two fronts. [Online, 8 February]. Available at: http://www.msnbc.msn.com/id/11203844 [accessed: 28 October 2009].

National Counter Terrorism Security Office (NaCTSO) 2007 *Counter Terrorism Protective Security Advice for Stadia and Arenas*. London: NaCTSO.

National Institute of Justice (NIJ) 2003. CCTV: constant cameras track violators. *National Institute of Justice Journal*, 249: 16–23.

National Public Radio 2008 Mexico's 1968 Massacre: What Really Happened? broadcast 1 December. [Online]. Available at: http://www.npr.org/templates/story/story.php?storyId=97546687 [accessed: 2 January 2010].

Ness, A. 2002. Blue skies for the Beijing Olympics. *China Business Review*, March.

New Lammas Lands Defence Committee (NLLDC) 2008. *The New Lammas Lands Defence Committee*. [Online]. Available at: http://www.lammaslands.org.uk/wwd2008.html [accessed: 12 July 2010].

The New York Times 1992 French government is struggling to limit damage in Habash case. [Online]. Available at: http://www.nytimes.com/1992/02/03/world/french-government-is-struggling-to-limit-damage-in-habash-case.html [accessed: 29 October 2009].

The New York Times 1995. Designs in a land of bombs and guns. 28 May.

The New York Times 2007. China finds American allies for security, 28 December.

Newburn, T., and Hayman, S. 2001. *Policing, Surveillance and Social Control: CCTV and Police Monitoring of Suspects*. Cullompton: Willan.

Newman, A. 1981. *The Jewish East End, 1840–1939*. London: Jewish Historical Society of England.

Newman, O. 1972. *Defensible Space: Crime Prevention Though Urban Design*. New York: Macmillan.

Nikelly, A. 2006. The pathogenesis of greed: causes and consequences, *International Journal of Applied Psychoanalytic Studies*, 3: 65–78.

Norris, C. and Armstrong, G. 1999. *The Maximum Surveillance Society*. Oxford: Berg.

North West Regional Development Agency 2004. Commonwealth Games Benefits Study. Warrington: Faber Mansul.

Nunn, S. 2003. Seeking tools for the War on Terror: a critical assessment of emerging technologies in law enforcement. *Policing: an International Journal of Police Strategies and Management*, 263: 454–72.

The Observer 2005. The day Coe won gold. [Online, 10 July]. Available at: http://www.guardian.co.uk/uk/2005/jul/10/olympics2012.olympicgames6 [accessed: 12 July 2010].

Odell, R. 1965. *Jack the Ripper in Fact and Fiction*. London: Harrap.

The Observer Sport Monthly 2005. August's 10: The ten greatest sporting muggings. [Online, 7 August]. Available at: http://www.guardian.co.uk/sport/2005/aug/07/features.sport1.

Office of Public Sector Information (OPSI) 2006. *London Olympic Games and Paralympic Games Act 2006*. [Online]. Available at: http://www.opsi.gov.uk/acts/acts2006/ukpga_20060012_en_1 [accessed: 2 May 2010].

Office of the Deputy Prime Minister (ODPM) 2003. *Sustainable Communities: Building for the Future*. London: HMSO.

Office of the Deputy Prime Minister (ODPM) 2004. *Safer Places: The Planning System and Crime Prevention*. London: HMSO.

Office of the Deputy Prime Minister (ODPM) 2005 *Planning Policy Statement 1 – Delivering Sustainable Development*. London: HMSO.

Olds, K. 1998. Urban mega-events, evictions and housing rights: the Canadian case., *Current Issues in Tourism*, 1(1): 2–46.

Oliver, P. and Furman, M. 1989. Contradictions between national and local movement organisational strength: the case of the John Birch Society. *International Social Research*, 4: 155–77.

Olympic Delivery Authority (ODA) 2007. ODA Security Industry Day, call for security tenders. Available at: http://www.london2012.com/documents/oda-industry-days/oda-security-industry-day-presentation.pdf [accessed: 3 December 2008].

Olympic Delivery Authority (ODA) 2009. *Olympic Park CCTV Code of Practice*. London: ODA.

Olympic Delivery Authority (ODA) 2010. Design and construction: Health, Safety and Environment Standard, 4th edition, March. [Online]. Available at: http://www.london2012.com/documents/oda-publications/oda-health-safety-and-environment-standard.pdf.

The Oquirrh Institute 2002. T*he 2002 Olympic Winter Games: Security Lessons Applied to Homeland Security*. Salt Lake City, UT: The Oquirrh Institute.

Organisationskomitee der XII Olympischen Winterspiele, Innsbruck (OOWI) 1976. *Final Report of the XIIth Winter Olympics, Innsbruck*. Innsbruck: OOWI.

Pawley, M. 1986. Electric city of our dreams. *New Society*, 13 June.

Pearson, G. 1973. *The Deviant Imagination*. London: Panther.

Pellew, Jill. 1989. The Home Office and the Aliens Act, 1905. *The Historical Journal*, 32(2): 369–85.

Piaspa, G., and Fonio, C. 2009. *The XXth Winter Olympic Games: Torino 2006*. Paper presented at The Surveillance Games research workshop, Simon Fraser University, Vancouver, BC, 21 November.

Poniatowska, E. 2003. *La Noche de Tlateloco*. Tlalpan, Mexico: Biblioteca Era.

Poulantzas, N. 1973. *Political Power and Social Classes*. London: Sheed Ward.

Poynter, G. 2009. The 2012 Olympic Games and the reshaping of East London, in *Regenerating London: Governance, Sustainability and Community in a Global City*, edited by R. Imrie, L. Lees and M. Raco. London: Routledge, pp. 131–50.

Poynter, G., and MacRury, I. eds 2009. *Olympic Cities: 2012 and the Remaking of London*. Farnham: Ashgate.

Prasad, D. 1999. Environment, in, R. Cashman and A. Hughes eds, *Staging the Olympics – The Events and its Impact*. Sydney: University of New South Wales Press, pp.83–92.

Preuss, H. 2004. *The Economics of Staging the Olympics: A Comparison of the Games 1972 – 2008*. New York: Edward Elgar.

Public Accounts Committee (PAC) 2008. *The Budget for the London 2012 Olympic and Paralympic Games: Fourteenth Report of Session 2007–08*, London: HMSO.

Quinten, I. 2009. *Developing a National Concept of Operation*. Olympic and Paralympic Safety and Security Conference, Royal United Services Institute, London, 13 November.

Raco, M. 2003. Remaking place and securitising space: urban regeneration and the strategies, tactics and practices of policing in the UK, *Urban Studies* 40(9): 1869–1887.

Raco, M. 2007. The planning, design, and governance of sustainable communities in the UK, in *Securing the Urban Renaissance*, edited by R. Atkinson and G. Helms. Bristol: Policy Press, pp. 39–56.

Raco, M and Tunney, E. 2010. Visibilities and invisibilities in urban development: small business communities and the London Olympics 2012, *Urban Studies* 47(10): 2069–2091.

Raine, R. 2009. *The Strategic Approach to Olympic Safety and Security*, Olympic and Paralympic Safety and Security Conference, Royal United Services Institute, London, 13 November.

Raine, R. 2009. *The Strategic Approach to Olympic Safety and Security*, Olympic and Paralympic Safety and Security Conference, Royal United Services Institute, London, 13 November.

Ranger, T., Samad, Y. and Stuart, O. eds 1996. *Culture, Identity and Politics: Ethnic Minorities in Britain*. Farnham: Avebury.

Rawlinson, P., and Fussey, P. 2010. Crossing Borders: migration and survival in the capital's informal marketplace. *Criminal Justice Matters*, 79, March.

Reeve, S. 2001. *One Day in September: The Full Story of the 1972 Munich Olympics Massacre and the Israeli Revenge Operation 'Wrath of God'*. New York: Arcade Publishing.

Reiner, R. 2000. *The Politics of the Police*, Oxford: Oxford University Press.

Reiner, R. 2007. *Law and Order: An Honest Citizens Guide to Crime and Control*, Cambridge: Polity.

Rendall, R. 2004. *The Olympics: Athens to Athens 1896-2004*. London: Weidenfeld & Nicolson.

Reuters 2010. Iraq official alleges Qaeda plotted World Cup attack. [Online, 17 May]. Available at: http://www.reuters.com/article/idUSTRE64G5AL20100517 [accessed: 17 May 2010].

Richie, J.R.B. 2000. Turning 16 days into 16 years Through Olympic Legacies. *Event Management*, 6(3): 155–65.

Rio 2016 2007. *Rio de Janeiro Applicant File – Theme 13: Security*, Rio de Janeiro: Brazil.

Rio 2016 2008. Rio 2016 seeks Chinese wisdom. [Online, 27 November]. Available at: http://www.rio2016.org.br/en/Noticias/Noticia.aspx?idConteudo=686 [accessed: 2 May 2010].

Roberts, P. and Sykes, H. ed. 2000. *Urban Regeneration: A Handbook*. Sage, London.

Roberts, R. 1973. *The Classic Slum*. Harmondsworth: Penguin.

Roche, M. 2000. *Mega-Events and Modernity: Olympics and Expos in the Growth of Global Culture*. London: Routledge.

Rogers, P. and Coaffee, J. 2005. Moral panics and urban renaissance: policy, tactics and lived experiences in public space, *City*, 9(3): 321–40.

Rose, N. 2000 Government and control. *British Journal of Criminology*, 40(2): 321–39.

Rose, R. 1979. Ungovernability: is there fire behind the smoke? *Political Studies*, 27(3): 351–70.

Royal Institute of Chartered Surveyors (RICS). 2004. Beijing revolution under way. News Release, 10 September.

Rumblelow, D. 1973. *The Houndsditch Murders and the Siege of Sidney Street*. London: Macmillan.

Russel, J. 2008. Should we mourn the cheesegrater? *The Week*, 67(9): 39–40.

Ryan, P. 2002. Olympic security: the relevance to Homeland Security, in *The 2002 Olympic Winter Games: Security Lessons Applied to Homeland Security*, The Oquirrh Institute, Salt Lake City: The Oquirrh Institute.

Ryan, P. 2007. Public Venue Security: Technology Support, paper presented at the *3rd Annual Science and Technology for Homeland Security and Resilience Conference*, Royal United Services Institute, London, 12th June.

Sadlier, D. 1996. Australia and Terrorism, in *Terrorism and the 2000 Olympics*, edited by A. Thompson. Canberra: Australian Defence Studies Centre.

Samatas, M. 2004. *Surveillance in Greece: From Anticommunist to Consumer Surveillance*. New York: Pella.

Samatas, M. 2007. Security and surveillance in the Athens 2004 Olympics: some lessons from a troubled story. *International Criminal Justice Review*, 173: 220–38.

Sampson, R.J., Raudenbush, S.W. and Earls, F. 1997. Neighbourhoods and violent crime: a multi-level study of collective efficacy. *Science*, 277: 918–24.

Samuel, R. 1994. *Theatres of Memory*. London: Verso.

Sanan, G. 1996. Olympic Security Operations 1972–94, in *Terrorism and the 2000 Olympics*, edited by A. Thompson. Sydney: Australian Defence Force Academy.

Sanan, G. 1997. *Olympic Security 1972–1996: Threat, response and international co-operation*, unpublished PhD thesis, University of St. Andrews.

Saul, B. 2000. Olympic street sweeping: moving on people and the erosion of public space. *Polemic*, 11(1): 34–7.

Scarman (Lord) 1981. *The Scarman Report: The Brixton Disorders, 10–12 April 1981*. London: HMSO.
Schaffer, K. and Smith, S. 2000. *The Olympics at the Millennium. Power, Politics, and the Games*. New Brunswick, NJ: Rutgers University Press.
Seager, A. 2004. Greeks are still hoping for gold. *The Guardian*, 30 August.
Searle, G. 2002. Uncertain legacy: Sydney's Olympic Stadium. *European Planning Studies*, 10(7): 845–60.
Searle, G. and Bounds, M. 1999. State powers, state land and competition for global entertainment: the case of Sydney. *International Journal of Urban and Regional Research*, 23: 165–72.
Security Products 2007. Beijing to invest more than $720 million for 2008 Summer Olympic Games security. [Online] Available at: http://secprodonline.com/articles/2007/08/14/beijing-to-invest.aspx [accessed: 10 March 2010].
Seed, J. 2007. 'Limehouse Blues': looking for Chinatown in the London docks, 1900–1940. *History Workshop Journal*, 62.
Segrave, J. and Chu, D.1996a. The Modern Olympic Games: A contemporary sociocultural analysis. *Quest*, 481: 2–8.
Segrave, J. and Chu, D. 1996b. *The Olympic Games in Transition*. Champaign, IL: Human Kinetics.
Senn, A. 1999. *Power, Politics, and the Olympic Games: A History of the Power Brokers, Events and Controversies that Shaped the Games*. Champaign, IL: Human Kinetics.
Sennet, R. 1996. *The Uses of Disorder: Personal Identity and City Life*. London: Faber & Faber.
Seoul Olympic Organizing Committee (SOOC) 1989. *Official Report of the XXIVth Olympiad*, Seoul: SOOC.
Sharma, A. 2005. Rich Mix in Brick Lane. *Rising East*, 2 [Online]. Available at: www.uel.ac.uk/risingeast/archive02/features/richmixinbricklane.htm.
Shaw, C.R. and McKay, H.D. 1942. *Juvenile Delinquency in Urban Areas*. Chicago, IL: University of Chicago Press.
Shearing, C. and Stenning, P.C. 1996. From the Panopticon to Disney World: the development of discipline, in *Criminological Perspectives: A Reader*, edited by J. Muncie, E. McLaughlin and M. Langan. London: Sage.
Shields, R. 1991. *Places on the Margin: Alternative Geographies of Modernity*. London: Routledge.
Sibley, D. 1995. *Geographies of Exclusion*. London: Routledge.
Silke, A. ed. 2004. *Research on Terrorism: Trends, Achievements, Failures*. London : Frank Cass, London.
Silke, A. 2010. Understanding Terrorist Target Selection, in *Terrorism and the Olympics*, edited by A. Richards, P. Fussey and A. Silke. London: Routledge. pp. 49–72.
Sinclair, J. 2007. Drivers face £5k VIP lane fines. [Online]. Available at: http://www.gamesmonitor.org.uk/node/491.

Slater, S. 2007. Pimps, police and filles de joie: foreign prostitution in interwar London. *The London Journal*, 32(1), March: 53–74.

Smith, G.J.D. 2007. Exploring relations between watchers and watched in controlled systems: strategies and tactics, *Surveillance & Society*, 44: 280–313.

Smith, N. 1996. *The New Urban Frontier: Gentrification and the Revanchist City* .New York: Routledge.

Sport England 2003. Young People and Sport in England: Trends in Participation 1996–2006) Research study conducted for Sport England Office of National Statistics (ONS). [Online]. Available at: http://www.statistics.gov.uk/cci/nugget.asp?id=718 [accessed: 17 September 2008].

Sport England 2005. *Understanding Participation in Sport: A Systematic Review.* [Online, September]. Available at: http://www.sportengland.org/research/idoc.ashx?docid=ae75441d-ff37-4922-822.

Srinivasa, S. 2006. *The Power Law of Information. Life in a Connected World.* London: Sage.

Stafford, A. 1961. *A Match to Fire the Thames*. London: Hodder and Stoughton.

Stedman-Jones, G. 1971. *Outcast London*. Oxford: Oxford University Press.

Stevenson, D. 1997. Olympic Arts: Sydney 2000 and the Cultural Olympiad. *International Review for the Sociology of Sport*, 32 (3): 227–38.

Stone, C. 1989. *Regime Politics: Governing Atlanta 1946–1988*. Lawrence: University of Kansas Press.

Sutton, A. and Wilson, D. 2004. Open-street CCTV in Australia: politics and expansion. *Surveillance & Society*, 22(3): 310–22.

Swanstrom, T. 2002. Are fear and urbanism at war? *Urban Affairs Review* 38(1): 135–40.

Swyngedouw, E., Moulaert, F., and Rodrigues, A. 2002. Neoliberal urbanization in Europe: large-scale urban development pojects and new urban policy. *Antipode*, 34(3): 542–77.

Talbot, J. 2003. Review of [B. Flyvbjerg, N. Bruzelius and W. Rothengatter] *Megaprojects and Risk, The Geographical Journal*, 170(2): 172–73.

Taylor, T. and Toohey, K. 2007. Perceptions of terrorism threats at the 2004 Olympic Games: implications for sport events, *Journal of Sport and Tourism*, 12(2): 99–114.

Teigland, J. 1999. Mega-events and impacts on tourism: the predictions and realities of the Lillehammer Olympics, *Journal of Impact Assessment and Project Appraisal*, 17(4): 305–17.

ThirdSector. (2007). Sector unconvinced about Milibands record on Olympics Lottery funding. [Online]. Available at: http://www.thirdsector.co.uk/Channels/Management/Article/647298/Sector-unconvinced-Milibands-record-Olympics-Lottery-funding.

Thomas, A. 2009. Letter from ACC Thomas to George Duncan, Civil Aviation Authority (CAA). [Online, March 2009]. Available at: http://www.whatdothey

know.com/request/south_coast_partnership_drone_do [UAV DISCLOSURE. pdf] [accessed: 2 May 2010].

Thomas, N. 2007. Let MPs debate Olympics – NCVO. [Online]. Available at: http://www.thirdsector.co.uk/Channels/Finance/Article/643380/Let-MPs-debate-Olympics-NCVO.

Thompson, A. 1996. Introduction: terrorism and the 2000 Olympics, in *Terrorism and the 2000 Olympics*, edited by A. Thompson. Canberra: Australian Defence Studies Centre.

Thompson, A. 1999. Security, in *Staging the Olympics – The events and its impact*, edited by Cashman, R and A. Hughes. Sydney: University of New South Wales Press, pp. 106–20.

Thompson, D. 2008. Olympic security collaboration. *China Security*, 4(2): 46–58.

Thompson, E.P. 1974. *The Making of the English Working Class*. Harmondsworth: Pelican.

Thomson, J. [1880] 2003. *City of Dreadful Night*. Gloucester: Dodo Press.

Tilley, N. 1998. Evaluating the effectiveness of CCTV schemes, in *Surveillance, Closed Circuit Television and Social Control*, edited by C. Norris, J. Moran and G. Armstrong. Farnham: Ashgate, pp. 139–75.

Tilly, C. 2004. *Social Movements, 1768–2004*. Boulder, CO: Paradigm.

The Times 2005. The two-man team on a secret mission who swung it for London. [Online, 7 July]. Available at: http://www.timesonline.co.uk/tol/sport/olympics/london_2012/article541242.ece [accessed: 12 July 2010].

The Times 2008a. CCTV and DNA advances add to bills but minister calls rises unacceptable. [Online, 28 February]. . Available at: http://www.timesonline.co.uk/tol/news/politics/article3448837.ece [accessed: 2 May 2010].

The Times 2008b. Renewed bomb attacks kill five in China. [Online, 10 August]. Available at: http://www.timesonline.co.uk/tol/news/world/asia/article4495365.ece# [accessed: 28 October 2009].

The Times 2008c. Boris Johnson's blond ambition key to London 2012. [Online, 26 August]. Available at http://www.timesonline.co.uk/tol/sport/columnists/matt_dickinson/article4607378.ece [accessed: 12 July 2010].

The Times 2009 General Sir David Richards demands Olympic security clarity. [Online, 27 January] Available at: http://www.timesonline.co.uk/tol/sport/olympics/london_2012/article5600583.ece [accessed: 4 February 2009].

Toohey, K. and Veal, A. 2007 *The Olympic Games: A Social Science Perspective*, Wallingford: CABI.

Tsoukala, A. 2006. The security issue at the 2004 Olympics. *European Journal for Sport and Society*, 3(1): 43–54.

Tufts, S. 2001. Building the competitive city: labour and Toronto's bid to host the Olympic Games, *Geoforum*, 35(1): 47–58.

United Kingdom Parliament 2007. 28 Jun 2007: Column 694. [Online]. Available at: http://www.publications.parliament.uk/pa/ld200607/ldhansrd/text/70628-0002.htm.

United Nations Security Council 1988. Provisional Verbatim Record of the Two Thousand Seven Hundred and Ninety-First Meeting. [Online, 16 February]. Available at: http://www.undemocracy.com/S-PV.2791.pdf [accessed: 3 February 2010].

Urban Task Force 1999. *Towards an Urban Renaissance*. (Department of Environment, Transport and the Regions (DETR). London: E & FN Spon.

Ure, A 1835. *Philosophy of Manufactures or, an exposition of the Scientific, Moral, and Commercial Economy of the Factory System of Great Britain*. London: Charles Knight.

US Senate Committee on Commerce, Science and Transportation 2004. *Lessons Learned from Security at Past Olympic Games*. [Online]. Available at: http://www.iwar.org.uk/homesec/resources/olympic-security/05-04-2004-cst-hearing.htm [accessed: 28 October 2009].

Venzke, B. and Ibrahim, A. 2003. *The al-Qaeda Threat: An Analytical Guide to al-Qaeda's Tactics and Targets*. Alexandria, VA: Tempest.

Vidal, J. 2004. Village damned – Olympic hosts fail green test. *The Guardian*, 25 August, p. 18.

Visit London 2007. Major sporting event – Le Grand Départ. [Online]. Available at: http://business.visitlondon.com/case_studies/major-sporting-event [accessed: 8 March 2010].

Wacquant, L. 2008. *Punishing the Poor: The Neoliberal Government of Social Insecurity*. Durham, NC: Duke University Press.

Walkowitz, J.R. 1992. *City of Dreadful Delight: Narratives of Sexual Danger in Late-Victorian London*. Chicago, IL: University of Chicago Press.

Waller, P.J. 1985. Immigration into Britain: the Chinese. *History Today*, 35(9): 8–15.

Ward, K. 2001. Entrepreneurial urbanism, state restructuring and civilising New East Manchester, *Area*, 35(2): 116–27.

Warning, D. 1980. *A Political History of the Summer Olympic Games*. Masters thesis, Longbeach: California State University Press.

Warrell H. 2007a. Big Lottery Fund reveals revised funding schedule. [Online]. Available at http://www.thirdsector.co.uk/channels/Finance/Article/663735/Big-Lottery-Fund-reveals-revised-funding-schedule.

Warrell H. 2007b. Social enterprises ask for Olympic contract change. [Online]. Available at: http://www.thirdsector.co.uk/News/Article/745133/Social-enterprises-ask-Olympic-contract-change.

Washington Post. 1998. False Olympic bomb threat reported. [Online, 23 February]. Available at: http://www.washingtonpost.com/wp-srv/sports/longterm/olympics1998/nagano/articles/bombthreat.htm [accessed: 23 October 2009].

Washington Post. 2008. Crew foiled an attack on airliner, China says; separatists in region were raided earlier. [Online]. Available at: http://www.washingtonpost.com/wp-dyn/content/article/2008/03/09/AR2008030900774.html [accessed: 28 October 2009].

Watson, R. 2007. Presentation to chief officers and Kent Police Authority. [Online, September]. Available at: http://www.whatdotheyknow.com/request/south_coast_ partnership_drone_do [UAV DISCLOSURE.pdf] [accessed: 2 May, 2010].

Watt, P. 2006. Respectability, roughness and 'race': neighbourhood place images and the making of working class social distinctions in London. *International Journal of Urban and Regional Research*, 30(4): 776–97.

Webster, C.W.R. 2004. The evolving diffusion, regulation and governance of closed circuit television in the UK. *Surveillance & Society*, 22(3): 230–50.

Wekerle, G.R. and Jackson, P.S. 2005. Urbanizing the security agenda: anti-terrorism, urban sprawl and social movements, *City*, 9(1): 34–49.

Wells, A. 2007. *The July 2005 Bombings*, Local Government Agency 2007 CCTV Conference: The Development of a National Strategy, Innovative Systems, Effectiveness and Standards, Local Government House, London, 4 July.

Welsh, B.C. and Farrington, D.P. 2002. *Crime Prevention Effects of Closed Circuit Television: A Systematic Review, Home Office Research Study 252*, London: Home Office. [Online]. Available at: http://www.homeoffice.gov.uk/rds/pdfs2/ hors252.pdf [accessed: 1 February 2010].

Wenn, S. and Martin, S. 2006. 'Tough Love': Richard Pound, David D'Alessandro, and the Salt Lake City Olympics bid scandal. *Sport in History*, 26(1): 64–90.

West (Lord) 2009. *Olympic and Paralympic Safety and Security*, Keynote Address, Olympic and Paralympic Safety and Security Conference, Royal United Services Institute, London, 13 November.

Wheeler, J. 2002. Airport Security Report. Unrestricted briefing available online at: http://www.parliament.uk/briefingpapers/commons/lib/research/briefings/ snbt-01246.pdf [accessed: 12 July 2010].

White, J. 1980. *Rothschild Buildings: Life in an East End Tenement, 1887–1920*. London: Routledge and Kegan Paul.

White, J. 2007. *London in the Nineteenth Century: A Human Awful Wonder of God*. London: Cape.

Whitson, D. and MacIntosh, D. 1996. The global circus: international sport, tourism and the marketing of cities. *Journal of Sport and Social Issues*, (23): 278–95.

Wieiwick, J. 1999. Urban design, in *Staging the Olympics: The Event and its Impact*, edited by R. Cashman and A. Hughes. Sydney: University of New South Wales Press, pp. 70–82.

Williams, C. 2003. Police surveillance and the emergence of CCTV in the 1960s. *Crime Prevention and Community Safety*, 53: 27–38.

Williams, R.J. 2004. *The Anxious City: English Urbanism in the Late Twentieth Century*. London: Routledge.

Wood D., Konvitz, E and Ball, K. 2004 The constant state of emergency?: surveillance after 9/11, in *The Intensification of Surveillance: Crime, Terrorism and Warfare in the Information Age*, edited by K. Ball and F. Webster. London: Pluto Press, pp. 137–50.

Woodman, E. 2004. Stratford's glamour gameplan. *Building Design*, 30(8), January.

www.PetitionOnline.com. n.d. No London 2012 Olympic bid. Available at: http://www.petitiononline.com/nolympic [accessed: 8 April 2008].

Yiftachel, O. 1994. The dark side of modernism: planning as control of an ethnic minority, in *Postmodern Cities and Spaces*, edited by S. Watson and K. Gibson. Oxford: Blackwell, pp. 216–42.

Young, J. 1999a. Cannibalism and bulimia: patterns of social control in late modernity. *Theoretical Criminology*, 3(4): 387–407.

Young, J. 1999b. *The Exclusive Society: Social Exclusion, Crime and Difference in Late Modernity*. London: Sage.

Young, M. and Wilmott, P. 1957. *Family and Kinship in East London*. London: Routledge and Kegan Paul.

Yu, Y., Klauser, F., and Chan, G. 2009. Governing security at the 2008 Beijing Olympics. *The International Journal of the History of Sport*, 26(3): 390–405.

Zedner, L. 2009. *Security*. London: Routledge.

Zirakzadeh, C.E. 1997. *Social Movements in Politics: A Comparative Study*. New York: Longman.

Zukin, S. 1995. *The Culture of Cities*. Oxford: Blackwell.

Index

References to illustrations are in **bold**